DISTRIBUTIVE JUSTICE AND
WORLD TRADE LAW

What does justice demand in international trade regulation? And how far does WTO law respond to those demands? Whether our focus is developing countries, struggling industries, or environmental protection, distributive conflict is a pervasive feature of international economic law. Despite this, we lack an adequate theory of distributive justice for this domain. Drawing on philosophical approaches to global justice, this book advances a novel theory of justice in trade regulation, and applies this to explain and critique the law of the WTO. Integrating theoretical and doctrinal approaches, it demonstrates the potential for political theory to illuminate and inform the progressive development of WTO law, including rules on border measures, discrimination, trade remedies, and domestic regulation. Written from an interdisciplinary perspective, accessible to lawyers, philosophers, and political scientists, the book will appeal both to theorists interested in building bridges from theory to practice and to practitioners seeking new perspectives on existing problems.

OISIN SUTTLE is a Lecturer at Queen's University, Belfast, having previously taught at the University of Sheffield and University College London. He teaches political philosophy, public international law and WTO law. He holds degrees in law (University College Dublin) and international relations (University of Oxford), and a PhD on the philosophy of international economic law (University College London). His research has been published in leading international journals, including the *European Journal of International Law*, the *Modern Law Review*, and the *Journal of International Law and International Relations*. He formerly practiced commercial law and is qualified both in Ireland and in England and Wales.

CAMBRIDGE INTERNATIONAL TRADE AND ECONOMIC LAW

Series editors

Dr Lorand Bartels, *University of Cambridge*
Professor Thomas Cottier, *University of Berne*
Professor William Davey, *University of Illinois*

As the processes of regionalization and globalization have intensified, there have been accompanying increases in the regulations of international trade and economic law at the levels of international, regional, and national laws.

The subject matter of this series is international economic law. Its core is the regulation of international trade, investment, and cognate areas such as intellectual property and competition policy. The series publishes books on related regulatory areas, in particular, human rights, labor, environment and culture, as well as sustainable development. These areas are vertically linked at the international, regional, and national level, and the series extends to the implementation of these rules at these different levels. The series also includes works on governance, dealing with the structure and operation of related international organizations in the field of international economic law, and the way they interact with other subjects of international and national law.

DISTRIBUTIVE JUSTICE AND WORLD TRADE LAW

A Political Theory of International Trade Regulation

OISIN SUTTLE

CAMBRIDGE
UNIVERSITY PRESS

CAMBRIDGE
UNIVERSITY PRESS

University Printing House, Cambridge CB2 8BS, United Kingdom

One Liberty Plaza, 20th Floor, New York, NY 10006, USA

477 Williamstown Road, Port Melbourne, VIC 3207, Australia

4843/24, 2nd Floor, Ansari Road, Daryaganj, Delhi – 110002, India

79 Anson Road, #06–04/06, Singapore 079906

Cambridge University Press is part of the University of Cambridge.

It furthers the University's mission by disseminating knowledge in the pursuit of
education, learning, and research at the highest international levels of excellence.

www.cambridge.org
Information on this title: www.cambridge.org/9781108415811
DOI: 10.1017/9781108235235

© Oisin Suttle 2018

First published 2018

Printed in the United Kingdom by Clays, St Ives plc

A catalogue record for this publication is available from the British Library.

Library of Congress Cataloging-in-Publication Data
Names: Suttle, Oisin, 1980– author.
Title: Distributive justice and world trade law : a political theory of international
trade regulation / Oisin Suttle.
Description: Cambridge [UK] ; New York : Cambridge University Press, 2017. | Series:
Cambridge international trade and economic law ; 36 | Includes
bibliographical references and index.
Identifiers: LCCN 2017030746 | ISBN 9781108415811 (hardback)
Subjects: LCSH: Foreign trade regulation. | World Trade Organization. | Distributive
justice. | Foreign trade regulation – Political aspects. | Free trade.
Classification: LCC K3943 .S89 2017 | DDC 343.08/7–dc23
LC record available at https://lccn.loc.gov/2017030746

ISBN 978-1-108-41581-1 Hardback

CONTENTS

PREFACE

It is a strange time to be thinking about justice and fairness in the rule-governed global economy.

I first became conscious of global politics in the 1990s, during that optimistic post-Cold War, pre-9/11, liberal internationalist moment that we were told was to be history's end state. That moment produced the WTO, but also the International Criminal Court, the Maastricht Treaty, the Millennium Development Goals, and a general sense that nations and nationalism were becoming a bit passé. When I began thinking seriously about international economic governance in the mid-2000s, the main criticisms of the trade system came from environmentalists, human rights activists, and advocates for the Global South. Nobody imagined that the trade regime was perfect: the debacle in Seattle made that clear. But the biggest challenge was that the trade rules were insufficiently cosmopolitan, preferring the interests of rich countries and industries over the globally most vulnerable.

Those days are over. In the months when I was finishing this book, two votes happened that made that eminently clear: the UK referendum on leaving the European Union; and Donald Trump's election as president of the United States. Whatever else these two votes mean, they signal a reassertion of economic nationalism in two countries that, over two centuries, have done most to advance an open international economic order. The political sentiments they express are a reminder of something that liberal economists know well, but often neglect to mention: that while trade may benefit countries as a whole, its costs and benefits are unevenly spread. They represent a demand, on the part of those who see themselves as losing out from globalization, to have their pain recognized and their interests accommodated, even if this means shifting that pain onto someone else. They are, in consequence, a rejection of many economic shibboleths on which the postwar – and especially the post-Cold War – liberal economic order was built. And in both the United Kingdom and the United States, they have brought to power governments unashamedly committed to advancing their national interests, above all, in international economic governance.

However, they are more than that. This is not just a reassertion of the interests of particular groups. Rather, in the rhetoric of "Take Back Control" and "Make America Great Again," there is a substantial normative component. There is a sense that aggrieved groups have been sacrificed unfairly, whether for the benefit of domestic elites, immigrants, or foreign economies. The antiglobalization rhetoric is one of fairness, and of sovereign rights, rather than purely of self-interest. It is not just that foreign manufacturers, or immigrants, or liberal elites, are doing well, but that they are cheating, or taking advantage, or otherwise getting more than they should. These are political rallying calls, but they are also something more. They are claims of political morality. And as claims of political morality, we can and should look for ways to evaluate them.

This book is an attempt to answer some of the fundamental questions that these kinds of claims raise. What exactly does it mean to say that international trade regulation is unfair, or unjust? In a world of independent states, where is the line between those things a state can permissibly do, even if this has effects on outsiders, and those that constitute wrongs to those outsiders? How should states reconcile the claims of their own citizens, including especially those least well-off, with the demands of outsiders with whom they do, or might, economically interact? And how far does the existing trade regime correctly answer these questions? For too long, the liberal international economic order assumed it was legitimized by an economic theory that showed international trade was in everyone's interests. As that assumption is challenged, it becomes more urgent directly to address the questions of distributive conflict and distributive justice that it obscured. It is precisely when liberal internationalism is going out of fashion that we must look again at the arguments that might support it.

I have not sought to engage directly with these recent political developments. This is not that kind of book. It may, in consequence, seem a little old-fashioned, a throwback to the optimistic days of the 1990s, or even the 1960s. However, it is motivated by a set of ideas that remain central to political discourse across many countries: that persons are free and equal; that the exercise of power requires to be justified to those over whom it is exercised; that peoples have rights to equality and self-determination. These are the ideals of the United States Declaration of Independence; of the Universal Declaration of Human Rights and the two International Covenants; and of the liberal tradition that, in

European and American thought, runs from Hobbes and Locke through Kant and Mill to constitute the dominant position in contemporary political thought. While today we may find these ideas invoked to motivate policies quite contrary to those with which they were formerly associated, they remain the firmest ground from which to build a shared political morality. Their meaning may not be fixed and eternal, but it also does not change with each shift in the political winds. We can thus examine what taking them seriously in the context of international economic governance would mean, without worrying overly whether our conclusions fit the political fashions of the moment. These liberal ideas will, I am confident, outlive our present reactionary moment. I hope this book might also.

Writing this book has been a journey. I have incurred many debts along the way.

My first and greatest academic debts are to Professor John Tasioulas and Professor Fiona Smith, who supervised my PhD at University College London, on which this book is based. The hours they spent reading and discussing drafts, and pressing me to clarify and strengthen my arguments, were crucial in turning a vague concern with global economic governance into the work here presented. I came to this project with training in law and political science, but relatively little experience of either philosophy or international trade law. I benefited enormously from having experts in both to guide me as I took my first steps as a scholar at this interdisciplinary boundary. I also benefited greatly from comments of my PhD examiners, Professors John Linarelli and Joanne Scott.

I first became interested in problems of fairness in global governance while completing a master's degree in international relations at the University of Oxford. My supervisor there, Professor Kalypso Nicolaidis, encouraged my research interests in economic governance and the trade regime, and has been a continuing source of encouragement ever since. I am also grateful to Professor Jennifer Welsh, who first introduced me to international political theory; many of the questions I try to answer in this book are ones I first asked in her seminars.

During the years of their gestation, the ideas herein benefited from conversations with colleagues too numerous to name. The Faculty of Laws at UCL, and particularly the community of graduate students working there, provided the perfect environment in which to develop my ideas; it took leaving to realize how unique that community was. The Political Philosophy Working Group at UCL provided a valuable source of interdisciplinary conversations. After leaving UCL, colleagues at the University of Sheffield provided a frequent sounding board as I continued to develop my views.

I received valuable comments from participants at various conferences and workshops where I presented parts of the argument, including: Northeastern University Workshop in Applied Philosophy, September 2012; American Society for International Law International Economic Law Interest Group Biennial Meeting, George Washington University, December 2012; Brave New World, University of Manchester Department of Political Theory, June 2013; British Institute of International and Comparative Law Annual Conference on WTO Law, May 2014; University College Dublin Workshop on WTO Law, May 2014; Junior Faculty Forum for International Law, European University Institute, June 2015.

Two papers presenting parts of my argument have been previously published. A shorter version of parts of Chapter 3 appeared as "Equality in Global Commerce: Towards a Political Theory of International Economic Law" (2014) *European Journal of International Law* 25(4) 1043–1070. Parts of Chapters 5 and 7 are included in abridged form in "What Sorts of Things Are Public Morals? A Liberal Cosmopolitan Account of Article XX GATT" (2017) *Modern Law Review* 80(4) 569–599. I am grateful to reviewers and editors of both journals for their comments, which improved those papers, but also informed other sections of this book. An EJIL:*Live!* interview with Professor Joseph Weiler discussing the first of these papers was another valuable source of feedback.

Financial support was provided by a UCL Faculty of Laws Research Scholarship. Revisions to the manuscript were completed during research leave from the University of Sheffield School of Law. University College Dublin School of Law kindly hosted me while I was finalizing the manuscript.

Finally, I am grateful to friends and family for support and encouragement. I owe particular thanks to my wife Maeve Bateman: for encouraging me to take the leap in beginning this project; for patiently enduring countless evenings and weekends when writing took precedence over all else; for keeping smiling and keeping me smiling through the crises of confidence that will be familiar to anyone who has undertaken a major piece of writing; and for constantly reminding me that there are more important things in life than getting that last footnote just right.

TABLE OF CASES

GATT Dispute Settlement Reports

Short Title	Full Citation
Belgium – Family Allowances	Belgian Family Allowances (Allocations Familiales), G/32, circulated November 6, 1952, adopted November 7, 1952, BISD 1S/59
EEC – Bananas I	*EEC Member States' Import Regime for Bananas*, DS32/R, circulated June 3, 1993, unadopted
EEC – Bananas II	*EEC – Import Regime for Bananas*, DS38/R, circulated February 1994, unadopted
EEC – Apples I (Chile)	*EEC Restrictions on Imports of Apples from Chile*, L/5047, circulated October 31, 1980, adopted November 10, 1980, BISD 27S/98
EEC – Dessert Apples (Chile)	*European Economic Community – Restrictions on Imports of Dessert Apples – Complaint by Chile*, L/6491, circulated April 18, 1989, adopted June 22, 1989, BISD 36S/93
EEC – Sugar (Brazil)	*European Communities – Refunds on Exports of Sugar – Complaint by Brazil*, L/5011, circulated October 7, 1980, adopted November 10, 1980, BISD 27S/69
Japan – Alcohol I	*Japan – Customs Duties, Taxes and Labelling Practices on Imported Wines and Alcoholic Beverages*, L/6216, circulated October 13, 1987, adopted November 10, 1987, BISD 34S/83
Norway – Textiles	*Norway – Restrictions on Imports of Certain Textile Products*, L/4959, circulated March 24, 1980, adopted June 18, 1980, BISD 27S/119

Short Title	Full Citation
Spain – Unroasted Coffee	*Spain – Tariff Treatment of Unroasted Coffee*, L/5135, circulated April 27, 1981, adopted June 11, 1981, BISD 28S/102
US – Autos	*United States – Taxes on Automobiles*, DS31/R, circulated October 11, 1994, unadopted
US – Malt Beverages	*United States – Measures Affecting Alcoholic and Malt Beverages*, DS23/R, circulated March 16, 1992, adopted June 19, 1992, BISD 39S/206
US – Section 337	*United States Section 337 of the Tariff Act of 1930*, L/ 6439, circulated January 16, 1989, adopted November 7, 1989, BISD 36S/345
US – Tuna (Mexico)	*United States – Restrictions on Imports of Tuna*, DS21/R, circulated September 3, 1991, unadopted, BISD 39S/155
US – Tuna (EEC)	*United States – Restrictions on Imports of Tuna*, DS29/R, circulated June 16, 1994, unadopted

WTO Dispute Settlement Reports

Short Title	Full Citation
Argentina – Footwear (EC)	DS121 *Argentina – Safeguard Measures on Imports of Footwear*
	Panel Report June 25, 1999, WT/DS121/R
	Appellate Body Report December 14, 1999, WT/DS121/AB/R
Argentina – Hides and Leather	DS155 *Argentina – Measures Affecting the Export of Bovine Hides and Import of Finished Leather*
	Panel Report December 19, 2000, WT/DS155/R
Argentina – Preserved Peaches	DS238 *Argentina – Definitive Safeguard Measure on Imports of Preserved Peaches*
	Panel Report February14, 2003, WT/DS238/R
Australia – Salmon	DS18 *Australia – Measures Affecting Importation of Salmon*

Short Title	Full Citation
	Appellate Body Report October 20, 1998, WT/DS18/AB/R
	Article 21.5 Panel Report February 18, 2000, WT/DS18/RW
Brazil – Aircraft	DS46 *Brazil – Export Financing Programme for Aircraft* Panel Report April 14, 1999, WT/DS46/R
Brazil – Tyres	DS332 *Brazil – Measures Affecting Imports of Retreaded Tyres* Panel Report June 12, 2007, WT/DS332/R Appellate Body Report December 3, 2007, WT/DS332/AB/R
Canada – Aircraft	DS70 *Canada – Measures Affecting the Export of Civilian Aircraft* Appellate Body Report August 2, 1999, WT/DS70/AB/R
Canada – FIT	DS426 *Canada – Measures relating to the Feed-in Tariff Program* Panel Report December 19, 2012, WT/DS426/R Appellate Body Report May 6, 2013, WT/DS426/AB/R
Canada – Periodicals	DS31 *Canada – Certain Measures concerning Periodicals* Appellate Body Report June 30, 1997, WT/DS31/AB/R
Canada – Pharmaceutical Products	DS114 *Canada – Patent Protection of Pharmaceutical Products* Panel Report, March 17, 2000, WT/DS114/R
Chile – Alcoholic Beverages	DS87 *Chile – Taxes on Alcoholic Beverages* Appellate Body Report December 13, 1999, WT/DS87/AB/R
China – Audiovisual	DS363 *China – Measures Affecting Trading Rights and Distribution Services for Certain Publications and Audiovisual Entertainment Products* Panel Report August 12, 2009, WT/DS363/R Appellate Body Report December 21, 2009, WT/DS363/AB/R
China – Rare Earths	DS431 *China – Measures Related to the Exportation of Rare Earths, Tungsten and Molybdenum* Panel Report March 26, 2014, WT/DS431/R Appellate Body Report August 7, 2014, WT/DS431/AB/R
China – Raw Materials	DS394 *China – Measures Related to the Exportation of Various Raw Materials*

Short Title	Full Citation
	Panel Report July 5, 2011, WT/DS394/R
	Appellate Body Report January 30, 2012, WT/DS394/AB/R
Dominican Republic – Cigarettes	DS302 *Dominican Republic – Measures Affecting the Importation and Internal Sale of Cigarettes*
	Appellate Body Report April 25, 2005, WT/DS302/AB/R
EC – Aircraft	DS316 – *European Communities – Measures Affecting Trade in Large Civil Aircraft*
	Panel Report June 30, 2010, WT/DS302/R
	Appellate Body Report May 18, 2011, WT/DS316/AB/R
EC – Asbestos	DS135 *European Communities – Measures Affecting Asbestos and Products Containing Asbestos*
	Appellate Body Report March 12, 2001, WT/DS135/AB/R
EC – Fasteners	DS397 *European Communities – Definitive Anti-Dumping Measures on Certain Iron or Steel Fasteners from China*
	Appellate Body Report July 15, 2011, WT/DS397/AB/R
EC – Hormones	DS26 *European Communities – Measures Concerning Meat and Meat Products (Hormones)*
	Appellate Body Report January 16, 1998, WT/DS26/AB/R
EC – Sardines	DS231 *European Communities – Trade Description of Sardines*
	Panel Report May 29, 2002, WT/DS231/R
	Appellate Body Report October 23, 2002, WT/DS231/AB/R
EC – Seal Products	DS400 *European Communities – Measures Prohibiting the Importation and Marketing of Seal Products*
	Panel Report November 25, 2013, WT/DS400/R
	Appellate Body Report May 22, 2014, WT/DS400/AB/R
EC – Tariff Preferences	DS246 *European Communities – Conditions for the Granting of Tariff Preferences to Developing Countries*
	Panel Report December 1, 2003, WT/DS246/R
	Appellate Body Report April 7, 2004, WT/DS246/AB/R
India – Quantitative Restrictions	DS90 *India – Quantitative Restrictions on Imports of Agricultural, Textile and Industrial Products*

Other Cases

TABLE OF TREATIES, INSTRUMENTS, AND OFFICIAL DOCUMENTS

GATT/WTO Treaties

General Agreement on Tariffs and Trade of October 30, 1947, No.814, 55 U.N.T.S. 194
(GATT 1947)

Marrakesh Agreement Establishing the World Trade Organization of April 15, 1994, No.
31874, 1867 U.N.T.S. 14 (WTO Agreement)

*General Agreement on Tariffs and Trade 1994, Marrakesh Agreement Establishing the
World Trade Organization, Annex 1A* (GATT or GATT 1994)

*Agreement on Agriculture, Marrakesh Agreement Establishing the World Trade
Organization, Annex 1A* (AoA)

*Agreement on the Application of Sanitary and Phytosanitary Measures, Marrakesh
Agreement Establishing the World Trade Organization, Annex 1A* (SPS)

*Agreement on Technical Barriers to Trade, Marrakesh Agreement Establishing the World
Trade Organization, Annex 1A* (TBT)

*Agreement on Implementation of Article VI of the General Agreements on Tariffs and
Trade 1994, Marrakesh Agreement Establishing the World Trade Organization,
Annex 1A* (ADA)

*Agreement on Subsidies and Countervailing Measures, Marrakesh Agreement
Establishing the World Trade Organization, Annex 1A* (SCM)

*Agreement on Safeguards, Marrakesh Agreement Establishing the World Trade
Organization, Annex 1A* (SA)

*Understanding on Rules and Procedures Governing the Settlement of Disputes,
Marrakesh Agreement Establishing the World Trade Organization, Annex 2* (DSU)

Other Treaties

International Covenant on Civil and Political Rights, of December 16, 1966, No. 14668,
999 U.N.T.S. 172

International Covenant on Economic, Social and Cultural Rights, of December 16, 1966,
No. 14531, 993, U.N.T.S. 3

Vienna Convention on the Law of Treaties of May 23, 1969, No.18232, 1155, U.N.T.
S. 331

EU-Canada Comprehensive Economic and Trade Agreement, signed October 30, 2016

GATT/WTO Documents

L/3464 *Report by the Working Party on Border Tax Adjustments* of December 2, 1970

L/4903 GATT Decision *Differential and More Favourable Treatment Reciprocity and Fuller Participation of Developing Countries* of November 28, 1979 (the Enabling Clause)

WT/L/304 *General Council Decision on Waiver: Preferential Tariff Treatment for Least-Developed Countries* of June 15, 1999

WT/MIN(01)/17 *Doha Ministerial Decision on Implementation-Related Issues and Concerns* of November 20, 2001

WT/MIN(01)/DEC/1 *Doha Ministerial Declaration* of November 20, 2001

WT/MIN(01)/DEC/2 *Declaration on the TRIPS Agreement and Public Health*, November 20, 2001

WT/L/540 *General Council Decision on Implementation of Paragraph 6 of the Doha Declaration on the TRIPS Agreement and Public Health*, August 30, 2003

WT/L/579 *General Council Decision on the Doha Work Programme*, August 1, 2004

WT/MIN(05)/DEC *Hong Kong Ministerial Declaration* of December 18, 2005

WT/l/754 *General Council Decision: United States – African Growth and Opportunity Act* of May 27, 2009

WT/L/759 *General Council Decision on Extension of Waiver: Preferential Tariff Treatment for Least-Developed Countries* of May 27, 2009

TN/RL/24 *Negotiating Group on Rules, Report by the Chairman*, March 22, 2010

WT/MIN(13)/38, *Bali Ministerial Decision on Public Stockholding for Food Security Purposes*, December 7, 2013

TN/RL/W/255 *Negotiating Group on Rules, Report by the Chairman*, March 14, 2014

WT/MIN(15)/DEC, *Nairobi Ministerial Declaration*, December 21, 2015, para 32

WT/MIN(15)/44-WT/L/979 *Nairobi Ministerial Decision on Public Stockholding for Food Security Purposes*, December 21, 2015

WT/MIN(15)/45-WT/L/980 *Nairobi Ministerial Decision on Export Competition*, December 21, 2015

United Nations Documents

E/CONF.46/3 United Nations Conference on Trade and Development (1964) *Towards a New Trade Policy for Development: Report by the Secretary-General of the United Nations Conference on Trade and Development*

A/RES/25/2625 – United Nations General Assembly (1970) Resolution 2625 (XXV) *Declaration on Principles of International Law concerning Friendly Relations and Cooperation among States in accordance with the Charter of the United Nations*

UN Human Rights Committee (HRC), *CCPR General Comment No. 12: Article 1 (Right to Self-determination), The Right to Self-determination of Peoples*, March 13, 1984

A/RES/60/1 – United Nations General Assembly (2005) *Resolution 60/1/2005, 2005 World Summit Outcome*

Other Official Documents

ABBREVIATIONS

ADA	Agreement on Implementation of Article VI of the General Agreement on Tariffs and Trade 1994 (Anti-Dumping Agreement)
ADD	Anti-Dumping Duty
AoA	Agreement on Agriculture
CVD	Countervailing Duty
DDE	Doctrine of Double Effect
DEM	Domestic Economic Measure
DSU	Understanding on Rules and Procedures Governing the Settlement of Disputes
EGC	Equality in Global Commerce
ETM	External Trade Measure
GATT	General Agreement on Tariffs and Trade
GATS	General Agreement on Trade in Services
ICCPR	International Covenant on Civil and Political Rights
ICESCR	International Covenant on Economic, Social, and Cultural Rights
MFN	Most Favored Nation
NIEO	New International Economic Order
NPRPPM	Non-Product Related Production Process and Methodology
NT	National Treatment
PT	Protectionism Theory
SA	Safeguards
SCM	Agreement on Subsidies and Countervailing Measures
SDT	Special and Differential Treatment
SPS	Agreement on the Application of Sanitary and Phytosanitary Measures
TBT	Agreement on Technical Barriers to Trade
TRIPS	Agreement on Trade Related Aspects of Intellectual Property Rights
TTT	Terms of Trade Theory
WTO	World Trade Organization

PART I

Foundations

1

Introduction

1.1 Distributive Justice in International Trade

We live in an unequal world. This much is beyond dispute.

We can describe that inequality in many ways. In terms of national income: in 2015, per capita GDP in the United States, adjusted for purchasing power, was $55,836; in China, $14,238; in the Democratic Republic of Congo, $728.[1] In terms of life expectancy: in the United States today, 81.2 years; in China, 76; in the Democratic Republic of Congo, 59. Similar inequalities appear in access to key services like clean water, electricity, and healthcare, and in access to education, with the manifold economic and personal opportunities it brings. Regardless of the metric, we find radical inequalities across countries that directly impact on individuals' chances of living long, healthy, and flourishing lives.

We also live in a world that is economically connected. Through international commerce, goods, services, capital, and (less often) labor move across borders. Clothes made in Dhaka are worn in Dublin, while lawyers in New York advise clients in New Delhi. And global value chains mean production is rarely limited to individual countries. Despite their differences, the countries mentioned above have at least one thing in common: they directly contributed to producing the computer on which this book was written. It was designed in the United States, assembled in China, and used raw materials from – among many others – the Democratic Republic of Congo. We are citizens of states, but we are also – in varying ways and to varying extents – participants in a global economy that transcends those states.

---

[1] (World Bank, 2016).

Often, when we talk about justice in the global economy, it is these two facts, of inequality and interconnectedness, that we emphasize. For some, as scholars and citizens, the fact of inequality alone is determinative of the justice or injustice of the global economy: no world in which such inequalities exist could possibly be just. For others, it is the fact that we enjoy such radically different benefits from an economy in which we all participate: it is not just that there are inequalities, but that we benefit unequally from something in which we are all involved. This sense of justice finds various expressions in the trade context: in the Fair Trade Movement; in World Trade Organization rules on Special and Differential Treatment for Developing Countries; and in the remnants of the post-colonial New International Economic Order.

But in practice, these inequalities are rarely the most prominent issues in debates about justice and fairness in international trade regulation. Here, we are more often concerned with trade barriers, where one country reduces tariffs or other obstacles, but others do not reciprocate; or discrimination, where goods from one country are treated differently from those of another; or competition between a struggling domestic industry and cheap foreign imports; or national regulations that impact on, and indeed target, exporters in other jurisdictions, including through their environmental, labor, and human rights practices. It is these issues that are the bread and butter of the trade regime; and while not unrelated to questions of economic inequality, they do not reduce to them.

What all these issues have in common is that they express competing claims that cannot all be satisfied. The claim that coffee growers in the developing world should enjoy a greater share of benefits from production is necessarily a claim that others, whether farm owners, processors, distributors, retailers, or consumers, should relinquish some of their gains. But the trade unionist's claim to protection from low-priced foreign imports is similarly a claim to deprive foreign workers of employment, to deprive foreign producers of some of the gains they hoped to make, and to deprive consumers at home of the opportunity to consume those cheaper imports. And the environmentalist's claim to dictate the conditions under which imported tuna are caught requires that foreign fishermen give up some of their opportunities for catching fish, and limits exporting countries' freedom to decide for themselves the balance between economic development and environmental protection.

It is the fact that claims conflict that makes these issues difficult. Few deny it would be better if the world's poorest enjoyed greater opportunities and higher standards of living, closer to those enjoyed in high-income countries. Where we disagree is about whether and to what extent others have duties to act, and to sacrifice, to bring that about. Similarly, most can recognize the suffering of workers in declining industries, and the value of protecting endangered species. But we disagree about how much we should be doing to address either, about who should make the decisions, and about who should bear the costs.

The fact of conflict is similarly what makes these issues of distributive justice. David Hume identified two features of the world as constituting the "circumstances of justice": first, moderate scarcity – there is enough so that all can have enough, but not so much that all can have everything they desire; and second, limited altruism – we can acknowledge the claims of others, but our primary focus remains on our own goals and projects.[2] These facts together constitute a moral landscape in which we must choose between the competing claims of different individuals and groups.

As sketched so far, these issues pose a question of political morality: how should the competing demands of different constituencies be reconciled, given that not all can be fully satisfied? However, in the world in which we live, they also raise questions of international economic law, which may fall to be debated and resolved under the rules of the World Trade Organization (WTO). Faced with import duties to protect infant industries, or subsidies to promote clean energy, or regulations to protect seal welfare, we can ask whether these are prudent, fair, or just: but the more practically relevant question will often be whether they are lawful by the standards of the WTO. By prohibiting and permitting particular measures, WTO rules endorse the claims of some groups over those of others, making judgments about how far the demands of each should be satisfied. And in each case, different rules would lead to different results, improving the lot of some while disappointing others. WTO law cannot avoid taking some position on these questions of distributive justice.

Distributive conflict and distributive justice are thus unavoidable concerns for international trade regulation. That inevitability is often obscured by economists' emphasis on the mutual gains that derive from international cooperation. Certainly, few would deny that great gains are possible through international trade. But after we have done all we can through cooperation to enlarge the collective economic pie, we will always and necessarily face questions of how that pie is to be divided,

---

[2] (Hume, 2000: §3.2.2) Cf. (Rawls, 1971: 126–127).

given the many competing claims thereon. Once this fact is acknowledged, we need some way to answer the questions of distributive justice that the international trading system poses. Yet we lack any adequate theory of what distributive justice means or demands in the context of international trade regulation, or of the implications this has for international trade law. We need a theory of justice for international trade law. That is the task of this book.

1.2   Why Trade Law Needs a Theory of Justice . . .

International trade law is not a new pursuit. The trade regime has existed in its present form since 1994, while central elements of the goods regime date from the General Agreement on Tariffs and Trade 1947. At least from the late 1970s, that regime has been substantially legal in character, including quasi-judicial organs applying legal methods to interpret agreements and adjudicate members' compliance therewith. It is frequently cited as the most successful system of legalized international governance that we have. Having got by so well for so long, we might wonder whether the trade regime really needs a theory of justice.

A theory of justice can play at least three important roles for the trade regime. The first is explanatory and justificatory. The second is critical. And the third is interpretive. Notwithstanding the apparent successes of the trade regime, the under-fulfillment of these functions weakens the legitimacy of both its rules and its decisions, and particularly of its quasi-judicial organs.

First, a theory of justice might tell us what the rules of the trade regime are for, and why we have reason to endorse them. There are, of course, various existing theories of the function of the trade regime. The most prominent explain the trade rules as realizing economic efficiency. Those explanations have serious defects in accounting for the specifics of the trade rules. They also struggle to justify those rules to critics who doubt that economic efficiency is an overriding value, and worry that trade law gives insufficient weight, on the one hand, to environmental, human rights, and development concerns, and on the other hand, to the ways the costs and benefits of international trade are distributed, both within and between countries. A theory of justice might hope both to better account for the rules, and to offer a more compelling justification.

Second, a theory of justice plays an important critical role. Justice, Rawls reminds us, is "the first virtue of social institutions, as truth is of systems of thought."[3] A theory of justice can propose an ideal, against which to judge actually existing institutions, and towards which we might hope to reform them. Different groups will have different views about what is right or wrong with the trade regime. Again, economists are prominent here, but so are environmentalists, trade unionists, human rights lawyers, and anti-poverty activists. When critics disagree, their different concerns mean they can often seem to talk past each other. It is only by thinking hard about the merits and demerits of their respective claims, and ultimately seeking to integrate these into a coherent system, that we can aspire to a rational moral critique of the trade regime.

Third, and perhaps most relevant for lawyers, a theory of justice can play an important interpretive role. Ambiguities and lacunae are pervasive features of law, which we must resolve as best we can. In approaching hard cases, we necessarily look to standards beyond the texts we are tasked to interpret, both to guide reasoning and to justify conclusions. Without such standards, legal reasoning becomes formalistic, circular, and question-begging. In the context of trade law, we often look to economic analysis to evaluate competing interpretations. But this is equally a function that a theory of justice can fulfill, particularly given the frequency with which economic explanations of WTO rules break down in practice. And indeed, to the extent we take seriously the priority of justice, political theory surely has a better claim than economic analysis to guide interpreters in these hard cases.

1.3   ... and Why It Doesn't Have One

Given the various roles a theory of justice can play, we might wonder why so little has been done to develop such a theory for the trade regime. It is certainly not for lack of relevant sources. Admittedly, until relatively recently, theorists of justice focused predominantly on justice within states, but the past four decades have seen distributive justice beyond the state become a major concern of political philosophy. The result has been a variety of substantive theories of global distributive justice, ranging from strong cosmopolitan views that argue the same economic duties apply between states as within them, to statist views that emphasize the distinctness of the domestic and international domains, and restrict most distributive concerns to the former.[4] Yet international economic lawyers in general, and trade lawyers in particular, have shown little interest in

---

[3] (Rawls, 1971: 3).   [4] I discuss a number of existing theories in Chapter 2.

these theoretical developments; while theorists have been slow to engage with the specifics of economic governance.[5] Given the obvious overlap in the concerns of these two groups, we might wonder why there has been so little interdisciplinary dialogue.

One answer, which undoubtedly has some truth, is that the hegemony of economic analysis has, for many years, limited the scope for alternative approaches.[6] Posner and Sykes observe that international economic law is the only area of international law where economic analysis has historically played a significant role.[7] In fact, it would be only slightly inaccurate to say that economics has constituted the sole respectable standard against which trade law has been judged. Trade lawyers know what their discipline is about: it is about economic efficiency; and other values, whatever their attractions elsewhere, are simply a distraction here.

Another answer is that there is a limit to how many disciplines any of us can be expected to master. World Trade Law is, after all, an arcane specialism within the already narrow field of international law; and while most lawyers will have encountered some legal and political philosophy along the way, global political theory is a relatively recent subfield, and quite far removed from most law school philosophy courses. To demand that scholars travel so far down both legal and philosophical rabbit holes may seem unreasonable, particularly given expectations that they should also have a working knowledge of (at least) economics, political economy, and international relations.

However, a third answer is, I think, the most relevant. This is that the theory of distributive justice beyond the state, as developed by political philosophers, has struggled to generate principles that can meaningfully engage with the kinds of distributive questions that arise within the trade regime.[8] Strong cosmopolitans, who deny the moral distinctiveness of the state, and argue for identical principles of justice globally to those they endorse locally, end up with conclusions that appear hopelessly over-demanding, and struggle to provide principled accounts of international law for a world where states remain the fundamental units. By contrast, moderate cosmopolitan and statist thinkers, who place greater weight on the distinction between local and global, and endorse different principles to govern these different contexts, require contestable and contingent empirical claims to connect their normative principles with legal and

---

[5] Some honorable exceptions include: (Carmody et al., 2012; Garcia, 2003, 2013; Linarelli, 2006; Moellendorf, 2005; Pogge, 2002; Trachtman, 2003).

[6] (Garcia, 2006).   [7] (Posner & Sykes, 2013: 3).

[8] The points in this paragraph are developed in more detail in Chapter 2.

political practice; and even then have little to say about the merits and demerits of large parts of international trade law. The upshot has been the effective exclusion of political theory from debates about international economic law, which have instead been informed predominantly by legal positivism and economic theory.

The upshot is that seriously engaging with questions of distributive justice in WTO law requires more than a willingness from lawyers to read the work of political philosophers. We cannot simply take an existing theory off the shelf and apply it to answer the particular questions raised by international trade regulation. Rather, serious theoretical work is required to develop an account of global distributive justice that is appropriate for the trade regime, before we can begin to examine the practical and doctrinal questions that arise therein.

1.4 Overview

This book is about distributive justice in international trade regulation. It is about the standards that we do, and should, use to adjudicate the competing claims that individuals and groups have upon the complex of rules and institutions that govern the international economy. It is also about those rules and institutions themselves, and the extent to which the law of the trade regime does, or could, express those standards.

I seek to answer two questions: first, what does justice demand in the regulation of international trade? And second, to what extent does the existing regime for trade in goods respond to those demands?

The first question raises broader questions, about economic justice, and justice beyond the state, that are the subject of ongoing debates in political philosophy. A key question in those debates is whether, and to what extent, duties of distributive justice, including in particular egalitarian concerns, that we recognize within the state, have implications for thinking about economic justice beyond the state. We have much more experience arguing about economic justice domestically than internationally, so how we translate our commitments from the domestic to the international will have a significant impact on the conclusions we reach about the latter. I develop a distinctive response to this question, building on existing approaches that emphasize state coercion as a key factor triggering distributive duties domestically. These, I argue, cannot support a strict division between domestic and international economic justice; rather, a suitably nuanced understanding of coercion beyond the state suggests important international distributive principles, albeit principles quite different to those applying domestically. Inequality matters for international justice, but not in the ways many assume. Rather, because distributive duties are a consequence of coercive relations, and coercive relations look quite different internationally, egalitarian duties also look quite different here. While the argument takes me far from the practical concerns of the trade regime, it ultimately yields principles appropriate to evaluating the justice of international trade regulation, and adjudicating the distributive conflicts that arise therein. These principles I label, collectively, Equality in Global Commerce, or EGC. I provide an initial specification of these at the end of this introduction. Articulating and defending them in detail is the task of Chapters 2, 3, 4, and 5.

The second question requires evaluating the existing positive law of the World Trade Organization in light of these principles. It requires detailed engagement with the treaties and case-law that together constitute that law, and with the existing scholarship thereon. However, my goal here is not simply to measure the positive law of the trade regime against the normative ideal prescribed by EGC. Rather, I examine whether, and to what extent, the law can be understood as expressing that ideal. In answering this latter question I contrast the explanations suggested by EGC with those proposed by the dominant existing theories of the trade regime, highlighting the ways those existing theories fail to account for the specifics of the trade rules, and how EGC might remedy this. While it is not strictly necessary to approach the question in this manner, doing so serves two additional goals: it strengthens the claim that EGC provides an appropriate standard of justice for the trade regime; and it shows how its interpretive implications differ from existing theories, and how EGC might thus guide the interpretation and progressive development of WTO law. These are the tasks of Chapters 6, 7, 8, and 9.

The argument is developed in four parts.

Part I   Foundations

Chapter 1   Introduction   This introduction locates the project and provides an overview of the approach adopted in the book as a whole. It also provides an initial specification of the principles of distributive justice that I label Equality in Global Commerce (EGC), which I argue are appropriate to international trade law, and which the rest of the book is concerned to defend and apply. This includes defining two categories of measures, External Trade Measures (ETMs) and Domestic Economic Measures (DEMs), and outlining the distinct justificatory standards appropriate to each.

Chapter 2   Why World Trade Law Needs a Theory of Justice
Chapter 2 provides a more detailed account of the motivation, existing
literature, and methodology. I begin by clarifying the concept of distributive justice, its distinctness from other concepts in political morality, and its role in the evaluation of legal and political institutions. I
then examine a number of prominent positions in debates about global
distributive justice, highlighting their inability to answer the kinds of
questions that arise in trade regulation. As well as the principal positions in the philosophical debate, I also examine views that, while rarely
defended by theorists, represent the unstated assumptions from which
many legal scholars and practitioners begin. Chapter 2 also examines
existing explanatory theories of international trade law, in order both to
clarify the relation between the present project and existing theoretical
work on IEL, and to explain why that existing work fails to answer the
questions of distributive justice that are my focus. Finally, I outline and
defend the methodology adopted throughout the book. This includes a
brief account of the Rawlsian constructivist approach that I adopt in
Part II, and the standards for testing theories' explanatory and interpretive claims against the legal doctrine examined in Part III.

Part II   Justice

Part II is predominantly a work of normative political philosophy. It
argues for an approach to global distributive justice that I claim is
better suited than existing approaches to address concrete problems
of legal and political practice, and thus avoids the problems identified
in Part I.

Chapter 3   Towards a Political Theory of World Trade Law   Chapter 3
sets out the core of the positive argument for EGC.
    I begin by reviewing a number of approaches that link duties of dis-
tributive justice to state coercion, and purport thereby to distinguish the
thick egalitarian duties that apply within the state from thinner sufficientarian duties beyond the state. I endorse and defend the emphasis that
these approaches place on coercion, understood as the imposition of
nonvoluntary institutions. However, I argue that they fail adequately to
distinguish the variety of coercive relations that exist in international
economic regulation, and the justificatory demands that these imply.
    To redress this weakness, I construct a typology of coercive relations,
built up from three crosscutting distinctions: between direct and indirect
coercion; between inclusive and exclusive coercion; and between self-

authored and external coercion. In each case, I argue that distinct justificatory demands arise in respect of measures on each side of the relevant
distinction.

Having established the moral significance of these various distinctions, I bring them together to articulate two normatively distinct
classes of measure, External Trade Measures (ETMs) and Domestic
Economic Measures (DEMs), which each give rise to distinct justificatory demands. I argue that ETMs are only justifiable in egalitarian
terms, subject to a reasonable principle of self-determination; whereas
DEMs can be justified in less demanding, broadly sufficientarian,
terms.

Chapter 4 Sovereignty and the Limits of Statism   In Chapter 4 I
anticipate and rebut objections that might be raised against my approach
from various statist and nationalist positions.

I first consider objections from Hobbesian international relations
realists. I distinguish two forms of the realist challenge: the first, I suggest,
is plausible but does not in fact constitute a challenge to EGC; the second,
while directly challenging EGC, is implausibly strong, constituting an
objection not just to EGC, but to international morality and international
law generally.

I next consider objections from anti-cosmopolitan Rawlsians, that my
approach ignores the differences between the basic structures underpinning
domestic and international cooperation. I examine three possible interpretations of this objection, arguing that the first is implausible, the second is
irrelevant, and the third in fact further supports the view that I defend.

I third examine nationalist views that claim we owe special duties to
our fellow nationals that are not due to outsiders. Rather than directly
challenging this claim of national priority, I show the limits on its scope,
and the consequent compatibility between EGC and the strongest plausible form of national priority.

Finally, I consider two arguments that, while commonly advanced by
nationalist thinkers, are separable from nationalism. The first claims that
egalitarian judgments are incoherent in the international context, given the
absence of shared values in terms of which to make those judgments. The
second claims that egalitarian duties between political communities are
incompatible with individual communities' legitimate claims to make
choices about the shared lives of their members. While both have force
when directed against strong cosmopolitan approaches, I argue that
neither constitutes an objection to the view I defend.

Chapter 5   Self-Determination and Trade Regulation   Chapter 5 completes the elaboration and defense of my preferred principles of economic justice, and pre-empts the objection that these give inadequate weight to the right of particular communities to self-determination, including their right to make collective choices, and to determine their economic systems and foreign economic policies. This requires establishing the extent of the policy autonomy that properly falls under self-determination.

In the first part of the chapter, I examine legal conceptions of self-determination, arguing that invoking these to determine the extent of policy autonomy a people can claim is either circular or wholly indeterminate.

This leads me, in the middle part of the chapter, to examine three categories of theoretical arguments for self-determination, which I label intrinsic, expressive, and instrumental arguments. Intrinsic arguments identify an intrinsic value in self-determination as a component of the autonomy of persons. Expressive arguments ground self-determination in the equal status of political communities. Instrumental arguments justify it by reference to its role in the sustainable realization of other valuable goods, including in particular the preservation of encompassing cultures and the protection of individual rights and social justice. In each case, I examine the extent of the powers that the relevant arguments imply that a people must have in order to be self-determining.

The final part of the chapter integrates these three approaches to identify the proper scope of the self-determination that states can claim in economic matters. While this extends to the enactment of DEMs generally, in the case of ETMs it is limited to measures necessary to preserve a state's capacity to provide certain public goods and make certain decisions; and measures advancing shared goals to which outsiders affected thereby have freely committed themselves. These two classes, thus, constitute the reasonable principle of self-determination accommodated by EGC.

Part III   Law

Part III is predominantly a work of applied theory and doctrinal analysis and reconstruction. It has two goals. First, it delivers on the claim that the principles defended in Part II are in fact capable of answering the practical questions of justice that arise within WTO law. Second, it shows how WTO law can itself be understood as an expression of the conception of justice defended in Part II, and how that explanation in fact fits better than the existing conventional wisdom. It thus demonstrates EGC's potential as a justificatory and interpretive, rather than purely critical, theory.

Chapter 6   Border Measures, Discrimination, and External Trade Measures   Chapter 6 examines the core principles of the GATT on border measures and nondiscrimination.

In the first part of the chapter, I examine the GATT's received wisdom, according to which these rules are justified by their function in solving economic problems of protectionism and terms-of-trade manipulation. I outline the various implications of these explanations, and contrast them with the explanation suggested by EGC, namely that these rules serve to discipline ETMs that are not justified under EGC.

The second part focuses specifically on nondiscrimination, given both its prominence in practice, and the recurring interpretive problems it raises. I suggest that these doctrinal problems themselves reflect the absence of an adequate justificatory theory of these rules. I next examine the various approaches to discrimination in GATT and WTO jurisprudence, and the difficulties reconciling these with standard economic accounts of these rules. Finally, I consider the existing jurisprudence's compatibility with EGC, suggesting EGC is better placed to make sense of that jurisprudence, and to guide its progressive development.

Chapter 7   Equality, Self-Determination, and GATT Exceptions   Chapter 7 examines the principal qualifications to the core disciplines: the general exceptions in Art XX GATT; and the various development provisions in Art XVIII, Part IV, and the Enabling Clause.

The first part of the chapter examines the development provisions. It highlights the difficulties reconciling these with the economic arguments supporting them or the economic justifications of the core disciplines. It next outline's EGC's explanation of these exceptions, as exempting ETMs justifiable under EGC's primary, egalitarian limb. Finally, it examines these provisions' treatment in the case-law, and particularly the AB's approach to the Enabling Clause. That approach makes little sense from the perspective of economic theories, but can be readily explained in terms of EGC's concerns with equality and interpersonal justification.

The second part of the chapter examines the general exceptions. Again, it highlights the problems of fit between economic explanations of trade agreements and the specific exceptions in Article XX. It suggests an alternative account of both specific exceptions and chapeau, arguing Article XX is best understood as exempting ETMs under EGC's secondary self-determination limb. It then considers a number of aspects of the AB's Article XX jurisprudence, suggesting this is better explained and justified by EGC than alternative theories.

Chapter 8   Trade   Remedies   and   Fairness   in   International Trade Regulation   Chapter 8 examines the WTO rules on trade remedies, including subsidies, safeguards, and anti-dumping, again arguing that these are better understood from the perspective of EGC than competing theories.

I begin with the persistent disagreements about the function of the trade remedies rules, and the general economic skepticism of their justifiability and compatibility with the economic rationales for trade agreements. I argue that this skepticism reflects a reluctance to take seriously the role of fairness in trade remedies rules, and the absence of a plausible account of fairness for these purposes.

The middle part of the chapter derives an account of fairness, and in turn of the trade remedies disciplines, from EGC. It argues the various trade remedies rules can each be explained as restricting the unjustifiable use of ETMs, or licensing the use of ETMs in response to their unjustifiable use by others, or in order to preserve the self-determination – in the limited sense discussed in Chapter 5 – of the regulating state.

The final part examines recurring problems in the trade remedies jurisprudence. I focus on the concepts of benefit in the definition of a subsidy, foreseeability, and causation in safeguards, and zeroing in anti-dumping. In each case, I argue the AB's difficulties developing and justifying its approach reflect the inadequacy of existing theories of these rules' functions. I show how EGC can both provide a more plausible account of what is at stake in disputes about these concepts, and offer guidance and justification for the AB's approach going forward.

Chapter 9   Regulation, Self-Determination, and Domestic Economic Measures   Chapter 9 examines the Agreement on Technical Barriers to Trade (TBT) and the Agreement on Sanitary and Phytosanitary Measures (SPS), as typifying the ostensibly more intrusive post-Uruguay Round trade regime.

I first identify the most significant innovations in these agreements: their emphasis on harmonization, minimum trade restrictiveness, and legitimate regulatory purposes, and SPS's focus on science as an all-purpose arbiter of the justifiability of regulation. As in earlier chapters, I argue that existing theories cannot account for the various features identified, and propose an alternative explanation derived from EGC. This understands these agreements as concerned, in the first instance, with imposing limited disciplines on DEMs in line with EGC's permissive attitude towards such measures; and second, disciplining ETMs not otherwise disciplined under the GATT.

The next three sections examine three elements of these agreements in detail: the concept of legitimate objectives in TBT; the role of science in SPS; and the aspiration towards harmonization in both agreements. In each case, I examine how far EGC can explain the relevant rules and jurisprudence, and how far it, or any of the other approaches examined, might guide the continued development of the jurisprudence on these issues.

Part IV   Progress

Chapter 10   Conclusion: Where to from Here?   Part III is concerned primarily with relating my normative approach to the existing positive law, and showing how it might play a role in that law's interpretation and progressive development. In Part IV, I consider briefly its implications for current developments in international trade politics, including the apparent demise of the Doha Round, and the turn towards regionalism and plurilateralism. I show how EGC can provide a standard for judging these developments, including suggesting which issues should be addressed multilaterally, which can appropriately be advanced among like-minded subsets of liberalizing states, and ultimately, what might constitute completion of the multilateral trade governance project. I also identify a number of wider implications and outstanding questions raised by the argument in the book as a whole.

1.5   On the Merits and Challenges of Interdisciplinarity

This book is an exercise in both political philosophy and international economic law. As such, I hope it will be of interest to scholars working in both disciplines, as well as potentially interesting economists, political scientists, and international public policy scholars generally.

Writing for these distinct audiences poses its own challenges. First, it invites judgment by the standards of multiple disciplines. And while standards of sound reasoning are in many ways transdisciplinary, each discipline has its own assumptions, methods, and preoccupations that require to be respected. Second, it requires care in deciding how much detail to provide, so as to avoid boring, confusing, or failing to satisfy any particular audience. Different disciplines have different assumed background knowledge, and indeed different basic premises. In consequence, something that one sees as too obvious to mention, another might want both explained and justified. Some objections may also be particular to one group rather than another, so that some will see addressing a particular worry as essential to the argument's success, while others see it as an unnecessary tangent.

I have tried to address these challenges in three ways. First, at each stage of the argument, whether theoretical or doctrinal, I have included some brief introductory remarks to orient readers otherwise unfamiliar with the issues discussed. Second, I have leaned heavily on footnotes, whether to elaborate points passed over relatively quickly in the text, to point readers towards sources providing more extensive discussion, or to answer objections that some might see as crucial, but others will regard as distractions. Third, I have presented the argument in two stages, the first self-consciously theoretical, and the second more explicitly legal and doctrinal. The result is, I hope, an argument that can be appreciated by both lawyers and political theorists, that is not overburdened with explanations that either will find unnecessary, but that is sufficiently rigorous to pass muster by the standards of both.

My hope is that the book as a whole will be of interest to both lawyers and political theorists. While some sections are more explicitly theoretical, and others more doctrinal, I believe there are lessons that specialists in each can learn from the other. These disciplines share a common concern with the terms on which economic and political institutions can and should be organized, so there should be scope for fruitful interdisciplinary conversations.

This may be clearest for lawyers, who are well accustomed to looking to other disciplines for inspiration in explaining and interpreting legal rules and principles. The dominance of economic approaches means that political theory may be less familiar territory for international trade lawyers. However, just as when borrowing from economists, it is not enough to simply take the conclusions of philosophical arguments, and plug them into our legal work. Doing so misses both the nuance of those conclusions, and the opportunities to interrogate their premises, and the reasoning from premise to conclusion. In consequence, while the conclusions of my theoretical argument can be (and are) stated in a few brief slogans, understanding both their force and their implications in legal practice will be greatly enhanced by engaging with the four main theoretical chapters through which they are developed.

However, I am not advocating a one-way traffic of ideas from philosophy to law. There is also much that philosophers might learn from the more doctrinal discussions in later chapters. First and foremost, those chapters illustrate the kinds of practical legal and political questions that actually arise within the trade regime. A major objection that I levy against existing philosophical approaches in Chapter 2 is their inability to speak to those questions. I hope the doctrinal discussions in later chapters exemplify the kind of practical engagement to which normative theorists should aspire. Second, there is wisdom in practice, and law is nothing if not practical. The rules discussed in later chapters constitute practical responses to the problems of cooperation, seeking to balance the conflicting claims that arise in the global economy, subject to the unavoidable limitations of international governance. This gives them an implicit, albeit contingent, normative warrant; they represent pragmatic efforts by those directly involved to solve pressing problems. By giving due respect to the tools that legal and political practitioners have fashioned, theorists can more securely embed their own approaches in political practice, avoiding challenges of irrelevance or normative chauvinism. And third, insofar as these chapters seek to elaborate in more detail the implications of my theoretical argument, they also, and in consequence, clarify that argument itself.

That said, not all readers will be equally interested in all parts of the book, so it is perhaps helpful to provide some guidance for those who prefer the *à la carte* approach.

There is very little law in the first half (Chapters 2–5) of the book. There is a lot of law in the second half (Chapters 6–9).

The main conclusions of my theoretical argument are summarized in the final section of this introduction. Those whose principal interest is legal might be tempted to move from there straight to Chapter 6. I have included cross-references from the later doctrinal chapters back to the earlier theoretical ones, so those who do skip directly to the law will be offered many opportunities to go back and dig deeper into the underlying theory. In addition to these later doctrinal chapters, some of the methodological points in Chapter 2 will be of particular interest to lawyers, including especially on the relation between political morality and legal interpretation.

Theorists may find more that is to their taste in the first half, which develops my main theoretical claims. Again, there are cross-references to later chapters, where ideas developed at the level of theory are put to work in explaining and interpreting the law. However, these are less frequent than in later chapters, reflecting the ways the argument develops. The theoretical argument really gets going in Chapter 3. However, Chapter 2 outlines and defends a number of the assumptions from which I work, and critically reviews existing theoretical approaches, so should repay attention from the more theoretically inclined.

1.6 Equality in Global Commerce

Having outlined the structure of the argument, this final section introduces the principles that I together label Equality in Global Commerce (EGC), which I argue constitute the appropriate standard of justice for international trade regulation. The presentation at this stage is necessarily preliminary and a little superficial, outlining in a few sentences the principles that I spend the rest of the book elaborating and defending. What is presented sparsely here is fleshed out in discussions throughout the later chapters.

1.6.1 Two Classes of Measure

EGC is not a grand blueprint, describing the structures, processes, and outcomes of a just global order. For reasons explained in the following chapters, such blueprints are not especially useful for our purposes. Nor do I think they accurately describe what justice demands in a world like our own. Rather, EGC provides a standard for judging the justice or injustice of the most important institutions that we find in the world, namely states, and of the measures they adopt.

It begins with a distinction between two classes of regulatory measure.

External Trade Measures (ETMs) are measures that pursue their goals specifically through regulating international economic activity.

Domestic Economic Measures (DEMs) are measures that pursue their goals through regulating domestic economic activity, or through regulating economic activity generally. They may affect international economic activity, and indeed may directly regulate such activity, but they do so only in so far as international economic activity is a subset of economic activity generally.

The essence of the distinction lies in the means by which measures of each type pursue their goals, rather than the formal status of the measures or the nature of the goals they pursue. A measure is understood in terms of (i) the specific actions that it requires or prohibits, (ii) the goals that it pursues, and (iii) the proposed causal chain linking the two.[9]

For example, a tariff on imported wine might be understood in terms of the specific action it requires, namely the payment of a duty on imports of wine; the goals that it pursues, for example the protection of livelihoods in the domestic wine sector; and the proposed causal chain linking the two, namely an increase in the price of imported wine leading to an increased market share for domestic wine and increased prices in the domestic market to the benefit of the domestic wine industry. As described, this would constitute an ETM, as it pursues its goal specifically through regulating international economic activity, namely wine imports. Note that it is an ETM because of the goal it pursues, and the means by which it pursues it, not because it falls within a prior category of "tariff" or "trade barrier." While tariffs and quotas will often constitute ETMs, they may not always do so, and many other forms of regulation, including apparently domestic and nondiscriminatory measures, will constitute ETMs under the definition above.

A more difficult case is regulations governing the characteristics of products for sale. Consider the German Beer Purity Law, the *Reinheitsgebot*, which strictly controlled the ingredients in beer sold in Germany, including imported beer. It regulated both domestic and international economic activity. The specific action that it prohibited was the sale of beer, whether domestic or imported, that included proscribed ingredients. Whether it constituted an ETM depends on the goals that it pursued, and the proposed causal chain linking the specific actions regulated to that goal. Two alternative goals could be suggested for the *Reinheitsgebot*. On one interpretation, it ensured the quality and safety of beer sold on the German market. Insofar as this was its goal, the causal chain linking the measure to its goal was concerned only with regulating economic activity generally, and did not specifically focus on international economic activity. However, an alternative interpretation understands its

---

[9] Other distinctions might be made between measures that are the exclusive concerns of a single community and those in which outsiders have a legitimate interest. Obvious candidates include an effects-based test, adopted by the United States Supreme Court in jurisprudence under the Commerce Clause, and a burden-based test, adopted by the European Court of Justice in its free movement jurisprudence. However, neither can make sense of boundary problem from which my argument in Chapter 3 begins.

goal as protecting initially Bavarian, and subsequently German, brewers from foreign competition. If this was its goal, it pursued it specifically through regulating international economic activity, namely the import and sale of non-German beers. Its effect on international economic activity was not simply incidental; rather, it was the only means whereby it could achieve that goal. Thus, if this was its goal, it would constitute an ETM. Note again, however, that it is the fact that the measure pursues its goal through regulating international economic activity, rather than its protectionism, that identifies it as an ETM.

By way of further illustration, consider the EU's prohibition on seal products.[10] There is little suggestion this prohibition is protectionist; rather, it is driven by genuine concerns for animal welfare.[11] However, to the extent it is concerned to improve animal welfare in exporting countries, it constitutes an ETM. It pursues its goal by prohibiting the marketing of seal products in the EU. The causal chain from measure to goal includes reducing economic incentives for commercial seal hunting in exporting countries, and thereby changing hunters' behavior. It thus pursues its goal specifically though regulating international economic activity, and so constitutes an ETM. However, again, the seal products regime might be understood in purely domestic terms. One might argue that its goal was to protect European consumers from the moral taint of exposure to immoral products.[12] On this interpretation, the measure is concerned only indirectly with international economic activity; its main concern is with activities within the EU, and it arguably constitutes a DEM.[13] Whether this is a plausible interpretation in this case seems doubtful; but other examples of moral restrictions, such as non-Kosher foods in Israel or beef in India, are more readily interpreted in these terms.[14]

These last two examples illustrate two slightly different ways in which a measure might pursue its goal specifically through regulating international economic activity. The protectionist interpretation of the *Reinheitsgebot* addresses international activity through its differential impact on foreign as compared with domestic products. It is the fact that foreign products are impacted more than domestic products that is the mechanism whereby the

---

[10] *Regulation (EC) 1007/2009 on trade in seal products.*

[11] Some concerns about political motivations for particular exemptions were raised in the WTO dispute: *EC-Seal Products*, (Panel), §7.350.

[12] I take up this point further in Chapter 4.   [13] Cf. (Charnovitz, 1997: 695).

[14] I take these examples from (Howse & Langille, 2012: 369). Although, at least among Muslim-majority states, such religious import restrictions are rare: (Bhala & Keating, 2014: 345) Cf. (Van den Bossche & Zdouc, 2013: 571).

measure has its effect. We cannot even describe that mechanism without referring to the foreign origin of the products affected. The animal welfare interpretation of the seal regime, on the other hand, pursues its goal through regulating international economic activity because it is only through altering patterns of international trade, viz. demand for seal products, and thus the behavior of foreign producers, that it can achieve its goals. It is not the fact that it targets foreign over domestic producers, but rather that it seeks, through regulating international trade, to change the behavior of those producers.

The mere fact that a measure affects, or even necessarily affects, international economic activity is insufficient without this link between action, goal, and causal chain. Consider, for example, the French prohibition on asbestos products in *EC-Asbestos*. That measure regulated a product, asbestos, that was not produced in France. All asbestos was therefore a product of international economic activity. However, the measure targeted asbestos as such. The fact that asbestos was a foreign product, or that the measure impacted foreign producers, was no part of its goal or of the mechanism whereby it pursued its goal. Nor was it necessary, in order to achieve that goal, that through altering patterns of international trade, it would change the behavior of foreign asbestos producers. The measure was concerned to prohibit asbestos in general, in so far as it might come onto the domestic French market from any source, domestic or international. In the context of an internationally traded product, such measures will necessarily impact on international trade, but this will not alone make them ETMs.

1.6.2   Identifying Measures

As these examples make clear, identifying a measure's goals and the means whereby they are pursued are not mechanical processes. They will always involve some degree of judgment, based on an examination of the measure, in the context of its domestic enactment, antecedents, wider economic and legal framework, etc. To identify both goals and means, I adopt Dworkin's method of constructive interpretation.[15]

Dworkin distinguishes conversational interpretation, which seeks to understand a practice through the intentions of its authors, from constructive interpretation, which he describes as "imposing purpose on an object or practice in order to make of it the best possible example of the

---

[15]   See generally: (Dworkin, 1986: ch. 2).

form or genre to which it is taken to belong."[16] The range of individuals involved in adopting economic measures and the likely diversity of their purposes mean that we cannot conversationally interpret measures to determine whether they constitute ETMs; but we can do so constructively.[17] While Dworkin divides interpretation into three stages, I here focus on the second, interpretive, stage, in which we seek "some general justification of the main elements of the [relevant] practice."[18] In our case, we seek a justification for a particular measure or complex of measures.

Where multiple interpretations are possible, as in the cases noted above, we adjudicate among them based on two criteria: how well they fit the object of interpretation, and how far they show it as valuable or justified, placing it in its best light. However, in adapting this approach to identifying ETMs, I adopt a variation on the latter criterion, asking what interpretation is best from the perspective of those in whose name the relevant measures are adopted.[19] In a democratic state, this is the citizenry as a whole. It is from their perspective that we must interpret measures to understand their goal and the means by which they pursue it. Best, then, means best having regard to the values of the public culture of the relevant state.[20] Identifying the appropriate values in a given case may lead to further contested interpretive questions, but at least we can form meaningful judgments on these without recourse to subjective intentions of decision-makers.[21]

As well as making the problem more tractable, constructive interpretation fits the judgments I hope to make about ETMs and DEMs. We commonly regard political acts as the acts of a community. The officials who take and implement decisions act as agents for the population as a whole. As Nagel notes, "the society makes [its members] responsible for its acts, which are taken in [their] name and on which, in a democracy, [they] may even have some influence."[22] Further, to the extent others react to state measures, it is the citizens who will feel the impact. Thus, in considering the justice of measures adopted by a state, we start with the

---

[16] (Dworkin, 1986: 52).

[17] Lamond notes this difficulty in attributing intentions to laws generally (Lamond, 2000).

[18] (Dworkin, 1986: 66).

[19] On the problems with Dworkin's use of justification: (Simmonds, 2008: 224–226).

[20] Dworkin suggests a similar move in interpreting foreign legal systems: (Dworkin, 1986: 107).

[21] The approach described parallels the objective intent approach favored by the Appellate Body. See e.g. *Japan-Alcohol II*, (AB), p. 29; *China-Rare Earths*, (AB), §5.96.

[22] (Nagel, 2005: 129) Cf. (Pogge, 2011a).

understanding of those measures that is available to those who we hold responsible for them, namely the society as a whole.[23]

How might this work in practice? Returning to the *Seals* example, we seek an interpretation that both reflects the values of the public culture of the adopting community (justification) and corresponds in so far as possible to the actual features of the relevant practice (fit). To adjudicate the justification criterion, we might consider how far the public culture of the European Union, as reflected in its institutions and legislation, national, and regional, and in its wider public discourse, reflects concerns to prevent animal cruelty, and/or to address the kinds of moral concerns evoked by exposure to inhumanely produced products. We might examine whether similar bans applied to other products, and if so, whether these were purely forward-looking (suggesting concerns about animal cruelty), or also included products produced before the relevant ban (suggesting concerns about moral taint). We might also consider whether, more generally, the relevant public culture had a practice of legislating moral questions. As regards fit, we would need to consider whether there were characteristics of the measure that were better explained by one interpretation or the other. Again, the question of how products produced prior to the ban were dealt with would be relevant; but we might also consider how it deals with goods in transit, whether it addresses the manufacture of seal-hunting paraphernalia, and perhaps even how it deals with synthetic seal products. We might also consider whether any public debate about this specific measure, or about similar measures, suggested that one of these concerns was dominant.

Finally on identifying ETMs, there may be cases where a measure genuinely pursues multiple goals, or pursues its goal though multiple channels, at least one of which would constitute it as both an ETM and a DEM. Such a measure should be regarded as an ETM *to the extent that* it pursues its goals specifically through regulating international economic activity. Thus, it may be possible to distinguish between elements of a

---

[23] This approach may require modification in considering nondemocratic states. Nagel suggests that, even in nondemocratic and colonial states, the coercion of law is generally exercised in the name of the population. However, there must be some threshold of social legitimacy below which we cannot attribute to the ruled the actions of the ruler. In these circumstances, it may be more appropriate to interpret measures from the point of view of the governing elite. However, we are still engaged in interpreting public measures, rather than identifying private motives, with what a measure means, rather than what its author means by it. See (Hollis & Smith, 1990: 74). The AB draws a similar distinction, observing that "[t]he government's reason for granting a subsidy only explains *why* the subsidy is granted. It does not necessarily answer the question as to *what* the government did.": *EC-Aircraft*, (AB), §1052.

measure that constitute it as an ETM, and other elements reflecting its nature as a DEM. Alternatively, we might look at the context in which the measure was adopted to consider whether it could have been adopted solely on the basis of its characteristics as a DEM; if this is not the case (for example, because the constituency concerned with the goals that constitute it as a DEM lacked the required political influence), then the measure as a whole should be considered as an ETM.[24]

The distinction between ETMs and DEMs is necessarily somewhat abstract at this stage. I have sought here to identify the conceptual distinction, and to show how, in practice, measures can be located within each category. However, the significance of the categories derives not from the definitions above, but from the way these map onto further distinctions drawn in Chapter 3. Thus, to the extent these categories remain unclear, the argument in Chapter 3 may further clarify them. Further discussion in Chapters 6 through 9, which links these categories more closely to existing WTO practice, should further illustrate the distinction.

1.6.3 Equality in Global Commerce

EGC proposes a standard by which ETMs should be judged:

> **EGC Principle:** ETMs are just if and only if they pursue global equality of individual opportunity, through improving the position of less advantaged individuals, subject to a reasonable principle of self-determination.

The language of EGC echoes that of Rawls' Difference Principle, discussed further in later chapters. It is individualist at the level of justification, and focuses on equality of opportunity. This reflects the view that inequalities of opportunity are particularly troubling,[25] and the fact that ETMs are primarily concerned in practice with distributing opportunities for economic activity, rather than directly distributing goods or resources.[26] However, I

---

[24] Cf. (Regan, 2006: 952). Note, however, that we inquire into the political constituencies supporting a measure to inform its interpretation from the perspective of the community as a whole.

[25] Thus, Rawls gives the principle of fair equality of opportunity lexical priority over the difference principle, and indeed one way to understand liberal equality is as simply the working out of a fundamental commitment to equality of opportunity: (Kymlicka, 2002: 57–60).

[26] Consider, the effect of a trade barrier will often be to divert consumption from a less expensive imported product to a more expensive domestic product: (Krugman et al., 2012: 225–226). While the anticipated result is an increase in welfare for the domestic producer, the immediate effect is to divert the transaction opportunity.

suggest, in practice, EGC is applied by considering per capita income of groups, as a proxy for the opportunity sets enjoyed by individuals within those groups. I discuss further in Chapter 4 the rationale for this approach.[27]

Two aspects of the principle of self-determination are relevant to EGC.

First, some ETMs may be justifiable under that principle, rather than under EGC's principal, egalitarian limb. I take up this point further in Chapter 5. I there distinguish two ways this might be the case: first, measures protecting peoples' capacity for effective self-determination, including their capacity to provide essential public goods; and second, measures advancing contingently shared goals and projects, to which particular states have jointly committed themselves. In both cases, I highlight the limits of these justifications.

Second, the reference to self-determination highlights the role of national choice in deciding when an ETM is justifiable, and when it is to the advantage of less advantaged individuals. I assume that the members of a political community, acting through their government, are best placed to determine what measures are likely to be for their benefit.[28] In the context of contested economic theories, it is particularly important that decisions about the most appropriate economic policies for a community be made by those directly responsible to that community.[29] I take up this point further in Chapters 3 and 7.[30]

So described, EGC is a partial principle of global justice, addressing a specific class of measures. It says nothing about the justice of measures other than ETMs, or of global distributions generally. It must therefore be complemented by another principle dealing with these issues. For ease of presentation, let me here borrow some elements from Rawls's *Law of Peoples*.[31] I discuss this further in Chapter 2. For present purposes, it suffices to note that Rawls rejects any comparative standard of global economic justice, while proposing a positive duty of assistance to burdened peoples[32] and a negative obligation to refrain from measures that undermine the capacity of peoples to become or remain well ordered, a concept that for Rawls imports domestic legitimacy and a capacity for

---

[27] See §4.5 below.   [28] For similar views: (Beitz, 1999: 83–122; Jackson, 2006: 74).

[29] For a review of the debate on interventionist trade policies and development: (Krugman et al., 2012: ch. 9–12). For views skeptical of the free trade orthodoxy: (Chang, 2005; Lindauer et al., 2002; Rodriguez & Rodrik, 1999; Rodrik, 2000, 2006).

[30] See §3.6, 7.2.2.

[31] Alternative arguments might adapt EGC to other moderate theories, including Buchanan's or Pogge's human rights approaches, or Miller's liberal nationalism.

[32] For Rawls's rejection of a global egalitarianism: (Rawls, 1999: 113–121). On the Duty of Assistance: (Rawls, 1999: 105–113).

effective self-determination and to vindicate basic human rights.[33] I adopt these latter elements from Rawls to govern measures not directly addressed by the EGC Principle. This is not simply *ad hoc*, however; as the argument in Chapter 3 makes clear, these elements derive from the same premises that generate EGC. So while I borrow the standards from Rawls, I will offer my own arguments to support them.

This yields the following proviso:

> **DEM Proviso:** *DEMs are externally just, provided they do not impair the basic rights of outsiders or undermine the capacity of other peoples to become or remain well ordered.*

Both principle and proviso are of course unmotivated at this stage. Arguing for them is the task of the next four chapters.

---

[33] (Rawls, 1999: 63–67, 106–112). The negative obligation is an obvious corollary of the Duty of Assistance. While not explicitly stated, some textual support appears in Rawls's discussion of cooperative organizations: (Rawls, 1999: 42–43). Freeman identifies a negative duty in Rawls's theory: (Freeman, 2007: 280). Variations on such a negative duty can be found in e.g. (Miller, 2007: 47, 163–201; Pogge, 2002: passim).

Why World Trade Law Needs a Theory of Justice

2.1 The Problem of Distributive Justice in International Trade Regulation

Many recurring problems in trade regulation seem to raise questions of distributive justice. As a political slogan, "fair trade" is frequently invoked to oppose "free trade," whether by developing countries demanding special and differential treatment, by trade unions seeking protection from low-wage countries, or by civil society activists raising social, environmental, and human rights concerns.[1] In each case, justice and fairness are co-opted to support arguments that existing or proposed rules give insufficient weight to some important interest, usually that of its advocates, and that costs and benefits from international cooperation should be distributed differently.[2] These are claims of distributive justice. However, whereas claims of justice and fairness seem inevitable and pervasive, there is little consensus on their implications for specific questions. In many cases, it seems, they appear on both sides of an issue. How should we reconcile developed countries' claims to equal treatment with developing countries' claims to policy space? How can we weigh the interests of threatened workers in developed countries against their low-wage competitors overseas? Should activists' concerns for environmental goods restrict exporting countries' rights to choose their own standards? Many of us have conflicting intuitions in these cases. We see some value on both sides and struggle to explain why we prefer one answer over another, or to convince others of our answers' merits.

There are, of course, extensive literatures on these, and many other, distributive questions in trade regulation. Much of the

---

[1] E.g. (Cass & Boltuck, 1996: 351–354; Hudec, 1996: 1–4).
[2] On the political function of fairness claims: (Lim, 2012).

"linkages" debate, for example, is squarely addressed to distributive questions, as is the literature on trade and development.[3] More generally, various accounts of the function of the trade regime, whether understood in terms of efficiency, human rights, or embedded liberalism, endorse particular answers to these questions.[4] However, those answers are not always made explicit; and to the extent that they are, they are rarely fully theorized.[5] We make judgments about distributive questions in trade regulation, but we lack a theory of distributive justice for this domain, which can integrate those judgments, articulate a consistent basis for them, and ground them securely in deeper or more general claims, about value, the right, and the good.[6]

Making sense of these distributive questions is the task of this book. In this chapter, I lay some of the essential groundwork for the argument that follows, clarifying the nature of the project, locating it in relation to various existing literatures, and outlining and justifying the methodologies adopted in subsequent sections.

I begin by clarifying the concept of distributive justice, distinguishing it from other concepts in political morality. This allows me to locate the project in relation to existing trade law scholarship, much of which either neglects specifically distributive questions or addresses them in a partial or under-theorized manner.

From there, I turn to the existing philosophical literature on global distributive justice, showing how that literature struggles to engage with the specific distributive questions that arise within the trade regime. I examine three prominent philosophical positions – global egalitarian, statist, and human rights approaches – as well as three less theoretically

---

[3] E.g. (Evenett & Hoekman, 2006; Francioni, 2001; Lang, 2011; Nielsen, 2007). On linkages and "fairness": (Charnovitz, 2002b: 39–41). Maduro clearly recognizes the relation between "linkages" and distributive justice: (Maduro, 2001). Cf. (Trachtman, 2002: 87) Admittedly, many other linkage accounts adopt a more positivist approach. E.g. (Kelly, 2006). On linkage debates' structure and their relation to debates about the WTO's role: (Lang, 2007). On the value of making questions of value and purpose explicit in analyzing linkage: (Lang, 2007: 540–542).

[4] See §§2.5.6, 2.6.2 below.

[5] Trachtman, for example, while by no means eschewing theory, assumes uncontroversially that "[t]he fundamental basis for responding to [linkage] is welfare, broadly understood: does it make individuals, in the aggregate, better off to do so?": (Trachtman, 2002: 77). For skepticism of such generalized answers: (Jackson, 2002: 118–120).

[6] On these roles of political theory: (Kymlicka, 2002: 3–7; Rawls, 2001: 1–5) Cf. (Cohen, 2008: 3–6).

prominent alternatives – internalism, positivism, and economic efficiency – to demonstrate the failings of existing approaches.

Having thus established the need for a new approach, I set out the methodology and assumptions on which my project rests. This is done in three sections: first, I outline the normative premises and constructivist methods through which, in Part II, I argue for the principles that I label Equality in Global Commerce (EGC); second, I outline the explanatory and interpretive standards that I adopt in Part III to apply and test EGC against the existing positive law of the trade regime; and third, I explain how the combination of normative and explanatory claims gives rise to critical implications for adjudicators, states, and the trade regime as a whole.

2.2   Distributive Justice and Political Morality

My concern is distributive justice in international trade regulation. By distributive justice, I mean those principles of political morality concerned with the distribution, given competing claims, of what John Rawls calls social primary goods.[7] These are the things that we all require, to a greater or lesser extent, to advance our plans of life, whether individually or collectively. They include economic goods, but also rights and liberties. They are wholly social in their origin and allocation, in contrast to the natural primary goods of health and vigor, intelligence, wit, and charm. Most of us would regard their distribution as an appropriate object of moral concern, believing that some ways of allocating these goods are better than others. Our social institutions, including our political, economic, and legal systems, distribute these goods; and different institutions can be expected to produce different distributions. Distributive justice is thus an aspect of the justice of social institutions.[8]

Clearly, distributive justice, so understood, is not the whole of political morality.

First, we distinguish distributive justice, which specifies a just distribution, from corrective justice, which addresses deviations from that distribution.[9] In the trade regime, the latter seems most relevant to the operation of the Dispute Settlement System, and the remedies it affords, while the former addresses the underlying distribution of substantive rights and obligations that is policed through that system.

[7] (Rawls, 1971: 62, 1996: 75–76).
[8] I address further in Chapter 3 the relations between institutions and distributive justice, and the significance of particular institutions for this purpose.
[9] See e.g. (Coleman & Mendlow, 2010: §3.1; Weinrib, 1995: ch. 3).

Second, we distinguish distributive justice, which addresses the substance of a distributive scheme, from procedural values, including democracy, participation, and due process, which concern the ways that scheme is selected. Justice no doubt demands in many contexts that particular procedural values be observed. Further, in so far as justice concerns the distribution of rights, which in turn protect choices, questions of substance at one level translate into questions of procedure at the next. However, the two issues are at least conceptually distinct.

Third, we distinguish distributive justice from legitimacy. Legitimacy commonly denotes either the propriety of a particular agent or institution determining a particular matter (the right to rule) or the extent to which others are bound by such determinations (the duty to obey).[10] Again, legitimacy is related to, but distinct from, distributive justice. Legitimacy concerns who decides, while distributive justice concerns what is decided.[11]

Fourth, we distinguish duties of justice from duties of humanity.[12] Justice is concerned with moral rights. Duties of justice are owed to particular agents, such that those agents have a moral claim to their fulfillment and are wronged when they go unfulfilled. Duties of humanity, by contrast, need not be owed to particular agents. So, for example, we might think that persons have duties of charity, which require them to donate some of their income to worthy causes; but this does not mean that potential beneficiaries are wronged if we fail to act on those duties. Such duties may be mandatory, in the sense that failing to act on them means acting wrongfully, making us appropriately subject to guilt and blame. But in acting wrongfully, we need not thereby wrong anyone else.[13]

Fifth, we distinguish distributive justice, as an aspect of the political morality of institutions, from the interpersonal morality of individual action.[14] My concern is with the institutions that govern the international

---

[10] See generally: (Raz, 2006; Simmons, 1979).

[11] Subject, again, to the recognition that the distribution of rights is often ultimately a distribution of choices.

[12] See generally: (Barry, 1982).

[13] The justice/humanity distinction is sometimes drawn in terms of enforceability: where I fail to comply with a duty of justice, others can coerce me to do so, whereas compliance with duties of humanity, or interpersonal morality more generally, is a matter of conscience. Depending on the content of a moral view, these two distinctions may or may not line up. One objection to understanding justice in terms of rights correlativity is that it denies that utilitarianism, at least understood teleologically, is a theory of justice at all. While this will strike some as problematic, others happily bite this bullet. E.g. (Kymlicka, 2002: 36).

[14] The distinction here is related but, at least in some versions, orthogonal to that between justice and humanity.

economy, rather than directly with the duties of individual participants therein.[15] The factors relevant to my choice whether to purchase ethically sourced products, for example, may be quite different to those determining whether the law should require, permit, or indeed prohibit, me from doing so.[16] Law and institutions define the space within which individual choice is exercised. While the two are closely related, care is required to ensure they are not conflated.

Finally, we distinguish justice from other institutional virtues, including in particular efficiency. This distinction is less straightforward than the others, because – at least on some interpretations – efficiency proposes answers to the same questions as distributive justice. Two conceptions of efficiency are prominent in trade scholarship: Pareto efficiency, which regards an institution or distribution as efficient if no agent can be made better off under any alternative institution or distribution without, at the same time, making another worse off[17]; and Kaldor-Hicks efficiency, which regards an institution or distribution as efficient if no agent can be made so much better off under any alternative that they would be able to compensate those who do worse as a result.[18] Both provide standards against which distributions may be judged. Indeed, the utilitarian injunction to maximize aggregate utility effectively equates Kaldor-Hicks efficiency and distributive justice[19]; and Rawls's difference principle, on which I draw below, incorporates elements of Pareto efficiency.[20] I say more later about the implications of moving from efficiency to justice in thinking about trade regulation. Suffice to note here that the two constitute alternative, and potentially conflicting, ideals.[21]

2.3   On the Scope of Justice: Domestic vs. International vs. Global

Distributive justice, then, is distinct from these various other aspects of political and indeed interpersonal morality and is characterized by a concern with the ways institutions distribute social primary goods. Before

---

[15] On the need to distinguish among potential objects of moral evaluation and to ensure the appropriate principles are applied to each: (Rawls, 2001: 10–12).

[16] On the distinct interpersonal morality of fair trade: (Kurjanska & Risse, 2008; Risse, 2007).

[17] (Coleman, 1979: 512–513).   [18] Ibid., 513–514.

[19] On the relation: (Posner, 1979). One upshot is that, to the extent we reject utilitarianism as a moral theory, we should be suspicious of approaches that single-mindedly pursue economic efficiency. For accessible introductions to the merits and demerits of utilitarianism: (Kymlicka, 2002: 10–52; Smart & Williams, 1973).

[20] (Rawls, 1971: 58).   [21] See e.g. (Cohen, 2008: 315–323).

proceeding, however, we must draw one further distinction, this time among different senses of distributive justice. These are distinguished by the classes of agents and relations over whom distributive judgments are made.

Domestic distributive justice refers to the justice of distributions as among members of a given polity. This is the most familiar sense of distributive justice, in both political theory and practice. When we worry about inequalities among citizens, we are addressing questions of domestic distributive justice. When we worry that a domestic law unfairly burdens some citizens for the benefit of others, our concerns fall under domestic distributive justice. However, domestic distributive justice might also serve to critique international institutions. When we worry, for example, that liberal trade rules depress wages for workers in developed economies, our concern might be one of purely domestic distributive justice: that these rules benefit some citizens (employers) at the expense of other citizens (workers). What matters is that we are making judgments of justice based on distributive outcomes for insiders, without regard to the implications for outsiders.[22]

International and global distributive justice both relax this constraint, at least potentially admitting the distributive claims of outsiders. They are distinguished by the identity of the agents whose claims are admitted.[23]

International distributive justice refers to the justice of distributions among states or, more generally, among political communities. If we claim, for example, that developing countries are unfairly disadvantaged by international trade rules, we make a claim of international distributive justice: our focus is on the state as a unit, rather than on the claims of its individual citizens. It can seem natural to consider justice beyond the state in terms of the claims of particular states. The international system is organized in terms of states, and when we think of foreigners we often identify them in the first instance with the states of which they are members. An approach to distributive justice in which political communities are the exclusive bearers of rights and obligations is a theory of international distributive justice.[24]

By global distributive justice, I mean an approach that is not restricted, either to members of particular political communities, as domestic approaches are, or to states, as international approaches are. Global distributive justice thus looks through the state, acknowledging potential

---

[22] Freeman argues for just this reason that taking domestic distributive justice seriously leaves little space for international or global justice (Freeman, 2007: 289–290).

[23] For some efforts to draw this distinction, and a sense of its fluidity: (Blake & Smith, 2015; Brock, 2015).

[24] Rawls's *Law of Peoples* is largely international in this sense.

justice claims across political boundaries, including those of members of one political community against another or against the international system as a whole. After all, while the international system is organized into states, international economic activity is not limited by national borders, and for many people it is outcomes for individuals, not states, that are most obviously of moral concern. In a world where many injustices are perpetrated by governments against their own populations, and many of the world's poorest live in countries where others enjoy great wealth, an exclusively international lens risks missing very significant injustices.[25] A theory of global distributive justice might subsume domestic distributive justice entirely, drawing no distinctions between relations among members of a community and relations with outsiders; or it might limit itself to addressing cross-border claims, leaving space for various domestic approaches within particular communities. However, it will not assume that either domestic or international distributions can be analyzed wholly independently of each other, or that conclusions on either can pre-empt, without examination, the kinds of claims that arise, for both individuals and groups, in the more variegated world in which we actually live.

I draw these distinctions in order to frame my inquiry, not prejudge its outcome. It might be that the proper domain of distributive judgments is the political community, or that only states have justice claims at the international level. However, we cannot reach either of those conclusions by assumption: they require an argument.[26] I therefore approach distributive justice in trade regulation as a question of global distributive justice; and while my conclusions include both significant space for domestic distributive justice within particular communities and a prominent role for states as bearers of rights and duties, these emerge as part of an answer to that global question.

2.4   What Trade Law Theory Is (and Is Not) About

Our concern, then, is global distributive justice in international trade regulation. In the next section, I discuss a number of existing approaches to distributive justice beyond the state, highlighting their weaknesses in

---

[25] Taking one stark example, at the time of writing China had 391 US dollar billionaires, more than any country apart from the United States. Yet in 2013 11.9% of its population – 163 million people – lived on less than US$3.10 per day.

[26] Contrast Rawls, who (in *Theory of Justice*) imposes the domestic scope limit by assumption, but subsequently (in *Law of Peoples*) treats the conclusions of domestic theory as given for the purposes of international theory: (Rawls, 1971: 8, 1999: 32–35).

addressing trade regulation. However, let me first distinguish the project pursued here from a number of existing theoretical approaches to the trade regime.

Efficiency often provides the default standard against which the trade regime is measured, leading to the virtual colonization of much trade law scholarship by economic approaches.[27] Because efficiency answers the same questions as distributive justice, my account necessarily challenges such scholarship. In the next section, I briefly examine the normative foundations of efficiency approaches, while much of the discussion in later chapters elaborates the different implications of thinking about trade regulation in terms of justice or efficiency.

Legitimacy, democracy, and various procedural virtues are similarly prominent concerns.[28] In so far as these address *how* decisions are made, they are compatible with various views about *what* decisions should be made. I therefore do not address them in detail. It is worth noting, however, that much of this literature implicitly endorses a statist view on the scope of justice: in assuming domestic political choice is prior to international obligation, it implicitly denies that outsiders have claims against a state's policy choices.[29] Others do recognize such claims, and that trade law might provide a tool for raising them, but no answer is offered to the subsequent question of how such claims should be adjudicated.[30]

Many scholars approach questions of value in the trade regime from a broadly sociological perspective, seeking to recover the normative assumptions expressed therein.[31] Most prominent here is embedded liberalism, which understands the trade regime as expressing a contingent political bargain balancing trade liberalization and domestic stability.[32] In some cases, these approaches are limited to empirical questions about the goals the trade regime pursues, as distinct from the normative question of which values it should pursue. In others, they support normative judgments; but those judgments are themselves grounded in implicit and undefended statist assumptions about distributive justice.[33]

[27] Garcia characterizes efficiency as the dominant distributive principle in the trade regime: (Garcia, 2006: 378).

[28] E.g. (Howse, 2002c; Howse & Nicolaidis, 2001, 2003; Joseph, 2009; Keohane & Nye, 2001; Krajewski, 2011; McGrew, 2011; Nanz, 2006).

[29] E.g. (Howse & Nicolaidis, 2003: 17; Keohane & Nye, 2001; Trebilcock et al., 2013: 89). I discuss in the next section some of the problems with this assumption.

[30] E.g. (Scott, 2004a). For some initial thoughts on integrating democratic choice and duties to outsiders: (Suttle, 2016: 831–833).

[31] E.g. (Cho, 2015; Eagleton-Pierce, 2013; Lang, 2011).   [32] See further: §2.6.2 below.

[33] For this point in relation to embedded liberalism: (Lang, 2006: 100).

Those assumptions might or might not be sound, but they require an argument to support them.

Other approaches are more explicitly normative, but adopt a narrow focus, articulating and defending one or a number of values, for example sustainable development or labor rights, without locating these in their wider normative context or resolving the distributive conflicts they imply.[34] The most prominent and wide-ranging approaches in this vein emphasize human rights.[35] Human rights claims are claims of distributive justice, as defined above, but they are not the whole of distributive justice. As such, these approaches speak to a subset of distributive questions and can support all-things-considered judgments only once integrated into a broader account of distributive justice.[36]

Finally, there is an extensive literature on the distributive effects of trade regulation.[37] However, that literature rarely engages with theoretical questions of whether, and how, justice is implicated in those effects. In some cases, it works from bare intuitions, as that rules imposing disproportionate burdens on less developed countries, or measures impeding their economic development, are obviously unjust.[38] In others, a familiar account of domestic distributive justice is transplanted and applied to the trade regime, but without considering how the move from domestic to international might affect the distributive principles that apply, or the radical implications of internationalizing domestic distributive claims.[39] Others make international distributive implications secondary to the domestic distributive effects of various trade policies.[40]

Once these various literatures are distinguished, we find distributive justice in trade regulation is substantially under-theorized. There are no more than a handful of studies that directly tackle it. Further, the wider literature on global distributive justice is ill fitted to answer the questions that seem regularly to arise in considering justice in trade regulation. In consequence, while global political theory and international economic

---

[34] For example, much of the linkage literature is implicitly statist, emphasizing states' claims to pursue their own conceptions and weightings of relevant values. E.g. (Francioni, 2001). For this criticism, with a North/South emphasis: (Bhagwati, 2002: 126–134).

[35] See further: §§2.5.3, 2.6.2 below.   [36] (Suttle, 2014a: 1078–1080).

[37] E.g. (Rodrik, 2001; Rolland, 2012).

[38] E.g. (Deardoff, 2001; Schefer, 2013). In many cases, the difficulty of defending substantive answers to distributive questions leads to a focus instead on procedure and legitimacy. E.g. (Howse, 2002b; Zampetti, 2001: 44).

[39] E.g. (Stiglitz & Charlton, 2005; Trachtman, 2003), both of whom simply apply Rawls's domestic theory internationally.

[40] E.g. (Maduro, 2001; Rodrik, 2011: xix, 55–61; Sapir, 2001).

law address closely related questions, about right action in international economic cooperation, there has been very little interdisciplinary dialogue. In the next section, I discuss the problems with existing approaches, before outlining how my approach solves these.

2.5 Existing Approaches to Distributive Justice in Trade Regulation

Trade regulation is, in the first instance, a species of regulation, and as such an exercise of political power.

This claim seems straightforward. The nature of the underlying practice (trade) may be relevant to the form that regulation takes, but it does not change its quality as regulation. This point is sometimes missed and so bears emphasis. Recall, for example, Fried's account of contract as expressing a Kantian morality of promising.[41] As critics have noted, this elides the difference between institutional justice and interpersonal morality.[42] Promising may be essential in explaining the reasons that a promisor has to comply with his promise; but it has no necessary role in explaining why a third party, the state, should coercively enforce that promise or respond to its breach.[43] These are simply different questions, and quite different considerations may be relevant to them. Similarly, Garcia has recently proposed an account of justice in trade that emphasizes consent as what makes economic exchange "trade" rather than, for example, theft, coercion, or exploitation.[44] From this, he argues that trade regulation should be based on consent, albeit the consent of states rather than individual traders.[45] Like Fried's approach, this conflates two different questions: what is essential for trade to be trade; and what is essential for trade regulation to be just. Regardless of the normative significance of the former question, it cannot directly answer the latter. If we want to know what a just trade regime looks like, we must look to the theory of political institutions rather than the morality of interpersonal interaction.[46]

This does not mean, however, that we can simply derive an account of justice in trade regulation from existing political theories of global justice.

---

[41] (Fried, 1981).   [42] E.g. (Barnett, 1991: 1024–1026).
[43] An analogous point appears in: (Freeman, 2001: 111–112).   [44] (Garcia, 2013: 205).
[45] Ibid., 219–221.
[46] On the latter in the context of trade, see the references at fn. 16 above. For an attempt to integrate the two perspectives, albeit in ways that may struggle to connect with many of the concerns of the trade regime (Risse and Wollner, 2014).

To do so would be to risk missing what is distinctive about trade regulation as a subject of justice, and in turn fail to answer the pressing questions of legal and political practice it raises. Rather, we need an account of global justice that is appropriate to this task, something existing approaches have yet to provide.[47]

To illustrate, I next consider three prominent approaches to global justice: a global difference principle, advocated by, inter alia, Charles Beitz and Darrel Moellendorf[48]; the social liberalism advocated in John Rawls's *Law of Peoples*[49]; and Thomas Pogge's rights-based cosmopolitanism.[50] I also examine three less prominent alternatives: the internalism advocated by Aaron James and Frank Garcia[51]; the egoistic positivism that is, I suggest, the default assumption of many legal scholars; and the economic approaches that constitute the dominant policy perspective on the trade regime. In each case, I enquire what, if anything, these approaches can tell us about justice in trade regulation.

2.5.1   Equality and a Global Difference Principle

The modern political theory of global justice arguably begins in 1979, with Charles Beitz's *Political Theory and International Relations*. One of the main claims in that book was that the arguments that lead liberals to worry about inequality domestically should make them equally concerned with inequalities internationally, motivating a global egalitarianism that remains a significant position in the philosophical debate.[52]

In the domestic context, the liberal concern for inequality finds its most prominent expression in what John Rawls labels the *difference principle*. The difference principle, which Rawls advocates as part of his theory of domestic justice, provides that inequalities are permissible only where they are to the greatest advantage of the least advantaged members of society.[53] Put simply, policy is judged by how it affects the worst off, and it should make them as well-off as they can possibly be. Beitz, extending Rawls's theory to the international context, advocates a *global difference principle*, requiring that political institutions be organized to the greatest advantage of the globally least advantaged representative person.[54]

As Beitz acknowledges, taking this idea seriously means dispensing with the existing state-centric international order, with its assumptions

---

[47] On the need to tailor principles to institutions/practices: (Rawls, 2001: 10–14).
[48] (Beitz, 1979; Moellendorf, 2002, 2005, 2009).   [49] (Rawls, 1999).   [50] (Pogge, 2002).
[51] (Garcia, 2013; James, 2012a).   [52] (Beitz, 1979).   [53] (Rawls, 1996: 6).
[54] (Beitz, 1979: 170) Cf. (Freeman, 2007: 259).

about states' relative freedom of action and about the restricted scope of their responsibilities.[55] In consequence, international trade as a distinctive object of analysis disappears. All state action becomes focused on improving the position of the globally least advantaged; but pending that reorganization, this approach has little specific to say about how we regulate international trade in particular.[56]

This becomes clear when global egalitarians address specific problems in trade regulation.

Moellendorf, for example, argues developed country protectionism is incompatible with a global difference principle,[57] but accepts non-protectionist domestic regulations as permissible, even where these restrict imports.[58] Given the welfare effects of such measures, it is difficult to see how this can be the case. A developed country regulation that is domestically welfare enhancing, while reducing market access for developing country exporters, and in consequence welfare for developing country workers, clearly benefits more advantaged persons at the expense of those less advantaged.[59] The same will be true of almost any measure adopted by a developed country that adversely affects developing country trade. The upshot is that it is not just protectionism that is condemned on this account; it is the territorial state.

Garcia's application of a global difference principle to trade law faces similar problems.[60] Like Moellendorf, he identifies developed world protectionism as problematic.[61] However, while acknowledging his principle invites a radical reordering of the international system, he steps back from this conclusion.[62] Instead, he implicitly reformulates the difference principle, asking not whether inequalities are to the greatest advantage of the least advantaged, but only whether they work to their benefit, a standard that is both less demanding and largely indeterminate.[63] The upshot is that

---

[55] (Beitz, 1979: 170).   [56] Ibid., 174–175.   [57] (Moellendorf, 2002: 55, 2009: 96).

[58] (Moellendorf, 2002: 58–59).

[59] To the extent the welfare gain from regulation for insiders exceeds the costs for outsiders, such regulation will be (Kaldor-Hicks) efficient, and so pass muster in economic terms. But egalitarians care not only about the total welfare effect but about who gains and who loses; and in this example, regardless of its efficiency, the regulation is clearly antiegalitarian.

[60] (Garcia, 2003).   [61] Ibid., 148–155.

[62] (Garcia, 2000: 1023, 2003: 207–211). A similar recognition and retreat appears in: (Razavi, 2013: 114). Both this problem and the challenges for social liberalism are recognized, but not resolved, in: (Broude, 2010: 79–80). Cf. (Brown & Stern, 2011: 10–11).

[63] (Garcia, 2003: 134, 147, 2013: 88, 90). While Rawls also uses this language, the context differs, such that in Rawls's usage its meaning is identical to the difference principle, while in Garcia's it expresses an indeterminate duty of benevolence on the part of the more advantaged that doesn't meaningfully challenge the underlying inequalities (Rawls, 1971: 75, 102).

like Moellendorf, he is skeptical of developed country protectionism affecting less developed countries, but has little to say on the many other questions arising elsewhere in the trade regime.

The problems are overdemandingness and lack of fit.[64] If strong egalitarian claims hold, then reforming the trade system will be only one element in the program of reforming the international institutional structure.[65] Further, there is no reason to believe it is the most urgent or the most important element of that program. Nor, pending those other reforms, can we even know how far the reform of the trade regime should go. And the sheer scale of the reforms demanded makes it relatively easy for decision-makers to dismiss exponents as utopian.[66] In these circumstances, global egalitarianism offers a mandate for making poverty and underdevelopment central concerns of the trade regime, but few tools for answering specific questions about the form that regime should take.

2.5.2   Social Liberalism and the Law of Peoples

While Beitz and others have argued Rawls's domestic theory commits liberals to globally egalitarian conclusions, Rawls himself takes a different approach.[67] In Law of Peoples, he examines international justice in substantially statist terms, emphasizing concerns for political independence, nonintervention, and compliance with treaty commitments.[68] Beitz labels Rawls's approach social liberalism: an international society providing background conditions in which a variety of distinct and independent domestic societies can flourish and can each take responsibility for the well-being of their own citizens.[69]

A striking contrast between Rawls's domestic and international theories is that concerns with economic inequality play no role in the latter.[70] Economic concerns are not entirely ignored. Recognizing that some peoples lack essential resources, including economic resources, Rawls advocates a duty of assistance owed to such "burdened peoples."[71] However, he rejects any international distributive principles analogous to the difference

---

[64] Wenar presses these objections against cosmopolitan theories generally: (Wenar, 2006: 107).

[65] This problem also appears in accounts that attempt to apply Rawls's principles to specific aspects of the trade regime. E.g. (Cedro & Vieira, 2010).

[66] For this worry about ideal theory generally: (Sen, 2009: 24–27).

[67] Many of the points here are equally applicable to other statist accounts: e.g. (Freeman, 2007; Miller, 2007; Nagel, 2005).

[68] (Rawls, 1999: 37).   [69] (Beitz, 2000: 677).   [70] (Rawls, 1999: 120).   [71] Ibid., 106.

principle, which would apply on a continuous basis to determine a just distribution of economic benefits, including those deriving from international cooperation.[72] The duty of assistance is understood to apply only below the threshold where peoples have the resources, whether material or institutional, to become *well ordered*, a term that for Rawls includes the capacity for effective self-determination and domestic legitimacy.[73] Once a people reaches this threshold, the duty of assistance ceases. No distributive duties apply among well-ordered peoples. Admittedly, in his discussion of international cooperation, Rawls makes passing references to "unjustified distributive effects between peoples," but it is unclear what this concept imports.[74] Similarly, he refers to the unfairness of developed countries "conspir[ing] to form a cartel or to act as an oligopoly," but it is unclear whether this reflects concerns for self-determination, or a broader, unarticulated, distributive principle.[75]

While avoiding the challenge of poor fit, Rawls's approach has been instead criticized as unduly conservative, legitimizing a deeply unjust international system.[76] The duty of assistance aside, on economic matters Rawls demands little more than that states comply with whatever agreements they enter into. In consequence, he lacks resources to address many questions of justice arising within the trade regime.

His emphasis on the value for peoples of being well ordered provides a basis for criticizing international cooperative schemes that undermine that capacity.[77] This suggests a justification for safeguards, understood as protecting a state's capacity to implement its scheme of domestic cooperation, as well as some special and differential treatment, understood as expressing the duty of assistance.[78] Further, his emphasis on consent suggests considering when and how consent is binding[79]; but his theory cannot tell us to what terms states should consent. This is assumed to be a matter for domestic choice and international bargaining. Yet without a principled account of what constitutes a fair international agreement, bargaining inevitably reduces to relative power.[80] Otherwise, Rawls's

---

[72] Ibid., 113–120.   [73] Ibid., 63–67, 106–112.   [74] Ibid., 43.

[75] Ibid., 43. On this ambiguity: (Reidy, 2007: 203–204).   [76] See e.g. (Buchanan, 2000).

[77] (Rawls, 1999: 106).   [78] For a critique of IFIs in these terms: (Clements, 2013).

[79] Cf. Garcia's concern for consent as a marker of trade: (Garcia, 2013).

[80] We can either argue based on principles or bargain based on power and interests; absent an effective mechanism for equalizing the relative power of peoples, there is no third way. Cf. (Muller, 2004; Risse, 2000). We might alternatively interpret Rawls's approach as restricting the use of certain kinds of power. However, this raises new problems, of specifying and identifying when and how particular kinds of power are deployed in international negotiations. Cf. (Miller, 2007: 77).

emphasis on international negotiation and binding agreements makes his approach indistinguishable from legal positivism across much of international economic relations.[81] In so far as arguments about distributive justice in international trade address the content of the agreements states make, rather than simply the fact of their having been agreed, Rawls simply has nothing to say.

2.5.3   Human Rights and Realization-Focused Comparison

A third prominent alternative is Thomas Pogge's rights-based cosmopolitanism, which emphasizes international institutions' complicity in violations of human rights, particularly antipoverty rights in developing countries.[82] The core of Pogge's argument is the claim that there exists an international institutional regime that foreseeably and avoidably produces massive human rights deficits. To the extent this is the case, we have collective obligations to reform those institutions to better realize the human rights of all persons. This approach allows Pogge to directly address existing institutions, and has grounded a sustained criticism of a number of features of the existing state system, including in particular what he terms the natural resource and borrowing privileges afforded to nondemocratic states.[83]

There are two principal difficulties with this as an approach to justice in trade regulation.

First, in emphasizing basic human rights, it is silent on questions of justice that arise above this threshold. Few theorists regard human rights as the whole of justice.[84] Pogge himself explains his focus on human rights as strategic; there are injustices that are not human rights violations.[85] Yet many contested questions in the trade regime are of this latter kind.[86] A

---

[81] (Rawls, 1999: 37) Cf. (Pogge, 1994: 211–214). The minimal constraints on international agreements that Rawls does acknowledge are surprisingly similar to those expressed in Embedded Liberalism, discussed further below.

[82] For Pogge's earlier egalitarian approach: (Pogge, 1989). His more recent approach is most comprehensively discussed in: (Pogge, 2002). Pogge has done more than most political philosophers to work out the implications of his views for international economic institutions. However, the criticisms noted here apply equally to other rights theorists, and indeed lawyers applying positive human rights law to the trade regime. E.g. (Cottier et al., 2005; Risse, 2012: ch. 14, 18; Wenar, 2008, 2011). Cf. (Moon, 2011; Waincymer, 2009: 25–31).

[83] (Pogge, 2002: 97–123). For a recent restatement of this position: (Pogge, 2011a).

[84] (Besson, 2013: 412; Harrison, 2007: 17–21).   [85] (Pogge, 2002: 25).

[86] A similar objection might be raised to using Scanlon's Principle of Rescue for these purposes, on which see (Linarelli, 2006: 216–218). On the limits of Scanlonian contractualism as an approach to global justice generally: (Nagel, 1991: 170–174).

concern for human rights tell us nothing about the appropriate balance between stability and liberalization, or relative rates of liberalization in developed and developing countries, or the permissibility of export subsidies, for example.

Second, in building justice on outcomes for individuals, the human rights approach requires contestable empirical premises.[87] The difficulties establishing these mean arguments about trade and human rights get diverted into debates about the economic merits of free trade, about multicausality and responsibility, about alternative paths to development, and about whether the trade regime is the appropriate venue in which to consider these questions.[88] If we need a perfect understanding of how the global economy works before we can apply our principles of justice to it, then those principles are for all practical purposes mute. Rather, we need principles that can be applied notwithstanding such uncertainties.

The first objection similarly disqualifies another recent innovation in global justice theory that seeks to place practical relevance ahead of theoretical purity. This is Amartya Sen's advocacy of what he labels *realization-focused comparison*, in opposition to the *transcendental institutionalism* of Rawls *et al.*[89] Transcendental institutionalists, on Sen's account, focus on identifying what a perfectly just system would look like. This, Sen worries, distracts from the practical task of making the world less unjust, which we can do by comparing reasonably achievable possible worlds, and working towards those that are better. We do not need to know what a perfectly just world looks like in order to agree that certain evident injustices require to be remedied; and in fact, in the absence of its realization, a blueprint for a perfectly just world may have perversely unjust effects.[90] Like Pogge's approach, however, this move is only helpful in respect of a subset of especially egregious justice-relevant issues. But most of the problems of the trade regime are not of this kind. In consequence, Sen's approach, while motivated by concerns of practicality, in fact precludes him addressing precisely those questions of international economic governance we are seeking to answer.[91]

---

[87] For this challenge to Pogge: (Freeman, 2007: 311–312).

[88] See e.g. a recent exchange between Pogge and two critics: (Howse & Teitel, 2011; Pogge, 2011b). Cf. (Risse, 2012: 264–266). For concerns about multicausality in particular: (Meckled-Garcia, 2014).

[89] (Sen, 2009: 7–8).   [90] Ibid., 9–18.

[91] Sen shares Pogge's focus on outcomes for persons, and may in consequence be vulnerable to the second objection also, but I do not explore the point here.

2.5.4   Internalism and Interpretivism

These approaches, then, seem ill-equipped to provide a theory of justice for the trade regime. In each case, their externally derived principles fail to "bite" on the problems of trade regulation. This leads others to approach justice in trade as an "internal" or interpretive question.[92] Instead of measuring the trade regime against an independent standard, they approach it as a distinct social practice, looking for the shared understandings that are expressed therein, and seeking to derive therefrom "internal" principles appropriate to its evaluation. I have already touched on one of these approaches, Garcia's account of trade as consent. James advances another, characterizing international trade as a practice of mutual reliance on international markets.[93] From this he derives principles of "structural equity," requiring that trading nations protect persons from the harms of trade; that gains be distributed equally among countries, unless unequal gains flow to poor countries; and that they be distributed equally within countries, unless inequalities are justified under special principles.[94]

The internal approach promises principles that are directly applicable to the problems of international trade, avoiding problems of fit by starting with the relevant practice.[95] Nevertheless, I do not pursue the internal approach for three reasons.

First, I doubt internalism can avoid the trap of relativism. If we derive our principles exclusively from the practices to which they are applied, then we will struggle to criticize fundamentally unjust practices. To the extent we can do so, we must invoke external principles to confirm our moral judgments.[96] However, it then becomes

---

[92] (Garcia, 2013; James, 2005, 2012a, 2012b). Methodologically, these theorists owe much to Walzer and, to a lesser extent, Dworkin: (Dworkin, 1986; Walzer, 1983). A similar enterprise in the context of private law is: (Weinrib, 1995).

[93] (James, 2012a: 19).

[94] Ibid., 17–18. Risse's identification of injustice where "[persons'] contributions to the production of goods or the provision of services for export do not make them better off (than if they were not producing those goods at all) to an extent warranted by the value of these contributions (and they did not voluntarily accept such an arrangement)" seems to have a similar, internal, structure (and to similarly beg many moral questions). However, in denying that such injustices sound internationally absent human rights violations, his account of global justice in trade reduces to a variant on Pogge's: (Risse, 2012: 273–274). Cf. (Risse & Wollner, 2014).

[95] Whether James's approach in particular delivers this seems doubtful.

[96] I thus suggest the normative attraction of both James's structural equity and Garcia's consent theory reflect external, rather than purely internal, values. See in particular James's invocation of Scanlon's contractualism: (James, 2012b: 206–210). Cf. (Garcia, 2013: 216–217). For a critique on these lines: (Valentini, 2011b).

difficult to see what distinctive contribution internalism makes, beyond mandating that we address principles to practices to which they appropriately apply.[97]

Second, and related, internalism commits theory to unnecessary conservatism.[98] While both James and Garcia propose critical standards, they are committed to holding fixed much of the practice they seek to criticize. Given the contested nature of the international economy, this is not obviously justified.[99] James, for example, assumes autarky as a morally neutral baseline; yet autarky is itself a political choice that is potentially subject to criticism.[100] Similarly, Garcia emphasizes consent in trade negotiations, potentially obscuring questions of justice in unilateral trade policies.[101] It seems preferable, at least initially, to assume all aspects of the relevant practice are open to criticism and revision.[102]

Third, I worry that internalism, when applied to individual practices, risks missing the ways those practices are embedded within, and interact with, wider social processes and institutions. It is certainly important, as Garcia and James emphasize, to recognize the distinctiveness of particular practices, including international trade; but it is also important to see those practices as elements within a comprehensive system of social institutions, and to consider how the justice of the specific practice may be tied up with, and require judgment in terms of, the justice of the system as a whole.[103] My concern is justice in trade regulation, and it is on this that I focus; but a successful theory must be cognizant of, and compatible with, judgments we may want to make about other aspects of global economic and political order.

---

[97] Sangiovanni advances a moderate internalist approach, which he labels practice dependence: (Sangiovanni, 2008).

[98] This concern also appears in: (Valentini, 2011c).

[99] For Garcia's view that trade is not *prima facie* objectionable, and so an appropriate object of internal interpretation rather than external criticism: (Garcia, 2013: 238). Criticisms of linkage's prioritization of trade in "trade and . . ." questions reflect a similar concern: (Lang, 2007: 534–536).

[100] (James, 2012a: 19–20).

[101] (Garcia, 2013: 240–262). Garcia might reply that these questions are better addressed under his liberal "first take." This, however, simply raises questions of how the approaches should be integrated, while also conceding the limited scope of internalism.

[102] A third criticism queries how objective internalist interpretations can be: (Moellendorf, 2013).

[103] For this point: (Rawls, 1971: 59–60).

2.5.5 *Moral Positivism*

A further potential approach, rarely defended in theory but commonly adopted in practice, combines international moral egoism with consent-based positivism. On this view, states' economic obligations derive exclusively from agreement. We have no economic duties to outsiders beyond those we have agreed to accept; and WTO law requires no normative warrant beyond the fact of that agreement. While few political theorists explicitly adopt this position,[104] it is clearly dominant among practitioners and adjudicators, and is implicit in a number of theorists' disinterest in international organizations.[105] It also provides the background for many economic and rational choice models of trade governance. These generally assume a baseline of egoistic states acting independently, and show how coordination through agreement can allow each to improve its own position, without any state concerning itself with the good of others, or of the community of states as a whole.[106]

I note four objections to this approach here.[107]

First, as with any argument based on state consent, it requires an account of why consent should bind dissenting minorities, subsequent populations, and nondemocratic populations.[108] Second, it assumes that the only object of concern is the agreement, obscuring concerns about states' undisciplined policies, about power in negotiations, and about the content of agreements.[109] Third, because it reduces state obligation to prior agreement, it cannot offer guidance on the content of those obligations

---

[104] A prominent exception is: (Nagel, 2005). In the domestic context, the view described has much in common with Nozick's libertarianism and Gauthier's contractarianism: (Gauthier, 1986; Nozick, 1974: 140).

[105] (Freeman, 2001: 307; Rawls, 1999: 37, 42–43). The Appellate Body's positivism emerges clearly in *Japan-Alcohol II*, (AB), p. 15:

> The WTO Agreement is a treaty – the international equivalent of a contract. It is self-evident that in an exercise of their sovereignty, and in pursuit of their own respective national interests, the Members of the WTO have made a bargain. In exchange for the benefits they expect to derive as Members of the WTO, they have agreed to exercise their sovereignty according to the commitments they have made in the WTO Agreement.

[106] E.g. (Dunoff & Trachtman, 1999).   [107] For the first two: (Howse, 2002b: 106–108).

[108] For some of these concerns in the WTO context: (Gian, 2014: 247–248, 253–255).

[109] For this objection, albeit with a more limited account of global economic justice: (Kumm, 2013). These concerns are exacerbated for post-Uruguay Round accessions where power imbalances are particularly prominent: (Tyagi, 2012).

without circularity.[110] And fourth, its egoism is unmotivated, and incompatible with our shared practice of moral criticism of international rules, in terms of their substantive content as well as their source-based legitimacy. It is also incompatible with liberal justice domestically; but vindicating this last claim must await the argument in later chapters.[111]

2.5.6   Economic Efficiency

I noted earlier that economic efficiency constitutes the default lens through which many scholars, critics, and policy-makers approach international trade regulation, and that – at least in some versions – it constitutes a competing standard to the justice-centered views discussed above.

It is not my purpose to deny the value of economic analysis. It would be perverse to deny the connections between trade law and economics, and at various points I help myself to the conclusions of economists to support arguments and interpretations. Nor is it my purpose to argue with the conclusions reached by economists within their domain of expertise. As a scholar of the international economy, I need some familiarity with the economic literature on international trade, but I am not an economist. Those expecting a radical critique will be disappointed to find that the economic views I invoke are generally quite mainstream. I have no desire to pick fights I cannot win, and arguing economics with economists is just such a fight.

Notwithstanding these caveats, there are two important reasons why efficiency cannot take the place of justice in international trade.

First, while aspiring to greater predictive power than other social sciences, economics remains probabilistic and deeply contested. There are certainly things economists can say with confidence: that productivity gains are possible through trade, for example. However, elsewhere, consensus is rarer, whether about the robustness of claims, or their scope of application. Particularly relevant here are debates about trade and development.[112] Economies are not like engines, whose design can be simply left to the experts. Rather, political judgments are required, raising consequent questions about who should make those judgments, on what

---

[110] We might hope to avoid this objection by invoking the collective intention of states parties to those agreements. However, problems of collective intention in the context of multilateral agreements prevent this yielding significant guidance.

[111] See in particular the discussion of statist approaches in Chapter 4.

[112] See e.g. (Chang, 2005; Rodrik, 2001).

grounds, and for whose benefit. Economics provides only part of the answers we need.

Second, economic efficiency itself is either an indeterminate, or a normatively doubtful, goal.

If we understand efficiency in Pareto terms, then it is plausibly (though not uncontestably) a desideratum of a just social system: a system that is Pareto-inefficient is one in which at least one person would be better off in some alternative system in which no other person is worse off. Pareto inefficiency thus indicates that someone is bearing a cost that there is no good reason to impose. However, Pareto efficiency does not pick out one unique solution to questions of institutional design. Rather, in any given situation, there may be infinitely many Pareto-efficient alternatives, which vary in the way benefits are distributed among agents. Pareto efficiency cannot choose between these.[113]

On the other hand, if we understand efficiency in Kaldor-Hicks terms, then it may uniquely identify a single answer to questions of institutional design, but it will struggle to justify it. Recall, Kaldor-Hicks efficiency is substantially the economic translation of the utilitarian injunction to maximize welfare. Like the utilitarian principle, its focus is the total amount of the good (wealth, preference satisfaction, well-being) in the system, rather than its distribution. In consequence, it can endorse radically unequal outcomes that leave the majority in dire economic conditions while a minority enjoy vast wealth. It prefers the fabulously wealthy pharaoh and his 99 slaves to the 100 peasant farmers. To the extent such inequalities condemn utilitarianism as a political theory, they condemn Kaldor-Hicks efficiency as the sole benchmark for judging international trade regulation (or indeed any other social institution).[114]

This is not to say that efficiency, whether Pareto or Kaldor-Hicks, has no role to play. Rather, I expect both will be invoked in any serious discussion of trade regulation. I certainly appeal to both, at least implicitly, at various stages; and much of Part III is a conversation with their explanatory and interpretive implications. However, their limits mean that neither is a plausible candidate as the exclusive critical standard for the trade regime.

---

[113] For this point: (Dworkin, 1980: 193). As Sen observes, many Pareto-efficient outcomes will be highly objectionable, and disastrous from at least some perspectives: (Sen, 1985: 10).

[114] It is this indifference to distribution that Rawls challenges when he suggests that utilitarianism "does not take seriously the distinction between persons": (Rawls, 1971: 27). Dworkin raises the further objection that the move from utilitarian welfare-maximization to economic wealth-maximization renders economic efficiency normatively unattractive, even in utilitarian terms: (Dworkin, 1980: 199–201).

2.6   Structure and Methodology

It seems, then, that existing approaches, whether self-consciously concerned with global distributive justice, or approaching the issue from perspectives of economics or law, are unable to answer the kinds of questions of distributive justice that arise in the regulation of international trade. A new approach is required. In the remaining sections of this chapter, I outline the methodology and assumptions that I adopt in developing such an approach. The next section introduces my approach to normative theory, its basis in liberal thought, and my focus on the state as the dominant institution in the international economy. Thereafter, I outline the explanatory and interpretive task that I undertake in later chapters, and the criteria that are appropriate to adjudicating among competing explanations of the trade rules. Finally, I sketch the critical implications of my approach, from the perspective of adjudicators, negotiators, and national governments.

2.6.1   Normative Theory

I approach justice in trade regulation as a special case of global distributive justice. I take as a starting point debates about global distributive justice in normative political philosophy. These are driven in large part by what I label, in Chapter 3, liberalism's boundary problem. This is the problem of whether, and to what extent, duties of distributive justice that we acknowledge within the state apply beyond the state and, to the extent they do not, why this is the case. International trade centrally concerns interactions across borders, so this boundary problem seems a promising place to begin. Justice in trade regulation need not be identical with justice in the domestic economy: but we might hope to reason from our relatively firm intuitions and developed theories about domestic economic justice to an account of justice in regulating relations between economies.[115]

At its most general, the methodology is constructivism: we identify principles of justice by inquiring what principles agents would accept under ideal choice conditions.[116] We thus construct our principles from an account of the kinds of agents to whom they will apply, and of the conditions under which they are chosen. While advanced in different forms by Kant and various social contract thinkers, the leading exponent

---

[115] On the structure of such arguments: (Caney, 2005: 107).
[116] See generally: (Bagnoli, 2011).

of constructivism in modern political thought is John Rawls. Many readers will be familiar with Rawls's use of the Original Position for this purpose.[117] This is a thought experiment, in which we imagine representatives, whose interests are carefully specified, placed behind a veil of ignorance, which prevents them from knowing key facts about their own characteristics and places in society. These representatives are tasked with agreeing principles to govern the society in which they will find themselves, once the veil of ignorance is lifted. Provided that agents and choice conditions are properly specified, this imagined procedure allows us to identify principles of justice that are appropriate for us, as we exist here and now. In the domestic context, Rawls argues, this will yield the two principles of justice, including the Difference Principle, that he together labels *Justice as Fairness*.

Rawls develops *Justice as Fairness* for a single society.[118] In consequence, all representatives in the Original Position are symmetrically situated; there are no insiders or outsiders to consider.[119] The plural agents, relations, and institutions to which my account is addressed mean that the Original Position thought experiment does not play so central a role in my argument; but the structure of the argument and the status of the conclusions are identical.[120] I work from an idealized account of the agents for whom we are seeking principles of justice, to an account of the principles to which those agents would themselves agree, abstracting away from many of the specific circumstances that, in real situations, are likely to bias or simply obscure our judgments.

Because this approach constructs principles for the agents and relations to which they will apply, we must begin with an account of those agents. In Chapter 3 I adopt for this purpose Rawls's conceptions of persons and peoples as free and equal, rational and reasonable. This is not uncontroversial. Indeed, Rawls himself denies his conception of the person is appropriate to theorizing justice beyond the state, reflecting his commitment to a particular political form of liberalism in his later work.[121] Political liberalism, as Rawls understands it, requires that we

---

[117] For various presentations: (Rawls, 1971: 118–150, 1980, 2001: 14–18).

[118] (Rawls, 1971: 8).

[119] (Rawls, 2001: 18). This symmetry is maintained in the Law of Peoples through Rawls's exclusive focus on peoples, who are symmetrically situated in respect of the law of peoples, and his denial that the institutions of peoples themselves are subject to justification at this stage.

[120] On the specificity of Rawls' original position: (Scanlon, 1998: 243–246).

[121] (Rawls, 1999: 82–83). On political liberalism, and the criticisms motivating it: (Mulhall & Swift, 1996: 170–190).

draw exclusively on ideas that are found in our shared public political culture and practice to construct our conceptions of justice.[122] The conception of persons as free and equal forms part of the public political culture of liberal democratic states. However, Rawls suggests, it is not shared by nonliberal states, nor does it form part of our international political practice, which is predominantly statist in character.[123]

There are, however, at least three reasons to reject Rawls's view on this point, all canvassed in existing literature. First, it is plausible this conception of persons is indeed shared in our international political practice, at least rhetorically.[124] Further, in so far as the principles I derive are themselves recognizable in World Trade Law, it suggests that this conception is also latent therein.[125] Second, assuming a liberal theory of global justice is a theory for liberal states, the fact that this conception is not shared by nonliberal states does not *ipso facto* license its denial, at least in liberal states' policies.[126] Put simply, the fact that others do not share our values does not mean that we must, or indeed can, refrain from acting on them ourselves. In circumstances of disagreement, we still need some basis for our own choices. There are, admittedly, difficulties in circumstances where the demands of respecting persons, so understood, and respecting peoples, conflict.[127] However, while I touch on this conflict, its resolution is not essential to my argument.[128] Third, to the extent the liberal conception of the person is not shared internationally, political liberalism simply is not a normatively attractive position for liberals.[129] This is not to deny the practical constraints on pursuing liberal politics in an illiberal world, but before accommodating ourselves to those constraints, we must first know what genuinely liberal principles demand.[130]

---

[122] (Rawls, 2001: 33).   [123] (Rawls, 1999: 33–34, 82–83).

[124] See generally: (Teitel, 2011). On the disconnect between international human rights practice and Rawls's restrictive approach: (Macleod, 2008; Nickel, 2008).

[125] Cf. (Emerton, 2009: 141).

[126] Recall Rawls describes the Law of Peoples as the foreign policy of liberal states: (Rawls, 1999: 82). See, in the trade context: (Garcia, 2003: 67–69, 2013: 67–68).

[127] For an excellent discussion of this problem: (Tan, 2000).

[128] This problem arises more directly for projects addressing civil and political rights: (Mulhall & Swift, 1996: xvii).

[129] (Mulhall & Swift, 1996: 192–194, 207–210). For this point internationally: (Tan, 2000: 2122, 28–30).

[130] For this view: (Kymlicka, 1996: 171). As well as political liberals, political realists, drawing on the work of Bernard Williams, are likely to raise objections at this point. See (Williams, 2005).

The argument is developed within liberalism. A defense of liberalism itself is beyond its scope.[131] My normative ambitions are, in this sense, limited. I tell a story about liberal equality and the trade regime, answering competing liberal stories. I do not claim that these are the only stories we can tell. Utilitarians and libertarians, for example, will tell very different stories, supporting different prescriptions in particular cases. For those committed to liberal equality, I suggest mine is the better story, but in the practical domain of trade regulation, it may be one story among many.

I make trade *regulation* my object of analysis. This reflects a view, developed further in Chapter 3, about why distributive justice matters within the state. We have recourse to principles of distributive justice because domestic cooperation proceeds subject to nonvoluntary institutions; and it is those institutions that we evaluate in terms of distributive justice. Similarly, when we consider justice in the international economy, our concern should be, in the first instance, the institutions subject to which cooperation proceeds. We ask what those institutions would have to look like, and what they would have to do, in order to be reasonably acceptable to persons and peoples subject thereto.

This approach ensures that the principles that we derive will speak directly to existing problems. I derive principles *for* the international trade regime, starting with an account of what the institutions that govern international trade are actually like. However, I do not seek to derive principles *from* that regime. Rather, I invoke premises and apply methods familiar from reasoning about domestic distributive justice, and specifically Rawls's approach, to identify principles appropriate to regulating the international economy. This is, of course, not the first attempt to do this: both Beitz's global difference principle and Rawls's *Law of Peoples* pursue the same goal.[132] However, by focusing on the role of nonvoluntary institutions, and the diverse ways that persons and peoples are subject to those institutions, I derive a novel set of principles that I argue are both a better expression of Rawls's approach internationally, and of more practical value in assessing justice in international trade regulation.

---

[131] This necessarily limits the reach of the argument. However, given the centrality of Rawlsian liberalism in contemporary Anglo-American political philosophy, it seems a reasonable starting point: (Kymlicka, 2002: 10).

[132] As do, taking a non-exhaustive sample of book-length treatments: (Brock, 2009; Garcia, 2003; Moellendorf, 2002; Pogge, 1989; Tan, 2004).

I focus on one institution in particular: the state. This may seem counterintuitive, given my ultimate concern for the justice of the trade regime, the archetype of an effective, legalized, international institution.[133] It might also be challenged as obscuring the role of private actors, and in particular transnational economic interests, in shaping the international economy.[134] My starting with the state reflects three important assumptions: one empirical, one methodological, and one normative.

The empirical assumption is that the state remains the most important institution in the international system, including the international economy.[135] I do not deny that other institutions exist, or matter greatly. However, they matter because, and in so far as, they are compatible with the state.[136] Of course, states vary greatly. Some larger multinational enterprises may be more important in explaining distributive outcomes than some smaller states; but even the largest such enterprises are necessarily subject to the authority of at least some of the states in which they operate.[137] Similarly, the rules of the World Trade Organization are undoubtedly important in explaining outcomes; but their power is likewise referable to their support by leading states.[138] The WTO matters because states make it matter.[139] It is therefore with states that we begin.[140]

---

[133] (Jackson, 2003: 799).   [134] For this criticism of Rawls's approach: (Buchanan, 2000).

[135] This need not imply the degree of control assumed by traditional models of sovereignty, but only that states remain the most basic institutions for this purpose. Cf. (Raustiala, 2003). On the merits, and limits, of placing the state at the center of theories of international politics: (Lake, 2008). For a review of the literature on the continued role of the state in economic governance: (Wren, 2006).

[136] (Gilpin, 1971; Mearsheimer, 2014: 17).

[137] As Waltz argues, claims about interdependence and the decline of the state often obscure the power of larger and more developed states at the expense of smaller ones: (Waltz, 1979: 143–151). Similarly, contemporary arguments about globalization and sovereignty tend to focus on governance challenges for small, open, and developing countries. E.g. (Ronzoni, 2012).

[138] The "member-driven" quality of WTO law provides a further justification for my choice to build an argument from within liberalism. WTO law (and international law generally) has a different logical structure to coercively enforced domestic laws. We cannot approach it exclusively from the perspective of the system as a whole. Rather, we must consider its role in the practical reasoning of individual states. And for liberal states, that means understanding it from within liberal political theory.

[139] This perspective on international institutions is most obviously reflected in realist and neoliberal institutionalist international relations theories. For reviews of these approaches: (Hasenclever et al., 1997; Stein, 2008). However, it could also find support among many moderate social constructivist scholars, to the extent these see institutions as operating primarily for and through states.

[140] Cf. (Eskelinen, 2011). For a similar point, albeit in support of a quite different argument: (Blake, 2013: 111–112). A similar point might of course be made in respect of any

The methodological assumption is that, *ceteris paribus*, normative argument should, to the greatest extent possible, avoid contestable empirical premises. By starting with the state, I avoid premises about the power of either transnational corporations or international institutions. This does not mean denying that the latter play an important role in the international economy. It is only if they wholly eclipse the state that my argument is undermined. By contrast, an argument invoking the power of international institutions and transnational actors in the first instance is exposed to challenge on the validity of such assumptions. I therefore prefer to work from the firm ground of the state, only later introducing other elements.

The normative assumption is that states play valuable roles in persons' lives. It is the state, in the first instance, that makes social life possible, stabilizes rights and expectations, and (ideally) instantiates the distinctive virtues of freedom, equality, and democracy.[141] It is not logically necessary that the institution that fulfills these functions is territorial; but it is a plausible empirical necessity.[142] Further, the state is a locus of political agency; starting with other entities would risk prematurely absolving the state, and us as its authors, of moral responsibility. As such, to the extent possible, we should consider whether and how far the state can be justified, and can in turn justify the international economy, before dispensing with it in favor of other, perhaps less attractive, objects of inquiry.

Distributive justice in trade regulation then becomes a question of whether, and under what conditions, states and the measures they adopt are reasonably acceptable to those, whether insiders or outsiders, subject thereto. This, then, becomes the starting point for our inquiry. Of course, we need to do a lot more work to answer this question. We need to know about the kinds of persons and peoples to whom justification is owed. We

---

institution, including the state itself. It exists, and exerts authority, only to the extent that the agents comprising it give it being, supporting, and complying with it, and coordinating their actions around it. There are agent/structure questions here that are beyond the scope of my project. It suffices to note that coordination problems are radically different in large-N systems, such as the state, than small-N systems, such as the international system. This leads us to focus, in the former, on extant coordinating institutions to the exclusion of individual units. In the latter, however, the coordination effected by institutions is rarely controlling, so our focus must remain primarily on the individual subunits and their systemic interactions.

[141] For elements of this (hopefully uncontroversial) idea: (Hobbes, 1996: 117, 121; Kant, 1991: 73–79; Rawls, 2001: 5–12; Rousseau, 1997: 53–54).

[142] (Rawls, 1999: 36) Cf. (Wenar, 2006: 108).

need to know in what ways those persons and peoples are subject to states. And we need to know what kinds of justifications they have reason to accept. Only then will we get a sense of what just or unjust trade regulation might look like. Constructing answers to these questions, and rebutting possible counterarguments, is the task of the next three chapters.

2.6.2 *Explanation, Interpretation, Evaluation*

My argument begins with the state. The principles I label EGC provide a standard of justice for state measures affecting the international economy. They are not, at least directly, principles for formal international institutions. However, in so far as WTO law provides a code of conduct for states, it occupies the same logical space as EGC. Both provide standards for measures affecting the international economy.[143] One way to approach WTO law is therefore to examine whether, and how far, its prescriptions track EGC. In answering that question, we will also see how far EGC offers principles that are not only normatively plausible, but also capable of answering practical questions arising in the trade regime. That is the task of the later chapters.

I cannot examine all aspects of WTO law, so some selectivity is unavoidable. I have focused on the goods regime, and within that on those areas that seem most significant, whether in the history, contemporary practice, or continuing evolution of that regime. Chapter 6 addresses the core disciplines on border measures and nondiscrimination in the General Agreement on Tariffs and Trade (GATT). The GATT was the whole of the trade regime for most of its history, and remains a central element of the World Trade Organization. Chapter 7 examines the main qualifications to the GATT disciplines: special and differential treatment for developing countries, and General Exceptions in Art. XX. Chapter 8 examines disciplines on subsidies, safeguards, and anti-dumping, which together constitute the most litigated specialized agreements.[144] Chapter 9 addresses domestic regulation under the Agreement on Sanitary and Phytosanitary Measures (SPS) and the Agreement on Technical Barriers to Trade (TBT), as typifying the ostensibly more intrusive post-Uruguay Round goods regime. Within each chapter, I present a "T-shaped" analysis, examining the relevant rules as a whole, before drilling in detail into one or

---

[143] As Ruggie notes, "the domain of international regimes consists of the behavior of states, *vis-à-vis* one another and *vis-à-vis* the market-place, not the market-place itself.": (Ruggie, 1982: 383).

[144] (Leitner & Lester, 2016: 294).

more specific issues. Again, there is a degree of selectivity here, but I know of no better way to present an analysis that is at once both broad and deep.

In focusing on these areas, I omit many others that might merit discussion. I do not address regionalization, customs unions and free trade areas, or related issues of rules of origin.[145] I seek to understand the generally applicable principles, rather than tackling every deviation therefrom; and regionalization, despite its pervasiveness in contemporary practice, constitutes a discrete and exceptional domain.[146] (I do offer some general thoughts on regionalization in Chapter 10.) Accession protocols and WTO-plus rules are, for the same reason, addressed only in passing.[147] The perceived status of the agriculture rules as a (largely unprincipled) exception similarly explains why I do not address these.[148] Furthermore, I limit myself to goods rules as a reasonably distinct body of law. Extending the analysis to services, investment, or intellectual property would constitute separate projects. While I suspect my approach is applicable, with limited modifications, to these areas, I make no claim here about how EGC might understand them.[149] Finally, I do not analyze ongoing negotiations: my normative argument has implications for negotiation outcomes, which I sketch in Chapter 10, but my explanatory analysis is limited to the existing law.

My goal is not simply to measure WTO law by the yardstick of EGC. Rather, I inquire whether we can understand WTO law as expressing EGC. This question is as much explanatory as it is critical, asking whether EGC provides a plausible account of what WTO law does. However, it is an explanation of a particular kind: neither historical[150] nor genealogical,[151] but justificatory. It shows how we can understand the trade regime as pursuing a goal that we, in fact, have reason to pursue. This in turn implies an interpretive question: if we can understand WTO law as expressing, if imperfectly, EGC, then how should we understand its specific provisions, in order best to realize that purpose? The task here has much in common with what Dworkin labels constructive interpretation, which we encountered in

---

[145] For an overview of the issues: (Bartels & Ortino, 2006).

[146] Mathis labels these rules "a self-standing regime" and "inherently exceptional": (Mathis, 2006: 79).

[147] See generally: (Charnovitz, 2008). On the "irrationality" of this exceptional treatment: (Qin, 2012).

[148] For an overview: (Trebilcock et al., 2013: 434–471).

[149] For some thoughts on the application of EGC to sovereign debt, which might more readily be translated to thinking about investment and intellectual property: (Suttle, 2016).

[150] E.g. (Douglas et al., 2008).   [151] E.g. (Lang, 2011).

Chapter 1.[152] However, mine is not a straightforward application of Dworkin's approach for two reasons.

First, I am doubtful whether Dworkin's model of law as integrity is a normatively attractive conception of international trade law.[153] Law as integrity explains the role of prior political decisions in adjudication through the value of legality and the judge's relation to the community as the author thereof.[154] However, the trade regime's decentralized enforcement mechanisms and doubtful democratic credentials undermine both of these premises.[155] Its positive law therefore commands a different status in the practical reasoning of adjudicators and policy-makers. Both have reasons to have regard to that law, but these reasons are primarily instrumental, and secondarily epistemic. Instrumentally, adjudicators' views are more likely to be accepted if they are expressed in terms of prevailing, socially sanctioned, norms, and policy-makers are less likely to be challenged if policies are justified in such terms.[156] Epistemically, the outcomes of multilateral negotiations, while lacking democratic legitimacy, may express values shared by the parties thereto. While many factors shape negotiated outcomes, social constructivists argue normative arguments and beliefs play an important role.[157] We can thus grant IEL provisional epistemic authority.[158] However, neither reason justifies the strong sense of respect for prior political decisions expressed in law as integrity.

Second, while Dworkin begins with the object of interpretation, I begin with normative theory.[159] It is only having elaborated and motivated my normative position that I address the positive law. Obviously, the correspondence between normative theory and law is not purely coincidental. Both respond to the same problem, specifying terms of cooperation in an international economy. The same features of negotiations that give them provisional epistemic authority make them likely to reflect, albeit

---

[152] (Dworkin, 1986: 52). Note that, while in Chapter 1 we were concerned with the interpretation of national measures, in these later chapters the focus is on interpreting WTO rules.

[153] See generally: (Dworkin, 1986: 177–224).   [154] (Dworkin, 2006: 176–178).

[155] On the different role of legality internationally: (Waldron, 2006).

[156] See generally: (Franck, 1990; Johnstone, 2003). For a skeptical account, see (Goldsmith & Posner, 2005: ch. 6) Cf. (Dworkin, 2006: 174–175).

[157] E.g. (Albin, 2001; Lang, 2011; Odell & Kell, 2006; Ruggie, 1982). For an illuminating study from outside the trade regime: (Crawford, 2002). A less optimistic perspective is: (Eagleton-Pierce, 2013).

[158] Cf. (Dworkin, 2006: 172–173).

[159] This distinguishes my approach from Garcia's and James's, discussed above.

imperfectly, the prescriptions of constructivist political theory. Further, as noted above, among the defects of existing global justice theories is their failure to address specific problems raised by the trade regime. Some correspondence between theory and law is therefore built into my methodology. However, it is on freestanding constructivist argument, rather than correspondence with positive law, that my normative claims rest. This is not simply an arbitrary choice; rather, the same reasons that make integrity a dubious model for international law mean normative principles must be grounded in something other than positive law. This is, in turn, reflected in my approach in later chapters, which focuses more on relating contested questions to conflicting theoretical approaches than on doctrinal exegesis; the latter is pursued primarily to highlight the need for and appropriateness of the former.

What constitutes a good account for these purposes?

I follow Dworkin in regarding fit and justification as key considerations. Justification matters because we are trying to explain the value of the trade regime *for us*, why we should continue to have and to support that regime. Fit matters because we are trying to explain *this* trade regime, rather than an imagined alternative. It is in part because of their failures of fit that I rejected a number of the existing approaches canvassed above. Further, a justificatory explanation that does not fit will fail to provide interpretive guidance. However, what constitutes a good fit depends in turn on the instrumental and epistemic reasons for considering existing legal materials in our practical reasoning.

Any adequate explanation must account for the most significant features of the WTO Agreements themselves (the Covered Agreements[160]). These constitute fixed points in the trade regime. An explanation of why we should value that regime must at least account for these. Further, to the extent we seek shared values emerging from negotiations, the agreements provide their most direct expression.

An adequate explanation must also account for key features of practice under that regime; but legal practices and interpretations as such are less important than explaining them as manifestations of political practice.[161] As legal practice becomes accepted and entrenched, however, its explanation becomes more important.

---

[160] WTO Dispute Settlement Understanding (DSU) Art 1.1 and Annex 1.

[161] This is particularly so given decisions' at best limited precedential weight in WTO law: DSU Art. 3.2. But cf. *US – Stainless Steel (Mexico)*, (AB), § 158–162.

Some failures of fit matter more than others. Trade agreements are negotiated among states with radically different interests and influence.[162] As such, it would be surprising if they could be comprehensively explained by any one theory. Where they diverge from a theory's prescriptions in ways readily explained by interests of dominant states, or dominant constituencies within those states, this constitutes a lesser objection than divergences that appear either to express alternative principles or to favor less powerful states or constituencies.[163]

I argue, in these later chapters, that much of the trade regime can be understood as expressing EGC. In doing so, I contrast EGC with existing accounts that explain trade agreements as solving particular economic problems, and thereby realizing economic efficiency. Efficiency is itself a distributive principle, and by contrasting EGC with efficiency-centered approaches, we see more clearly how EGC differs, in both its explanation of particular rules and the interpretations it suggests. I make economic approaches my focus because of their prominence in trade scholarship, their detail, and their breadth: while other approaches address specific provisions or agreements, economic explanations have been offered, or can be deduced, for almost every element of the Covered Agreements. Addressing these also has the added benefit of showing how focusing on two competing virtues, justice and efficiency, imply quite different understandings of WTO law.

These are not, however, the only explanatory theories of the trade regime.[164] It is therefore worth noting briefly here how EGC differs from other explanatory theories, and why I do not focus on these. I consider three groups of approaches: embedded liberalism, governance approaches, and human rights theories.

Originally advanced as a sociological account of the GATT, embedded liberalism has been developed more recently as a normative claim that the WTO should respect the particular relationship between state, society, and market reflected therein.[165] The trade regime, on this account, is not simply concerned with rooting out inefficiency. Rather, its focus is addressing specific mutually harmful practices, and policing

---

[162] See generally: (Narlikar, 2003; Odell, 2006).

[163] The confounding role of power imbalances provides an additional reason why I do not make accession protocols and WTO+ obligations a significant focus. Cf. (Qin, 2003: 515–516) On the fairness concerns these raise: (Bienen & Mihretu, 2010).

[164] For an overview in terms of competing "frames": (Charnovitz, 2002b).

[165] See generally, in respect of the trade regime: (Dunoff, 1999; Howse, 2002b; Lang, 2006, 2011; Ruggie, 1982). For the origins of embedded liberalism: (Polanyi, 2001).

defection from shared understandings of legitimate state action and regulatory diversity. Those understandings overlap with, but do no reduce to, various economic orthodoxies. Indeed, many economically dubious policies, including safeguards and anti-dumping, are permitted because they are regarded as acceptable tools for managing the economic and political challenges of exposure to international markets.

That I do not make embedded liberalism my focus reflects its logical form. As a sociological account of the contingency of the GATT bargain, its normative claims rested ultimately on consent, albeit understood flexibly.[166] In its recent reformulation, it expresses a normative commitment to national autonomy, and standardly comprises three claims: that the trade regime should respect domestic choice[167]; that the trade regime should limit itself to anti-protectionism[168]; and that positive law is legitimized through political process and not economic theory.[169] These in turn reflect two further ideas: a normative claim that social institutions are justified by political choice[170]; and a sociological claim, that markets are contingent social tools, embedded in, and in the service of, social institutions.[171] The sociological claim reinforces the normative, against the technocratic ambitions of economists.

So understood, normative embedded liberalism reduces to a partial anti-protectionist view or an implicitly positivist one. The former I discuss in detail. The latter cannot provide an explanation of the right form, counseling deference to political choice, rather than explaining or justifying its content. In so far as embedded liberalism leaves a remainder after these are subtracted, it is an emphasis on states' claim to manage their own economies, in pursuit of domestic social and economic stability and justice, which is understood as in tension with anti-protectionism.[172] However, embedded liberalism theorists do not justify a particular balance between these concerns, beyond emphasizing the need to respect democratic choice.[173] We are

---

[166] In emphasizing contingency, embedded liberalism can also subsume commercial liberal arguments about the links between free trade and international peace. E.g. (Dunne et al., 2007: 97). However, reflecting Ruggie's original insight, while these motivate a stable, relatively open, trade regime, they tell us little about the form that regime should take: (Ruggie, 1982: 382–383).

[167] (Dunoff, 1999: 738–739).   [168] Ibid., 738–739.   [169] (Howse, 2002b: 114–115).

[170] (Howse & Nicolaidis, 2001: 243–246).   [171] See generally: (Polanyi, 2001).

[172] (Howse, 2002b: 95) Cf. (Rodrik, 1997: 69–71, 2011: xix).

[173] E.g. (Howse, 2002b: 104). Lang highlights the need to interrogate the continued normative attraction of the embedded liberalism bargain, particularly given the exclusion of developing countries therefrom: (Lang, 2006: 98–100) Cf. (Howse & Nicolaidis, 2001: 245; Steger, 2002: 143–145).

thus led back, again, to a qualified positivism, rather than a normative account of the trade regime's content.[174] Indeed, embedded liberalism's commitment to domestic choice suggests any such account is undesirable, as imposing a false – and antidemocratic – coherence on contingent political settlements.[175] Embedded liberalism thus seems to constitute, not an alternative explanatory theory, but rather a negation of such theories.[176]

It is worth noting one similarity and one difference between embedded liberalism and EGC. They share a concern for effective self-determination, including economic self-determination; although for embedded liberalism this is assumed, while EGC embeds it within a comprehensive normative theory. They differ in that embedded liberalism emphasizes political claims being resolved domestically; whereas EGC makes justification to outsiders a central concern, seeing domestic choice as potentially constrained by outsiders' claims.[177] EGC is, in consequence, less deferential to arguments from subsidiarity or democracy, enquiring why a particular community should be entitled to make a particular choice, notwithstanding its effects on others.[178]

Structure similarly explains why I don't focus on governance theories. Governance is here a catch-all term for approaches emphasizing the WTO's role, actual or potential, as a tool, agent or venue of international governance, whether through rule making,[179] monitoring,[180] judicial

[174] A positivism that is further undermined by doubts about whether embedded liberalism even accurately describes the WTO as opposed to the GATT: (Howse & Nicolaidis, 2001: 232–233).

[175] (Howse, 2002b: 110). As noted, linkage accounts emphasizing particular values, for example health or sustainable development, frequently have a similar, ultimately positivist, structure. Further, such linkage accounts generally focus on countervalues, assuming economic arguments explain the default case. E.g. (Epps & Green, 2010: 74–77) While embedded liberalism requires accommodating elements of protectionism, these other approaches are more concerned to ensure that addressing protectionism does not inadvertently lead to other values being sacrificed. Direct conflicts do arise, however, when linkages are extended from products to state policies: (Harrison, 2007: ch. 5).

[176] This conclusion seems implicit in Lang's more recent work: (Lang, 2014) Cf. (Howse & Nicolaidis, 2001: 230–232). More generally, embedded liberalism's commitment to excavating and respecting shared understandings is incompatible with the modern, legalized trade regime. For a version of this point: (Lang, 2011: 240–253).

[177] E.g. (Howse, 2002b: 99–100; Howse & Nicolaidis, 2001: 237–238; Rodrik, 1997: 77–81, 2011: 233–250). In this, embedded liberalism has much in common with Rawls's social liberalism.

[178] Contrast: (Howse & Nicolaidis, 2001: 249), although invocations of global deliberative democracy suggest some qualification of this position: (Howse, 2002b: 115; Howse & Nicolaidis, 2001: 248).

[179] (Guzman, 2004b).   [180] (Bown, 2011).

review,[181] regulatory dialogue,[182] socialization,[183] constitutionalism,[184] jurisdictional transactions,[185] or corrective justice.[186] Despite their differences, these approaches share an emphasis on the mechanisms whereby the WTO affects outcomes, rather than the specific outcomes it brings about.[187] They are, to that extent, compatible with various accounts of the distributive scheme expressed in WTO law.[188] Understanding WTO law as a mechanism for giving outsiders voice in states' regulatory choices does not answer what weight, if any, their claims should be given. Understanding it as a transaction in regulatory authority does not answer what allocation of authority it expresses. Governance theories are concerned with procedure and form rather than distributive outcome: it is the latter that concerns me.

Third, human rights approaches might be divided into three categories: human rights critiques, highlighting the ways particular rules undermine, or fail to vindicate, human rights[189] (I have touched on these above); instrumental human rights defenses, showing how the trade regime contributes to the enjoyment of particular human rights, most prominently antipoverty rights[190]; and intrinsic human rights justifications, which characterize the trade regime as directly protecting particular human rights, specifically market freedoms of contract, property, and exchange.[191] The first two do not constitute alternative explanations: rather, critiques challenge the trade regime, while instrumental

---

[181] (Scott, 2004a).   [182] (Lang & Scott, 2009a, 2009b; Steinberg, 2009).

[183] (Cho, 2015).   [184] (Dunoff, 2006a; Joerges & Petersmann, 2006).

[185] (Trachtman, 2006; Trachtman, 2007).   [186] (Carmody, 2008).

[187] Constitutionalism theorists may also be committed to institutionalizing a particular distributive scheme, such as Petersmann's human rights approach, discussed below, or a particular economic view. E.g. (Trachtman, 2006: 631–634). However, the two questions are conceptually distinct, and some focus exclusively on governance issues. E.g. (Cass, 2001, 2005; Cho, 2015: 164–167). For mixed approaches: (Armingeon et al., 2011; Cottier & Jackson, 2000).

[188] The same point applies to theories emphasizing the value of certainty or predictability in economic governance: such theories are compatible with a range of accounts of the ends such governance should serve.

[189] E.g. (Choudhury et al., 2011) and various contributions in (Cottier et al., 2005). Pogge's philosophical human rights approach also fits here, as do approaches examining how the WTO might reconcile trade and human rights. E.g. (Armingeon et al., 2011: 77–78; Harrison, 2007; Howse & Teitel, 2009; Marceau, 2002; Petersmann, 2002: 645–646) Cf. (Cottier, 2002).

[190] E.g. (Harrison, 2007: 38–40; Petersmann, 2002: 630–632; Sykes, 2006b; Waincymer, 2009: 23–25).

[191] (Petersmann, 2008b; Petersmann, 2002: 639–644). Much of this work clearly shades from explanatory to critical, e.g. (Petersmann, 2008a).

defenses commonly reduce to economic approaches. By contrast, intrinsic human rights approaches, of which Petersmann's is the most prominent, do provide alternative explanations.

My choice to focus elsewhere thus reflects, not logical form, but a substantive judgment about the prominence, fit, and attractiveness of the intrinsic human rights approach. First prominence: whereas Petersmann's approach constitutes a sustained research agenda, it has gained limited traction with other scholars[192]; when more doctrinally or practically inclined scholars analyze specific issues they refer constantly to economic explanations, but only rarely to the human rights approach.[193] Second, fit: because Petersmann's approach focuses on citizens' rights against governments,[194] the lack of an individual complaint procedure seems an insurmountable obstacle.[195] Third, attractiveness: the market freedoms Petersmann defends are themselves of doubtful moral significance, and incompatible with the liberal egalitarian premises from which I begin[196]; anyone prepared to grant my normative argument a hearing is thus unlikely to regard Petersmann's approach as attractive.[197] I do not claim these points defeat Petersmann's views, or establish my own approach as superior: rather, they explain why I have not made challenging Petersmann my focus.[198]

2.6.3   Critical Implications

Much of my discussion of the positive law is explanatory and interpretive. But of course, as Marx teaches, it is not enough simply to interpret the world: the point is to change it. The principles defended in Part II, and applied in Part III, are not simply an account of how the law is. Rather, they describe what justice demands in trade regulation. As such, they aspire to guide action: but this may mean quite different things from different perspectives.

---

[192] For this point: (Alston, 2002: 817).

[193] For a rare exception: (Howse, 2010: 92–95). But cf. (Howse, 2002d).

[194] (Petersmann, 2008a: 58–59) Cf. (Cottier, 2002: 122).

[195] (Petersmann, 2008a: 55–57). To this extent, the approach better fits the European and federal systems from which it derives: (Petersmann, 1992). It is better understood as an evolutionary proposal internationally. See (Petersmann, 2008a: 60–61, 2012: 61–78).

[196] (Alston, 2002; Howse, 2002d: 654–655, 2008: 946–949; Kymlicka, 2002: 138–153).

[197] I have elsewhere argued that the kinds of market rights that Petersmann defends are incompatible both with substantive liberal commitments domestically, and with the methods standardly adopted in answering domestic political questions: (Suttle, 2016).

[198] Of course, to the extent the normative and explanatory arguments in later chapters are accepted, their incompatibility constitutes a refutation of Petersmann's views.

At various points in later chapters, I highlight interpretive debates where EGC might guide adjudicators. Positivists and interpretivists will understand these suggestions differently. Positivists, to the extent they recognize hard cases as lacunae, may accept adjudicators' reference to extra-legal norms – including those advanced here – to resolve these.[199] For interpretivists, the explanatory claims in Part III provide grounds for interpreting WTO rules in light of these principles, and hence allowing them to guide adjudicators.[200]

Art. 31(1) *Vienna Convention on the Law of Treaties'* requirement to interpret treaties in light of their object and purpose provides a doctrinal basis for this approach.[201] That provision raises problems of collective intentions for multilateral treaties: in circumstances where parties pursue diverse, and often conflicting, goals, whose "object and purpose" is relevant?[202] Even where, as with the GATT, a few states are the effective authors, there is little reason to interpret other parties' obligations in light of their object and purpose.[203] Preambles may provide some guidance, but the preambles to the WTO agreements are often scant, contradictory, or at odds with the operative parts.[204] Adjudicators have little alternative but to engage in constructive interpretation of the agreements, identifying their object and purpose from their provisions, and from the motivations appropriately attributable to the parties thereto.[205] At this point my normative and explanatory arguments together provide a plausible doctrinal basis for understanding the object and purpose of the WTO agreements in terms of EGC.

This may sound like a mandate for judicial activism that risks undermining the legitimacy of international trade law, or making it the vehicle of values not shared by the regime's members as a whole. Better, some argue, to limit ourselves to narrow textualism and established doctrinal techniques, and otherwise defer to other domestic and international

---

[199] On whether adjudicators must reach conclusions in such cases: (Bartels, 2004: 873 et seq).

[200] Subject, of course, to the caveats noted earlier. I do not advance an interpretivist theory of international law. For efforts in that direction: (Çali, 2009; Tasioulas, 1996: 55 et seq). An obvious objection queries the appropriateness of liberal legal theory in a pluralist world. For this objection, among others: (Beckett, 2001). For Dworkin's own efforts in this direction: (Dworkin, 2013).

[201] On the VCLT's status in WTO law: *US-Gasoline*, (AB), p. 17

[202] (Jonas & Saunders, 2010: 581).

[203] On the GATT's negotiating history: (Mavroidis, 2012: 9–13).

[204] (Howse & Neven, 2003: 157).

[205] For this point, albeit from an economic point of view: (Mavroidis, 2007: 6–7).

decision-makers.[206] This challenge is particularly relevant to my argument, given its acknowledged basis in liberal thought. However, I follow Horn and Weiler in thinking that, by avoiding explicit acknowledgement of value questions and choices that are an unavoidable part of adjudication, textualism undermines the regime's legitimacy far more than the alternative.[207]

Readers might here object that Article 3.2 of the Dispute Settlement Understanding rules out this approach. Article 3.2 provides that the Dispute Settlement System serves "to preserve the rights and obligations of members under the covered agreements," and that recommendations and rulings cannot "add to or diminish" those rights. However, while this certainly suggests a cautious interpretive approach, it does not remove the need to interpret the agreements. Legal theorists of all stripes recognize that, in hard cases, interpretation cannot proceed exclusively by deduction from the language of legal texts.[208] Textualism obscures judicial discretion: it does not avoid it. Once this is acknowledged, the approach proposed here seems as compatible with Article 3.2 as any other.

For negotiators the implications are more straightforward. There are undoubtedly practical impediments to the further incorporation of these principles in the positive law of the WTO: most obviously, the disappointment of the Doha Round underlines the difficulties of achieving meaningful progress in multilateral trade negotiations. However, those agreements and amendments that have been achieved, including most recently the Bali Trade Facilitation Agreement and the Nairobi Ministerial Decision on Export Competition, demonstrate that progress is possible. EGC aspires to point the way. Further, through offering a principled argument for a just trade regime, it suggests standards around which negotiations might converge, independent of the narrow self-interest that traditionally characterizes trade agreements.[209]

EGC also has immediate normative significance for states in their regulation of international trade. As noted above, WTO law can claim limited practical authority. States, in determining their economic

---

[206] For this argument in respect of international law generally: (Beckett, 2001). In the trade regime: (Bacchus, 2005; Howse, 2001; Howse & Nicolaidis, 2003).

[207] (Horn & Weiler, 2005) Cf. (Diamond, 2008: 675–678). On the role of legal argument in constructing a community of values: (Cho, 2004). On the implications for social legitimacy: (Cho, 2015: 211–213).

[208] See e.g. (Hart, 1958: 607–608).

[209] On this role of principled argument, see sources at fn. 157 above.

policies, must therefore have direct recourse to the first order reasons applying to them, including those expressed in EGC. For example, in many cases WTO law affords permissions to states to do or refrain from particular actions; however, EGC might suggest that states' moral freedom of action is significantly constrained. Similarly, there are cases where EGC suggests states should have greater freedom than is accorded by WTO law, for example, in respect of development policies. In such cases, EGC implies other states should refrain from demanding strict compliance with legal obligations, or taking enforcement action. Exactly how states should respond in such circumstances is a difficult question, given the undoubted value of a stable, legalized trade regime, and the importance of clear signaling for maintaining that regime. I offer no general answer to this question. I doubt there is one. But there will be circumstances where individual states have the flexibility to refrain from exercising their rights under, or demanding compliance with, the positive law of the trade regime. In these circumstances, EGC requires that they do so.[210]

2.7   Conclusion

The purpose of this chapter has been to lay the groundwork for what comes later. I have sought to clarify the questions I am trying to answer, to show the defects in existing approaches to those questions, and to outline the methodology that I use in answering them in later chapters. The next chapter begins my argument in earnest, as I lay out the central elements of my constructivist argument for EGC.

---

[210] This links to another question that I address only in passing: whether and to what extent the WTO is the appropriate venue to institutionalize the principles I here advance. There are certainly plausible arguments that its limited epistemic capacities and social legitimacy would counsel caution. E.g. (Howse et al., 2015). However, the substantial authority in fact enjoyed by WTO dispute settlement, exceeding that of any competing locus of international governance, together with the WTO's status as a member-driven organization, in which dispute settlement outcomes inform actions by individual states, supports an argument that the answers the DSU produces to questions of WTO legality should seek to approximate, insofar as possible, the all-things-considered reasons that apply to members. Of course, for various reasons, this may not be possible, something I highlight at various points below.

PART II

Justice

Towards a Political Theory of International Economic Law

A liberal theory of justice in international economic law must start with liberalism's unresolved boundary problem. Until we have a satisfactory account of the obligations that states and their citizens owe to insiders and outsiders, we cannot construct a moral theory of the regimes governing international economic interaction. The goal of the present chapter is to advance and defend such an account, and thereby to argue for EGC as a standard of justice appropriate to international economic law.

3.1 Introduction

Many people endorse duties of economic justice within states, including a concern for excessive inequalities. That concern finds expression in various ways, including through progressive taxation, unemployment insurance and welfare systems, minimum wage and labor rights legislation, and the public provision of healthcare, education, and other basic services. While we differ on exactly what these duties require, we commonly assume that they are owed primarily or exclusively to our fellow citizens or conationals. Our duties to foreigners, to the extent they are acknowledged, are assumed to be of a different, and lesser, kind. Yet, when pressed, we struggle to explain why we make this distinction, and to justify the different treatment that it accords to foreigners.

In political philosophy, the leading expression of that egalitarian sentiment is John Rawls's difference principle, which provides that social and economic inequalities are only permissible where, *inter alia*, they are to the greatest benefit of the least-advantaged members of society.[1] While Rawls advances the difference principle as applying to individual societies, some

---

[1] (Rawls, 1971: 83).

of the earliest responses to his *Theory of Justice* observed that his argument for that principle seemed to apply equally to the world as a whole.[2] Rawls argues from moral equality to the difference principle; but if moral equality implies the difference principle, and we are to respect the moral equality of all persons everywhere, which surely we must, then why does the difference principle not apply globally? Nor is this problem particular to Rawls; it seems that any view that concerns itself with economic inequalities within the state must explain whether, to what extent, and why, that concern does or does not extend to those beyond the border. This is contemporary liberalism's boundary problem, around which much contemporary global justice theorizing resolves.

Responses can be roughly divided into three groups, none entirely satisfactory: first, strong cosmopolitans, who accept that the logic of liberalism extends beyond the state and argue for the same distributive principles globally as they favor domestically[3]; second, communitarians, who reject the liberal derivation of distributive justice from moral equality, instead grounding distributive principles in social meanings and obligations within communities[4]; and third, liberals who defend Rawls's arguments domestically while arguing that specific features of social cooperation within the state distinguish the domestic and international contexts, making the difference principle appropriate to the former but not the latter.[5] Features emphasized have included interdependence, coercion, self-authored coercion, cooperation, cooperation in the production of basic public goods, political cooperation, and the presence of basic institutions or a basic structure; in each case, these face challenges querying the significance of the relevant feature in motivating egalitarian duties, and/or the extent to which it can effectively distinguish domestic from cross-border cases.[6]

Among those who reject the strong cosmopolitan position, a further distinction appears between those who deny any duties of economic

---

[2] (Barry, 1973: 128–133; Scanlon, 1972–1973: 1066–1067). Tamir identifies this boundary problem as a reason for favoring her nationalist, original position (Tamir, 1993: 111).

[3] (Beitz, 1983, 1999; Caney, 2005; Moellendorf, 2002, 2009; Pogge, 1989, 1992, 1994; Tan, 2000, 2004).

[4] (Miller, 1995, 1999a, 1999b, 2007, 2009; Tamir, 1993; Walzer, 1983, 1994).

[5] (Blake, 2001; Brock, 2009; Cohen & Sabel, 2006; Freeman, 2007; James, 2005, 2012b; Maffettone, 2009; Meckled-Garcia, 2008; Nagel, 2005; Rawls, 1999; Sangiovanni, 2007, 2008, 2011; Valentini, 2011c).

[6] For critical reviews of these approaches: (Abizadeh, 2007; Barry & Valentini, 2009; Buchanan, 2004; Follesdal, 2011; Julius, 2006).

justice beyond the state[7]; and those who, while denying that identical principles apply within and beyond the state, advocate less demanding principles of global economic justice. These latter principles are frequently sufficientarian rather than egalitarian: they measure outcomes against absolute standards (sufficiency), whether expressed in economic, political, or human rights terms, rather than making comparative judgments (equality) across different persons. Depending on whether these emphasize duties to nations, peoples, or persons, theories of the latter type are characterized as liberal nationalist,[8] social liberal,[9] or moderate cosmopolitan,[10] and collectively as moderate theories.[11]

It is against this background that I build the argument for EGC.

I begin, in Section 3.2, with existing moderate coercion-based accounts of global justice, which argue that the differences between domestic and international coercion explain why egalitarian obligations are limited to the domestic context. I argue that these cannot satisfactorily resolve the boundary problem, because they lack a sufficiently nuanced understanding of international coercion, and so cannot plausibly distinguish the domestic and international contexts. It is not enough to claim that domestic and international coercion are different; we need an account of how they differ, and how those differences affect the justifications that they evoke. This must allow us both to reconstruct our domestic principles, through a plausible account of the morally significant features motivating them, and to show how focusing on those same features produce different results in the international context. By providing such an account, this chapter makes the coercion-based approach more plausible, while also modifying the conclusions of that approach, leading us to EGC.

Sections 3.3–3.6 provide the account of coercion and its justification that existing coercion-based accounts lack. Section 3.3 highlights how the plurality of international institutions requires reconstructing the coercion approach to focus on distinct institutions and relations. Subsequent

---

[7] (Nagel, 2005; Walzer, 1983). This position is commonly associated with international relations realists, although contemporary realists generally avoid normative claims (Morgenthau & Thompson, 1985; Waltz, 1979). For a brief review of realism as a normative position: (Caney, 2005: 7–10).

[8] (Miller, 1995, 2007; Tamir, 1993). Although Valentini argues that Miller's later work is less easily classified: (Valentini, 2011c: 73 n.74).

[9] (Freeman, 2007; Rawls, 1999).

[10] (Brock, 2009; Buchanan, 2004; Pogge, 2002; Valentini, 2011c).

[11] For a definition of moderate cosmopolitanism capturing the essence of moderate theories generally: (Scheffler, 2001: 116).

parts seek to establish three claims. First, in Section 3.4, I argue that indirect international coercion may, within limits, be justified by invoking the principle of self-determination; while direct coercion must be justified to those subject to it by reference to ends that they themselves have reason to share. Second, in Section 3.5, I argue that the justification of exclusive coercion may be sufficientarian, while inclusive coercion requires justification in distributive (and generally egalitarian) terms. Third, in Section 3.6, I argue that where the subject of coercion is not also in some meaningful sense its author, it is particularly important to examine its justification from the perspectives of both parties.

Having established these claims, I turn in Section 3.7 to EGC, arguing that ETMs constitute direct, inclusive coercion of outsiders, and that as such they can only be justified in egalitarian terms; the same considerations do not apply to DEMs, which are justifiable in the sufficientarian terms of existing moderate theories.

3.2   Coercion, Nonvoluntary Institutions, and Distributive Justice

Various authors have argued that duties of distributive justice, understood as a concern for relative rather than absolute shares, derive from the nature of coercion in the domestic context, and that this explains why such duties are not applicable internationally.[12]

Blake argues that concern for relative shares reflects the need to justify coercion to those who are subject to it.[13] He builds his theory from a principle of autonomy that is violated when individuals are subject to coercion.[14] While he does not define coercion, he makes it clear that his concern is with situations where the options available to individuals are

---

[12] A separate approach, labeled political realism, draws on the work of Bernard Williams to refocus political theory from morality towards the legitimation of coercion. My argument is not realist in this sense. However, it reflects a similar recognition that the justification of coercion, albeit in moral terms, is the basic problem of politics; and I believe taking seriously in international politics what Williams labels the *critical theory principle* should lead realists towards something like the conclusions I defend here. See generally: (Williams, 2005).

[13] (Blake, 2001).

[14] Blake relies on Raz's perfectionist liberalism rather than Rawls's political account. For a discussion of the differences: (Nussbaum, 2011). While this raises questions about the compatibility of some aspects of Blake's approach with Rawls's theory, his account of coercion is transferable, and arguably (given criticisms below) fits better in the Rawlsian framework.

subject to the will of another.[15] Recognizing that state coercion, as so understood, is both prevalent and necessary, he argues that the violation of the principle of autonomy that this implies requires justification through the hypothetical consent of those who are subject to it.[16]

In the domestic context, Blake emphasizes the continuous nature of coercion, the unitary nature of the legal system, and the role of private law in particular in defining patterns of entitlements in society, including how citizens may hold, transfer, and enjoy property, and ultimately what sorts of economic holdings result from activities.[17] Egalitarian concerns derive from this role of the legal system in defining returns to individuals, and from the fact that the legal system applies to all individuals within a society. In consequence, that system must offer to all individuals who are subject to it, including those who do least well, reasons to accept it. This need to justify the legal system to all, including the least advantaged, in turn generates the difference principle as the only principle that the least advantaged could be expected to accept. Thus, Blake argues, the concern for relative shares in domestic theory in fact derives from an underlying concern for autonomy.[18]

While providing a plausible reconstruction of Rawls's argument for the difference principle, Blake's argument is weaker when he tries to distinguish between international and domestic contexts. At one point, he suggests that the state does not coerce outsiders, and therefore need not apply its principles of liberal justice to them.[19] However, he does not ultimately deny that coercion is present in the international context. Rather, he denies that international coercion is such as to require justification in distributive terms, primarily because it is not ongoing or directed against individual human agents, in the way that domestic coercion is.[20] It is only coercion of this type, and particularly coercion tied to the definition of economic returns to individuals, that requires egalitarian justification.

Nagel similarly emphasizes the distinctiveness of domestic coercion in his argument against international distributive justice. He cites Rawls for the view that "[i]t is the nature of sovereign states ... and in particular their comprehensive control over the framework of their citizens' lives, that

---

[15] (Blake, 2001: 268, 270–272).   [16] Ibid., 274–279.   [17] Ibid., 280–281.   [18] Ibid., 283.
[19] Ibid., 287.
[20] Ibid., 280–281. Blake does note in a footnote that "the entire international system might be based on coercion," but does not pursue this point except to suggest that the justification offered for that coercion would differ from the justification offered by a state to its own citizen. Risse invokes a similar concept of "immediacy" to make this distinction: (Risse, 2006) Cf. (Blake, 2013: 97–98, 102–107).

creates the special demands for justification and the special constraints on ends and means that constitute the requirements of justice."[21] Justice, on this view, is an associative obligation, applying among persons who stand in a strong political relation with one another. However, for Nagel, it is not simply the fact of being subject to the state's coercion that gives rise to obligations of socioeconomic justice; rather, what matters is that we are "fellow participants in a collective enterprise of coercively imposed legal and political institutions."[22] What is distinctive about state coercion is that it is coercion exercised *in the name of* its subjects: "we are both putative joint authors of the coercively imposed system, and subject to its norms."[23] It is this that gives rise to the demand for justification, which in turn grounds the argument for distributive justice.

International coercion, in Nagel's view, lacks this element of self-authorship. Domestic coercion invokes the will of its subjects, who are asked to accept it and who are held responsible for obeying the society's laws and norms, thereby supporting its institutions. Against outsiders, on the other hand, laws are merely enforced.

> [T]he laws are not imposed in their name, nor are they asked to accept and uphold those laws. Since no acceptance is demanded of them, no justification is required that explains why they should accept such discriminatory policies, or why their interests have been given equal consideration.[24]

Julius has defended an individualist variant of the coercion approach, focusing on what he labels "framing": acting with the intention of leading another to act in a way that advances one's own interests. It is the pervasiveness of individuals' mutual framing that constitutes the domestic basic structure and motivates its egalitarian demands.[25] In a critique of Nagel, he suggests that framing might similarly serve to distinguish domestic and international. However, because framing is not limited to the domestic case, this would not generate the stark contrast identified by Nagel; rather, Julius suggests it would motivate an intermediate principle, albeit one whose application is difficult to imagine.[26]

---

[21] (Nagel, 2005: 123).   [22] Ibid., 128.   [23] Ibid., 128.   [24] ibid., 129–130.
[25] (Julius, 2003).
[26] Julius observes:

> A continuous transition between [a national and a global difference principle] succeeds in acknowledging both circumstances [that many people have outgoing projects, while most people are locally concentrated] even as it ensures that the international difference principle eventually displaces the national one.

And, in a nearby footnote:

Most recently, the coercion-based account of global justice has been defended by Valentini, who adopts a broad definition of coercion as "foreseeably and avoidably placing non-trivial constraints on an agent's action," and argues that the function of principles of justice is to evaluate coercion so understood.[27] Like Blake, Valentini argues that it is differences in the scope of coercion that explain why specifically distributive obligations only apply domestically.[28]

3.2.1 Can Coercion Distinguish Domestic from International?

As an argument against strong cosmopolitanism, the coercion view has been subject to sustained criticism. In the narrower form advanced by Blake, it is challenged as relying on a straightforwardly false empirical claim, namely that states do not coerce outsiders, or that their coercion is not directed against individuals on an ongoing basis.[29] In so far as Blake accepts the existence of international coercion, he fails to convincingly explain why domestic coercion is distinctive and gives rise to distributive obligations.[30] Even in its narrowest form, focusing on the role of domestic coercion in defining economic returns, it is difficult to argue that international coercion does not also fulfill this function.[31] Nagel's extension of this theory, on the other hand, is criticized as relying on a problematic definition of what it means to accept a coercive

---

"Could it be something so Procrustean as

$$\max \left[\alpha \min_{i \in A} W_i + (1 - \alpha) \min_{j \in W} W_j \right]$$

with A the set of your fellow citizens, W the set of people in the world, w_i an index of i's goods, and α a parameter decaying from 1 to 0?": (Julius, 2006: 191).

[27] (Valentini, 2011c: 121–154, 180–182) Cf. (Valentini, 2011a, 2011b). Valentini's definition of coercion, while broad by contemporary standards, arguably maps directly onto Kant's definition as "a hindrance or resistance to freedom." Obviously, given the heavily moralized nature of freedom in Kant's account, this definition does not reduce to Valentini's. However, its recognition that what matters is "hindrance or resistance," as opposed to orders or threats, supports both Valentini's definition, and also my own approach: (Kant, 1991: 134).

[28] Risse develops a further variant on the coercion approach. While proposed as an improvement on Blake's approach, it is, I believe, subject to the same criticisms identified in the text: (Risse, 2006).

[29] (Abizadeh, 2007: 350–351).   [30] Ibid., 354–356.   [31] Ibid., 355–356.

system,[32] and a perverse normative premise that coercion without any pretense of accountability is somehow less objectionable than coercion that is administered in the name of those coerced.[33] More generally, it has been suggested that both Blake's and Nagel's arguments depend not on coercion, in the narrow sense, but on a broader concern for "the non-voluntary, de facto authority of a legal system,"[34] or the nonvoluntary "imposition of societal rules."[35] This reading makes it even harder to distinguish the international and domestic contexts in a convincing way, leading Sangiovanni to characterize the "voluntarist" turn in global justice theory as a dead end.[36]

There are, however, good reasons to maintain the focus on coercion, understood broadly as subjection to nonvoluntary institutions. The imposition on individuals of nonvoluntary institutions, and the effects those institutions have, are essential in motivating Rawls's account of domestic justice.[37] Blake is right in arguing that it is in large part because the institutions of the basic structure are nonvoluntary that we must rely on the hypothetical consent of individuals, as modeled in the Original Position, to identify appropriate principles of justice.[38] Indeed, in the domestic context, it has been argued that the justification of coercion, so understood, is the central problem of contemporary liberalism.[39] There is, therefore, good reason to think that, if the boundary problem can be resolved, coercion is a good place to start.

3.2.2   Why Does Coercion Matter?

While querying whether coercion can distinguish the domestic and international contexts, Sangiovanni also advances a more fundamental

---

[32] (Sangiovanni, 2007: 15–18) Cf. (Cohen & Sabel, 2006: 166–168; Julius, 2006: 180–184).

[33] (Abizadeh, 2007: 354–356) Cf. (Julius, 2006: 184–187). And, in an account anticipating both the argument and the objection: (Brilmayer, 1989, 90–93).

[34] (Sangiovanni, 2007: 12–14).

[35] Ibid., 15. The breadth of Valentini's definition of coercion arguably reflects a similar move, albeit retaining the language of coercion.

[36] (Sangiovanni, 2007). For a similar conclusion: (Tan, 2012: 160–163). Brilmayer, emphasizing legitimacy and political obligation rather than distributive justice, develops an analogous argument, to the effect that the externally coercive aspect of the state requires legitimation in similar terms, *ceteris paribus*, to its domestic aspect, a claim that she labels the "vertical thesis": (Brilmayer, 1989: passim).

[37] Thus, Rawls argues that "[t]he social role of a conception of justice is to enable all members of society to make mutually acceptable to one another their shared institutions and basic arrangements, by citing what are publicly recognized sufficient reasons, as identified by that conception.": (Rawls, 1980: 517).

[38] (Rawls, 2001: 10, 20, 40–41, 55).   [39] (Gaus, 2010).

challenge, denying that there is any connection between coercion and distributive justice, in either the domestic or international contexts.[40] The upshot, if this argument is accepted, is that any differences between coercion in these domains are irrelevant to the applicability of particular distributive principles. It is therefore necessary to address Sangiovanni's criticism before proceeding.

Sangiovanni first identifies three possible ways coercion might give rise to distributive claims. Two of these rely on a presumption that coercion constitutes a *pro tanto* wrong. The first, *Compensation*, claims that "special distributive obligations [are] meant to compensate for the wrong of forcing [the object] to do something."[41] The second, *Outweighing*, claims that "[the coercer's] infringement of [the object's] right to autonomy is … outweighed by the urgency or importance or weightiness of the interests protected by the more demanding distributive principle."[42] The third, *Fiduciary Obligation*, regards coercive relations as constituting a quasi-fiduciary relation between coercer and coercee, among whose incidents are distributive duties attaching to the coercer. Having rejected each explanation in turn, Sangiovanni provisionally rejects the coercion approach. He concedes that an alternative explanation might be offered that avoids his criticisms, but denies that such an alternative has been offered to date.

While it is unclear how far other scholars are committed to the views Sangiovanni criticizes, my goal here is not to defend them, but rather to show that a plausible link can be drawn between coercion and distributive justice which avoids Sangiovanni's objections. My approach might be labeled *Reconciliation*. Like much else in this text, it draws heavily on Rawls.[43]

Reconciliation begins with the idea of persons as free and equal. It sees coercion as both unavoidable, and also potentially problematic. It is unavoidable because, in order for persons to live minimally decent lives, and to benefit from social cooperation, some element of coercion is necessary.[44] It is potentially problematic because, to the extent it involves the options available to persons and the returns to their activities being determined by others, it is in tension with the idea of persons as

---

[40] (Sangiovanni, 2012). A similar objection, albeit less developed, appears in: (Caney, 2008).
[41] (Sangiovanni, 2012: 90).   [42] Ibid., 94.
[43] Blake's recent restatement of his position, which seems in part concerned to avoid Sangiovanni's objections, has elements in common with the view I outline in this section: (Blake, 2013, ch. 4).
[44] There is nothing new in this claim, which is simply Hobbes's argument for the state.

free and equal. *Reconciliation*, as its name suggests, seeks to reconcile these two ideas.

How do we move from here to the idea of distributive justice? In the absence of coercion, persons' choices are their own, and they can properly be regarded as responsible for the returns, both positive and negative, to their activities. While we may be concerned that they have access to essential resources required to take responsibility for their own lives, in general, our treating them as free and equal may require no more than leaving them alone to pursue their own projects, just as we pursue ours. We owe them no justification for the ways those projects turn out. Moral equality in this context carries no implication of economic equality.

However, in circumstances where persons are subject to coercion, neither their choices nor the returns to their activities are fully their own. The options they have and the returns that accrue from them are, in varying degrees, dictated by others. The need to reconcile these facts with the idea of persons as free and equal is what leads us into questions of hypothetical consent and original position reasoning. It does not explain why that reasoning in turn implies distributive obligations. However, it reframes the question of how we respect persons in a way that gives different answers from those that arise in its absence.[45] Coercion may not feature in those answers; rather, it is what leads to the question being asked. Sangiovanni's criticism thus elides the distinction between the reasons why a justification is required, and the form that a justification takes.

Reconciliation differs importantly from Sangiovanni's accounts of either *Compensation* or *Outweighing*. *Compensation* fails because it cannot identify a relevant baseline against which to assess the harm of coercion, and so cannot explain why distributive justice is an appropriate compensation.[46] *Outweighing* fails because it depends on the prior existence of reasons of sufficient moral weight to outweigh the wrong of coercion; but to the extent these reasons exist, Sangiovanni claims, it is they, rather than the fact of coercion, that must ground distributive claims.[47] To the extent Sangiovanni sees coercion altering the reasons applying in a given situation, he argues this is limited to a duty not to harm, meaning *Outweighing* faces the same baseline problems as *Compensation*.[48]

Reconciliation tells a different story. Under conditions of moderate scarcity, it recognizes extensive coercion as necessary for anyone to enjoy a minimally decent life. It follows Hobbes in regarding social life without

---

[45] For an analogous point, in the language of equal concern and respect: (Dworkin, 2002: 6).
[46] (Sangiovanni, 2012: 91–93).   [47] Ibid., 97.   [48] Ibid., 101–102.

institutional coercion as impossible.[49] In these circumstances, there is no question of this coercion requiring compensation; all persons are better off as a result of it than they are in the state of nature. Further, while *Outweighing* might play some role, we can assume that the benefits of stable social cooperation for all outweigh any *pro tanto* wrongfulness of that coercion. To this extent I agree with Sangiovanni: we cannot get to distributive justice through either *Compensation* or *Outweighing*.

However, whereas the benefits of stability justify some coercive scheme, they do tell us what shape that scheme should take. Let us assume for a moment that a coercive scheme creating radical and unnecessary inequalities would still benefit all persons subject to it, when compared with a counterfactual state of nature. In consequence, no subject has a claim to compensation, nor can they deny that the benefits of being coerced outweigh any *pro tanto* wrong involved. However, few would claim that this, without more, answers the question of whether the coercive scheme, and its authors, respect its subjects as free and equal. They may, but it requires further argument to explain how this is the case. Those arguments may or may not make reference to the coercive nature of the relevant scheme. However, even if they make no further reference to coercion, coercion remains important in constituting the need for those arguments in the first place. Coercion constitutes the relationship between persons without which these questions would not arise. If answers are provided then no wrong, *pro tanto* or otherwise, is committed. If they are not, then the wrong is not simply coercion, but rather a failure to respect persons as free and equal.

A major aspect of Sangiovanni's critique is the failure to explain why, assuming coercion requires some additional justification, that justification should be limited to the interests of those coerced, and should be in specifically egalitarian terms.[50] Certainly, the mere fact that justification is owed does not *ipso facto* imply egalitarian justice.[51] Does this constitute an objection to *Reconciliation*? As I argue below, the justification that coercion evokes will vary depending on the form that it takes, and only a subset of coercion evokes egalitarian justification. Where it does, the path from coercion to distributive equality goes through a version of Rawls's theory of justice as fairness, the elements of which are introduced in the next section. It invokes ideas of moral equality, reciprocity, and generality,

---

[49] Blake similarly endorses this view: (Blake, 2013: 84). [50] (Sangiovanni, 2012: 87).
[51] That said, I doubt either Blake or Nagel believes it does. Blake is quite explicit on this point: (Blake, 2013: 84).

as well as substantive conceptions of persons and peoples, that are not themselves limited to the context of coercion. It is the form these concepts take, rather than the bare fact of coercion, that explains why justification is distributive. However, like respect, these concepts have different implications in the presence of coercion. For example, whereas reciprocity might elsewhere be understood as voluntary bargain, under coercion it raises substantive as well as procedural questions. Further, the reason we invoke these concepts is to fill out the need for justification that coercion triggers.

Reconciliation thus suggests a preliminary answer to Sangiovanni's irrelevance challenge, showing how coercion can play a nonredundant role by changing what it means to treat a person as free and equal. A full answer to his challenge must further explain the form that treatment takes. This, I suggest, will vary depending on the form of the coercion, and the relation between coercer and coerced. Thus, a successful coercion account must explain how the particular coercive relations found domestically evoke distributive duties, and how the same considerations translate to the international context. This is the task to which I next turn.

3.3 Coercion and the Plurality of Global Institutions

Assuming that we can avoid Sangiovanni's irrelevance challenge, then, it seems the main weakness of existing coercion accounts is their failure to plausibly show how international and domestic coercion differ, and how this difference explains the different distributive obligations that apply internationally and domestically.[52] While both Blake and Nagel emphasize the elements of domestic coercion that demand distributive justification, they give only limited attention to the contrasting phenomenon of international coercion.[53] This must then be our focus in seeking to rehabilitate these arguments.

Drawing on Rawls's account of the basic structure, let us first recast the coercion argument as focusing on nonvoluntary subjection to institutions that distribute fundamental rights and duties and determine the

---

[52] Both Nagel and Freeman have noted the difficulties of providing a plausible account of how distributive obligations might vary with variations in some other independent variable: (Freeman, 2007: 289–294; Nagel, 2005: 140–143). For one such effort, see Julius' suggestion at fn. 26 above.

[53] While Valentini gives greater attention to the manifestations of coercion in the international system and the international economy, she fails appropriately to disaggregate globally coercive institutions or to consider the different qualities and justificatory structures of coercive measures and institutions: (Valentini, 2011c: 186–198).

division of advantages from social cooperation.[54] As well as tying the argument to a canonical account of contemporary liberalism, this formulation captures Blake's central concern with cases where the options open to individuals are subject to the will of another.[55] Its focus on institutions reflects Rawls's own starting point, which is shared by Blake and Nagel[56]; but by emphasizing subjection rather than participation, it avoids the status quo bias criticism leveled at some institutional theories.[57] Regardless of whether they are participants in Nagel's sense, an individual or community is subject to an institution whenever that institution shapes their fundamental rights and duties or determines the division of advantages from cooperation in which they participate. As a definition of coercion, this might be criticized for underemphasizing effects on the coercee's will, which constitutes coercion as a violation of autonomy.[58] However, on closer examination, we generally find such nonvoluntary institutions supported by coercion in this narrower sense.[59] Further, notwithstanding Blake's argument, the link to the will is not essential in the Rawlsian approach, which asks not "how can coercion of the will be justifiable to autonomous persons?," but rather, "how can coercion through nonvoluntary institutions be reconciled with the respect due to individuals as free and equal?."[60] This is the question

---

[54] (Rawls, 1971: 7, 1996: 258). The role of the basic structure in Rawlsian theories is discussed further in Chapter 4.

[55] (Blake, 2001: 268). It might be objected here, and elsewhere, that the sense of coercion used is too broad, capturing any situation where agents affect one another. However the focus on institutions substantially avoids this objection. That our actions affect others is an unavoidable upshot of sharing a world. It is when we solve the problems this raises through constituting nonvoluntary institutions, and thereby departing from the practical equality of the state of nature, that political justification becomes relevant. Once such institutions start determining outcomes, we can no longer rely on our mutual impacts simply balancing each other out, as the image of equal interacting agents invites us to do.

[56] For a critique of Rawls's institutional focus: (Cohen, 1997, 2008: 116–180; Murphy, 1998; Pogge, 2000).

[57] (Valentini, 2011b).

[58] For a discussion of recent approaches to coercion: (Anderson, 2011).

[59] (Rawls, 2001: 40). For a discussion of this point in the international context: (Abizadeh, 2008; Miller, 2010).

[60] Cf. fn. 37 above. On the move from autonomy to respect, and its implications: (Nussbaum, 2011) The view here defended need not limit justice, per se, to coercive institutions. Rather, the argument links specifically distributive claims to particular coercive relations. We might identify other duties of justice, including, for example, duties to refrain from harming and some positive duties in respect of basic rights, in noncoercive contexts. Alternatively, we might understand at least the latter in terms of exclusive coercion, as discussed further below; or as expressing duties of humanity rather than justice.

whose answer I suggested above motivates the most plausible form of the coercion approach.

Coercion in this sense is obviously not limited to the domestic context. International examples include territorial sovereignty,[61] border controls,[62] structural competition,[63] the internal laws of other states,[64] the global market economy,[65] and the system of international law and treaty institutions.[66] In each case, we find nonvoluntary institutions distributing fundamental rights and duties and determining the division of advantages from cooperation, for both individuals and communities. Further, these are not simply a function of nonideal conditions; as this list seeks to illustrate, even under ideal conditions, the international order is necessarily coercive.[67]

The mere fact that the international system is coercive need not evoke egalitarian justification. Recall Blake's starting point: coercion must be justified in terms that those subject to it can reasonably accept. For Rawls, this is the function of deliberation in the Original Position, which seeks to model fair agreement among participants conceived as free and equal moral persons.[68]

In the domestic context, the first subject of justice is the society's basic structure; and among free and equal persons symmetrically situated subject to that structure, the difference principle is selected as the only

---

[61] (Bull, 1977; Keene, 2002; Krasner, 1999; Reus-Smit, 1999).

[62] (Abizadeh, 2008; Miller, 2010, 2012).

[63] (Mearsheimer, 2014; Walt, 1987; Waltz, 1979).

[64] (Drezner, 2007; Freeman, 2007: 306–308; Hurrell, 2007: 71).

[65] (Inayatullah & Blaney, 1995; Strange, 1988).

[66] (Buchanan, 2004; Chayes & Chayes, 2005; Gaus, 2010; Hurrell, 2007: 61–62; Maffettone, 2009).

[67] It might be objected that my focus is unduly restricted, to material forms of power that impose on agents, constituting legal or economic barriers to their pursuing their goals. This necessarily elides other, more insidious forms of power through ideology and the promulgation of hegemonic ideas. This is Lukes's third face of power: (Lukes, 2004). While there is much to be said about power in this sense, a liberal view that emphasizes freedom, understood as the capacity to form revise and pursue a conception of the good, cannot make ideas a direct object of justification. We cannot emphasize individuals' capacity for choice while also seeing their choices as imposed through hegemonic ideologies. This is not to say that liberals have nothing to say on the subject. Rather, the standard liberal emphases on education, free speech, and political equality are substantially concerned with ensuring that actual persons have the opportunity to become the kinds of critical agents that liberal theory assumes them to be. More direct forms of noncoercive social authority may be analyzable in the terms I propose here.

[68] (Rawls, 2001: 6) Cf. (Rawls, 1980: 528).

basis on which that structure can be justified to all.[69] Rawls's egalitarianism is thus a consequence of his approach to justifying domestic institutions.[70]

Once we move to the international context, however, the situation becomes more complicated. Individuals are no longer symmetrically situated; rather, we must consider the different positions of insiders and outsiders, each of whom are subject to institutions in different ways. To the extent that they are subject to institutions, those institutions must be justified to them. But the form of justification may vary across persons.

Domestically, we start from the basic structure, understood as "the way in which the major social institutions fit together into one system, and how they assign fundamental rights and duties and shape the division of advantages and disadvantages that arises from social cooperation."[71] As the basic structure is responsible for the distribution of advantages and disadvantages, we can assess its justice in terms of distributive outcomes. The state and the various interrelated domestic institutions under which we live have pervasive impacts on how our lives go, so how our lives can be expected to go thereunder becomes an important element in how we evaluate those institutions. In the international context, however, while there are institutions that assign fundamental rights and duties, and shape the division of advantages and disadvantages from social cooperation, these do not fit together in the way that Rawls envisages the basic structure, and Blake the legal system.[72] Rather than a unified scheme, we find a plurality of institutions, which together have pervasive effects on individuals' life prospects, but each of which may alone have only limited power to affect outcomes. Distribution is effected by a range of different and largely uncoordinated institutions, some domestic, some international, and not subject to any common political authority.[73] Therefore, rather than asking whether the coercion of the system as a whole can be

---

[69] Persons are symmetrically situated in at least two senses. First, in the original position thought experiment, each has the same knowledge about themselves and about society, and the same influence on the choice to be made. But second, and more importantly for my purposes, they are symmetrically situated in society subject to the basic structure: each will find their life prospects comprehensively determined by that structure and, while they may occupy different positions, those differences are themselves constituted by that structure.

[70] Gosepath labels this logic "constitutive egalitarianism": (Gosepath, 2011).

[71] (Rawls, 1996: 258).

[72] I address further in Chapter 4 objections invoking the absence of a basic structure in this narrower sense.

[73] (Freeman, 2007: 287–288). For a fuller discussion of the different ways we can understand the distinctness between international institutions, and why we might choose one view over another: (Suttle, 2016: 815–821).

justified, as we do domestically, we must approach each institution separately, while always recognizing that whether one institution can be justified will necessarily depend on its interaction with others. Further, as no institution is wholly responsible for the distributive outcomes of individuals or peoples, their justification cannot depend entirely on those outcomes, although it may depend on how they affect them.[74]

To whom must these disparate institutions be justified? In the final analysis, they must be justifiable to those subject to them, persons and peoples as they are, in the world as it is; but in the first instance, we consider their justification to idealized persons and peoples, modeled as free and equal, rational and reasonable. The purpose of this abstraction is to help identify the reasons that apply to persons and peoples as they in fact are, the justifications they have reason to accept, and the ends they have reason to share.[75] I draw my conceptions of persons and peoples from Rawls's constructions of the original position in domestic and international theory.[76] As moral persons, individuals have two highest order interests, represented by their capacity for an effective sense of justice and their capacity to form, revise, and rationally pursue a conception of the good.[77] Peoples' interests are similarly modeled, save that liberal peoples, lacking a comprehensive conception of the good, substitute their reasonable conception of political justice, as identified in the domestic original position.[78] As rational, they seek to advance these highest order interests, which leads to their valuing basic liberties (at the level of

---

[74] (Freeman, 2007: 308; Meckled-Garcia, 2008). As will be clear from this discussion, I do not offer an argument for starting with a blank slate and choosing the existing international institutional structure. Rather, I follow Blake in asking "not what institutions we ought to have, but what the institutions we currently have would have to do to be justified": (Blake, 2001: 262). See further in §4.3.4 below.

[75] (Rawls, 1980: 516–517).   [76] (Rawls, 1980: 522–554, 1999: 30–35, 2001: 80–89).

[77] (Rawls, 1980: 525, 2001: 18–20). There are various explanations we might offer for starting with this particular conception of the person. Perhaps the most straightforward, simplifying Rawls' later view, highlights that persons and peoples, in the world in which we live, have very different ideas about what is valuable and important to them. Further, in relatively liberal contexts, this fact is unlikely to change. In consequence, we cannot hope to build our political principles on particular answers to these questions. However, in so far as we are each committed to our own particular answers, we are also in some sense committed to the importance of our having that commitment, and of being able to act on it. We cannot agree on what is important in life. But we might perhaps agree on the importance of each identifying and pursuing whatever it is that is important. So we abstract from actual persons and peoples, with their disparate commitments, to idealized persons and peoples, with an interest in forming, revising and pursuing those commitments, whatever they may be.

[78] (Rawls, 1999: 34).

persons), self-determination (at the level of peoples), and social primary goods, as the all-purpose means to advance their conceptions of justice and of the good.[79] As reasonable, they recognize the equal status of others, and are prepared to cooperate on fair terms provided others do likewise.[80]

Rawls relies on the veil of ignorance, symmetry of persons, and the focus on the basic structure to build reasonableness into the original position; persons are modeled as rational while their situation enforces reasonableness.[81] In particular, because in the original position nobody knows the position they will occupy in society, we are forced to consider how everyone will fare under a given institutional structure; enforcing ignorance makes it rational to be reasonable. However given the move, noted above, away from symmetry and the unified basic structure, I cannot rely solely on these structural constraints to model reasonableness, and must instead make it a more explicit element in the justification of principles. What does this require? While Rawls does not consistently define reasonableness,[82] it implies at least the following: recognition of the equality of persons/peoples and willingness to cooperate on fair terms[83]; acceptance of the principle of fair reciprocity, "that all who cooperate should share in the benefits and burdens of cooperation in some appropriate fashion as judged by a suitable benchmark"[84]; acceptance of the burdens of judgment – those limits on our reasoning and judgment that explain the persistence of disagreement among reasonable persons[85]; and acceptance of generality (that principles are not tailored to particular persons) and universality (that principles hold for all persons relevantly situated, in virtue of their moral equality) as formal constraints on principles of justice.[86] Where the concept of reasonableness appears below, it is used in this minimal sense. Our idealized persons and peoples are not therefore wholly egoistic. Rather, they have ends deriving from their capacity for justice and their status as reasonable that give them reason to accept, under appropriate circumstances, justifications deriving from the interests of others with whom they are linked through unavoidable, coercive institutions.[87]

This, then, is the problem. Coercive institutions are pervasive and unavoidable. In order to reconcile this pervasive coercion with our status as free and equal persons and peoples, it must be justified in

---

[79] (Rawls, 1980: 526–528, 1999: 39–45).   [80] (Rawls, 2001: 6–7).   [81] (Rawls, 1980: 528).
[82] (Rawls, 2001: 82).   [83] Ibid., 6–7.   [84] (Rawls, 1980: 528).   [85] (Rawls, 1996: 54).
[86] (Rawls, 1971: 130–133, 2001: 85–86).   [87] (Rawls, 1980: 530, 532).

terms that we, as free and equal persons and peoples, can reasonably accept. The various abstractions and hypotheticals of Rawlsian social contract theory serve to help us work out what that justification demands.

In the domestic context, this leads us to, *inter alia*, the difference principle. The challenge is to work out what will constitute a sufficient justification of international coercion. In the next three sections, I consider specific aspects of international coercion that I argue are relevant to its justification, before showing how these can be combined to reconstruct the coercion-based account of global justice as a defense of EGC.

3.4   Direct Coercion, Indirect Coercion, and Self-Determination

Let me first distinguish between being directly subject to an institution, such that the institution directly involves a person or makes them an intentional focus of its action; and being indirectly subject to an institution, such that the institution, while affecting the rights, duties, obligations or opportunities of a person, or determining the division of advantages from cooperation in which they participate, does not directly involve them or make them an intentional focus of its action.

This echoes, and relies on, the distinction between intending and foreseeing which grounds the doctrine of double effect (DDE). DDE is a controversial principle[88]; but I argue in this section that its underlying rationale is relevant to the justification of international coercion, and that its relevance here is not limited to those who accept the principle in its conventional form.

DDE claims that the difference between foresight and intention may make the difference between an action that is permitted and one that is prohibited. Specifically, as articulated by Warren Quinn:

> [DDE] distinguishes between agency in which [foreseeable] harm comes to some victims, at least in part, from the agent's deliberately involving them in something in order to further his purpose precisely by way of their being so involved (agency in which they figure as *intentional objects*) and harmful agency in which either nothing is in that way

---

[88] For an overview of current literature on DDE: (McIntyre, 2011). For critical examinations of double effect sympathetic to deontological concerns: (Foot, 1994; McIntyre, 2001). For critiques from more consequentialist perspectives: (Bennett, 1995: 194–225; Kagan, 1989: 128–182). For a defense of the slightly reformulated doctrine, on which I rely: (Quinn, 1989) discussed further in (Fischer et al., 1993; FitzPatrick, 2003; Kamm, 1992). For alternative treatments of the doctrine: (Kamm, 1989; Nagel, 1986: 180–185).

intended for the victims or what is so intended does not contribute to
their harm.[89]

In Quinn's formulation, it is not that harm is intended for the victim,
but only that something is intended for the victim, and that something
leads foreseeably to their harm. It is the fact that the victim is an object
of the agent's intention ("the agent's deliberately involving him"), and
that the agent pursues its objective by a causal chain which runs through
the involvement of the victim ("in order to further his purpose precisely
by way of their being so involved") that makes harming in this context
particularly troubling.

Why is harmful agency of this type (which Quinn terms direct agency)
particularly troubling? Quinn offers two arguments:First, he suggests,
direct agency shows "a shocking failure of respect for the persons who are
harmed."[90] There is undoubtedly also a lack of respect in cases of indirect
agency, where individuals are harmed as a side effect rather than as a
means; but the disrespect in cases of direct agency is greater, because it
involves the agent taking up a particular attitude towards his victims: "He
must treat them as if they were then and there *for* his purposes."[91] By
contrast, where victims are harmed as a side effect, they "are not viewed
strategically at all and therefore not treated as for the agent's purposes
rather than their own."[92] Ideally, we should treat individuals not as mere
means but as ends in themselves. Indirect agency, in so far as it harms
individuals incidentally on the way to achieving some goal, does not treat
them as ends and is to that extent objectionable; but at least indirect
agency does not treat individuals as means, which is regarded as worse
than bracketing their interests entirely.

Second, Quinn argues that the doctrine:

---

[89] (Quinn, 1989: 343). The inclusion of "foreseeable" reflects Fischer et al.'s point that, as
formulated in his paper, Quinn would characterize as direct agency any instance where
harm came to an individual as a result of their being deliberately involved in an agent's
plans, regardless of whether this harm was a foreseeable consequence of that involvement
(Fischer et al., 1993: 715). This seems to be a permissible clarification of Quinn's position
that reflects the overall thrust of his argument.

Most formulations of DDE focus on the subjective intention of agents. An exception is
FitzPatrick, who identifies the necessary quality in the structure of the available justifications: (FitzPatrick, 2003: 320). It is the existence of a justification that does not invoke the
relevant harm, rather than the subjective motivation of the agent, that he makes central.
While I do not adopt FitzPatrick's formulation, his emphasis on available justifications is
reflected in my strategy of constructing intention from the best interpretation of a measure.

[90] (Quinn, 1989: 348).   [91] Ibid., 348.   [92] Ibid., 348.

reflects a Kantian ideal of human community and interaction. Each
person is treated, so far as possible, as existing only for purposes that he
can share . . . People have a strong prima facie right not to be sacrificed in
strategic roles over which they have no say. They have a right not to be
pressed, in apparent violation of their prior rights, into the service of other
people's purposes.[93]

The claim is thus that (i) individuals should be treated as ends, not
means, and to treat a person as a means is more objectionable even
than discounting them entirely in pursuit of a goal; and (ii) individuals
should be treated as existing for purposes in which they can share, so that
making use of a person instrumentally for some collateral purpose is
more objectionable than simply discounting that person's interests in
pursuit of that same purpose.[94] As Kagan notes, in cases of direct agency,
"I am using that person – and it might plausibly be claimed that the other
person is not mine to use."[95]

Nagel takes a different approach to identifying what is distinctively
objectionable about such cases.[96] He develops his account of morality in
terms of the tension between the embedded personal view, which is
limited in its scope of concern and deontological (act-based) in structure;
and the detached impersonal view, which is universalizing in scope and
consequentialist in structure.[97] DDE exists within the personal view. He
argues that the quality of intentionality in direct agency[98] has the effect of
intensifying, in the personal point of view, the particular effects that are
aimed at over those that are merely foreseeable, or that exist independently of one's own actions.[99] Intentionality creates a relationship
between the agent and the victim, such that the harm caused to the victim
necessarily looms especially large in the personal view. Furthermore,
Nagel argues that the use of the victim in cases of direct agency represents
an especially egregious attack on him, "not simply because of the quantity
of the harm but because of the assault on his value of having [one's]
actions guided by his evil."[100] This seems to shade back into the points
made by Quinn; harming another through direct agency represents a

---

[93] Ibid., 350–351.
[94] My categorization of Quinn's arguments reflects the treatment in: (Bennett, 1995:
      220–221).
[95] (Kagan, 1989: 132).   [96] (Nagel, 1986: 175–188).   [97] Ibid., 185.
[98] For consistency, I will continue to use Quinn's terminology. Nagel does not use the
      terminology of direct and indirect agency.
[99] (Nagel, 1986: 180). This explanation of the salience of direct agency thus ties the rationale
      for double effect to the rationale for distinguishing doing and allowing.
[100] (Nagel, 1986: 184).

dehumanizing attack on the victim's status that is not present when the victim is harmed as a foreseen but unintended consequence.

The arguments for DDE thus rely on two ideas: first, that intentionality involves a disrespect for a person's moral worth, connected with the use of a person to serve the goals of another, that is not present in cases of foresight; and second, that intentionality establishes a closeness between subject and object, bringing the object's interests within the purview of the subject. Both ideas have implications for how we justify coercion internationally.

The idea that persons should not be used to serve the ends of others features prominently in liberal theory from Kant through Rawls to contemporary theorists.

In Kant, it is reflected in the claim, discussed above, that persons should be treated not as means only, but as ends in themselves. Thus, discussing contract, an archetypal case of instrumental use by one of another, Kant emphasizes that the contract right must derive from the will of the promisor. My own deed is quintessentially mine, so the right of another to that deed must derive from what is mine. In claiming rights under contract, the promisee does not reduce the promisor to an instrument of his will; rather, he enforces their joint will, and their shared end, as expressed in their prior agreement. A right to make use of another that does not derive ultimately from them is incompatible with respect for their freedom.[101]

A similar concern motivates Rawls's account of socioeconomic inequalities in domestic justice; but hypothetical consent in the original position replaces the prior act of will as the means by which the use of another is linked to ends that they have reason to share. The symmetrical situation of individuals in the original position reflects the fact that each is directly subject to the institutions of the basic structure; as such, reflecting Quinn's argument, each must be able to share in the ends for which they are so subject, a requirement that for Rawls implies the difference principle.[102] This claim may seem difficult to reconcile with

---

[101] (Kant, 1996: 421–426). Kant's concern to reconcile the rights we have over one another with the freedom of each to define our own ends is also reflected in his discussion of "Rights to Persons akin to Rights to Things": (Kant, 1996: 426–432). For commentary on this point in Kant: (Rauscher, 2012).

[102] Indeed, Rawls explicitly argues that the difference principle expresses Kant's injunction to treat individuals as ends rather than mere means: (Rawls, 1971: 180). See also and more generally: (Rawls, 1980). The direct/indirect distinction also appears in Rawls's account of neutrality: (Rawls, 1988: 260–263).

our daily practice, as citizens and market participants, of making use of our fellow citizens to meet our needs without asking them to share our ends, just as we similarly are used by them. However, the liberal basic structure itself does not pursue any end except the freedom of those subject to it; and the difference principle, by maximizing the position of the least advantaged, ensures that the basic structure can be justified to each as advancing their freedom to pursue their own ends to the greatest extent compatible with the like freedom of others.[103] Further, when as citizens we speak, vote and act politically, seeking to directly shape the coercive structure under which we all live, public reason constrains the grounds on which we may act to those that we can reasonably expect others to share.[104] Thus, while as individuals we may turn others to our own purposes, their use is ultimately referable to a coercive structure that serves ends that are their own.

Thus, both Kant and Rawls are concerned to reconcile the direct coercion of individuals with their status as free and equal moral persons, whose freedom implies a right both to define and to pursue their own ends. In each case, that reconciliation is effected by linking that coercion to the ends of those directly coerced.[105]

While individuals are directly subject to the basic structure of their domestic societies, in the international context much coercion is indirect. Outsiders may be adversely affected by a people's institutions, but these impact on them as side effects rather than as means to the desired ends, and so may be justifiable even where the relevant end is not one that those affected have reason to share. This does not mean that such coercion does not require justification, but only that it may be in different terms. In particular, the principle of self-determination provides a basis for justifying much indirect international coercion. While I address self-determination

---

[103] The relation between the way individuals within a society may seem to treat one another as means only and the way the basic structure treats each as an end in themselves is reflected further in Rawls's discussion of background fairness: (Rawls, 1996: 265–271). Contrast Julius's account of framing, discussed above.

[104] (Rawls, 1996: xlvii–lv).

[105] As noted above, Julius uses a similar concept of "framing," understood as acting with the intention of leading another to act in a way that advances one's own interests, to reconstruct Rawls's basic structure argument, and suggests some implications for global justice: (Julius, 2003; 2006: 187–192). However, in moving from individual framing to justice for the basic structure, he appears to adopt a less-demanding standard of intentionality than Quinn's direct agency: (Julius, 2003: 329). Further, his underlying focus is on individuals rather than institutions, which generates quite different implications for the structure of international obligations.

in detail in Chapter 5, some preliminary remarks are necessary here to see how it might be relevant to the justification of indirect coercion.

Self-determination itself may be justified on various grounds[106]: Miller defends it as a means of enforcing social justice, protecting a national culture, and expressing individuals' interest in collective autonomy[107]; Beitz interprets arguments for self-determination as grounded in reducing social injustice within a territory[108]; while for Rawls, self-determination expresses a fundamental interest of peoples "to preserve their free political institutions and liberties and free culture of their civil society,"[109] as well as reflecting a view that there is no practical alternative to a world of independent political communities.[110]

Howsoever justified, in its conventional form, self-determination asserts that communities are entitled to a sphere of autonomy, invoking "the right of individuals to a public sphere, thus implying that individuals are entitled to establish institutions and manage their communal life in ways that reflect their communal values, traditions, and history."[111] It asserts that there is a sphere of communal activity that is uniquely the concern of the relevant community, within which the community is entitled to govern its own affairs, with minimal reference to outsiders.[112] Further, in its liberal form, it asserts that all persons have an interest in self-determination.[113]

This sphere of autonomy provides a basis for justifying indirect coercion that has no analogue in the domestic context.[114] Where a community acts to regulate its own affairs, this may indirectly affect the rights and duties of outsiders, or shape the distribution of benefits from transnational cooperation involving them. Indeed, in the context of economic interaction, such indirect coercion is almost inevitable. If self-determination is a value that

---

[106] (Hurrell, 2007: 27–29).   [107] (Miller, 1995: ch. 4).   [108] (Beitz, 1999: 92–109).
[109] (Rawls, 1999: 29, 35, 111).
[110] Ibid., 36. Self-determination can also be understood as a manifestation of Rawls's idea of responsibility for ends: (Rawls, 1980: 545–546).
[111] (Tamir, 1993: 69).
[112] Although, as discussed in Chapter 5, there is some difficulty identifying exactly what might fall within this sphere.
[113] This distinguishes liberal nationalism from chauvinist nationalism, which values self-determination only for one's own nation: (Miller, 1995: 99–100).
[114] A parallel is sometimes drawn between national self-determination and individual freedom. However, whereas individuals can be regarded as constituting self-authenticating ends for themselves, not subject to external justification, the same cannot plausibly be claimed for collective institutions. While self-determination provides a ground for justifying institutions, freedom pre-empts the need for such justification with respect to the ends individuals choose for themselves.

all have reason to share, then respect for a community's right to self-determination provides a basis for outsiders to accept the indirect coercion that flows from it. Indeed, if we cannot justify indirect coercion under self-determination, then self-determination itself will be rendered nugatory. Such indirect coercion does not "use" outsiders in the problematic sense identified by Quinn; and so provided the underlying principle of self-determination is justified, those outsiders cannot argue that they are being made to serve ends that are not their own.

However, this justification cannot be extended to direct coercion. Self-determination asserts a right to self-government. It does not express any claim to govern others, and to the extent that a community purports to do so, respect for the moral equality of outsiders requires that their coercion be justified by reference to ends they have reason to share.[115] Self-determination may be relevant to such justification, where the direct

---

[115] I take up the scope of this justification further in Chapter 5. For now, it suffices to note that the standard arguments for self-determination in the literature, including those mentioned above, do not support a right directly to coerce outsiders. Thus, we elsewhere see self-determination defended as the "capacity of a people to politically determine their social and economic fate" (Freeman, 2007: 305), reflecting the need "to govern a territory in order to constitute a space in which the national aspiration can be realized." (Walzer, 1983: 45). In each case, the principle defended is primarily inward-looking. Miller is explicit in recognizing that self-determination may not even be sufficient to justify national control of all aspects of domestic governance (Miller, 1995: 100–102), and that border controls, insofar as they necessarily govern outsiders, cannot be subsumed under a general defense of domestic jurisdiction (Miller, 2012). In any event, in each case, the principle is addressed to matters that are primarily of concern to the relevant people. Indeed, Tamir emphasizes that self-determination is substantially concerned with the exclusion of outside interference, a view that is difficult to reconcile with using it to justify interference with others: (Tamir, 1993: 74).

It is a separate question whether the principles of self-determination and nonintervention, as commonly understood, include a right to directly coerce outsiders. Krasner, in his skeptical examination of the sovereignty norm, understands Westphalian sovereignty as primarily concerned with "relations between rulers and ruled": (Krasner, 1999: 73). Nonintervention is primarily concerned, for Krasner, with a state's power to regulate its own citizens. International legal sovereignty, on the other hand, is outward-facing, but does not assert any right to coerce. Indeed, Krasner argues that any effort by a state to coerce another, at least with respect to matters within that state's own domestic jurisdiction, would necessarily violate that state's international legal sovereignty, regardless of whether the means adopted otherwise violated existing norms of international law: (Krasner, 1999: 125). For an alternative view, querying whether these principles have any coherent content: (Brownlie, 2008: 292–294).

In practice, of course, such direct coercion is a pervasive part of international life, and provided the means adopted are not otherwise objectionable, it is not disciplined by international law. However, to the extent that this practice is not supported by good reasons, and is not essential to any other valued aspect of the international system, it constitutes no objection to the position advanced here.

coercion is specifically intended to protect that end; but in that case, the structure of the justification is different to that invoked in the case of indirect coercion. Rather than arguing that self-determination provides a basis for indirectly coercing outsiders in pursuit of particular ends of the self-determining people, it claims that self-determination is itself an end all have reason to share, providing a justification for the specific direct coercion.

The distinction is that between respecting another people's right to pursue a particular end, and having reason to pursue that end oneself.[116] If all peoples have reason to value self-determination, then we can justify direct coercion that is necessary to preserve that self-determination. But the ends that self-determining peoples in turn pursue are their own, and need not be shared by others. Others have reason to respect those ends, as a consequence of their valuing self-determination, and this provides a basis for justifying the resulting indirect coercion; but they have no reason to themselves share those ends, and so cannot be directly coerced in pursuit of them. We cannot justify direct coercion by reference to the ends self-determining peoples choose; but we may be able to justify it where it is necessary to allow them to be self-determining at all.[117]

There are here two distinct reasons why self-determination, while potentially justifying indirect coercion, cannot justify direct coercion. The first focuses on the arguments advanced in support of the principle of self-determination, and the related principle of nonintervention, and claims that these arguments do not support a principle that is so widely drawn as to encompass direct coercion of outsiders; while the second claims that any principle that was so widely drawn as to encompass generalized direct coercion of outsiders would be incompatible with their moral equality in so far as it necessarily treats them as means towards ends that are not their own.

A similar point appears in Rawls's account of the fundamental interests of peoples.[118] Peoples' interests are specified by their reasonable conception of political justice, and they strive 'to protect their political independence and their free culture with its civil liberties, to guarantee their security, territory, and the well-being of their citizens.' Further, peoples have an interest in their "proper self-respect of themselves as a

---

[116] Waldron makes a similar distinction in the domestic context: (Waldron, 1987: 145).

[117] This is obviously a difficult line to draw. Much of Chapter 5 is concerned with identifying what is required to say that a people is self-determining, and hence what might justify direct coercion to preserve that self-determination.

[118] (Rawls, 1999: 34–35).

people," which leads them to insist on receiving from others proper respect and recognition of their equality, while granting the same proper respect to others. Respect for the equality of others requires that peoples accept the indirect coercion that is a necessary consequence of other peoples exercising their right to self-determination. But their insistence on their own independence and equality means that they cannot be expected to share the ends that other peoples pursue; and so have no basis for accepting direct coercion in pursuit of them.[119]

---

[119] The argument can alternatively be articulated through Rawlsian original position reasoning, along one of three lines.

First, recall that for Rawls, the fundamental interests of peoples are given by their reasonable conception of political justice, which derives from the domestic original position. Their fundamental interests are thus self-regarding; they are concerned to pursue their own ends, and accept that it is for others to do the same. This necessarily implies some degree of indirect coercion resulting from each constituting their own institutions and pursuing their own ends. Given these assumptions, how might we expect them to evaluate a principle that permitted peoples to directly coerce outsiders, on a general basis, and without specific justification? Given the requirements of generality and reciprocity, such a principle would necessarily imply not only that each people be free to directly coerce others, but also that they would themselves be subject to such direct coercion. This would in turn imply a reduction in their own capacity to realize their reasonable conception of justice, specified as a basic interest, in return for a potential capacity to influence others, which forms no part of their basic interests. Given Rawls's own assumptions, we can expect such a principle to be rejected. This is particularly so where the alternative candidate principle permits such direct coercion where this is in fact necessary to allow a state to be self-determining, which is likely to include protecting its capacity to pursue its domestic conception of justice. The reasoning here is analogous to that supporting the priority of the basic liberties in Rawls's domestic theory.

Second, and alternatively, we might allow that peoples have an interest in directly coercing others, whether because their conception of justice extends to them or because the actions of those others, in turn, have consequences for them. The question then becomes whether a people's interest in coercing outsiders is outweighed by its interest in not being coerced by them. We might reasonably make two further assumptions. First, on average, direct external coercion is zero sum or (more likely) negative sum; the greater freedom of the coercer to pursue its goals is reflected in at least an equivalent loss of freedom on the part of the coercee. And second, larger and wealthier peoples, who in consequence of those characteristics already enjoy greater freedom to pursue their ends, will also gain most and lose least from a principle allowing direct external coercion, as they have both the resources to effectively coerce others, and the resources to resist such coercion themselves. Cf. (Waltz, 1979: 139–146). Behind the veil of ignorance, states will be more concerned by potential losses than gains in their freedom to pursue their ends, and so will reject a principle that would tend to further disadvantage those who are already disadvantaged in terms of size and wealth. They would therefore reject the proposed principle; the reasoning is analogous to Rawls's Maximin argument for the difference principle.

Third, we might note that the effect of the proposed principle is to increase the power of those who are already more advantaged, at the expense of those who are less advantaged. In these circumstances, the principle might be directly challenged as failing to respect the moral equality of less-advantaged peoples, insofar as it asserts that less- advantaged

An alternative argument links self-determination to the limited capacity of institutions to take account of individuals' interests. Scheffler argues that moral agency is made possible in part by the recognition of special obligations to those with whom we stand in special relationships[120]; the limits on our individual and collective cognitive capacities constitute a powerful argument against unrestrained consequentialism.[121] In the economic sphere in particular, the complexity of cause/effect relations makes it impossible to consider the implications of a measure for all individuals who may be affected by it; the principles of self-determination and national priority therefore provide a basis for institutions to focus in the first instance on their own members, who are directly subject to them.[122] However, where an institution directly coerces outsiders, this (following Nagel's account of double effect) constitutes a relationship with those outsiders that precludes bracketing their interests. As Anscombe observes, "[i]t is nonsense to pretend that you do not intend to do what is the means you take to your chosen end."[123] Similarly, one cannot, on the basis of limited cognitive resources, be excused from considering fully the implications of a measure for outsiders who you make directly subject to it and whose involvement is a means to your end.

The upshot of these arguments is that indirect coercion may be justifiable in circumstances where direct coercion is not, even though the actual effects of indirect coercion are the same as those of direct coercion. In particular, indirect coercion may be justified by invoking the principle of self-determination, provided that principle is itself justified, and provided the negative effects of the indirect coercion are not such as to outweigh it.[124] Direct coercion, on the other hand, must be justified to

peoples, who are *ex hypothesi* in a worse initial position to realize their own ends, should have even less freedom, solely in order that those who are more advantaged should have more. The argument here reflects Rawls's argument from reciprocity to the difference principle in the domestic context.

[120] See Scheffler's argument that the distinction between doing and allowing, and the recognition of special obligations to those with whom we stand in significant relationships, constitute important limits on normative responsibility in common-sense moral thought: (Scheffler, 2001: 36–38). Nagel's argument might be summarized as the claim that intentionality has the same effect.

[121] (Rawls, 1980: 560–564).

[122] On national priority see further the discussion in §4.4 below.

[123] (Anscombe, 1963: 71) quoted in: (Bennett, 1995: 214).

[124] As with the classical doctrine of double effect, it is not suggested that indirect agency will always be justifiable. The negative effects of indirect agency may be such that it cannot be justified. In particular, if indirect coercion is to be justified by reference to self-

those who are subject to it by reference to ends that they themselves have reason to share.

3.5   Exclusive Coercion, Inclusive Coercion, and the Fruits of Social Cooperation

We next distinguish between exclusive coercion, whose effect is to exclude those subject to it from participation in some productive cooperative practice; and inclusive coercion, which governs participation in such a practice and the distribution of the benefits therefrom.

To demonstrate the significance of this distinction, it is necessary to rehearse briefly Rawls's treatment of distributive justice in the domestic context. Recall first how Rawls characterizes the problem of distributive justice:

> The problem of distributive justice in justice as fairness is always this: how are the institutions of the basic structure to be regulated as one unified scheme of institutions so that a fair, efficient and productive system of social cooperation can be maintained over time, from one generation to the next? Contrast this with the very different problem of how a given bundle of commodities is to be distributed, or allocated among various individuals whose particular needs, desires, and preferences are known to us, and who have not cooperated in any way to produce these commodities.[125]

Justice as fairness is fundamentally a theory of how the benefits of productive cooperation are to be distributed among participants by the non-voluntary institutions that govern it. The difference principle is proposed as a basis on which we can justify that coercion to all participants.

In so far as society constitutes a scheme of cooperation, and that cooperation gives rise to benefits that would not otherwise exist, there is a need for some principle of distribution.[126] The selection of equality as a baseline reflects the moral equality of all persons, and the absence of any respectable alternative distributive principle.[127] Any principle that gives foundational significance to characteristics of individuals, whether these be

---

determination, then its effect cannot be to undermine the self-determination of other peoples; to hold otherwise would be to claim that the realization of this good for one people was sufficient reason to deny it to another. The claim is only that it can be more easily justified, and by a different route, than direct agency.

[125] (Rawls, 2001: 50).   [126] (Rawls, 1971: 62).

[127] Hence Rawls' extensive discussion and rejection of the principles of utility, dessert, and perfection.

social or natural characteristics, can be rejected as giving weight to characteristics that are "arbitrary from the moral point of view." Neither being born into wealth, nor being born with great natural talents, can be regarded as deserved in any morally relevant sense.[128] In consequence, the parties in the original position can be expected to reject any system of distribution that gives weight to these factors.[129] They are equally expected to reject the principle of utility, which gives insufficient weight to the separateness of persons and their interest in pursuing their own life projects. Instead, they insist upon equality, except in so far as a departure from equality is to the benefit of the least-advantaged member of society (and in this context, least-advantaged means least advantaged by the departure from equality, rather than least-advantaged in terms of any natural advantages).

In the course of developing the argument for the difference principle, Rawls rejects the possibility of distributing the benefits of social cooperation based on the contributions that individuals make (provided they are capable of making a contribution within the normal range), or based on their natural talents.[130] In part, natural talents are rejected because they are regarded as "morally arbitrary." However, both contribution and natural talents are also rejected because they are regarded as in a more concrete sense irrelevant to the distribution of the benefits of cooperation. Rawls does not deny that individuals are entitled to their natural talents, and to the benefits that flow from them. The benefits of social cooperation, however, flow not from the natural talents of any individual, but rather from cooperation between them:

> the difference principle represents, in effect, an agreement to regard the distribution of natural talents as in some respects a common asset and to share in the greater social and economic benefits made possible by the complementarities of this distribution.[131]

---

[128] Indeed, deservingness itself is problematic given pluralism. Without a shared account of virtue, we have no standard for determining dessert; and without knowledge of the basic structure, we have no way of knowing what will constitute a contribution worthy of reward.

[129] §4.4 below considers and rejects the relevance of nationality to my argument.

[130] Where individuals are not capable of making a contribution within the normal range, they cannot be regarded as participants on the same basis in the productive scheme. The coercion that they experience as members of society is therefore substantially exclusive rather than inclusive. This might ground an argument (which I do not seek to pursue here) that the claims such individuals may make against society are analogous to those made by outsiders.

[131] (Rawls, 1971: 101).

It is not natural talents but their distribution that is held in common.[132] Benefits emerge from cooperation rather than from the natural talents of any individual. They are a function of "complementarities between talents," both in degree and kind, which make possible benefits that simply are not available to individuals. What will count as a talent depends on a host of external factors, including available talents of others, their preferences, the form of our social institutions, and the availability of technologies. Consider: for much of human history, great physical strength was a valuable talent; yet in most developed countries today, beyond the sports field it confers little advantage. Equally, the mathematical faculties that are today most economically prized counted for very little throughout most times and places in human history. It is for this reason that we cannot regard any individual as having a privileged claim on the benefits of cooperation, and so cannot justify their distribution except on a basis that starts from equality, reflecting the moral equality of the participants.

It has been argued that international economic activity does not constitute cooperation of this kind, being better regarded as mere "exchange."[133] However, this position is difficult to sustain once we recognize that international trade, rather than simply representing the exchange of products and services between communities, facilitates the production of goods and services that would not be produced in its absence. The simplest two-product equilibrium models show the increase in overall production that results when two states with different comparative advantages engage in trade with one another[134]; this is one of the few uncontested claims of international economics. Like domestic cooperation, this trade dividend is a product of the differences between the parties involved; neither could have achieved it without the cooperation of the other. There may be differences between cooperation in the international economy and domestic cooperation, both in the intensity of interactions and the nature of the

---

[132] (Rawls, 2001: 75–76).   [133] Barry argues:

> Trade, if freely undertaken ... is not, it seems to me, the kind of relationship that gives rise to duties of fair play ... Trade in pottery, ornamentation, and weapons can be traced back to prehistoric times, but we would hardly feel inclined to think of, say, the Beaker Folk as forming a single cooperative enterprise with their trading partners. No more did the spice trade unite east and west. (Barry, 1982: 232–233) quoted with approval in: (Blake, 2001: 292).

[134] (Krugman et al., 2012: 64–65; Ray, 1998: 647–650).

goods produced[135]; but it still raises the fundamental problem of justifying the distribution of social goods that would not exist without cooperation.[136]

It is this concept of productive cooperation that creates the need for a distributive principle; and the claim that benefits accrue from the differences between participants, rather than the participants' own resources, makes equality the appropriate baseline. However, the logic of this argument need not extend to nonparticipants. We may not be able to distinguish between the claims that the various participants in a scheme of cooperation have on the benefits of that cooperation, but we can distinguish their claims from the claims of those who, in Rawls's words, "have not cooperated in any way to produce these commodities." It is because participants make a contribution that they have a claim on the resulting social product, which must be reflected in the justification of the institutions that govern it.[137]

Furthermore, it is those institutions, rather than any pre-institutional entitlement, that determine how the benefits of cooperation are shared. This is the essence of Rawls's anti-libertarian argument, and applies

---

[135] This is the central argument in: (Sangiovanni, 2007). I take up further in §4.3.3 below some implications of this view.

[136] We find little recognition of this problem in the *Law of Peoples*. While Rawls rejects egalitarian principles of international distributive justice, he makes little effort to put anything in their place. An important explanation of this omission is Rawls's assumption that most, if not all, significant social cooperation takes place within, rather than between, peoples. Peoples are characterized as "free and independent": (Rawls, 1999: 33). Indeed, this is the first principle of Rawls's Law of Peoples: (Rawls, 1999: 37). This freedom is assumed to include the freedom to decide autonomously on a people's level of wealth. "In a reasonably just (or at least decent) Society of Peoples, the inequalities of power and wealth are to be decided by all peoples for themselves.": (Rawls, 1999: 39) Later, he argues that:

> [t]he causes of the wealth of a people and the forms it takes lie in their political culture and in the religious, philosophical, and moral traditions that support the basic structure of their political and social institutions, as well as in the industriousness and cooperative talents of its members, all supported by their political virtues.

(Rawls, 1999: 108)

[137] Blake's own argument from coercion to economic equality does not seem to invoke cooperative production in this way, instead running through the value of democratic self-government, and the justification of private law: (Blake, 2013: 88–96). Blake's emphasis on democratic self-government seems significantly to explain his quite different conclusions about both what constitutes morally significant international coercion, and what its implications may be: (Blake, 2013: ch. 5). Contrast, for example, (Blake, 2013: 121–122) with the discussion in §3.7 below.

equally to international and domestic contexts.[138] If we accept that different institutions would result in different distributions, then the mere fact that a particular distribution emerges under one system provides no basis for those so benefited to object to an alternative system under which they receive less. Entitlement only arises within an institutional system, and is a function of that system. Where the system itself requires to be justified, invoking existing distributions would be circular. This is why the justification of inclusive institutions is intimately linked to their distributive effects.[139] Not all inequalities will require to be justified in this way; but where an institution creates an inequality among participants who stand in relevantly similar relations to it, then the institution cannot be justified without justifying that inequality.

The justification of exclusion, on the other hand, need not make reference to the benefits accruing to participants. Indeed, given the basis of participants' claims, it would be surprising if nonparticipants were entitled to make similar demands. In particular, the mere fact that, if they were admitted, they would be entitled to make distributive claims does not mean that their exclusion can only be justified in distributive terms.[140] We may recognize that whether someone is included or excluded is an accident of birth, and to that extent morally arbitrary; but in so far as distributive claims depend on participation and contribution, the mere fact of moral arbitrariness is insufficient to justify

---

[138] Dworkin makes a similar point in discussing the legal baseline implied by equality of resources: (Dworkin, 2002: 143–144).

[139] As will be clear from the earlier discussion, the link between coercion, production, distribution, and egalitarianism is recognized in existing coercion approaches. Rawls's view that distributive justice is about how institutions distribute goods among participants, rather than the transfer of resources from one party to another, is difficult to reconcile with his arguments against international distributive justice. Those arguments seem more concerned with allocative than distributive justice, although this may simply reflect the positions against which he is arguing in *Law of Peoples* (Rawls, 1999: 113–120). Pogge argues convincingly that Rawls, insofar as he adopts a distributive principle internationally, has implicitly endorsed the libertarian principle of entitlement: (Pogge, 1994: 211–214). While Freeman challenges this view (Freeman, 2007: 285–286, 310), it is difficult to find textual support for any other principle, although some of Rawls's references to free trade can be read as endorsing an unstated moderate egalitarianism (Rawls, 1999: 42–43).

[140] Nagel makes an analogous point when he argues that rights of equal concern are due to members of a society, but there is no obligation to allow outsiders to join and thereby accrue those rights: "Everyone may have the right to live in a just society, but we do not have an obligation to live in a just society with everyone.": (Nagel, 2005: 132).

egalitarian claims.[141] Exclusive coercion must be justified, but its justification need not mirror the justification of inclusive coercion.[142]

What constraints apply to the justification of exclusive coercion? Like all coercion, it must be justified in terms that those subject to it can reasonably accept. Furthermore, having regard to the moral equality of persons and peoples, the justification must accord with the principles of generality and reciprocity; in so far as it invokes the value of some end for one party, it must acknowledge its equal value for others.[143] Finally, building on the discussion in the previous section, in so far as it is direct, it must be justified in terms of ends those subject to it have reason to share.

What does exclusive coercion look like in the international context? Without prejudging whether it should also be regarded as inclusive, the most obvious example is border coercion, and specifically restrictive immigration policies.[144] Refusing a migrant entry excludes them from the scheme of productive social cooperation within a country; further, it may significantly restrict their opportunities and leave them significantly less advantaged than participants who benefit from that scheme. In short, the effect of this coercion is often significantly antiegalitarian.

However, this does not mean that the coercion cannot be justified in terms that the frustrated migrant can reasonably accept. As with the direct/indirect distinction, the principle of self-determination is important in justifying exclusive coercion in the international context. If we assume, as Rawls does, that persons and peoples value self-determination, and recognize its equal value for others, then this can provide a justification for border controls that migrants can reasonably accept. Certainly, the need for some degree of border control is recognized by most theorists who see self-determination as a value.[145] However, this justification will not suffice in all cases. Where, for example, the effect of exclusive coercion is to prevent the frustrated migrant living a minimally decent life, the excluding state's interest in self-determination cannot provide a sufficient

---

[141] In this respect, the Rawlsian argument is not luck-egalitarian. On the limits of the moral arbitrariness argument: (Sangiovanni, 2011).

[142] Exclusive coercion might alternatively be distinguished as a form of eliminative agency, which Quinn contrasts with opportunistic agency, suggesting that the former is easier to justify than the latter because it less obviously exploits its object: (Quinn, 1989: 350).

[143] On generality: (Rawls, 1971: 130–132); on reciprocity: (Rawls, 1980: 528–530, 1996: xliv–xlix, 16, 2001: 6–7).

[144] On the coercive nature of border controls: (Abizadeh, 2008; Miller, 2010).

[145] See e.g. (Miller, 1995: 128–129; Rawls, 1999: 39; Walzer, 1983: 38–51).

justification. Similarly, if the effect of exclusive coercion is to prevent another community from itself enjoying self-determination (for example, because they are prevented from accessing essential resources) then it would be unreasonable for the excluding community to seek to justify its coercion on this basis.[146]

What is important about these justifications, and their limits, is that they are sufficientarian rather than egalitarian. There are, we may assume, minimum prerequisites for an individual or community to enjoy self-determination. I examine further in Chapter 5 how we might specify these. For the present, it suffices to note some clear examples. Where an individual lacks basic resources or is subject to gross human rights violations, they cannot enjoy self-determination.[147] Similarly, if a community lacks the resources to organize itself internally and to provide for the basic needs of its members, it cannot be said to enjoy self-determination. To the extent that exclusive coercion leaves persons or peoples in these circumstances, it cannot be justified by reference to self-determination.[148] However, above these minimum thresholds, it is irrelevant that the excluding community is significantly more prosperous than the migrant's home community.[149] Their

---

[146] We might further, correctly, observe that in the present state of the world, border controls are not purely exclusive. Rather, they frequently serve to restrict individuals to particular positions within the system of cross-border economic cooperation, and to determine the returns they receive from that system. These paragraphs thus describe an idealization illustrating a conceptual distinction, rather than the justification of actual border controls, as they exist in the world as it is.

[147] We might make this connection in various ways, but the simplest highlights the extent to which the goods realized through self-determination, including *inter alia* collective autonomy and participation in a shared culture, can only be enjoyed by individuals who are first secure in their basic rights, and have access to adequate resources to ensure their subsistence. The strategy is thus analogous to Shue's argument for a basic right to subsistence: (Shue, 1996).

[148] This point may be limited to circumstances of moderate scarcity. Under conditions of absolute scarcity, in which resources are insufficient for all peoples to be well-ordered, it may be that the self-determination justification would apply, provided the excluding people takes all possible steps to vindicate the rights of those excluded, having regard to their own limited resources. Of course, at that point, we are no longer in Hume's circumstances of justice.

[149] I have assumed here that the relevant minimum threshold is that at which Rawls locates the duty of assistance. It has been argued that Rawls's standard of decency is too low a level, and that the appropriate threshold should be somewhat higher: (Tasioulas, 2005). Regardless of the precise threshold adopted, the key point for my purposes is that this is an absolute, rather than relative, standard. I discuss further in Chapters 4 and 5 some reasons for preferring a sufficientarian over an egalitarian conception of self-determination, including problems of comparison and responsibility that an egalitarian standard raises. However, these are not

exclusion is justified by an end that both enjoy and both have reason to share. Notwithstanding the adverse distributive consequences, the frustrated migrant can reasonably accept this justification, even if it leaves him worse off than he might otherwise be, and than those who are excluding him already are.[150]

3.6   External Coercion and the Interpersonal Test

A final aspect of international coercion that is relevant to its justification is the identity of the authors of that coercion, and those on whose behalf it is adopted.

Nagel notes that coercion in the domestic context is distinctive because it is coercion of citizens in their own name; they are, at least ideally, the authors of their own coercion. However, while Nagel takes this to imply that citizens are owed a greater justification than outsiders, the opposite conclusion seems more warranted.[151] The ideal liberal state can be understood as one wherein individuals become the authors of their own coercion. The justificatory apparatus of the original position models individuals' choices in respect of matters that they cannot in fact choose, with a view to reconciling the nonvoluntary institutions to which they are subject with their status as free and equal. For the same reason, democracy and political rights are valued as giving persons a stake in their political institutions, allowing them to accept decisions even where they disagree with them.[152] In so far as self-authored coercion is more easily reconciled with autonomy and equal respect, we have greater reason to be concerned about coercion by others than we have about coercion in

---

necessary for the present point. Rather, what matters is that egalitarian claims, at least on the Rawlsian view, derive from participation and cooperation, whereas both self-determination and basic rights, at least as conceived here, are invoked in contexts of exclusion.

[150] On this view, it is the principles of generality and fair reciprocity, reflected in the respect and recognition by just peoples of others as equals, that establish the outer limits of self-determination as a justification for exclusive coercion, requiring that the justification of coercion stands in a symmetrical relation to the end it pursues. Rawls's Duty of Assistance can also be understood in these terms. As Rawls emphasizes, this duty has a target and a cut-off. That target is the level at which other peoples have the resources necessary to be well-ordered. It is only once outsiders are at this level that well-ordered peoples can justify the exclusive coercion they deploy against them. A benefit of the present approach is thus more clearly to identify the basis for the duty of assistance and its quality as a duty of justice rather than humanity (Rawls, 1999: 105–113).

[151] As noted above, Abizadeh makes a similar point against Nagel.

[152] (Christiano, 2015: §2.2 esp. 2.2.1).

which the subject is also in some sense the author.[153] There may be some aspects of international coercion that can properly be regarded as self-authored in this sense, but in most cases, we are concerned with coercion exercised by one political community against the members of another.[154] A useful device for highlighting this is Cohen's interpersonal test:

> This tests how robust a policy argument is by subjecting it to variation with respect to who is speaking and/or who is listening when the argument is presented. The test asks whether the argument could serve as a justification of a mooted policy when uttered by any member of a society to any other member ... If, because of who is presenting it, and/or to whom it is presented, the argument cannot serve as a justification of the policy, then whether or not it passes as such under other dialogical conditions, it fails (tout court) to provide a comprehensive justification of the policy.[155]

Cohen proposes the test as a general constraint, but it has particular relevance in the international context, where we are significantly concerned with coercion of the members of one community by another. In these circumstances, the interpersonal test prompts us to consider not only whether that coercion can be justified in terms that its subjects could reasonably be expected to accept; but also whether they could reasonably be expected to accept the proposed justification when advanced *by the authors of that coercion*.

In what circumstances might a justification fail the interpersonal test? Cohen highlights cases where a justification invokes a factual premise for which the speaker is responsible, and the speaker cannot in turn justify their making that factual premise true.[156] His interest is in the role of incentives in justifying inequality under the difference principle, but similar situations arise in considering coercion in the international economy. Political economy arguments are commonly invoked, for example, to explain why safeguards provisions are necessary in trade

---

[153] Thus, the republican concept of nondomination reflects the view that coercion is not incompatible with liberty when the subjects of coercion are also in some sense its authors: (Lovett, 2014: §2.2).

[154] Valentini's concept of interactional coercion goes some way to capture this idea. However, she does not consider how the fact that coercion is interactional might impact its justification (Valentini, 2011c: 130–137).

[155] (Cohen, 2008: 42). For a critique of the interpersonal test: (Lippert-Rasmussen, 2008). The moral underpinnings are developed in more detail in: (Cohen, 2006).

[156] A similar scenario has been discussed in relation to coercive offers, where the offeror has, through his action, foreclosed preferable alternatives, leaving the offeree no option but to accept: (Alexander, 1983; Zimmerman, 1981).

agreements; they are justified by reference to the risk that, in their absence, greater protectionist pressures would result in even more restricted market access.[157] To the extent this is the case, it provides a good reason for outsiders to accept such provisions. However, if we consider this argument as articulated by the protectionist state, we recognize that the factual premise (i.e. the risk of protectionism) is attributable to the state making the argument, in so far as it is its own citizens who pose this risk. It is essentially an argument that you should accept me doing x, as if you do not, then I will do y, which is even worse. This may be a good reason for you to accept x, but it cannot constitute a justification for my doing it.

A second reason why a justification might fail the interpersonal test is because, while the measure proposed is desirable in itself, its author is not the appropriate person to adopt it. Again, the principle of self-determination is relevant here. In its conventional form, that principle would preclude a measure adopted by one state from being justified by the benefits it confers on another that is subject to it, not because the effects of the measure are objectionable, but because of the relative positions of those adopting and accepting it.[158] For example, the threat by a more developed state to restrict market access for less-developed states unless they open their markets on a reciprocal basis cannot be justified on the grounds that such market opening would benefit the less-developed state.[159] This may in fact be true, but it is not an argument that it is open to the more advantaged state to make.[160]

A third possibility, not unrelated to the second, is where the justification invokes the outcome of a process from which the addressee was themselves excluded. On many contested issues, we cannot expect to achieve consensus, even within relatively small and homogenous communities. Liberalism has two principal responses to this. The first is a strategy of privatization and toleration. We define as large as possible a domain of individual choice, within which persons can live in their own ways. The second is a strategy of proceduralization. We cannot achieve

---

[157] These arguments are discussed further in Chapter 8.

[158] This objections falls under the intrinsic and expressive accounts of self-determination discussed in Chapter 5.

[159] Arguments in this form are not uncommon, and were particularly visible in the context of recent negotiations between the European Union and African, Caribbean, and Pacific Countries. E.g. (Mandelson, 2010: 400).

[160] This does not mean that the economic wisdom of the less-developed state's policies is necessarily irrelevant. See further the discussion of development provisions in Chapter 7.

agreement on an outcome, so we define a set of decision-making procedures, usually though not exclusively democratic, in which all can participate on fair terms, and which all can thus reasonably accept. Where the state cannot avoid taking a position on some contested point, we can then invoke these procedures to explain why the disappointed minority has reason to accept laws whose substance they cannot endorse. They participated on fair terms in the process, and so cannot reasonably reject the outcome. Yet this justification cannot be offered to an outsider, who has neither participated, nor been afforded an opportunity to participate, in the process whereby the decision was reached. This need not mean that the outsider is wronged by being excluded; there may be many reasons why the democratic community is drawn as it is. But it does limit the justificatory relevance of the decision's democratic credentials towards that outsider.[161]

The interpersonal test constitutes a justificatory safeguard rather than necessarily an additional substantive requirement.[162] It forces us to step outside the impersonal abstraction of hypothetical consent to enquire how the justifications generated by that abstraction translate to the world as it is, and to agents and institutions as they actually are. It addresses directly the point made earlier about the plurality of internationally coercive institutions, and the plural relations in which individuals stand to those institutions. While original position reasoning can never be the whole of justification, which must always be translated from thought experiment to concrete practice, insider/outsider cases are more prone than closed cases to elide important considerations in this transition. The interpersonal test serves as a useful check on our reasoning in such cases.

3.7   From International Coercion to Equality in Global Commerce

In the previous sections, I identified three aspects of international coercion that are relevant to its justification. First, I argued that the effects of

---

[161] This point need not be limited to liberal or even democratic states. Assuming there exist legitimate nondemocratic states, they will have internal procedures and communal self-understandings that legitimize decisions towards their citizens. Provided those procedures and understandings are appropriately shared, they may constitute an effective justification to those citizens. But outsiders do not share in these, and so justifications invoking them are less relevant to them.

[162] In Cohen's approach, the interpersonal test provides a mechanism for applying the discrete value of community, which plays no part in my argument.

indirect coercion can, within limits, be justified by reference to the principle of self-determination, whereas direct coercion must be justified to those who are subject to it in terms of ends that they have reason to share. Second, I argued that exclusive coercion may be justified in sufficientarian terms, whereas inclusive coercion requires justification in distributive terms. Finally, given that international coercion is rarely self-authored, I highlighted the need to examine its justification from the perspectives of both its objects and its authors.

How do we move from this typology, through the coercion approach, to EGC?

First, recall the definition of ETMs as measures that pursue their goals specifically through regulating international economic activity. So defined, ETMs necessarily constitute direct coercion of outsiders. They pursue their goals specifically through the regulation of international economic activity and, by extension, by involving and affecting the interests of outsiders. ETMs logically presuppose the existence of international trade; in its absence, they would be meaningless.[163] Further, it is only by changing patterns of international activity that they pursue their objectives. In so far as international economic activity necessarily involves the activities and interests of outsiders, ETMs address those outsiders as intentional objects. They need not intentionally harm them; but they are intentionally and instrumentally used in the context of ETMs, in a way that they are not by DEMs.

To illustrate, recall the wine tariff discussed in Chapter 1. The tariff achieves its objective by raising the price of imported products, thereby either reducing the profits available to a foreign exporter, reducing his sales volume, or shutting him out of the market entirely. It is not open to the state imposing the tariff to claim that the negative effects this has on importers are merely unfortunate side effects of a policy intended to improve the position of domestic industry, or to claim that it did not

---

[163] A parallel can be drawn here between ETMs and Rawls's discussion of war powers in *the Law of Peoples*: (Rawls, 1999: 26–27). Rawls argues that war powers derive from the law of peoples as there would be no reason to adopt such powers in the domestic original position, which presupposes a closed society. The same point can be made about ETMs. It is not clear what turns on this point in Rawls's argument. However, one conclusion might be that, since these powers derive from agreement between peoples, their use is more directly subject to justification to other peoples, in a way that purely domestic powers are not. Alternatively, one might argue that, as a liberal people's fundamental interest is given by its conception of justice adopted in the original position, and as ETMs form no part of that conception, liberal peoples would be less concerned to protect their freedom to use ETMs than other measures.

intend to affect their interests; the effect on their interests *is* the causal mechanism whereby the tariff pursues its objective. The causal path runs from the tariff through the harm to importers' interests to the hoped-for benefits for the domestic industry.

Further, the coercion effected by ETMs is, in general, inclusive. As argued above, international economic activity constitutes productive cooperation, raising the problem of distributive justice. In so far as ETMs regulate international economic activity, they necessarily govern participation therein and the distribution of benefits therefrom. Thus, the effect of the wine tariff in our example is to divert opportunities from outsiders to insiders, conferring greater benefits on domestic wine producers or imposing costs on foreigners. The tariff, and ETMs generally, are distributive in the sense discussed above.[164]

A contrary view might claim that many ETMs constitute exclusive coercion, in so far as they exclude foreign products from the domestic market, preventing productive cooperation in the relevant area. In a limited number of cases, this may indeed be the case.[165] However, in most cases, we can assume that the effects of ETMs are inclusive for one of two reasons. First, the international economy cannot be simply divided into products, or indeed industries. Each area of the economy affects many others.[166] Excluding imports or exports of a particular product does not prevent economic cooperation; it merely changes its profile so that cooperation is concentrated in some areas rather than others, with consequent distributive effects.[167] With the exception of an entirely closed economy, restrictions in one area should therefore be regarded as inclusive. Second, the effects of ETMs cannot be entirely understood at the point of application; their objects and effects are usually dynamic rather than static.[168] Thus, the purpose of the wine tariff in the above example might be to increase the scale and in consequence the efficiency of the domestic industry, with a view to competing more effectively in international markets. By temporarily limiting cooperation, its goal is to shift the distribution of benefits from the wider scheme of cooperation in favor of the relevant state.

Contrast this with the position of DEMs. As defined, these do not directly regulate international economic activity, and as such cannot be

---

[164] A more direct argument for viewing tariffs as inclusive coercion, albeit less relevant in practice, would focus on their terms of trade effects: (Bagwell & Staiger, 2002: 13–41; Krugman et al., 2012: 255–256).

[165] See, for one possible example, §8.3.3 below.   [166] (Krugman et al., 2012: 142–146).

[167] Ibid., 146–157.   [168] Ibid., 286–298, 302–309; (Ray, 1998: 650–700).

said to directly coerce outsiders in the way that ETMs do. They may have effects on international economic activity, but these are side effects of their primary purpose, which is to regulate domestic economic activity.

Given these characteristics of ETMs, and bearing in mind the inter-personal test, we next ask how such measures can be justified. What reasons can a state adopting such measures offer to those who it thereby coerces, reasons that they can themselves be expected to share, and that justify the distributive effects of these measures? In the Rawlsian constructivist scheme equal freedom, expressed at the individual level in terms of individual liberties and social primary goods, including economic advantage, and at the collective level in terms of the self-determination of peoples, exhausts the ends that persons and peoples necessarily share. It is thus in terms of that equal freedom that ETMs must be justified in the first instance. However, as outlined above, self-determination can play only a limited role in justifying direct inclusive coercion. We must therefore look instead to the egalitarian considerations evoked by equal access to social primary goods and in particular, economic advantage. ETMs must be justified, if they can be justified at all, in terms of the effects they have on the distribution of economic advantage. However, such justifications will only be available where the interests invoked are those of the globally less advantaged. Reasonableness, and more particularly concerns of reciprocity, generality, and universality, precludes the justification of ETMs adopted in order to benefit globally more-advantaged individuals at the expense of those less advantaged; while at the same time precluding those more-advantaged individuals from objecting to ETMs adopted by others in pursuits of globally egalitarian goals. A concern for the justification of coercion thus leads us directly to the EGC Principle.

To illustrate, consider two states, Agraria and Industria, that trade various goods and services between themselves. Agraria proposes to impose a tariff on imports of widgets from Industria. Simplifying for clarity, assume that the effect of this tariff will be to divert sales of widgets from producers in Industria to producers in Agraria. The goal of the tariff is to protect the widget industry in Agraria, in the hope that it will grow and become more efficient, leading in the long term to a net increase in economic activity in Agraria, perhaps making it self-sufficient in respect of widgets, and ultimately allowing it to build an export widget industry. The effect of the tariff in Industria, on the other hand, is to exclude its widget manufacturers from a potential market for their products. If they have previously sold widgets into Agraria, then they can expect to see a reduction in sales as a result, and a consequent reduction in overall economic activity in Industria; if they have no history of selling into Agraria, then they may not suffer a loss, but they are deprived of the opportunity to benefit from future sales. In either case, the effect of the measure is that Agraria captures more of the benefits from the cooperation between Agraria and Industria than would otherwise be the case.

What arguments might the government of Agraria offer to the population of Industria to justify this action?

Consider, first, the case where Agraria is more affluent than Industria. Its citizens enjoy a higher standard of material wealth, and have access to a wider range of choices than do the citizens of Industria. Industria is not impoverished. Its citizens' basic needs are met, and it has sufficient resources to maintain a stable liberal democratic system of government. However, the lifestyle of Industria's citizens is sparse, and compared with the citizens of Agraria, they are relatively poor and enjoy fewer opportunities.

In these circumstances, could we expect the citizens of Industria to accept an argument advanced by Agraria that their purpose in imposing the tariff was to claim more of the benefits of the cooperation between their countries, with a view to the long-term benefit of their own citizens? Recognizing, as discussed above, that neither state has any pre-institutional claim to any specific share of the benefits of their cooperation, could we expect the citizens of Industria to accept that a greater share of those benefits should be extracted by the already wealthy citizens of Agraria? It is difficult to see how the citizens of Industria could be convinced to accept this outcome as just. If the effect of the tariff was to so injure the economy of Industria that it no longer had the necessary resources to remain well-ordered, this would certainly constitute a greater injustice; but even where this is not the case, Agraria can offer no justification for the measure that would meet the requirements outlined above.

Now consider the opposite situation. In this example, it is Industria that is wealthy, and Agraria that is relatively poor. Does Agraria have the same difficulties justifying its coercive imposition of this tariff against Industria? Unlike the former example, the citizens of Agraria can now make the following argument:

> You, in Industria, are rich, while we, in Agraria, are poor. A scheme of cooperation exists between our two states, which generates benefits for both of us. By imposing this tariff, we are coercing you in order to ensure that a

greater share of the benefits of our cooperation goes to certain of our citizens. In the absence of this tariff, the cooperation between our two states would result in greater benefit to your citizens than it does with this tariff in place. However, even with this tariff in place, your citizens continue to benefit from our cooperation (if they did not, then they presumably would not participate), and they continue to be wealthier than our citizens. To object to this tariff, you would need to claim that we, who are poor, should have less, solely in order that you, who are rich, can have more. It is not reasonable for you to make this claim.[169]

The citizens of Industria might certainly be disappointed that they were no longer receiving benefits they had previously or were deprived of benefits they hoped to gain from the cooperation. However, as discussed, they have no pre-institutional claim to any particular share of the benefits from their cooperation, so they cannot object that they have been deprived of something to which they are entitled. We might have great sympathy for the individual widget manufacturer in Industria, whose business is seriously damaged. However, we might reason, he is a citizen of an affluent state, and can expect protection and assistance from his fellow citizens; and if that protection and assistance is not forthcoming, then it is his fellow citizens who are guilty of an injustice towards him.[170] We know that Industria remains wealthy, so we need not worry overly about how our disappointed widget-maker will fare; certainly, he is still better off than the less-advantaged citizens of Agraria. There is nobody who cannot justify the imposition of the tariff, and nobody to whom it cannot be justified.[171]

---

[169] This argument intentionally echoes Rawls's argument from reciprocity to the difference principle: (Rawls, 2001: 122–124).

[170] This of course depends on Industria itself enjoying distributive autonomy, which falls under self-determination as discussed further in Chapter 5. A similar argument explains why the valid distributive claims of the less advantaged in Industria could not justify an ETM against less-affluent Agraria. While the less advantaged in Industria have claims of justice, they are claims against their fellow Industrians, and against the Industrian basic structure, which has constituted them as less advantaged, not against Agraria.

[171] It might be objected that this reflects the principle of redress, rather than the difference principle, as it justifies giving greater advantages to those who are less advantaged, instead of seeking to equalize the share each receives from international cooperation. There are three responses to this argument. The first notes that ETMs are not the only mechanism whereby the benefits of international cooperation are distributed, so that an ETM seeking to maximize the share that one group receives is compatible with that group in fact being less benefitted than others by the relevant cooperation. The second argues that the principle of redress is rejected in the domestic context in large part because it expresses disrespect for individuals; this concern does not arise in the international context. The third suggests that, whereas we can sensibly distinguish natural

Putting the argument in explicitly Rawlsian terms, we model both persons, and in turn peoples, as free and equal, rational and reasonable.[172] As reasonable, both persons and peoples recognize the equal rights of others, and do not claim for themselves what they are not prepared to allow to others. The recognition of peoples as free and equal implies recognizing their right to regulate their own affairs, and to exclude outsiders, but does not imply any right to regulate the cooperation between peoples, which is the effect of ETMs.[173] However, *ceteris paribus*, if the effect of an ETM is to confer a greater advantage on less-advantaged individuals, at the expense of more-advantaged individuals, reciprocity precludes those more advantaged individuals from objecting to this. The same principle would, however, prevent more-advantaged individuals from imposing on those less-advantaged ETMs that would have the effect of conferring greater advantages on them. Thus, ETMs can be justified only where they are to the advantage of less-advantaged individuals. Incorporating the concerns for opportunities highlighted in Section 3.3, this leaves us with the EGC Principle.

Are there justifications other than EGC that might support ETMs?

As I noted above, there may be ETMs that can be justified under the principle of self-determination. If we assume that all peoples have reason to value self-determination, and that they respect its equal value for others, then this provides a basis on which measures that pursue that end may be justified subject to the limitations discussed above. I discuss this point further in Chapter 5.

The ends of individual freedom and collective self-determination are the only ones that persons and peoples necessarily share. Whereas a given person or people may be firmly committed to other ends, for example

---

and social goods domestically, and thus pre-empt redress; in the international context, we are concerned with goods of the same kind, and deriving from complex causal processes, so it makes little sense to distinguish disadvantage in the distribution of international social goods from disadvantage generally. For a view that seeks to make this distinction, albeit with a qualification that immediately undermines it, and with little sense of how it might be operationalized: (James, 2012a).

[172] Of course, as discussed in Chapter 2, Rawls himself denies the appropriateness of this conception of the person in international theory.

[173] Because ETMs by definition regulate international as opposed to domestic economic activity, there is no question of their effecting a redistribution of resources that are the product of domestic as opposed to international cooperation. As such, Rawls's concerns that international distributive principles would be incompatible with national self-determination do not arise in connection with EGC: (Rawls, 1999: 117–118). See further in §4.5.2 below.

animal rights, they have no basis for directly coercing others in pursuit of them.[174] Others may share that commitment, which they might jointly pursue through international cooperation; but it can provide no basis for coercing outsiders.[175] Therefore, in the absence of clear evidence that the relevant ends are in fact shared by the relevant agents, it is difficult to see how they could justify ETMs.[176]

The constraints on justifying ETMs do not however apply to DEMs. In so far as these do not directly coerce outsiders, they do not require justification in terms of ends outsiders themselves have reason to share. The principle of self-determination provides a basis on which the effects of DEMs on outsiders can be justified, provided they respect outsiders' equal right to self-determination. The external effects of DEMs may be

---

[174] The interpersonal test is relevant here, and specifically its third, procedural, upshot, in explaining why the dissenting members of a given people may be directly coerced in pursuit of that people's chosen ends, whereas outsiders may not.

[175] This does not imply that states may not adopt regulations to reduce animal cruelty, but only that they may not use ETMs for this purpose. However, in many cases, regulations that on their face appear unrelated to international economic activity may in fact constitute ETMs where the specific good they are intended to promote will be affected only through the effects of the relevant measure on international economic activity. This will be the case with many (though not all) regulations of Non-Product Related Processes and Production Methods, a point taken up in Chapter 6. A somewhat different interpretation of the appropriate place of animal rights in international economic law, while still recognizing that the prevention of animal cruelty is not an interest that all can be expected to share, is advanced in: (Howse & Langille, 2012).

Cross-border pollution and climate change are more difficult as these represent cases where outsiders may directly harm members of a community. I am inclined to think that the prevention of serious harm to members of a community resulting from the actions of outsiders can provide a legitimate basis for coercing outsiders. However, in the case of much environmental damage, the relevant arguments can be better expressed in egalitarian or self-determination terms. This also has the benefit of bringing into view the equal right of outsiders to be protected from polluting activity by insiders, and potential historic claims of climate injustice.

Human rights are a further case where ETMs directed against repressive regimes may be justifiable; again, however, it may be possible to express this interest in self-determination or egalitarian terms, including under both aspects of the account of self-determination developed in Chapter 5. Its significance, however, is that it represents a case where ETMs might be adopted by one state for the benefit of individuals in another state, running against the presumption noted in §3.6. This might be explained on the basis that non-realization of basic rights indicates (or may indicate) an unwillingness of inability on the part of the relevant government, rebutting that presumption.

[176] I discuss further in Chapter 5 the relation between self-determination, international cooperation, and the justification of nonegalitarian ETMs. We might draw a parallel here to Rawls's argument against liberal states' efforts to export liberalism: EGC can endorse Rawls's conclusion on this point, albeit reaching it by a different route: (Rawls, 1999: 60–62, 83–85).

either inclusive or exclusive. In so far as they are inclusive, they shape the distribution of benefits and burdens from international cooperation. However, because they do not aim to do so, and do not use outsiders to pursue their goals in the way that ETMs do, they do not require justification in distributive terms in the same way. It is for this reason that, in considering DEMs, we can apply the domestic difference principle without concern for the effects they have on outsiders, subject to the side constraints implied by Rawls's Duty of Assistance.[177] The Duty of Assistance, with its negative corollary, does impose some constraints on states to consider the implications of DEMs for outsiders, but only where the effect of the relevant measure would be to impair basic human rights, or to deprive another people of the resources they require to become or remain well ordered. This may preclude a state adopting certain measures or (more commonly) require that measures be adapted to minimize the adverse effects on the relevant outsiders. This is not a general obligation, however, and applies only below the threshold where the effect of the measure would be to undermine the basic rights or effective self-determination of outsiders, and thus their capacity to become or remain well ordered. We are thus left, not only with EGC, but with the DEM Proviso that I described in Chapter 1.

The consequence of this argument, then, is that ETMs will be just only to the extent that they comply with EGC; while DEMs require justification only at the margin where they impact on the basic rights or self-determination of others. These two claims combine to provide a comprehensive account of the justice of state action in the international economic sphere.

3.8   Conclusion

In this chapter, I have advanced equality in global commerce as a principle of global justice applying specifically to external trade measures. I have argued that ETMs coerce outsiders in ways that DEMs do not. They represent a form of direct inclusive coercion that can only be justified in distributive, and specifically egalitarian, terms. I have further argued that other measures adopted by states, which I characterize as

---

[177] In so far as the indirect coercion of outsiders implicit in DEMs is justified by reference to the principle of self-determination, the duty of assistance can be regarded as a necessary element of that justification which vindicates the equal right of outsiders to self-determination as well-ordered peoples.

DEMs, do not have this character, and can generally be justified under the principle of self-determination, subject to a proviso analogous to Rawls's Duty of Assistance to burdened peoples.

I have thus set out the core of the positive argument for EGC. One element that remains to be explained is what exactly I mean when I refer to ETMs being justified under a reasonable principle of self-determination. I have touched on this possibility, but elaborating it requires a fuller account of what exactly it means for a people to be self-determining. I take up that task in Chapter 5. However, before doing so, I want to consider some of the major arguments *against* international distributive justice, to examine whether, and to what extent, these may constitute objections to EGC. That is the task of the next chapter.

4

Sovereignty, Nationality, and the Limits of Statism

The argument so far works from the assumption that state action requires justification to outsiders, in the same way as it does to insiders. While reflecting a widely shared belief in the moral equality of human persons, we might worry that this assumption underemphasizes a prominent feature of the international system: rather than a unitary political structure, it comprises a multiplicity of independent sovereign states. This chapter examines arguments emphasizing the moral distinctiveness of the sovereign state to preempt any objection to EGC from this perspective.

4.1 Introduction

One of the most striking differences between the legal, empirical, and philosophical literatures on the international system is the role of sovereignty in each. For positivist international lawyers, sovereignty is a foundational concept: neither the subjects nor sources of international law make sense without a prior account of sovereignty.[1] While perhaps less prominent in applied fields than in foundational scholarship, it remains both a persistent backstop on interpretive disputes, and a substantive value, frequently invoked to end debate and limit obligation.[2] For political scientists, sovereignty plays a different, but no less prominent, role. For realists, it is sovereignty that distinguishes the hierarchy and order of the state from the anarchy of the international

---

[1] (Brownlie, 2008: 289–290). As Koskenniemi notes, "For [classical international lawyers], the State's sphere of liberty was prior, and normative, and the principles of conduct between States simply followed as a description of what was required to safeguard the anterior liberties.": (Koskenniemi, 2005: 224). On humanity's challenge to sovereignty's predominance: (Teitel, 2011: 170–174).

[2] For an example in WTO practice, *Japan-Alcohol II (AB)*, p. 15.

system.[3] For institutionalists, it justifies bracketing domestic divisions and modeling international politics as the pursuit of state preferences. Even many social constructivists, while rejecting rationalists' reification of the state, recognize the roles different conceptions of sovereignty play in constituting both states and the international system, and explaining the emergence and persistence of distinct modes of order and disorder.[4]

Contemporary philosophical literature, by contrast, has had little time for sovereignty. Earlier cosmopolitan work dismisses it as incompatible with individual rights.[5] Anti-cosmopolitan thinkers are also reluctant to endorse any account of the state that depends on it. Thus, Rawls takes care to speak of peoples, distinguishing them from states *inter alia* by their lack of traditional sovereignty.[6] Similarly, Miller warns against "mak[ing] a fetish out of national sovereignty."[7] Nagel invokes the Hobbesian argument from sovereignty, as reflected in contemporary political realism, but shows little interest in the legal conception.[8] While debates on self-determination and secession, territorial rights, natural resources, migration controls, and human rights all necessarily touch on aspects of state sovereignty, few thinkers directly invoke that concept in support of their arguments. Rather, they have been concerned to explain, defend, or critique some aspect of sovereignty on the basis of other, more fundamental, values.[9]

This reflects two important features of sovereignty: first, its institutional character; and second, its disparate content. As an institution, philosophers find sovereignty at the end of an argument, not at its beginning. It is an object of justification; only once justified itself can it in turn ground further claims. Second, because diverse in content, sovereignty falls to be justified piecemeal. Legal sovereignty is neither essential nor indivisible; it is a bundle of rights, over territory, persons, and

---

[3] (Waltz, 1979: 93–97) Cf. (Krasner, 1999). Sovereignty's explanatory role in realist thought dates at least to Hobbes (Hobbes, 1996: 86–90).

[4] (Reus-Smit, 1999; Wendt, 1999). While not ostensibly constructivist, much English School scholarship reflects a similar concern to explain international politics in terms of conceptions of sovereignty (Bull, 1977; Keene, 2002; Wight, 1996).

[5] (Beitz, 1999: 67–125; Pogge, 1992: 57–61). For a qualified reconstruction of sovereignty on cosmopolitan premises (Tesón, 1998: 39–49, 57–58).

[6] (Rawls, 1999: 25–27). Kuper labels this qualified view of sovereignty "thin statism": (Kuper, 2000: 641).

[7] (Miller, 1995: 103).   [8] (Nagel, 2005: 115–117, 126).

[9] E.g. (Benvenisti, 2013; Endicott, 2010: 255–258).

policies, each of which falls to be separately justified.[10] The postwar evolution of legal sovereignty clearly illustrates this point.[11] It may be the case, as Hobbes argues, that some of these rights necessarily depend on others, such that a justification of one will necessarily constitute a justification of the others; but such iterative justifications require to be made out in each case.[12] We cannot assume that, once an argument for sovereignty is advanced, it necessarily justifies all aspects of the traditional doctrine.[13]

This last point is important for the present chapter, and indeed for my argument as a whole. Depending on how sovereignty is understood, it might ground an objection to the principles advanced in the previous chapter. Certainly, the traditional doctrine includes a right to adopt measures, including ETMs, without restriction as to either their purpose or their economic effects on outsiders.[14] We might pre-empt this objection in various ways. While they are clearly distinct principles, the principle of nonintervention, whether understood as an exception to, or an expression of, the principle of sovereignty, might on some interpretations overlap with the restrictions on ETMs expressed in EGC.[15] Further, to the extent that the positive law of the trade regime can be understood as expressing EGC, any conflict with the principle of sovereignty might be reconciled by invoking state consent.[16] However, the better response is to emphasize the evolving content of the principle of sovereignty, and to deny that any of the grounds that might justify sovereignty constitute objections to EGC. To the extent this is the case,

---

[10] (Koskenniemi, 2005: 240–255; Pogge, 1992: 59–61). In the WTO context, this point is emphasized in Jackson's "power allocation" approach: (Jackson, 2006: ch. 3).

[11] (Teitel, 2011: 8–11). That evolution appears most prominently in contemporary discussions of sovereignty as responsibility. (Report of the International Commission on Intervention and State Sovereignty, 2001: §2.14–12.15; UNGA Resolution 60/1/2005: §138). On the role of moral argument in this development: (Orford, 2013). However, equally significant for my purposes are the less controversial developments of human rights protections, and restrictions on the international use of force. Kratochwil identifies absolute territorial sovereignty with a brief postwar moment: (Kratochwil, 1986: 42).

[12] I take up this idea further in §5.5 below.

[13] Simmons analyses the various rights comprised in conventional sovereignty, and the justificatory relations between them: (Simmons, 2001). The need to disaggregate and separately analyze these rights is further emphasized in (Kolers, 2009: 34–35; Moore, 2012: 85). A number of thinkers analogize the variable character of sovereignty to that of property. E.g. (Kratochwil, 1986: 27–28). For a contrary view, (Freeman, 2007: 286).

[14] (Brownlie, 2008: 299).   [15] For an argument on these lines: (Bartels, 2002: 379–382).

[16] For the avoidance of doubt, I do not adopt or in any way rely on this view. To the extent I argue these principles apply apart from, and so constitute an appropriate basis for interpreting, WTO law, such a view would risk circularity.

any conflict between EGC and traditional sovereignty constitutes not an objection to EGC, but rather an argument for further revising sovereignty doctrine. The important question then becomes not whether EGC conflicts with sovereignty, but rather whether it conflicts with some value protected by sovereignty.[17] My purpose in the present chapter is to show that it does not. I do not argue either against sovereignty or against the disparate values that support it; rather I show that, properly understood, these are compatible with EGC. I thereby also show that sovereignty, properly understood, cannot provide an alternative basis for justifying measures addressed by EGC.

I consider four distinct sets of arguments. The first identify sovereignty as enabling justice within the state. The second analogize the sovereign state to Rawls's concept of a basic structure. The third challenge global justice based on priority for compatriots. Finally, the fourth raise conceptual objections to international egalitarian theories. None is exclusively concerned to justify national sovereignty. However, each, in different ways, makes a claim for the importance of states or political communities, or membership thereof, whether for persons or for the scope of justice. They support claims that states, in their choices, should pay attention to the interests of their own citizens, to the exclusion of outsiders. Many originate as objections to strong egalitarian cosmopolitan positions that I do not defend. My main concern is not therefore directly to challenge them; rather, I show that, regardless of their other merits, they do not constitute objections to EGC.

4.2   Sovereignty, Security, and Global Justice

A first objection identifies sovereignty, understood in the Hobbesian sense of an absolute political authority, as a prerequisite to justice, and hence denies that justice can play any role beyond the state. The objection is pressed in two variants; a strong variant, which closely follows Hobbes' formulation, and is reflected in contemporary neorealist international relations theory; and a moderate variant, which emphasizes coordination problems as requiring solution before claims of justice are appropriate. Nagel advances both.[18]

---

[17] For an analogous point, arguing for a revised approach to tax sovereignty: (Dietsch, 2011: 2115). Jackson advocates a similar approach to sovereigntist challenges to the WTO: (Jackson, 2006: 59).

[18] (Nagel, 2005).

4.2.1   Sovereignty and Security

The strong variant characterizes international relations as a Hobbesian state of nature in which states must look to their own protection or risk extinction. There is no international authority that can guarantee the security of individual states, in the way states guarantee the security of their citizens, so each must make their own security their highest priority. For Hobbes, this translates into an appetite for "power after power, that ceaseth only in death."[19] For contemporary realists, it mandates an overriding focus on the national interest, a concern for relative gains from cooperation, and a skepticism of international morality.[20] A state that sacrifices national interest to moral considerations, on this view, risks eclipse and ultimately domination by rising powers less naïve in their policies.[21]

The strong variant is an objection to international distributive principles, but also to international morality more generally, and indeed to most international cooperation and international law. As such, it is too strong an argument for its contemporary proponents' purposes.[22] This problem is not simply an *ad hominem* challenge; the clearest objection to the strong variant is the existence of relatively stable practices of international cooperation, institutions, and laws that seem to play a more substantial role than realists predict.[23] Beyond empirics, institutionalist and social constructivist international relations theories have challenged realist explanatory theories of the state and the international system, showing how both institutionalized mutually beneficial cooperation and morally motivated behavior are possible under anarchy.[24] Indeed, as constructivists, in particular, have emphasized, security may be better assured through cooperation and socialization than containment and conflict.[25] To the extent, this is the case, promoting and complying with normative principles like EGC might be the optimum strategy for

---

[19] (Hobbes, 1996: 70).   [20] (Donnelly, 2008: 155, 157–159; Stein, 2008: 209–211).

[21] For a particularly robust exposition, (Mearsheimer, 2014).

[22] This point is pressed against Nagel: (Cohen & Sabel, 2006).

[23] Although for a skeptical review: (Stein, 2008: 212). International realists' difficulties explaining pervasive international law and institutions stimulated the emergence of neoliberal institutionalism. More recently, debate between these schools has focused less on the truth of the strong sovereignty objection than on its proper scope, with most realists accepting that institutions play an important role in at least some spheres of international politics.

[24] For an overview: (Hasenclever et al., 1997). On solving prisoners' dilemmas under anarchy (Axelrod, 1984). On the causal role of moral considerations: (Crawford, 2002; Price, 2008; Tannenwald, 2007).

[25] (Wendt, 1992). This point was clearly recognized by early realists. E.g. (Carr, 1946).

states pursuing security. Certainly, moral behavior absent sovereignty is not necessarily irrational, even in narrowly egoistic terms.[26]

However, it is not necessary to reject the strong variant entirely. Instead, we might focus on the proper scope of that objection. It is most plausible in circumstances where complying with a moral principle would expose an agent to immediate, unforeseeable, and irrecoverable injury.[27] It is less plausible where the predicted injury is protracted, predictable, and remediable.[28] It is for this reason that realism remains more influential in matters of security than economics.[29]

Further, the prisoners' dilemmas described by the strong variant arise only among peer competitors capable of threatening one another's vital interests. Hobbes emphasizes men's relative equality to generate competitive dynamics[30]; internationally, realists have been explicit in recognizing that their theories describe only the relations among great powers.[31] In consequence, in relations between large and small states, the strong sovereignty objection is silent.[32]

To the extent EGC addresses relations between larger and smaller states, or between more developed and less developed states, and in so far as it addresses economic relations, it is thus substantially reconcilable with the realism underpinning the strong sovereignty objection. However, there remains some unavoidable conflict between these positions. In particular, to the extent EGC denies that a state may adopt ETMs to preserve its privileged position vis-à-vis a rising power, or that it can object to their use by that rising power itself, it directly conflicts with realist precepts.[33] If this necessarily involved sacrificing the state's vital interests, this would constitute a serious objection to EGC.[34] However, in

---

[26] Thus, Kapstein builds a theory of international fairness on narrowly rationalist premises: (Kapstein, 2006).

[27] (Hobbes, 1996: 89). Of course, many realists would deny that any other circumstances exist: (Waltz, 1979: 104–106, 111).

[28] (Axelrod, 1984: 124–141). Much institutionalist scholarship examines how international institutions transform risk of the former kind into the latter. Recent realists' focus on offense/defense balance and the fungibility of resources similarly addresses this distinction: (Wohlforth, 2008: 138–139).

[29] (Lipson, 1984).   [30] (Hobbes, 1996: 86–87).   [31] (Waltz, 1979: 129–131).

[32] (Caney, 2005: 137). This is clearest in hegemonic stability theory: (Snidal, 1985). Obviously, how a great power interacts with lesser powers might affect its standing towards peer competitors, but the policy implications will differ.

[33] For a study of the relation between economic and military power in this process: (Kennedy, 1987). Although even realists' positions will diverge: (Kirshner, 2012).

[34] And, indeed, to the possibility of either cooperation or justice in such circumstances. To this extent, we can read the realist objection as a claim that we are not in Hume's

respect of such cases, EGC can fall back on the alternative explanatory theories noted above to argue that moral behavior can reflect enlightened self-interest. This may not always be the case; but given plausible disagreement, those pressing the strong sovereignty objection must at least make out a stronger case in the specific circumstances.

4.2.2   Sovereignty and Coordination

The moderate sovereignty objection emphasizes the role of sovereignty in solving coordination problems.[35] The goods with which social justice is concerned are produced not through individual action, but rather through the coordinated action of numerous agents. Only a sovereign, on this view, can effectively coordinate those agents. In its absence, no purpose is served by imposing duties of social justice directly on individual agents. Doing so results in wasted effort, as individual agents cannot meaningfully contribute to the provision of the relevant goods; and/or unfairness among duty bearers, as some contribute more than their fair share, while others free-ride on their efforts.[36]

The strong sovereignty objection, emphasizing the sovereign's assurance function, regards the pervasive coercive power of the state as a prerequisite to justice. The moderate variant, by contrast, emphasizes its coordination function. However, this latter role demands neither hierarchy nor effective coercion. Indeed, neoliberal institutionalists explain much of contemporary international law and international organizations as helping to solve such coordination problems. This does not mean that the moderate sovereignty objection is irrelevant to thinking about international justice. However, we should not overstate its importance. International institutions are neither easy to construct, nor unlimited in their capacities.

---

circumstances of justice internationally; if we cannot cooperate with others without sacrificing our own vital interests, then we are faced with absolute, rather than relative, scarcity of security.

[35] (Nagel, 2005). Among cosmopolitans, some seek to accommodate this objection, while others deny its relevance: (Beitz, 1999: 158–160; Caney, 2005). For an extended treatment of both sovereignty objections: (James, 2012a: 77–130). There is a significant overlap between this objection and the agency interpretation of the basic structure objection, considered below.

[36] In fact, there are two different objections here, with quite different force. If coordination problems mean that effort will be wasted, and no meaningful progress made, then this is a compelling objection to any duty. If, on the other hand, the objection is only that duties may be unfairly allocated, such that some can free-ride, then we face a further question, of whether unfairness among duty-bearers is more problematic than underfulfillment of the primary duty.

There are undoubtedly candidate principles of international socioeconomic justice that should be rejected either because the coordination burdens they impose are beyond any plausible international institutions, or simply because the costs of constructing such institutions are too great. However, neither objection holds in the case of EGC. Because EGC addresses states in the first instance, it imposes minimal coordination requirements. To the extent such requirements arise, they do so under the DEM Proviso, and are no greater than those arising in any other moderate theory. Further, the WTO provides a venue in which EGC can be institutionalized with minimal cost.[37] As discussed in later chapters, much of the existing positive law of the trade regime can be understood as expressing, albeit imperfectly, the concerns of EGC. Certainly, fully implementing EGC would require progressive development of that law, through both interpretation and negotiation; but it is not unrealistic to think this could be done within the existing institution, and without imposing significantly greater demands on its coordinating capacities than at present. I take up this question of progressive development further in Chapter 10.

It thus does not appear that the sovereignty objection, in either its strong or moderate variants, constitutes a serious objection to EGC.

4.3   Sovereignty and the Basic Structure

A second sovereigntist objection identifies the state with a central element of Rawls's scheme, the basic structure, and denies that arguments developed for that structure can be applied beyond it. Thus, a number of theorists argue that, while there may be both international cooperation and international coercion, there is no global basic structure comparable to the basic structure of domestic societies and, in consequence, that we cannot apply distributive justice internationally.[38]

The focus on basic structures might tempt us to dismiss these objections as parochial, of limited interest except to dogmatic Rawlsian theorists. However, they pick out an important point. For many of us, there is something about the social and political organization of the state that is significant for our understanding of political morality. Arguments about the

---

[37] James makes a similar point in support of his own preferred approach: (James, 2012a: 103–107).

[38] This argument is most strongly pressed in: (Freeman, 2007: ch. 8, 9). However, versions also appear in: (Meckled-Garcia, 2008; Ronzoni, 2009). I understand Sangiovanni's reciprocity account as also falling under this heading: (Sangiovanni, 2007). For critical reviews of these approaches: (Abizadeh, 2007; Follesdal, 2011).

basic structure are in large part efforts to explain that moral significance, and its relevance for justice beyond the state. They are therefore potentially interesting, even for those not attracted by Rawls's approach generally.

I examine three versions of this objection, concluding that while they constitute a plausible objection to a global difference principle, they do not undermine, and on two interpretations support, EGC. I begin with Rawls's reasons for focusing on the basic structure, distinguishing those features that make it an appropriate object of justification from those that are required for it to be just.[39] I next examine cosmopolitan claims to identify a global basic structure, and statist objections to those claims. Finally, I distinguish three versions of the statist objection, which I label the Impact, Participation, and Agency Objections. The first, I suggest, is empirically implausible. The second is either normatively perverse or, to the extent it is plausible, supports EGC. The third, while constituting a valid objection to a global difference principle, similarly seems to support EGC.

4.3.1   Why the Basic Structure?

Rawls defines the basic structure as "the way in which the major social institutions fit together into one system, and how they assign fundamental rights and duties and shape the division of advantages that arise from social cooperation."[40] Domestically, it includes *inter alia* the political constitution, the legal system, the economy, and the family.[41] Rawls identifies it as the first subject of justice, and proposes *Justice as Fairness* as an account of justice for the basic structure.

There are three reasons for this focus.

The first is its role in defining and maintaining inequalities in life prospects.[42] The basic structure defines the social positions we occupy and the rights, opportunities, and returns we enjoy. On this view, we

---

[39] For this distinction: (Ronzoni, 2009).

[40] (Rawls, 1996: 258) Cf. (Rawls, 1971: 7, 2001: 10). Barry refers to "the institutions that together determine the access (or chances of access) of the members of a society to resources that are the means to satisfying a wide variety of desires": (Barry, 1989). Freeman identifies the basic structure domestically with the legal system: (Freeman, 2007: 268).

[41] Cohen objects that Rawls is imprecise and/or inconsistent in his treatment of nonformal and noncoercive elements of the basic structure, including in particular the family, suggesting that a focus on impact would tend to broaden the focus: (Cohen, 2008: 125). Answering that objection in part motivates Julius' account of framing and the basic structure, discussed in Chapter 3: (Julius, 2003).

[42] (Rawls, 1971: 7) Cf. (Rawls, 1996: 269–271, 2001: 55–57).

focus on the basic structure because it is the most important element of our social world, and so its effects are most in need of justification.[43]

Second, the basic structure is essential in maintaining background justice.[44] For Rawls, background conditions are important in assessing the fairness of interactions: the outcomes of agreements are fair only when background conditions are fair[45]; and given background justice, we can rely on procedural rules to ensure the justice of outcomes. However, no single set of rules, complied with by interacting agents, can reliably maintain background justice over time. In consequence, the basic structure must include mechanisms for adjusting rules and entitlements to maintain background justice.[46]

Third, under a just basic structure, individuals can pursue their own projects without constantly addressing problems of social justice. Van Parijs describes this as the "institutional division of moral labor": by catering for the demands of justice primarily through institutions, we allow individuals to focus on their own valued projects.[47] Provided we live under just basic institutions, and support and comply with those institutions, we need not worry about pursuing justice through our own actions.[48]

These three reasons have different structures. The first identifies a consequence of living under any basic structure: it has profound and pervasive impacts on persons' lives, making it an urgent object of moral inquiry. The second and third, by contrast, point to benefits of living under a *just* basic structure. They thus identify desiderata of such a structure: it maintains background justice and relieves individuals of the need to themselves pursue social justice. An institutional scheme that neither fulfills, nor plausibly could fulfill, these latter functions would remain an important object of moral inquiry for the first reason; albeit its inability to do so might affect our judgments about it, and about the obligations of agents living thereunder.[49]

---

[43] (Abizadeh, 2007: 341–344).   [44] (Rawls, 1971: 86–87).

[45] Rawls thus rejects the libertarian concept of entitlement: (Nozick, 1974: 151).

[46] (Rawls, 1996: 268, 2001: 52–55) Cf. (Abizadeh, 2007: 327–329).

[47] (Van Parijs, 2003: 229). See also (Murphy, 1998: 257–264; Porter, 2009).

[48] (Rawls, 2001: 50–52). On the natural duty to support and comply with just institutions: (Rawls, 1971: 114–117). For another argument along these lines: (Tan, 2012: ch. 2).

[49] This point is made clearly in: (Ronzoni, 2009). Abizadeh makes a similar distinction between senses in which distributive justice might be understood as requiring a basic structure, namely by presupposing, including, or demanding such a structure: (Abizadeh, 2007: 324).

If the basic structure is defined as institutions that distribute fundamental rights and duties and determine the distribution of advantages and disadvantages, then there are certainly institutions that meet that description internationally. Indeed, these are precisely the institutions that EGC addresses, and on which cosmopolitans have generally focused. Thus, Beitz refers alternately to "a global regulative structure" or "constitutional structure of the world economy," under which he includes financial and monetary institutions, "international agreements on tariff levels and other potential barriers to trade," and informal practices of economic policy coordination among national governments. He further identifies "political and legal institutions [that] influence the global distribution of income and wealth," including international property rights in respect of territory and natural resources, international investment protection, and the rule of nonintervention, the last of which "when observed, has clear and sweeping effects on the welfare of people everywhere."[50] Buchanan defines a global basic structure as "a worldwide cooperative scheme consisting of a complex pattern of institutions, including the international legal system, whose workings have profound, pervasive, and lifelong effects on individuals and groups." In the present international context, he identifies this structure with "a widely recognized system of private property rights (including intellectual property rights), the law of the sea, financial, and monetary regimes, basic trade regimes, and the systematic patterns of interaction among states under various aspects of public international law."[51] More recently, Føllesdal has distinguished between candidate global and international basic structures: the former importantly includes the domestic basic structures of states, in so far as these play an important role in structuring actions and outcomes globally, while the latter comprises international law, including multilateral treaties, and international organizations and tribunals.[52] That some such distributive institutions exist seems undeniable.[53]

Given this, the denial of a global basic structure can be understood in three distinct ways, which I label the Impact, Participation, and Agency Objections.[54]

---

[50] (Beitz, 1999: 148–149).   [51] (Buchanan, 2004: 81, 212–214).   [52] (Follesdal, 2011: 53).

[53] (Abizadeh, 2007: 344; O'Neill, 2000: 121). Nor is this necessarily a recent development. For accounts from the 1640s, 1910s, and 1940s: (Hobbes, 1996: 171; Keynes, 1919: 6; Polanyi, 2001: 18).

[54] Others divide up the arguments in different ways. Abizadeh, for example, distinguishes coercion, pervasive impact, and cooperation approaches: (Abizadeh, 2007) Cf. (Follesdal, 2011).

4.3.2   The Impact Objection

The Impact Objection directly challenges the cosmopolitan claim that there is a global institutional scheme that has pervasive effects on the life prospects of persons and peoples. So understood, the objection seems empirically implausible. Nonetheless, it is implicitly endorsed by leading anti-cosmopolitans. Rawls's explanatory nationalism, which locates the sources of economic and political success primarily at the national level, appears significantly motivated by this view.[55] Further, while ostensibly disclaiming the Impact Objection, Freeman makes a distinction between voluntary international institutions and nonvoluntary (and hence more "basic") domestic institutions that seems to depend on it.[56] Elsewhere, he emphasizes the far greater impact of domestic institutions on individuals' lives, the exit options available from international institutions, and the extent to which domestic rather than international institutions in fact distribute the benefits of international economic activity.[57]

Focusing on the claim that international institutions are voluntary, a number of responses are available. First, given the pervasive power inequalities that characterize international politics, we might query how far most states can meaningfully influence those institutions. Second, we might query how the possibility of exit is relevant, given Rawls's refusal to countenance it in his domestic theory.[58] Third, we might query whether exit is realistic, given the importance of international markets and the near-universal membership in key institutions including the WTO.[59]

---

[55] This appears most prominently in: (Rawls, 1999: 39, 106, 108). While there is some recognition of the distributive effects of international institutions in Rawls's discussion of cooperative institutions, he does not develop the implications for distributive justice: (Rawls, 1999: 42–43).

[56] (Freeman, 2007: 269). Contrast Franck's claim that domestic legitimacy importantly relies on international law: (Franck, 1990: 12). An alternative reading of Freeman's view is that, because the international basic structure works through the domestic basic structure, and because the latter is structured by the domestic difference principle, there is nothing left to which an international principle might apply. However, given the possibility of nesting such principles (as EGC does), and given the limited implications that Rawls's domestic theory has for institutions addressed by EGC, this seems implausible. See (Freeman, 2007: 269–270, 289–290).

[57] (Freeman, 2007: 288). We could alternatively understand this last point as one about immediacy or directness, as emphasized by Blake and Risse. However, it is not clear why either would matter categorically, in the way these writers assume: (Caney, 2008).

[58] (Follesdal, 2011: 58).

[59] (Maffettone, 2009) Cf. (Blake, 2013: 122–123; Follesdal, 2011: 57–59; Garcia, 2004). Freeman concedes that exit is not costless, but denies that this affects the voluntary quality of institutions. This seems to depend on a distinction between benefits and

Fourth, we might query whether peoples are in fact free to take that option, given the possibility of intervention to enforce continued participation in and compliance with the rules of the international economy.[60]

Alternatively, we might concede *arguendo* Freeman's claim, and instead focus on aspects of the candidate global basic structure that are clearly nonvoluntary, even in this narrow sense.[61] Recall Føllesdal's division of the global basic structure into an international basic structure, including the institutions to which the voluntariness argument is addressed, and the several domestic basic structures of states. Whereas the former may be voluntary in Freeman's sense, the latter are not. Further, as Freeman himself emphasizes, it is the domestic basic structures of individual states that directly distribute the benefits of international cooperation.[62] Indeed, as noted in Chapter 2, it is primarily by coordinating states' domestic policies that international institutions have distributive effects.[63] Whether a given people choose to participate in a particular formal institution will not affect whether they face an international institutional landscape that substantially determines their prospects, and those of their members.[64] Thus, even if we allow Freeman's claim of voluntariness in respect of formal institutions, there remains a substantial global institutional structure that is "basic" in Freeman's required sense.[65] The Impact Objection thus seems implausible.

---

costs that in turn faces baseline problems that a constructivist must struggle to answer. See also (Caney, 2008: 497–498; Loriaux, 2012: 27–28).

[60] (Cavallero, 2010).

[61] For a view conceding that international institutions, and specifically the WTO, are not basic in the required sense, but understanding states themselves in personal rather than institutional terms: (Eskelinen, 2011).

[62] (Freeman, 2007: 290).

[63] Risse characterizes this feature of domestic basic structures as "immediacy": (Risse, 2006).

[64] (Stein, 2008: 210–211).

[65] The same point can be made about informal international institutions, including in particular territorial sovereignty, which is emphasized by *inter alia* Beitz and Buchanan. Indeed Freeman himself, while arguing that sovereignty is not cooperative, highlights its nonvoluntary quality: (Freeman, 2007: 308). Critics might here object that, once we disaggregate the global structure into discrete institutions, as I did in Chapter 3, we can distinguish based on the extent of the impact different institutions have, and that the states we live in have infinitely greater impact on our lives than do other states. Three replies occur. The first concedes this point, but argues the fact of institutional impact still requires justification, albeit the impact requiring to be justified is lesser. The second denies the objection, pointing out that many measures adopted by foreign governments may be more significant for particular individuals than those adopted by their own: consider the relative impact of U.S. dietary regulations versus local veterinary licensing rules for a cocoa exporter in Ghana. The third, subsuming the first two, recalls that it is the

4.3.3   The Participation Objection

The Participation Objection concedes that there is a global institutional structure with pervasive impact, but denies that this constitutes a basic structure because it is not cooperative in the required sense. Thus, Freeman observes that the difference principle expresses "a principle or reciprocity, designed to apply under conditions of social cooperation to the basic structure of society, where the members of society are regarded as engaging in a complex web of political and social institutions that make up the basic structure."[66] This idea is elsewhere linked to Rawls's distinction between cooperation and coordination, the former being understood in moralized terms.[67] At base, the claim is that international institutions do not constitute a basic structure because they neither express a conception of reciprocity of the requisite kind nor reflect a "common social and political project" of all who are subject to them.[68]

As an empirical claim, this is plausible. Many international institutions do seem to benefit those better off at the expense of those worse off: this is precisely what cosmopolitans object to.[69] However, it cannot support the normative conclusion that there is no justice-relevant international basic structure. As Abizadeh argues, the Participation Objection relies on a confusion between the prerequisites for claims of social justice and their demands. Reciprocity, in the sense identified by Freeman, is a desideratum of a just basic structure, not a prerequisite to its evaluation in terms of justice.[70] The alternative conclusion, that only schemes of coordination that are *already* fair systems of cooperation can be evaluated in Rawlsian terms, would deprive Rawls's theory of any critical bite in respect of, for example, a libertarian minimal state.[71] Admittedly, on at least some readings of Rawls's political liberal methodology in his later work, this conclusion would be unsurprising.[72] However, as noted in

---

qualitative rather than quantitative difference between institutional and individual impacts that gives rise to the demand for justification.

[66] (Freeman, 2007: 286–287).   [67] Ibid., 266–267.

[68] Sangiovanni advances a similar claim, albeit in somewhat different terms: (Sangiovanni, 2007). Cf. (Barry, 1982). On the limits of reciprocity arguments: (Caney, 2011).

[69] Pogge's work on the natural resources and debt privileges is perhaps clearest in this regard.

[70] A similar point might be made against Franck's invocation of the concept: (Franck, 1995).

[71] Abizadeh presses this challenge against various possible interpretations of the participation objection: (Abizadeh, 2007: 330–341). Some implications of this argument are worked out in (Ronzoni, 2009) Cf. (Caney, 2008: 493–494; Follesdal, 2011: 48–49).

[72] (James, 2005: 290–306). For this critique: (Valentini, 2011b). That this is part of Freeman's view is clear from: (Freeman, 2007: 270–272, 305, 319–320).

Chapter 3, to the extent that (as this view implies) political liberalism reduces to bare interpretivism, its attraction is limited to liberal contexts. The Participation Objection would then constitute not an argument against global distributive principles, but rather a demonstration by *reductio* of the limits of interpretivism.[73]

An alternative understanding of this objection focuses not on the presence or absence of reciprocity, but rather on what it serves to produce, namely the political system that makes possible the "incredibly complicated system of legal norms that underlie economic production, exchange and consumption" and, more generally, that makes it possible for individuals to pursue their own diverse conceptions of the good.[74] Cooperation among citizens produces the framework that makes everything else possible, such that everything else is properly regarded as a product of that cooperation, and hence an appropriate object of distributive justice.[75] Outsiders do not cooperate in the maintenance of the political system in the relevant sense, and so are not owed the same egalitarian duties.

This interpretation, however, cannot ground an objection to EGC. Note that it starts not from the terms of cooperation/coordination, but rather from what it produces. Outsiders are not owed reciprocity because

---

[73] There is a slightly different interpretation available, which highlights the importance of relative social equality for the operation of political processes. Most obviously, in order to realize the fair value of the political liberties, it is plausible that all citizens require to have as large a share as possible of economic goods, in order to maximize their opportunities to influence the political process. More generally, a degree of mutual respect is necessary if we are to accept the results of political processes, and this may not be compatible with seeing some of our fellow citizens living in abject poverty. These kinds of arguments will not apply beyond particular political communities. However, they are at most complementary to Rawls's central argument for the difference principle. As such, their nonavailability internationally cannot significantly undermine that argument.

[74] See in particular: (Freeman, 2007: 267–269, 290, 307). This reading reflects the fact that proponents of the participation objection accept that outsiders make contributions, and Freeman even concedes that there is international cooperation, but not "social cooperation": (Freeman, 2007: 268, 307). In discussing sovereignty he implies that, where a political structure is imposed noncooperatively, contributions made under it will not ground reciprocity claims: (Freeman, 2007: 308). On a contractarian approach, this may follow: (Buchanan, 1990; Nussbaum, 2004: 7, 12). However, neither Rawls's own argument, nor the approach advanced in Chapter 3, is contractarian in this sense: (Quong, 2007: 78–82). Indeed, such perverse consequences seem a compelling reason to reject contractarianism: (Cudd, 2012: §5). Loriaux argues there can be fair but noncooperative social coordination, equating cooperation with the solution of prisoner's dilemmas. However, in so far as trade depends on property rights, which in turn solve prisoner's dilemmas, albeit sometimes nonvoluntarily, this argument fails: (Loriaux, 2012: 30).

[75] A similar argument is advanced in (Sangiovanni, 2007).

they do not contribute to the production of the basic institutions that make all social primary goods possible.[76] However, surely to the extent they contribute to the production of specific social primary goods, they may be owed reciprocity, and hence egalitarian justice, in respect of *those specific goods*.[77] And indeed, this distinction is clearly reflected in EGC, in the distinction between measures regulating international and domestic economic activity, and the application of egalitarian standards exclusively to the former.[78] It might be objected that this fails to distinguish between cooperation in the production of basic institutions and cooperation under such institutions. However, such an objection is vulnerable to the same challenge posed to Nagel's coercion account in Chapter 2. If cooperation in the production of institutions is limited to those with political agency, or those who voluntarily lend their support, it implies that slave states, and undemocratic regimes more generally, are *ipso facto* not subject to egalitarian duties. If, conversely, cooperation is understood simply in terms of compliance with such institutions, then outsiders cooperate in their maintenance to the extent that they are subject to them, and this revised Participation Objection reduces to the coercion approach, and more specifically, to EGC.[79] Where an institution directly and inclusively coerces me, it necessarily views me as a contributor. I may not sustain the system, but I sustain cooperation thereunder, for the purposes of those with political control over it; and I am due reciprocity in respect of my contribution.[80]

4.3.4   The Agency Objection

The Agency Objection focuses on Rawls's characterization of the basic structure, particularly in his later work, as "the way in which the major social institutions fit together into one system." We might accept that there were international basic institutions in the sense emphasized by the

---

[76] This is itself contestable, both because the international system constitutes the state in important ways (an argument Freeman fails convincingly to refute), and because other goods, arguably necessary for a successful human life, are produced through international activity. On the former point: (Caney, 2008). On the latter: (Armstrong, 2009).

[77] Armstrong terms this the continuum objection: (Armstrong, 2009: 311).

[78] Various authors express concerns about the possibility of such intermediate distributive principles: (Beitz, 1999: 165–167; Freeman, 2007: 315–318; Nagel, 2005: 141).

[79] Caney highlights this dilemma: (Caney, 2008) Cf. (Goodin, 1988: 677).

[80] Freeman might further object that such a partial reciprocity principle lacks an institutional structure to which it can be applied: (Freeman, 2007: 306–308). EGC's distinction between ETMs and DEMs, however, answers this objection.

Impact and Participation objections, but deny that these constitute a basic structure because they do not fit together into one system and, in particular, are not subject to the authority of any one political agent.

This objection arises in two ways

The first emphasizes that distributive principles are normative, in the sense of action-guiding, and as such must be addressed to some agent, and capable of guiding that agent's choices. Domestically, principles are addressed to governments, legislators, and citizens who, whether individually or jointly, control distributive institutions.[81] Internationally, by contrast, distribution is effected by diverse institutions under the control of a large number of disparate political agents.[82] Because distributive principles are concerned with the design of those institutions, the absence of any authoritative agent over them makes such principles inapplicable.[83] Combined with Rawls's assumption, following Kant, that a world state is neither desirable nor feasible, this implies that distributive justice neither applies nor can apply internationally.[84]

The second focuses specifically on the difference principle, emphasizing its complexity, and its consequent dependence on a degree of political agency unique to states.[85] As noted above, for Rawls maintaining background justice requires not only rules applicable to individuals, but also mechanisms for revising those rules and the resulting distributions. No set of rules for individuals could be sufficient: it requires a modern bureaucratic state to do this effectively. Similarly, there is no set of rules that could be acted on by individual states that would maintain background justice internationally. It may be possible, through international institutions, to coordinate the individual policies of states to some degree; but this could not approach the degree of coordination required to implement a global difference principle.[86] Again, combined with the denial of a global state, this suggests the difference principle cannot apply internationally.

Aspects of the Agency Objection are anticipated in the discussion of coercive institutions in Chapter 2, so my conclusions here will be unsurprising. If we accept the constraints on a world state, then the Agency

---

[81] (Freeman, 2007: 314) Cf. (O'Neill, 2000: 7).

[82] This point has already been touched on in §3.3 above.

[83] (Freeman, 2007: 290, 305–307, 316). Waltz makes an analogous point against macro-theory in international politics: (Waltz, 1979: 110). For this point with specific reference to the WTO, albeit expressed in terms of human rights: (Meckled-Garcia, 2014).

[84] (Rawls, 1999) Cf. (Reidy, 2007: 213–215).   [85] (Freeman, 2007: 268, 288).

[86] Ibid., 315–317.

Objection raises insuperable objections to an international difference principle. This does not mean international inequality is not a concern, but it precludes a direct translation from Rawls's domestic theory to global equality. It also precludes reliance on international institutions to maintain background justice and relieve other agents of social justice responsibilities. But EGC does not propose such a move, so I will not consider this point further.

As an objection to distributive principles more generally, however, the Agency Objection is overstated. It can be answered in two ways.

The first denies that the absence of agents capable of acting on a principle constitutes an objection to that principle generally, as opposed to a feasibility constraint on its immediate implementation.[87] The better conclusion, on this view, is that secondary obligations arise, whether on governments or on individuals, to constitute such agents through international cooperation.[88] The Agency Objection fails unless this is impossible, under any plausible conditions. Principles demanding a global state may fail on this basis; but less demanding principles will survive.[89]

The second strategy, which EGC pursues, fits principles to existing agents, rather than constructing agents to fit principles. As Freeman argues, it is states and their domestic basic structures that are primarily responsible for distributive outcomes in the international economy. Those domestic basic structures, however, are subject to identifiable political agents, namely the governments of the relevant states. To the extent principles can be applied directly to them, the Agency Objection fails.[90] EGC, in particular, can be implemented largely through principles addressed to states. International coordination problems remain, but these are less complex than those posed by the difference principle and, as noted earlier, can be addressed through international cooperation. The Agency Objection then becomes not an objection to EGC, but rather a reason for preferring it to alternative principles making implausible demands of international political agency.[91]

---

[87] This reflects Rawls's disagreement with Cohen about justice and principles of social regulation. In the international context: (Buchanan, 2000: 713; Caney, 2008: 495–496).

[88] Recall Rawls's invocation of a natural duty of justice. Cf. (Ronzoni, 2009). We will of course face coordination problems in allocating the duties to constitute such agents, but these are plausibly more tractable than the problems of coordinating distribution in their absence.

[89] On the limits of distributive justice without a state: (Dufek, 2013).

[90] For a similar move: (Blake, 2013: 112).

[91] Meckled-Garcia objects to claims that persons/states/international institutions violate human rights through causing global poverty, arguing that economic outcomes are

It thus appears that, regardless of how we interpret the basic structure objection, it does not constitute a plausible objection to EGC.

4.4   National Priority and Global Justice

A third potential objection to EGC invokes the special duties that we owe to our compatriots. Many people hold that we owe such duties, over and above those we owe to persons generally. These duties, critics might object, provide an alternative basis for justifying measures, including ETMs, which EGC overlooks. This section serves to rebut that objection.

Special duties to compatriots are defended on various grounds, but the most challenging refer to the particular value of conationality.[92] Unlike other views that recognize different duties within and between states, nationalists stand out in characterizing special duties to conationals as a fundamental starting point in thinking about justice beyond the state. The most sophisticated exponent of this view and its implications for global justice is David Miller.[93] I therefore focus on Miller in addressing the compatibility of nationalist views with EGC.[94]

---

multicausal and, absent a specific link, we cannot attribute responsibility for particular outcomes to particular agents or institutions: (Meckled-Garcia, 2014). EGC avoids much of this objection by emphasizing the justification of particular measures. While its DEM proviso, like other rights-based principles, may be exposed to this objection, integrating basic rights with egalitarian considerations and an emphasis on the justification of specific measures limits its significance.

[92] For alternative approaches: (Beitz, 1983; Goodin, 1988; Hurka, 1997; McMahan, 1997; Miller, 2010: 31–57; Primoratz, 2008). Obviously EGC, and indeed moderate accounts of global justice generally, ultimately endorse a distinction between duties to compatriots and outsiders. However, unlike the views considered in this section, they do so as a conclusion of arguments about global justice, rather than seeing priority as either a premise or an objection.

[93] (Miller, 2007). See also (Miller, 1995, 2009, 2011) Cf. (Miller, 1999b).

[94] I do not necessarily claim that Miller would disagree with the arguments here. He has himself recognized that his approach may not answer how benefits of international trade or costs of environmental protection should be divided: (Miller, 2009: 306). His views on international economic regulation are not developed in detail, but include the idea that poor countries "must be given reasonable opportunities to develop, and [allowed] to choose between different policies for achieving this." This is interpreted as requiring that international institutions not impose rigid guidelines on developing countries, and that they be granted broad market access by developed countries without being required to similarly open their own markets: (Miller, 2007: 253). The basis of these prescriptions, which appear in a discussion of international justice as grounded solely on human rights, is unclear in Miller's account. However, he would presumably reject any suggestion that they are motivated by global egalitarianism.

Before examining the relationship between Miller's position and EGC, we must first understand what that position is. Miller argues that individuals owe special duties to their conationals, such that it is legitimate for them to prefer the interests of their conationals over similarly placed foreigners, in appropriate circumstances. Acknowledging such duties, he suggests, is intrinsic to conationality.[95] Ethics and justice, on this view, are fundamentally linked to particular interpersonal relations.[96] Those relations generate obligations, and the different relationships between conationals and foreigners mean that thick duties of egalitarian social justice, which apply domestically, are simply inappropriate internationally.[97] Global justice, on this view, is sufficientarian rather than egalitarian.[98]

This reflects Miller's commitment to a particularist rather than universalist ethics generally; relations between persons matter at a basic level in identifying their moral obligations.[99] The same situation may impose different obligations and require different responses from different persons, depending on their relationships. We need to understand the context in which a person is acting, and their relations to the particular others involved, before we can say what moral obligations apply to them. On this view, impartiality as an ethical ideal means, not treating all persons equally, but rather acting faithfully on the moral reasons that apply to us.[100] There is therefore nothing problematic about giving priority to the interests of those with whom we share special relationships. Partiality is only problematic where it involves treating persons favorably in ways not justified by such particular reasons and relations.[101] Nationality is one such morally significant relationship, which shapes the moral landscape in which individuals act and justifies treating conationals and nonnationals differently.[102]

---

[95] (Miller, 1995: 49).   [96] Ibid., 50.   [97] Ibid., 8–70.   [98] Ibid., 73–75.

[99] Ibid., 49–58. See also (Tamir, 1993: 106). On the limits of this approach, and the error of subjectivism: (McMahan, 1997: 112).

[100] (Miller, 1995: 53–54).   [101] Ibid., 54.

[102] Miller thus characterizes as question-begging cosmopolitan claims that nationality is morally arbitrary: (Miller, 2011: 165–166). The source of nationality's moral significance is, however, unclear. In so far as Miller's particularism attributes fundamental moral significance to social relations, he implicitly denies that their importance needs explanation in other terms. For two competing discussions of potential bases for national priority: (Goodin, 1988; McMahan, 1997). For an argument grounding priority in the role of national communities in constituting moral agency: (MacIntyre, 1984). A particularly instructive non-reductionist account of special responsibilities is: (Scheffler, 1997).

This contrasts with EGC's universalist conceptions of persons and peoples. Indeed, the kind of abstraction from particular identities and contexts that EGC pursues makes little sense in an approach like Miller's. Miller does accept a limited sense of cosmopolitan equality, that all human beings are due moral consideration "of some kind," and that this involves treating their claims equally "in some sense."[103] However, he is careful to avoid equating equality of consideration with identity of treatment. This equality does not preclude treating different groups differently; rather, it precludes treating them differently without giving any grounds for the unequal treatment.[104] This translates into accepting the moral equality of suffering at home and abroad, while maintaining that responsibility for remedying that suffering may be distributed differently to different agents.[105] The special relationship in which I stand towards conationals means that I have a special responsibility to them, which justifies my prioritizing their interests over those of nonnationals.[106]

The nature of the priority required will vary depending on the relevant relationship.[107] Some duties apply entirely apart from such special relationships, but these are limited to human rights and non-oppression.[108] These duties arise from the relations we all stand in towards each other, simply in virtue of our shared humanity. Individuals then incur additional duties arising by virtue their particular relationships with others, the content of those additional duties being determined by the nature of the relevant relationships.[109] In the context of national priority, we look

---

[103] (Miller, 2007: 27). While some particularly strong nationalists might deny even this, the bulk of the literature accepts it.

[104] (Miller, 2007: 28).   [105] Ibid., 28–29.

[106] Miller's reconciliation of universalism and particularism thus seems to drain universalism of any force. MacIntyre argues any reconciliation that gives universalism significant weight must fundamentally compromise nationalism: (MacIntyre, 1984: 6).

[107] (Miller, 1995: 66) Cf. (McMahan, 1997: 118; Scheffler, 2001: 51).

[108] For Miller's account of human rights and the continuing relevance of national priority: (Miller, 1995: 73–80, 2007: 163–200). For an account focusing on the duty of non-oppression: (Miller, 1999a). On the difficulty of reconciling priority with more demanding background duties: (Arneson, 2005).

[109] Miller does not claim that special relationships are the only basis on which duties of distributive justice may be grounded. He acknowledges that participation in schemes of cooperation and the need to justify coercion provide additional bases for distributive justice, arguing that neither of these, nor special relationships considered on their own, can provide necessary and sufficient conditions for the application of social justice principles. In the domestic context, it is the overlapping civic, political, and national structures that ground social justice: (Miller, 2009). Elsewhere, Miller has argued that different distributive relationships apply in solidaristic, instrumental, and civic

to the public culture and common understandings of the relevant national groups to identify this. In so far as these cultures and understandings vary, the specific obligations that members acknowledge towards each other will similarly vary.[110] However, there is an immutable core to the special concern for conationals, including responsibilities "to support one another and to preserve [the] community."[111]

How might we reconcile this approach with EGC, which starts from moral universalism?

First, note that Miller's position does not require treating nationals and nonnationals differently in all contexts. Rather, this depends on whether the relevant "ethically sanctioned rules and procedures" call for the claims of two individuals to be treated equally or not; whether they fall into the same category *for the purposes of the relevant decision*. Miller does not elaborate on when a particular group may be relevant; but implicit in his approach is a recognition that not all groups will be relevant for all purposes.[112]

Tamir, whose account of national priority parallels Miller's, develops this point, arguing that the "morality of community" justifies preferring members over nonmembers where they "belong to the group relevant to the action in question."[113] Which groups are relevant will vary depending on the action in question: thus, she suggests, shared political affiliation and family connections will play different roles in deciding how to vote, as against whether to donate a kidney.[114]

Therefore, while accepting Miller's argument for national priority, we might consistently conclude that this applies to some decisions, but is

---

associations. He characterizes national communities as solidaristic, while citizens are in a civic relation to one another: (Miller, 1999b: 25–32). However, it is on special relationships that he grounds his defense of nationalism, so these are my focus here.

[110] (Miller, 1995: 66).

[111] (Miller, 2007: 40). MacIntyre similarly emphasizes communal preservation as motivating priority: (MacIntyre, 1984: 6–7). Of course, given EGC's self-determination proviso, it is difficult to see how it could conflict with this hard core. See further the discussion in Chapter 5.

[112] The subject-matter scope of priority is emphasized by various scholars. Thus, Primoratz, while generally skeptical of priority, sees its proper scope as a key question: (Primoratz, 2008). Goodin addresses this in terms of relationships as both magnifiers and multipliers of duties: (Goodin, 1988). Pogge examines priority in terms of both degree and scope, suggesting that human rights identify one scope limit, while leaving open whether others apply: (Pogge, 1997: 465, 471). Miller himself gives basic human rights an important role in determining what priority is appropriate, albeit denying that we must choose the basic rights of foreigners over the needs of compatriots: (Miller, 1995: 74–80, 2000: 177, 2007: 231–261).

[113] (Tamir, 1993: 114).   [114] Ibid., 114.

irrelevant to others.[115] We need to examine what groups (if any) are salient in each case. For example, as a private individual, I might prefer my conationals in making charitable donations, but it may seem improper to prefer them in making employment decisions, or in deciding to whom to provide services.[116] In these examples, it seems, the nature of the good being distributed determines what groups are relevant. Some goods are by their nature distributed having regard to special relationships, while others require some other distributive principle[117].

We might alternatively distinguish based on the capacity in which individuals act. We commonly expect that an individual acting in a public (qua public official) or quasi-fiduciary (qua agent, employee, company director etc.) capacity should consider different factors to those they might consider when acting in a private capacity.[118] Miller's archetypal example of a special duty, that of a parent towards their child, exhibits this quality.[119] Miller argues that, where a child goes missing, a father has an overwhelming moral reason to devote all of his time and energy to finding that child. But if that father is also a Chief Constable, the parental relationship is surely of secondary relevance in deciding how he should make use of the powers and resources at his disposal. If two children are missing, Miller presumably would not claim that there was any duty on the Chief Constable, in his capacity as Chief Constable, to prioritize the search for his own child.[120] We might not blame him if he did, but this is

---

[115]   Miller recognizes this point in his discussion of human rights: (Miller, 2007: 48–49). This is the only case where I am aware Miller expressly recognizes a limit on the scope, as opposed to the degree, of national priority. However, some such limit is also presumably implicit in his reference to duties arising from reciprocity and coercion, discussed at fn. 109 above.

[116]   Such a distinction commonly appears in anti-discrimination legislation.

[117]   Walzer's claim that different distributive criteria apply to different social goods, and that the appropriate distributive criterion is a function of the social meaning of the relevant good, suggests a similar conclusion: (Walzer, 1983: 9). Miller elsewhere adopts Walzer's analysis on this point: (Miller, 2000: 169–170).

[118]   Administrative laws impose strict requirements on the matters to which public decision-makers have regard. Similarly, agency and company laws require agents/directors to avoid conflicts of interest, and to act in the best interests of their principals/companies, without regard for their own priorities. While drawing different conclusions, Pogge highlights the importance of such role relations in thinking about priority and special relationships: (Pogge, 1997). Sangiovanni interprets Nagel's argument from coercion as expressing such quasi-fiduciary duties: (Sangiovanni, 2012: 103–107).

[119]   (Miller, 2007: 29).

[120]   Miller notes that "there are some agents, for instance the police, who should devote equal resources to finding the child in all instances." My point here is that police officers are also persons, with morally significant relationships, but in their capacity as police

because we understand why he has failed in his duty of impartiality, not because we think he has acted properly.[121] In making decisions qua Chief Constable, and in determining how to allocate public resources, impartiality requires considering the needs of each member of the public equally, without regard to any personal relationships.[122]

How does all this relate to EGC? In Chapter 3, I showed how, within a broadly Rawlsian framework, we can distinguish distinctive justificatory considerations relating to ETMs. That discussion did not address the role of nationality and special relations. However, those same considerations can distinguish ETMs as measures in respect of which national priority is not appropriate; and the distinction can be restated in terms found in these theories.

Consider, first, the nature of the good being distributed. ETMs by definition regulate international economic activity, distributing opportunities in the international economy. These are not goods that are within the exclusive power and control of any national community. Under autarchy, one might argue that each nation had an exclusive right to control its own domestic market; but existing conditions of economic integration mean it is not clear what that would mean. We can no longer conceive of the global economy as merely a cumulation of discrete national economies, each of which is the exclusive concern of the relevant nation. Nor, however, need we regard the global economy as an undifferentiated whole, such that all economic activity takes place in the same

---

officers, we expect them to bracket those relationships and act impartially in their public role. (Miller, 2007: 29).

[121] Pogge, in discussing national priority, assumes that some partiality is permitted to public officials, and proposes human rights as a possible limit. However, the better view is that, to the extent we accept any partiality by public officials, we regard it as an excuse rather than a justification. Pogge's analysis is confused by his conflation of citizens, political representatives and public office-holders, and by his concern to identify duties of impartiality as binding the first two categories as such. In fact, in our political practice we generally distinguish between these. Thus, a political representative might be expected to show strong priority for his constituents when acting as such; but once appointed as a minister, such priority would cease to be appropriate. Limits on partiality undoubtedly apply in each case; but the fact that a person acts *qua* office-holder imposes stricter requirements (Pogge, 1997).

[122] Miller's discussion of social justice in the domestic context is also instructive. In distinguishing between solidarist, instrumental, and civic associations, each subject to different distributive principles, he recognizes that the capacity in which an individual acts will impose different duties on him, such that the same individual might be required to prioritize their fellow members in one context, while this would be inappropriate in another: (Miller, 1999b: 28–35). The capacity in which an agent acts also seems to explain Tamir's example of friendship in hiring decisions: (Tamir, 1993: 111).

space, and all regulatory measures can be regarded as acting on some part of that space. It makes more sense to conceive of both aggregated domestic economies, which continue to have their own discrete character; and a conceptually distinct but practically integrated international economy, which is shared between the disparate nations that participate in it, without any nation having a claim on any discrete part of it.[123] In so far as this is the case, when a nation acts to regulate any part of the international economy, whether allocating opportunities or setting standards, it is distributing a good over which it does not have exclusive title. Where it acts in respect of its own economy, it can properly prefer its own nationals; but when it acts on the international economy, its actions must be judged by a standard that is impartial between all of those who share in that economy.

Alternatively, we might look to the nature of the choices being made and the capacity in which they are made. ETMs express choices about the allocation of opportunities between nationals and foreigners; or choices to trade off the good of one against another, including imposing costs on foreigners in order to provide goods to conationals. These are quintessentially external, and by analogy public, actions, in contrast to domestic measures that are internal and by analogy private.[124] When a state acts to regulate the international economy, its action is not simply an exercise of domestic authority, a private act in which it may legitimately prefer the interests of nationals; rather, it is an international quasi-public act, analogous to the action of an agent or officeholder in the domestic setting.[125] It acts as a trustee for the collective participants therein, and the relevant group whose interests it must consider is wider than simply its own nationals.

If either of these arguments is accepted, it provides a basis for distinguishing ETMs from other measures that a state adopts, such that we can

---

[123] Gravity model studies of size, distance and borders provide some empirical support for this mixed model. E.g. (McCallum, 1995).

[124] An analogy can be drawn to immigration decisions, another case where the interests of foreigners are directly traded off against those of conationals. Abizadeh argues the coercion border controls exert over outsiders means they require democratic justification towards both insiders and outsiders: (Abizadeh, 2008). While Miller rejects Abizadeh's specific claims about democratic justification, he seems to accept that such measures raise particular justificatory demands: (Miller, 2010: 115).

[125] The idea that exercises of foreign and domestic power are subject to distinct considerations appears implicit in Rawls's discussion of war powers: (Rawls, 1999: 26–27). Polanyi highlights both the historical distinctness of international and domestic markets, and the ways the former predate the latter: (Polanyi, 2001: 61–68). Cf. (Graeber, 2011).

maintain the appropriateness of national priority, while still judging ETMs by a globally egalitarian standard.

Proponents of national priority might here object that distinguishing an area in which priority is permissible from one where it is not is insufficient, without addressing the content of the priority claim, and the reasons for it. Otherwise, we risk reconciling EGC not with national priority in its valuable sense, but rather a diluted, universalist shadow.[126] However, given the arguments advanced for national priority, this objection seems ill founded. If there is a hard core of national priority, it is in the areas of mutual support and national preservation. But to the extent these are in issue, the self-determination proviso will exempt the relevant measures. Beyond this, some element of priority may be necessary to express the valuable relations between conationals, to maintain trust and community, or to express gratitude and reciprocity (taking three common arguments); but these cannot specify the particular areas where priority is appropriate, and so cannot ground this objection.

A nationalist might still assert, following Miller, that priority in some area simply is an incident of membership in their particular national community. To the extent this reflects a strong moral relativism, which reads moral obligation directly off the particular norms of a given community, I know of no way to answer it on its own terms. However, to the extent that its proponent seeks to universalize this claim, addressing it to outsiders by invoking the value of national cultures and communities, it similarly falls under the self-determination proviso, and in particular the instrumental argument for self-determination, with the limits that implies.[127] If, on the other hand, the argument is not universalized in this way, then its force cannot extend beyond the relevant group, and it has no role to play in either the justification or the (third party) evaluation of such measures.[128] National priority thus constitutes no objection to EGC.

4.5   Further Statist Objections

As well as a positive case for national priority, Miller advances two negative arguments against global egalitarianism, which he labels the metric and dynamic problems. Both have been challenged directly[129]; I

---

[126] (MacIntyre, 1984: 6).   [127] See further §5.4 below.

[128] That "radically particularist" arguments lose purchase in this way is noted in: (McMahan, 1997: 110). Cf. (Caney, 2005: 32; Franck, 1995: 16–18).

[129] (Holtug, 2011). With regard to the metric problem: (Butt, 2012: 10–11).

do not do so here. Rather, regardless of their force as objections to cosmopolitan egalitarianism more generally, I show that neither constitutes an objection to EGC.

4.5.1   The Metric Problem

The metric problem claims global egalitarianism is incoherent because there is no plausible metric in which to make the comparative judgments it requires; if there is no way to compare the positions of two persons, then we cannot take steps towards equalizing those positions.[130] The objection is developed against two common conceptions of global egalitarianism: equality of resources and equality of opportunity.[131] Neither, Miller argues, provides a credible metric for the good it claims to distribute. As regards equality of resources, he focuses on the disparate nature of global resources, the significant social component in resource value (particularly land values), and the extent to which value is added to resources through local factors.[132] As regards equality of opportunity, he first argues that this must mean access to equivalent opportunity sets, rather than identical opportunities.[133] However, he suggests, equivalence is indeterminate in this context. Judging equivalence requires a thick set of cultural understandings about what opportunities are equivalent to one another. These shared understandings only exist to a sufficient degree within national communities, forming part of their public culture.[134] In cases of radical disparity, he concedes it may be possible to conclude that the opportunity set available in one community is on all measures larger than that available in another (Miller uses the examples of France and Niger). However, in most cases such a judgment requires a fine-grained understanding of the value and meaning of particular goods that simply cannot be made across disparate cultures.[135]

---

[130] (Miller, 2007: 56–68).

[131] On the metric problem and equality of opportunity: (Brock, 2009: 58–63). Some anti-cosmopolitan implications of the metric problem for natural resources are addressed in: (Miller, 2012: 258–264). As Holtug observes, metric problems are not limited to global justice. For an overview: (Gosepath, 2011 §3).

[132] (Miller, 2007: 51–62).

[133] (Miller, 2007: 62–63). In fact, at least some cosmopolitans would deny this. E.g. (Moellendorf, 2002).

[134] (Miller, 2007: 64–66). Garcia suggests there is an emergent global community expressing at least some such shared meanings: (Garcia, 2013: 38).

[135] Ibid., 67–68. This reflects Walzer's claim that we must understand "what [a social good] is, what it means to those for whom it is a good" before we can know "how, by whom, and

Can we accept these arguments, while still defending EGC? EGC does not require equalizing either resources or opportunities. Rather, it requires that ETMs should pursue equality of opportunity. We might hope that this would make problems of measurement less urgent. However, we still need some means of measuring opportunity sets across borders to determine whether a measure meets this standard, so does Miller's objection not still apply?

I believe the objection can be avoided on at least three grounds.

First, note that ETMs are, by definition, concerned with the regulation of economic activity. This may interact with a range of educational, cultural, and social goods, but it is defined by its economic character. As such, it may be possible to apply EGC without engaging with the kinds of contested value questions that Miller identifies. While ETMs may have secondary effects on the distribution of other goods, their primary effect is distributing economic opportunities. As such, it is economic opportunity, whether measured in per capita GDP or some other suitable economic unit, that is the appropriate metric for these purposes.[136] Such opportunities are of largely instrumental value; but they are important prerequisites to thicker measures of intrinsic value, such as capabilities.[137] Economic goods constitute the material basis for social goods, even while they also depend on them.[138] We therefore make international

---

for what reasons it ought to be distributed": (Walzer, 1983: 9). For Miller, such understanding is a prerequisite for comparison. Cf. (Miller, 2000: 168–169).

[136] Both GDP and GNP are rightly criticized as measures of development, reflecting as they do economic activity without any sensitivity to distributive considerations, or noneconomic aspects of development. E.g. (Sen, 1999: 43–51). While flawed as metrics of development, they provide reasonable proxies for the absolute size of per capita opportunity sets within a community. As discussed below, how opportunities are distributed within a community is a matter of domestic social justice. In a radically unequal society with high per capita GDP, most persons will have relatively limited opportunities. However, this need not reflect any international injustice; rather, it reflects a failure of domestic justice (albeit that failure might be traced further back to the international system). One merit of these metrics is that they avoid problems of valuing "potential" or noninstrumental resources, and thus undermining local understandings about their role and value: (Moore, 2012: 93–94). Further, by applying them at the level of communities, we avoid the objection that a focus on opportunities misses important considerations of equality of status: (Brock, 2009: 60–61).

[137] (Sen, 1999: 87).

[138] Ibid., 90–92. Capabilities, social primary goods, and any other unit that is directly relevant to persons' lives, are of course a function of both domestic and international factors. We do not expect a comparison in terms of GDP to tell us much about the wellbeing of individuals in the states concerned. However, in so far as our concern is justice at the international level, we can bracket these domestic factors. They may give rise both to claims of justice domestically, and indeed to international claims where these

comparisons in economic terms, both because what is exchanged is the bare economic good, and because those economic goods are translated within states into Miller's incommensurable social goods.

Second, many of the disparate goods that Miller discusses (education, employment, religious facilities, recreation) require, for their provision, both economic activity and economic choice. While not readily fungible in the short term, over the medium term the disparate provision of opportunities for (to take Miller's example) education and recreation within a community reflect to a significant degree choices made by individuals and public authorities to prioritize one good or the other. (Should a local authority build a public swimming pool or increase funding to the public school system?) Provision of particular goods will also be shaped by external factors (England's university system benefits from the global success of the English language. Portuguese leisure opportunities are enhanced by a clement climate.). However, where one good is provided to a greater extent than another, this will generally be a function of social choice.[139] Indeed, such choices are at the core of national self-determination. By contrast, the goods with which Miller is concerned all require for their provision some degree of economic development. Before a community can choose to build a school or a church, it must first accumulate sufficient capital for construction, and expect sufficient revenues to cover running costs. The international economy does not directly distribute either schools or churches; it distributes the opportunity for communities to provide themselves with whichever goods they deem necessary. Conceding Miller's claim, it may not be possible directly to compare the opportunity sets of specific individuals in different communities, and thereby implement a general redistributive principle of equality of opportunity; but if the absolute size of opportunity sets within a community in the medium term is a function of economic activity, then this need not be a barrier to applying EGC as an evaluative principle to determine the justice of international economic regulation.

Third, and related, the structure of international economic regulation is substantially statist in character. The WTO agreements do not directly regulate international trade; rather, they regulate measures states adopt to regulate trade. While ETMs can obviously affect individual traders, it is

---

are necessary for their remedy; but they are not relevant to the comparison proposed by EGC.

[139] The explanatory nationalist thesis, to which Miller is partially committed, relies on this assumption.

at the level of industries and national economies that their effects primarily manifest.[140] In an important sense, ETMs and their regulation are not about the opportunities of individuals, but rather the opportunities for economic activity and development of industries, communities, and entire states.[141] EGC is limited in its field of application, and even within that field, its scope is limited by a reasonable principle of self-determination. This recognizes that it is for each community, acting together, to regulate matters within its exclusive concern.[142] It is domestic policies that most directly distribute resources and opportunities to individuals and, except in so far as they address international activity, diversity in those decisions is compatible with EGC. In short, international economic regulation does not distribute opportunities to individuals; it distributes them among self-determining national communities, which in turn distribute them to their members.[143] This is a stylized account, but its central point holds. Opportunity sets might be equally distributed at the international level, while unjust domestic policies create radical inequality within a given country, as a result of elites monopolizing opportunities; while this no doubt constitutes an injustice towards the excluded individuals, that injustice exists at the domestic rather than the international level.[144] If self-determination is to be respected, EGC can

---

[140] This reflects the fungibility of both production and consumption opportunities. Whether the appropriate unit of analysis is individual, firm, industry, factor of production, or state will presumably vary depending on the particular measure at issue. The literature on the determinants of protection may be instructive here: (Rodrik, 1995). For present purposes it suffices to note that, in an effective state, the first four are subject to the distributive choices of the fifth, a feature Buchanan labels distributional autonomy. In other contexts, assuming fungibility might beg the question the metric problem raises. However, we are here concerned with economic activity, and hence with instrumental rather than intrinsic value. To the extent noninstrumental values are implicated, these can be addressed under the self-determination proviso.

[141] Petersmann defends a contrasting view, defending restrictions on trade policy as protecting the market freedoms of individuals. However, this remains a minority and contested view, relying on an account of fundamental market freedoms that is incompatible with contemporary left-liberalism, including in particular the Rawlsian approach on which I draw: (Petersmann, 2002). Cf. (Alston, 2002; Howse, 2002d; Tomasi, 2012).

[142] See further Chapter 5.

[143] Cf. (Freeman, 2007: 310). In so far as EGC identifies a privileged sphere in which communities can distribute goods in accordance with their meanings for members, nationalists have good reason to support this view. What EGC denies is that these locally held meanings are determinative of measures distributing opportunities internationally.

[144] This does not preclude outsiders having obligations to remedy that injustice, whether because it is a function of international institutions, or simply by virtue of its victims' shared humanity. However, such obligations do not fall under EGC. For the former argument: (Pogge, 2002). For the latter: (Caney, 2005).

only directly address the distribution of opportunities *between* peoples. It is the total opportunity set available to such peoples that then becomes the working metric; and while economic activity is not the same as opportunity, at the national level standard economic metrics are a plausible proxy for these purposes.[145] This does not alter the underlying individualist concern expressed in EGC. ETMs are justified to the extent they pursue global equality of individual opportunity, by improving the position of the globally least advantaged. However, EGC's application to a statist international system and its interaction with peoples' domestic basic structures leads us to focus in practice on aggregate measures of economic activity at the level of states.[146]

This last point highlights a further attraction of EGC: as developed here it is relatively agnostic about the way peoples, including in particular nonliberal peoples, organize their domestic affairs. As such, it avoids many of the objections of moral chauvinism that might be advanced against a more intrusive view.[147]

4.5.2   The Dynamic Problem

The dynamic problem arises where the different decisions taken by different nations, as to economic policy, resource allocation, levels of investment and a multitude of other factors, result in differing rates of economic growth or contraction.[148] A commitment to self-determination requires that states have at least some control over these decisions[149]; but their result is that, even if two nations initially have equal access to opportunities and resources, over time their different choices are likely to

---

A further question is whether an ETM adopted by a domestically inegalitarian state can be justified under EGC. I think it can, for one of two reasons: (i) it is for domestic governments, within a reasonably wide margin of appreciation, to determine their path to development, and this may require inegalitarian policies to develop the forces of production before more egalitarian policies become possible; (ii) even absent long term egalitarian motivations, the possibility of subsequent political change may make any measures that increase national wealth in less-advantaged states ultimately egalitarian in their effects.

[145] See the discussion at notes 136, 138, and 140 above.

[146] Buchanan highlights both the relation between individual opportunity and aggregate wealth, and the way international and domestic distribution of opportunities interact: (Buchanan, 2000: 711).

[147] I touch further in Chapter 5 on the extent to which intervention in the affairs of other peoples might be relevant to EGC, and the conception of self-determination I endorse.

[148] See generally: (Miller, 2000: ch. 10, 2007: 68–75).   [149] (Miller, 2000: 163–164).

upset this equality.[150] Further, this is not simply a matter of brute luck; the implications of different policies for economic development are often predictable, while investment decisions may reflect preferences for present consumption over future growth. Miller is committed to holding nations responsible for their choices, and hence argues it is unfair that one should subsidize another for the predictable results of its own choices, especially if this means subsidizing historically higher levels of consumption.[151] As well as the fairness problems, this creates perverse incentives towards overconsumption.[152]

As a problem of fairness, this depends for its force on a strong commitment to national responsibility; if the units of analysis are individuals then it only arises for those committed to defending inherited wealth, which will exclude most liberals.[153] As a problem of perverse incentives, global egalitarians reply that it can be addressed at the point of implementation without undermining egalitarianism as a fundamental principle.[154]

We need not adjudicate these questions here. At most, the dynamic problem challenges principles that redistribute resources and opportunities among national groups without regard to the existing distribution, or the reasons why that distribution came about.[155] Because EGC is not such a principle, it is not vulnerable to this objection.

EGC evaluates ETMs by reference to a globally egalitarian standard. As developed further in later chapters, this implies some priority for less advantaged over more advantaged peoples in the international economy. It precludes measures that shift the benefits of international commerce in favor of wealthier peoples, while permitting those that benefit less advantaged peoples. However, this is an advantage in distributing the benefits of international cooperation, rather than an attempt to equalize the

---

[150] For the analogous claim challenging domestic egalitarianism: (Nozick, 1974: 160–164).

[151] Rawls makes a parallel argument: (Rawls, 1999: 117–119) Cf. (Freeman, 2007: 290–291, 312–313). Martin reads the dynamic problem as Rawls's principal argument against global equality: (Martin, 2006: 228). Other proponents include: (Cappelen et al., 2007).

[152] (Miller, 2007: 71).

[153] This is a standard challenge to Rawls's account of the dynamic problem. See e.g. (Tan, 2004: 73). Unlike Rawls, Miller provides a clear theoretical defense of national responsibility, thus strengthening this argument. While some degree of collective responsibility is an upshot of the view that I defend, this is so only in order to realize the distinct good of self-determination. It is not intrinsically valued in the way that Miller argues, and that Rawls seems to assume. See further the discussion in Chapter 5.

[154] (Holtug, 2011: 157).

[155] This recalls Rawls's distinction between distributive and allocative principles: (Rawls, 2001: 50).

position of persons or peoples. If we accept Miller's assumption that less advantaged peoples are so through their own choices, this might ground a presumption against compensating them fully for the consequences of those choices; but it need not preclude all attempts to prioritize their interests or facilitate their recovery. Those who, at the domestic level, accept any claims of social justice beyond bare starting-gate equality should see no contradiction in prioritizing the interests of less wealthy nations while recognizing (for the sake of argument) that their economic condition is their own doing.[156] To the extent EGC reflects such intuitions, I have argued for it in Chapter 3; my concern here is only to show that the dynamic problem does not undermine it.

As an argument about practicalities and perverse incentives, the dynamic problem similarly does not challenge EGC. EGC does not equalize the positions of less advantaged and more advantaged peoples. Large inequalities would likely persist in a world that was fully just by this standard, whether because of domestic factors, or international factors other than ETMs. As such, a people that chose to consume instead of investing, or whose economy stagnated as a result of poor economic choices, could not invoke EGC to demand resource transfers from more prudent peoples. EGC respects the choices of both more successful and less successful peoples, allowing the former to enjoy the fruits of their success, and the latter to take responsibility for their own failures. In so far as perverse incentives result, their effects will be minimal. In marginal cases, a people might choose a lower level of development, while benefiting from EGC, over pursuing growth and, eventually, dispensing with those benefits.[157] However, unlike the unqualified egalitarianism that Miller criticizes, the "free-riding" nation in these circumstances will remain at a lower level of economic development. International economic regulation is only one factor determining economic growth, so EGC will not generate equality of resources or opportunities unless combined with prudent domestic policy choices by less advantaged

---

[156] Thus, recall that Rawls's difference principle is sensitive to the distribution of social goods, but insensitive to the reasons for that distribution. (Rawls, 1971: 75–80). Anderson highlights the weaknesses of luck egalitarianism compared to a view largely (though not entirely) insensitive to the self-inflicted nature of many inequalities: (E. S. Anderson, 1999). I do not argue that either approach is directly applicable in the international context. However, both suggest there is nothing contradictory in recognizing an inequality as self-inflicted and seeing reasons of justice to ameliorate it.

[157] Studies of graduation under GSP schemes highlight the effects immediate withdrawal of preferred status can have, suggesting at least some potential perverse incentives. E.g. (Stevens et al., 2011).

peoples (and a host of other factors that may be outside the control of either international regulation or domestic policy). Peoples hoping to enjoy high standards of living must still therefore choose responsible policies to bring this about.

Thus, neither in principle nor practice is the dynamic problem an objection to EGC. One further point merits mention, however. The discussion here has assumed for the sake of argument that the determinants of growth are primarily domestic, and that peoples can be regarded as responsible for their economic performance. This claim, which Pogge labels "explanatory nationalism," is essential in motivating the dynamic problem. However, it is also heavily contested.[158] If, by contrast, economic development is significantly externally determined, it makes less sense to suggest peoples take responsibility for it.[159] I do not claim to resolve this issue here; it remains a contested question among economists, but it must surely be economics, rather than law or political theory, that is best placed to answer it.[160] Note, however, that EGC will have egalitarian effects only to the extent international factors are relevant to economic success. If economic development was purely a function of domestic factors, EGC would have negligible effects, and the dynamic problem becomes irrelevant. If, however, economic development is significantly shaped by international factors, then nations cannot be held wholly responsible for their own success, and can reasonably expect the international factors shaping their prospects to be arranged to their benefit.

4.6   Conclusion

This chapter has continued the case for EGC. Whereas in Chapter 3, I advanced a positive case for that view, this chapter has been largely defensive. I have sought to address potential objections from various statist perspectives, and thereby to strengthen the case for EGC. In each

---

[158] When Miller first introduces this claim, he accepts that it "is not, in general, a very realistic assumption": (Miller, 2007: 69, 239–244). However, he accepts its importance in establishing the dynamic problem, and in later sections seems to adopt it as part of his position. Rawls, in developing the same argument, provides even less support for his crucial empirical claim that the causes of a people's wealth are domestic in origin: (Rawls, 1999: 108–111, 117).

[159] For arguments along these lines: (Caney, 2005: 129; Pogge, 2002; Tan, 2004: 70–72).

[160] A prominent recent contribution emphasizing domestic factors is: (Acemoglu & Robinson, 2012).

case, I have sought to argue that, whatever the merits of the relevant positions generally, they constituted no objection to EGC.

One significant issue remains to be addressed to complete the normative elaboration of EGC. This is the scope of the "reasonable principle of self-determination" to which I have suggested EGC is subject. I touched on self-determination at various points in the previous chapters. However, in the next chapter, I make it my focus, in order fully to elaborate this proviso, before proceeding in subsequent chapters to examine the relation between EGC and the positive law of the trade regime.

5

Self-Determination and External Trade Measures

5.1 Introduction

In the previous chapter, I examined arguments invoking what we might broadly label statist or sovereigntist concerns, whether grounded in Hobbesian, Rawlsian, or Nationalist views. However, I did not address what is perhaps the most obvious value grounding sovereignty, namely self-determination. The reason for this omission is that, unlike the other positions considered, self-determination is incorporated as a proviso to EGC. As such, the question it poses is not whether self-determination constitutes an objection to EGC, but rather what is the scope of the proviso so incorporated. This does not mean, of course, that self-determination cannot pose problems for EGC. Most obviously, in order for EGC to remain an interesting principle, the self-determination proviso cannot be too broad, or EGC will simply collapse into its proviso. If any economic measure could be justified under self-determination, then there would be nothing left to say. It is therefore necessary to identify the proper scope of this proviso. That is the task of this chapter.

My concern here is not with self-determination in general. Rather, it is with self-determination as a justification of measures adopted by states. The argument in earlier chapters proceeded on the basis that measures require to be justified. We might expect that justifications offered to outsiders will often invoke self-determination: either "this measure is an exercise of our self-determination" or "this measure is necessary to preserve our self-determination." What we need to know is when these justifications in fact apply. In what circumstance can we, or can we not, invoke self-determination as an adequate justification of our measures to outsiders? And in particular, when might such claims suffice to justify ETMs under EGC's self-determination proviso?

Before trying to answer these questions, it is worth briefly recalling a distinction that I drew in Chapter 3, between two ways that self-determination might be relevant to the justification of a measure: where the measure is an exercise of self-determination; and where it is necessary to protect self-determination.[1]

Consider first the claim to exercise self-determination: the state adopting the measure is acting for its own reasons, whatever those may be; and self-determination provides a ground for justifying the measure to outsiders, as falling within a privileged domain of choice, where the state is entitled to act on its own reasons, and outsiders are not entitled to second guess these.[2]

This contrasts with the claim to protect self-determination: here, the state adopting the measure is acting to protect a value, self-determination, that is threatened in some way; and because both insiders and outsiders recognize the value of self-determination, and their equal claim to it, the protection of that value provides a sufficient justification for the particular measure adopted. Rather than acting on reasons that are its own to choose, the regulating state is acting in pursuit of the shared value of self-determination, albeit in respect of itself.

These are two distinct claims, with quite different structures. I suggested in Chapter 3 that DEMs could generally be justified under a claim of the first kind, whereas, to the extent ETMs could be justified under self-determination, this would involve a claim of the second kind. However, the two are also closely linked. In particular, we need to know what kinds of choices fall under self-determination, as it is invoked in the first claim, before we can identify when self-determination is threatened, grounding the second claim. So an account of which powers and choices are required to be exercised by a particular group, in order for it to be regarded as self-determining, is a necessary step in identifying the proper scope of both the claim to exercise self-determination, and the claim to protect it.

How might we construct such an account?

Self-determination is a slippery concept, both legally and morally. It is most frequently discussed in connection with national self-determination

---

[1] §3.4.

[2] The claim of self-determination here is obviously only relevant as a justification to outsiders: from the point of view of insiders, it is irrelevant, and they can presumably expect justification in whatever terms are appropriate given their domestic conceptions of justice and legitimacy.

and secession.[3] In that context, the discussion is complicated by problems of identification (Which groups are entitled to self-determination?), stability (What implications would a robust principle of self-determination have for the stability of existing states?), and conflicting claims (How do we reconcile the claims of the majority in an existing state, the majority in a particular region, and any dissenting minorities in that region?). It is on these questions, rather than the scope of the powers claimed, that much of the literature focuses.[4] Self-determination is generally understood to comprise a claim to statehood or, where this is not possible (usually, though not always, in response to the conflicting values noted above), some lesser form of self-government.[5] The precise powers a group requires to be able to exercise in order to be self-determining, and the choices that it must be free to make, are rarely discussed.[6] Yet, it is precisely these questions that we need to answer. This literature can still provide a starting point, however, as by examining the various arguments advanced for self-determination, we can in turn identify the scope of the powers each supports. This is the strategy I pursue here.

I begin with legal doctrine, where self-determination has found expression primarily in the context of decolonization and, more generally, the right of particular groups to political independence. However, it is not limited to this, extending also to rights for particular groups to participation and to the protection of their own cultures and ways of life. Unfortunately, the former doctrine, concerned with a right to statehood, tells us little about the kinds of powers a self-determining state should have. The latter, addressing especially the rights of minorities, is potentially more fruitful but its extent is unclear and, precisely because it represents a second-best to self-determination, the lessons we can take from it are quite limited.

---

[3] For an overview: (Miscevic, 2010).

[4] Much of the debate has focused on whether nations, as opposed to other groups, have a privileged claim to self-determination. To the extent possible, I avoid referring to nations, as the claims I address can be evaluated without adjudicating this question. On the diversity of plausible groups: (Margalit & Raz, 1990: 447). On disaggregating questions about territories and the powers and duties that attach to them: (Goodin, 1988: 682). In bracketing questions about the groups claiming self-determination, I necessarily emphasize the ways self-determination realizes value for individuals. Self-determination is thus understood as a group right only in the sense that it is claimed by, and realized through, groups: but in each case, the arguments discussed here understand the underlying value as being one for individuals.

[5] (Miller, 1995: 81).   [6] An excellent example is: Ibid., 100–103.

I therefore turn to consider self-determination as it is defended in the philosophical literature. There, arguments for self-determination fall into three categories: intrinsic, expressive, and instrumental.[7] Intrinsic arguments see self-determination as an aspect of autonomy, and as such, intrinsically valuable. Expressive arguments see it as necessary to express or respect some other value, most obviously fairness or equality. Instrumental arguments see it as valuable because it makes more likely the sustainable realization of some other value. In each case, those arguments have implications for the kinds of powers a self-determining entity must have, in order for self-determination to realize its particular value, and hence for us to say that a people is in fact self-determining. I draw out these implications for each category in turn, and then integrate them to show how they can identify the scope and limits of self-determination as a justification of state measures affecting outsiders.[8]

It might seem contradictory to explore the powers of states in terms of a concept, self-determination, which is commonly attached to peoples, and asserted *against* existing states. The contradiction is dissolved, however, once we recall that the claim to self-determination is itself a claim to constitute a political unit, and includes within it subsidiary claims about the powers that unit should have. The state is thus both the addressee of self-determination demands, and the vehicle through which these seek realization. To the extent that states claim legitimacy, they do so in part as vehicles for their peoples' self-determination. We can thus reason from

---

[7] I do not separately examine arguments from territorial rights to self-determination. Simmons develops such an argument on Lockean premises. However, he concedes that it has little relevance to the world as it is: (Simmons, 2001: 315). Like property, Lockean genealogies of territory have implications only if they are true, which they obviously are not. We must therefore look to consequentialist or contractualist accounts: (Waldron, 2004: §4). But the scope of the rights these support will depend directly on the arguments for those rights, running only contingently through territoriality. Cf. (Philpott, 1995: 370).

[8] Some readers might be tempted to reject this approach as falsely reductionist, in assuming that the scope of self-determination can be identified in the value it realizes and its relation to other values. Rather, they might assert that self-determination simply is the irreducible right of particular groups to exercise certain powers and make certain choices. While I offer no argument against such a view, I also see no reason to accept it. Self-determination, as it is understood in modern practice, is clearly historically contingent rather than necessary: international politics in previous eras got by without it. If we are to endorse self-determination, whether in general, or in some particular form, then this must be based on some argument about the value it realizes, whether for some particular persons or peoples, or for the international system as a whole. And once we accept the need for such arguments, we can in turn interrogate them to identify the scope of the right they support.

self-determination to the powers ostensibly legitimate states properly claim.

5.2   Self-Determination in International Law

Accounts of self-determination in international law traditionally begin by invoking the intellectual inheritance of the Enlightenment, before recalling its problematic experience in inter-war Europe, and eventual blossoming in decolonization. Moving into the present, we find discussions of, *inter alia*, the breakup of Yugoslavia and the status of Quebec, invoked to clarify the extent of self-determination in noncolonial settings. While writers disagree at all stages of the story, there is a broad consensus that this is the story that they are disagreeing about.[9]

At each stage, the principal question examined is whether self-determination grounds a claim on the part of a particular community to secede from an existing state, and to constitute its own state. When Robert Lansing described self-determination, as espoused by Woodrow Wilson, as an idea "loaded with dynamite," he had in mind this sense of self-determination, as a principle of state-making and state-breaking. In the colonial context, self-determination was understood as posing, for the people of a given colonial territory, the choice among "the establishment of a sovereign and independent State, the free association or integration with an independent State, or the emergence into any other political status freely determined by a people."[10] While the recognition of statuses other than independence and integration opens space for more textured outcomes, the question posed remains one of who should determine the political status of the relevant territory; and in practice, in the vast majority of cases, self-determination was identified with independent statehood.[11] And of course, the contemporary cases, whether violently in the Balkans, or peacefully in Canada, ask this same question: who is entitled, and under what conditions, to separate from an existing state and to constitute a new state for themselves?

So described, self-determination seems unlikely to yield much guidance on the questions we are trying to answer, which concern the extent of the powers that a political community, including in particular a state,

[9] See e.g. (Borgen: 6–10; Brownlie, 2008: 579–582; Cassese, 1999; Shaw, 2014: 183–188).
[10] UNGA Resolution 2625 (XXV) (1970).   [11] (Quane, 1998: 551–554) Cf. (Kirgis, 1994).

must exercise in order to be regarded as self-determining. The emphasis on either statehood, or such other status as the relevant population may choose, gives us no sense of what essential substantive powers, if any, the resulting entity must exercise.

However, self-determination, as understood in international law, is not exclusively concerned with the choice of sovereignties. For example, Common Article 1 of the International Covenant on Civil and Political Rights and the International Covenant on Economic, Social, and Cultural Rights understands self-determination as including a people's right, not only to freely determine their political status, but also to "freely pursue their economic, social, and cultural development."[12] While this has been argued to confer a claim to participation in government, it also clearly includes a substantive element, in terms of the powers and capacities a people must have under its control. It must condemn at least some restrictions to which an ostensibly self-determining people might be subject, in so far as these limit its capacity to pursue its economic, social, and cultural development.[13] And it suggests, without stating, that the absence of material resources necessary for this purpose would similarly conflict with the principle of self-determination. In this latter respect, we might note that Common Article 1 also protects a people's right freely to dispose of its natural wealth and resources, and against being deprived of its means of subsistence. However, the exact content of the substantive powers required under Common Article 1 remains unclear.[14]

Another place we might look for legal expression of the powers of a self-determining people is the protection of minority rights. It seems plausible that, whatever powers a people must have in order to be self-determining, they must include at least those powers implied by the *ex hypothesi* less-extensive protections of nonsovereign minorities. However, this again offers little guidance for two reasons. First, the exact status and content of minority rights in international law is a matter of significant controversy: while particular minorities have been accorded special protection, in general, protection extends to little more than the observation of (individual) human rights and some

---

[12] *ICCPR*, Art. 1; *ICESCR*, Art. 1.

[13] For an argument on these lines, focusing on protection against external interference: (Cassese, 1995: 52–58).

[14] See e.g. CCPR General Comment No. 12, 1984. For an overview highlighting the neglect of economic aspects of self-determination in particular, and linking Common Article 1 to the New International Economic Order: (Oloka-Onyango, 1999: 169–177).

concern to protect minority cultures and languages.[15] Second, to the extent minority protections are recognized, they are understood as second-best solutions, implying rights less extensive than those accorded to fully self-determining peoples.[16] In so far as we are concerned with the latter, we cannot identify them by reference to another, *ex hypothesi* lesser, status.

It might here be objected that expecting self-determination, as a legal principle, to elaborate the powers of states confuses its role with a number of related ideas, including most obviously independence, sovereignty, and nonintervention. While self-determination is a claim to constitute, and thereafter to maintain, a state, the powers of states fall under the concept of sovereignty. This move does not assist us however, as it is unclear what, if any, concrete powers are required to be exercised in order for a state to be sovereign.[17] Thus, the ICJ in *US Nationals in Morocco*, for example, accepted that Morocco remained sovereign, notwithstanding a protectorate alienating complete control over its foreign affairs[18]; and while the PCIJ held that a customs union between Germany and Austria involved an alienation of Austria's economic independence, this reflected quite particular circumstances.[19] In general, political, economic, and legal restrictions on states' powers are not regarded as undermining their sovereignty, unless they place them under the authority of another state.[20]

There is a further, more fundamental, reason why understanding self-determination in terms of sovereignty is unlikely to be helpful for our purposes. As noted in Chapter 4, sovereignty plays a foundational role in positivist international law, constituting the basis for all legal obligations. It is because sovereign states consent that international law constitutes law at all. This brings with it a corollary: that whatever sovereign states consent to is, *ipso facto*, international law. The essence of sovereignty, on this account, is not the exercise of any particular substantive powers, but

---

[15] See e.g. *United Nations Declaration on the Rights of Ethnic, Religious and Linguistic Minorities*, Art. 1; ICCPR, Art. 27. For an overview: (Musgrave, 1997: 126–147). For an argument that minority protections can only be effective given some form of autonomy, and drawing the connections between minority protections and self-determination: (Wright, 1999).

[16] Models of "internal" self-determination, and Klabbers' reconceptualization of self-determination as a procedural "right to be heard" face the same challenge: (Klabbers, 2006; McCorquodale, 1994). On the limits, and indeterminacy, of internal self-determination: (Summers, 2013: 237–242).

[17] This point was touched on in §4.1 above.

[18] *France v United States* [1952] ICJ Reports 176 at 188.

[19] *Customs Regime between Germany and Austria* [1931] PCIJ Reports 37 at 52.

[20] (Shaw, 2014: 153). The evolution of sovereignty in recent decades constitutes a further objection to reading the relevant powers off it. See §4.1 above.

rather the capacity, *qua* sovereign, to give or withhold consent to a potentially binding obligation. But if we understand sovereignty in this way, then it makes little sense to enquire whether particular restrictions on a state's powers are compatible with its sovereignty. Rather, such restrictions are an expression of that sovereignty.[21]

It seems, then, that legal doctrine is unlikely to assist us in giving content to the self-determination proviso to EGC. Instead, in the next three sections, I examine arguments advanced in the theoretical literature, to identify the scope of the powers that these suggest a self-determining community must exercise for itself. I begin in the next section with intrinsic arguments, which see self-determination as an aspect of autonomy, and as such, intrinsically valuable. From these, I move in subsequent sections to consider expressive and instrumental arguments.

5.3   Intrinsic Arguments

Philpott advances an intrinsic argument for self-determination.[22] Beginning from a Kantian account of autonomy, he argues that this implies not only individual liberty, democracy, and distributive justice, but also self-determination, which he understands as promoting "participation and representation, the political activities of an autonomous person."[23]

Two separate claims about democratic autonomy motivate Philpott's argument.

The first is that self-determination promotes participation. Persons are more likely to, and can more effectively, participate in the political process of a community in which they feel at home, than one from which they are alienated.[24] It is participation in the political process, rather than agreement with its outcome, that constitutes us as free citizens, and reconciles our individual freedom with the coercion of the state.[25] Autonomy is therefore better realized when we are members of self-determining political communities.[26]

---

[21] (Brownlie, 2008: 290). The same problem arises if we recast the question in terms of the scope of states' domestic jurisdiction: (Brownlie, 2008: 292–294).

[22] (Philpott, 1995).   [23] Ibid., 358.   [24] Ibid., 359–360.

[25] Philpott invokes both Kant and Rousseau in developing this account of autonomy through political participation.

[26] Arguments for the intrinsic value of participation in shared political projects, and for collective self-authorship, have a similar structure: (Miller, 1995: 88–90, 2000: 162, 164–165). A similar argument is conditionally endorsed in (McMahan, 1997: 111).

The second is that persons' interests are more effectively represented when they are not aggregated with the interests of disparate others. We are not required to "constantly combat or be drowned in the dissonance of foreign ways," and can thus "more directly shape [our] political context and are thus, more autonomous."[27] On this latter claim, it is outcomes that matter. We are more autonomous when politics in fact represents our interests, regardless of our own participation in the political process.[28]

That political authority should be under the control of those over whom it is exercised is a liberal commonplace. Philpott's argument goes further, claiming that delineating political communities by reference to the political self-identification of members more effectively realizes autonomy. Democratic participation in a wider political community is, on this account, a second-best.[29]

What implications do these arguments have for the content of the powers claimed?

Turning first to the participation claim. This can be understood in one of two ways. First, we might understand autonomy as an interest of persons, one component of the good. To satisfy that interest, we require a sufficiently large range of options for our choices to be meaningful, and to thereby make us authors of our own lives.[30] If we assume that our autonomy extends to the political, it implies access to a political sphere in which we can effectively participate. However, it does not identify the scope of the choices that fall to be made within the political sphere. They must be sufficient to give us a meaningful sense of ownership over our shared lives. If our choices relate only to ephemera, or are wholly frustrated by external factors, then autonomy is not realized.[31] However, this cannot require that we control all factors that might affect how our lives turn out. Just as individual autonomy must be reconcilable with living together with other autonomous agents whose choices may

---

[27] (Philpott, 1995: 359–360).

[28] As a claim about autonomy, this latter argument seems suspect. Whatever political autonomy consists in, given pluralism, it cannot require actually having one's preferences reflected in political decisions. We might also query whether, given political economy concerns, domestic decision making is more likely to achieve this: (Kapstein & Rosenthal, 2006: 70–71). We might alternatively understand this argument as relating not to the fact of particular outcomes, but rather to their likelihood.

[29] For an argument combining aspects of participation and outcome claims, together with instrumental arguments: (Tamir, 1993: 69).

[30] (Raz, 1986: 373–377).

[31] On what this might mean internationally: (Brock, 2009: 224; Miller, 2000: 163–164).

affect us, so collective autonomy must respect the shared context in which polities act and the impacts they have on each other. Where the questions that fall to be decided affect more than one community, then one's maximizing claim of autonomy necessarily conflicts with the similar claims of others. Some other argument is required to explain where the balance between such maximizing claims should be drawn.[32]

An alternative interpretation understands the participation claim as identifying conditions for equal respect. Individuals' claims to equal respect may be denied where they cannot participate in political choices that affect them, regardless of the adequacy of the options available.[33] However, given the pervasiveness of cross-border effects, and assuming we are committed to a world comprising different political communities making their own decisions, we cannot all participate in all decisions that affect us.[34] Rather, we again find ourselves in need of a criterion for allocating particular decisions to particular communities.[35] The participation claim itself contributes nothing to this inquiry.

A similar point counts against the outcome claim. We might accept that persons are more autonomous when their preferences are more frequently reflected in the outcomes of political decisions. However, as with the participation account, this tells us nothing about whose preferences should be reflected in outcomes that affect those both inside and outside the community.

Philpott recognizes these problems in his discussion of secessionists' obligations to former compatriots, observing that self-determination applies only to "affairs that are truly [our] own," but not matters affecting the larger state.[36] However, what we understand to be exclusively the affairs of a particular community will depend on our theory of global/international justice, including importantly of economic justice.[37] Just as, domestically, liberal commitments lead us to endorse both liberty rights and socio-economic rights that reconcile the freedom of each with all, so internationally they imply both a core of self-determination, and a complex of restrictions to respect the equal rights of others.

---

[32] An obvious example is the limits of democratic autonomy in justifying borders: (Abizadeh, 2008).

[33] For such an equal respect interpretation: (Copp, 1997).

[34] Moore presses this boundary problem against Copp's approach: (Moore, 1998: 20).

[35] The argument in Chapter 3 can be read as defending one such criterion.

[36] (Philpott, 1995: 363) Cf. (Margalit & Raz, 1990: 456). In the trade context, this is recognized in: (Howse, 2001: 67; Jackson, 2006: 59).

[37] See generally: (Philpott, 1995: 362–364) Cf. (Fine, 2010: 345–347, 353).

The intrinsic argument, then, offers little guidance on the scope of the choices over which communities can expect to be self-determining. It demands a sufficient range of choices to provide meaningful self-authorship[38]; and it suggests the need for adequate resources, to allow communities to organize themselves and to allow individuals the capacity to participate therein; but it tells us little about the relationship between self-determination and decisions affecting outsiders.[39] It can endorse EGC's identification of the category of DEMs as requiring only limited justification to outsiders, but cannot tell us what role – if any – self-determination plays in the justification of ETMs.

In consequence, the intrinsic argument offers a very limited account of *external* self-determination.[40] To the extent external decisions necessarily relate to outsiders, the argument from autonomy seems not to extend this far, with one significant exception. We can motivate treaty powers from autonomy, by analogy to Fried's argument for contracts.[41] In the individual case, as Fried develops the argument, it relies on the extent to which a power of binding ourselves expands the scope of our autonomy, through making possible cooperation, and the realization of projects and outcomes that would be impossible acting alone. Given the many contemporary problems (including, but not limited to, environmental degradation) whose solution depends on joint action, and the extent to which these affect individuals in precisely the ways highlighted in Philpott's intrinsic argument, it seems straightforward to argue that, to the extent

---

[38] Moore includes some choices about land use and property regimes in this category: (Moore, 2012: 87–88).

[39] We might try to resolve this problem by examining the extent to which different persons are affected: those who are most affected by a decisions have, we might think, the strongest claim to participate in that decision, and to have their interests reflected in it. However, given the ways the effects of a measure can fall disproportionately on outsiders, it seems unlikely that this approach would lead us to anything like the existing system of self-governing territorial states.

Consider an example: a state's regulations on the safety of any given product are likely to impact substantially more on manufacturers of that product, including those outside the state, than they do on any individual consumer within the state. It may be that the aggregate impact on consumers is greater than the aggregate impact on producers. However, we cannot appeal to this sort of aggregation without circularity. In order to compare the impact on the class of domestic consumers with that on any given foreign producer, or indeed the class of foreign producers, we have to first decide that these are the classes that are relevant. But this is precisely the question we are trying to answer. The aggregation solution is therefore circular.

[40] Put otherwise, it explains Westphalian Sovereignty, but not International Legal Sovereignty: (Krasner, 1999: 14–25).

[41] (Fried, 1981: 7–21). Simmons labels this the "federative" power: (Simmons, 2001: 306).

autonomy motivates a claim to self-determination, this should include a power of self-determining communities to attach themselves to shared goals, standards, and projects.

Of course, this raises further questions as to when we can regard a community as having made such a commitment, and how we should define both its duration and its limits. In Chapter 4, I suggested that, in many cases, states' participation in international agreements cannot be regarded as voluntary. In the world as it is, peoples may have no meaningful choice but to agree to many treaty obligations. The upshot is that a legally binding treaty obligation may be neither sufficient, nor indeed necessary, to conclude that such a commitment exists. Rather, if we see contracting as a way for peoples to expand their autonomy then we need first to identify a baseline of precontractual moral rights and obligations before examining how far this has been varied through exercise of this aspect of self-determination.[42]

The power of communities to enter into commitments and to attach themselves to shared projects is an important one, on which I will draw in later chapters. However, as this last point highlights, as an account of external self-determination, the intrinsic argument is at best incomplete. This seems particularly unsatisfactory given the history and contemporary practice of self-determination. External self-determination, including the power to act as well as to agree, is commonly regarded as central to that concept. Control of a dependent territory's foreign and defense policy was an important mechanism of colonial control; and the establishment of an independent foreign policy has been a key step for postcolonial states in asserting their independence.[43] If the intrinsic argument cannot make sense of this, then it cannot be the whole of self-determination. But if such claims cannot be grounded in autonomy, how should we understand them?

5.4   Expressive Arguments

The second class of arguments for self-determination are expressive arguments, including in particular arguments from fairness and equality. These neither ascribe intrinsic value to self-determination, nor claim it serves instrumentally to promote or protect some other value. Rather,

---

[42] On the importance of this distinction: (Hart, 1955). Freeman's discussion of contracting in liberal and libertarian theories may also be instructive in this regard: (Freeman, 2001).

[43] (Brownlie, 2008: 73–74).

they claim that according self-determination to particular populations expresses or respects some other value that, while not comprised in self-determination, is connected to it.[44]

Consider, for example, the position of colonial peoples. Their colonial status might substantially undermine their autonomy, grounding an intrinsic argument for self-determination. However, in many cases, colonial peoples were accorded substantial self-government, particularly in respect of those domestic affairs that are "truly [their] own." We might imagine a particularly restrained imperialist affording self-government in all matters where the intrinsic argument uncontroversially applies, controlling only the dependent territory's foreign and defense policies. While the intrinsic argument does not apply in these circumstances, we would presumably still regard the situation as unjust. The explanation, on the expressive account, is that external control over foreign and defense policy is unfair, denying the equality of peoples. The imperialist exercises these powers for itself, but denies them to the colonial people. They might have neither intrinsic nor instrumental value; but their exercise by one people for another denies their equal status, and is to that extent, unjust.[45] The wrong lies in the disrespect expressed towards the colonial people, whether that be expressed in self-interested or paternalistic terms.[46]

The expressive argument explains key features of colonial self-determination. The principle *uti possitedis* is difficult to reconcile with the intrinsic argument, but readily accords with the expressive account; by affording colonial peoples the same political rights as others, we respect their equal status. Whether subsequent settlements might be required to reflect the disparate political identities and aspirations within particular territories is a separate question, on which the expressive argument is silent. It similarly explains the one-off nature of colonial self-determination, and the menu of options available. Self-determination does not demand independence: free association, integration, and "any other political status" are all compatible with self-determination, provided they are freely chosen by the self-determining people.[47] This makes little sense on

[44] E.g. (Waldron, 2010: 399–400, 411–412). Elements of this view appear, albeit as arguments against statist self-determination, in: (Gans, 2003: ch. 3).

[45] Elements of this idea appear in (Copp, 1997: 292; Philpott, 1998: 83). A similar idea appears in: (Berlin, 1997: 226–230).

[46] The sense of respect here is distinct from the equal respect interpretation of the intrinsic argument. There, we focused on the disrespect to persons of excluding them from decisions that affect them. Here, we are concerned with the disrespect to peoples of denying them a status that we accord to others.

[47] (Brownlie, 2008: 580).

the intrinsic account; but if we assume the wrong of colonialism lies not in the limited political powers of the colonial people, but rather in disrespect that this expresses, then integration, freely chosen, cures that wrong.[48]

What does the expressive argument tell us about the content of self-determination?

First, note that it does not identify any intrinsic value in self-determination. Rather, it is motivated by concerns for fairness or equal respect. To that extent, it is compatible with a world where no peoples are self-determining. It is similarly compatible with a world where peoples exercise limited self-determination, provided the limits are fair having regard to those imposed on others.[49] However, it will necessarily question any arrangement under which some peoples' self-determination is limited while others' is not. It need not necessarily condemn this; countervailing concerns might trump self-determination claims of some peoples but not others. However, such unequal self-determination is at least *prima facie* objectionable.

This might suggest that the expressive argument was silent on the content of self-determination. Provided self-determination is equal, it may be more or less restricted without objection. However, the requirement of equality may itself generate limits in at least two circumstances.

First, the expressive argument can directly condemn measures whereby one people exercises power over another. This, recall, is the objection to colonialism. To the extent one people makes choices for another, it necessarily expresses the disrespect that this argument addresses. There are, admittedly, difficulties identifying when this is the case. The argument in Chapter 3 defends one answer to this question; the problem with ETMs is in part that they assert a right on the part of one community to make choices for another. Admittedly, in wholly symmetrical cases, the expressive argument for self-determination cannot alone identify a wrong in such measures.[50] However, states' diversity in size and influence means such cases are vanishingly rare in practice, and are in any event condemned on other grounds; we can therefore dispense with them here.

---

[48] If a state ceases equally to represent all its citizens, an expressive argument for secession might arise: (Philpott, 1995: 359–360). However, remedial claims secession might be better understood as instrumental: (Buchanan, 2004; Margalit & Raz, 1990: 457).

[49] The argument does assume that political authority in general has value; if it didn't, then we simply wouldn't be concerned with how it was distributed. However, we need not assume that there is some general case for allocating it to individual political communities to recognize the injustice of allocating it to some but not to others.

[50] A Hobbesian state of nature, in which each equally violates the rights of others, may be both unjust and abhorrent, but it is neither unequal nor unfair.

Second, consider the frequent claim that small and developing states are more exposed than others to developments in international markets and the international system. This might be due to their reliance on export earnings, international capital markets, or foreign investors[51]; or to the perverse incentives international law poses for domestic institutions.[52] In either case, the objection is in terms of self-determination, but, more specifically, it is in terms of *equal* self-determination. It is not simply that the relevant states are subject to external influences. All states in an interdependent world are subject to such influences. Rather, the objection is that they are more exposed to such influences than larger and more developed states. Formally equal rights obscure substantively unequal freedom.[53]

Is this the kind of inequality that the expressive claim addresses? Certainly, if there are plausible alternative institutional arrangements that more effectively assure the equal self-determination of peoples, we might regard the choice of this particular arrangement as expressing disrespect towards those disproportionately burdened by it. However, we might worry that such alternatives, while reducing inequality, would also impair self-determination for all peoples.[54] This obviously assumes that self-determination has some value, whether intrinsic or instrumental; but to the extent it does, we might conclude that greater self-determination for all is preferable, even for those least benefited by it.[55] The argument then becomes, not that some are less self-determining than others, but rather that some are less self-determining than they might themselves be under some plausible alternative arrangement.

It is hard to know how such an argument might be applied in practice. The challenges noted in Chapter 4 against global egalitarianism apply *a fortiori* against an egalitarianism of self-determination. We might plausibly identify when peoples fall below some absolute standard of self-determination, defined in intrinsic or instrumental terms. It is harder to see how we could construct a robust comparative metric, given the diverse goals peoples pursue. In Chapter 4, we relied on domestic choice to defend EGC's egalitarian limb from the metric

---

[51] (Garcia, 2000: 987–988; Margalit & Raz, 1990: 441–442; O'Neill, 2000: 140–141; Ronzoni, 2012).

[52] (Pogge, 2011a: 29).   [53] (Loriaux, 2012: 28; Ronzoni, 2012: 581).

[54] Most obviously, because equalizing the self-determination of more and less economically advantaged peoples over time would – as the dynamic problem emphasized – require depriving both of significant economic freedom.

[55] The argument is analogous to that for the difference principle.

problem; but we cannot use the same technique when comparing self-determination itself. And even if we could construct such a metric, it is hard to know how it could be implemented without a global state that would likely, perversely, impair the self-determination of all peoples.

That does not however dispense with this argument. We might derive less-demanding standards from the expressive argument that avoid these difficulties. In particular, to the extent that we identify a threshold for regarding a state as self-determining, the expressive argument motivates a duty to protect it. If we can say, not that one people is more self-determining than another, but rather that one enjoys self-determination while the other does not, then the expressive argument can be invoked. I discuss further below how we might define that threshold.[56]

The expressive argument, then, has some relevance for our inquiry, but like the intrinsic argument, it cannot explain which powers a people must exercise for themselves in order to be self-determining. We therefore turn to a third cluster of arguments, which identify an instrumental value in self-determination.

5.5   Instrumental Arguments

Instrumental arguments defend self-determination as making more likely the sustainable realization of some other good, to which it is causally linked. They claim that, to the extent we are concerned to ensure those other goods are realized, we have reason to accord to each particular community the powers necessary to realize them for themselves.

A number of broadly nationalist thinkers advance instrumental arguments for self-determination as protecting national cultures.[57] These depend on a prior claim about the value of such cultures for persons. Margalit and Raz, for example, argue that culture is a prerequisite to our forming and pursuing worthwhile goals and relationships, which are in turn understood as essential components of wellbeing.[58] To the extent this is the case, persons have a fundamental interest in the continued flourishing of the cultures into which they are born, and in their adherence thereto. Protecting that

---

[56] In fact, none of the arguments through which I elsewhere give content to self-determination provides reasons to understand it in maximizing, as opposed to sufficientarian, terms. So it is not that, given practical constraints, we refrain from understanding self-determination in strongly egalitarian terms; but rather that there are few reasons for doing so, even apart from these constraints.

[57] (Gans, 2003: ch. 2; Miller, 1995: 85–88; Nielsen, 1997: 121–125; Tamir, 1993: 69–77).

[58] (Margalit & Raz, 1990: 448–449).

continued flourishing may in turn require that the relevant group enjoy "political sovereignty" over its own affairs.[59]

This protective argument suggests possible boundaries on the rights it will justify. If self-determination is understood as protecting a group's culture, then it must accord to peoples at least such powers as are necessary to do that.[60] This might seem to substitute one ill-defined term ("culture") for another ("self-determination").[61] However, by explaining why culture is valued, namely as a context for individuals to form and pursue goals and relationships, it suggests some possible boundaries on that concept. In particular, it suggests that the culture requiring protection is that which exists within the territory of the relevant state, in so far as it is there that goals and relationships are formed and pursued. This will not always be the case. We can imagine peoples whose encompassing culture was expressed externally, and for whom that external expression is valuable in the sense invoked by Margalit and Raz.[62] However, we might doubt whether, even in these cases, the fact of external expression, as opposed to the aspiration, was valuable in the relevant sense. There are also obvious fairness problems with such externally expressed cultures: if the only way one people can maintain its valued culture is through seeking to change the culture of others, then such a culture may simply be incompatible with the equality of peoples.[63] An analogy can be drawn to individual conceptions of the good that deny the equal claim of others to pursue their own conceptions.[64] We need not deny that peoples can have reasons to pursue changes in the cultures and practices of others; but this cannot be justified solely through the instrumental value for them of preserving their own encompassing culture. Something more than self-determination is required.[65]

---

[59] This argument is not limited to a distinctively national culture. It depends only on being attached to some culture: (Gans, 2003: 42–43; McMahan, 1997: 121). However, a further set of identity-based arguments pre-empt the objection that any culture, and not only persons' original culture, will suffice for this purpose: (Kymlicka, 1996: 84–89; Miller, 1995: 86).

[60] Miller tentatively distinguishes the implications of this argument for social, economic, and defense powers: (Miller, 1995: 100–102).

[61] Thus, Miller assumes that the powers required will vary with the relevant culture. Gans distinguishes between protecting cultures, and protecting individual practices comprised therein: (Gans, 2003: 55 et seq.).

[62] E.g. (MacIntyre, 1984: 7).

[63] It might also conflict with the expressive account of self-determination.

[64] For a similar point, (Hurka, 1997).

[65] Dworkin makes a similar point in arguing that liberty cannot justify departures from equality, properly understood; to the extent departures are plausible, something more is required (Dworkin, 2002: 128–131).

There is a second, less culturally focused, protective argument. Margalit and Raz locate the value of culture in its stabilizing role. However, for persons to form and pursue goals and relationships, more than just a stable culture is required. They also require a stable institutional, political, and economic environment.[66] Consider, for example, the choice of career, which will often have pervasive effects on a person's life. While stability may not be a prerequisite to choice, relative stability is a plausible prerequisite to meaningful choice. If I choose to pursue an academic career, for example, that choice may be frustrated if, some years later, all the universities in my country close. This is likely significantly to impair both my material wellbeing and my sense of autonomy. We need not suppose that I have any right to pursue any particular career, or indeed to continue in my chosen career, to recognize the value that a stable context of choice offers for individuals.[67] What is at issue here is not the range or quality of choices available, but rather their stability. How much stability is required is an open question. Some risk is presumably inevitable, and need not prevent individuals taking control over, and responsibility for, their own lives. Further, some individuals may flourish in uncertain environments, while others prefer stability. More generally, at a societal level, stability may be valuable, to the extent that it protects expectations; but it may also be costly, impairing growth and restricting opportunities, particularly for new participants. While there is no logical necessity that stability be protected at the national level, the value judgments required, as well as informational considerations, suggest that it is best done at the level of individual peoples. We might also highlight the links between economic and broader social change, tying this argument more closely to the previous, cultural, version. Instrumental and intrinsic arguments thus combine to suggest that peoples should have the powers necessary to maintain this stability.[68] However, this argument is similarly subject to fairness constraints. A people cannot expect reliable access to the international economy, with implications for the stability of others, while at the same time pursuing

---

[66] It is on this aspect of self-determination that theorists of embedded liberalism focus: (Lang, 2011: 190–200; Polanyi, 2001: passim, esp. ch. 12, 18, 21; Ruggie, 1982: 386–388). Cottier argues that such stabilizing mechanisms are a prerequisite to effective market liberalization: (Cottier, 2013).

[67] On the perils of ignoring these concerns with commodity labor: (Polanyi, 2001: 76).

[68] The assumption that stability is best provided domestically may also reflect the extent to which we have come to identify the trade regime with unregulated markets, eliding earlier assumptions about the role of social order in international trade regulation.

perfect stability domestically at the cost of others' market expectations. Policing this boundary is an important function of the trade regime.

A third instrumental argument emphasizes the role of the state in managing the provision of public goods, including in particular security of persons and property, which are themselves prerequisites to autonomy. We label as "failed" states that cannot provide physical security for their populations. However, the concern here is broader. States provide diverse public goods, most prominently security, stability, cultural protection, and political and socio-economic justice, including the protection of basic rights.[69] For various reasons, it makes sense to provide such goods at the level of individual political communities.[70] However, their value lies in their provision to individuals, rather than the individual's role in and power over their provision. This distinguishes this point from the intrinsic argument discussed earlier.[71] To the extent this is the case, the capacity to make and to implement choices about such goods is a necessary element of self-determination. However, we must again be careful to recognize the limits of this argument. Its focus is the state's role in making choices about and managing the provision of public goods, not the acquisition of resources required to provide those goods. In so far as such resources are valuable for all peoples, they are the objects of distributive rather than self-determination claims.[72]

---

[69] This includes what Buchanan labels "distributional autonomy": (Buchanan, 2000: 705).

[70] Kratochwil identifies the failure to provide these as a stimulant for the move from feudal to territorial sovereignty. Ronzoni and Dietsch make a similar point in arguing for a move to cooperative sovereignty. Kolers examines a number of arguments for defining state borders by reference to the efficient scope of public goods. (Dietsch, 2011; Kolers, 2012: 34–39; Kratochwil, 1986; Ronzoni, 2012) Cf. (Chayes & Chayes, 1995; Risse, 2006).

[71] The underprovision of basic rights also goes to the intrinsic argument, insofar as it prevents persons participating in political life, and thus undermines their enjoyment of the intrinsic value of self-determination.

[72] Where peoples lack the resources to provide essential public goods at a level sufficient to assure basic rights of citizens and allow them to take effective control of their own affairs, this will ground a separate self-determination justification, which can be understood in instrumental or intrinsic terms. However, in most such circumstances, a straightforward distributive justification will also be available.

A complication arises where the decisions states make about the provision of public goods in turn affect their access to resources. A poorly designed revenue and welfare regime, for example, might significantly undermine a state's economy, thereby restricting its access to resources required to provide essential public goods. As we acknowledged when discussing the dynamic problem in Chapter 4, that peoples' choices carry costs is not itself a problem: however, where those costs would leave them below the relevant minimum threshold, we might reasonably regard this as undermining their self-determination. Some notion of reasonableness, in an economic rather than moral sense, may be relevant in judging whether and to what extent this is problematic. I do not claim to have fully resolved this question here.

A fourth instrumental argument highlights the role of peoples as custodians of territories, and of the resources therein. Two separate arguments can be made here. The first parallels Hume's conventionalist and consequentialist argument for property.[73] It claims that resources will be better managed, to the benefit of all, if they are under the control of particular peoples.[74] The second highlights the importance of natural resources for other aspects of self-determination, including in particular, autonomy and cultural stability.[75] Peoples who control territories and the resources therein are more secure in their enjoyment of these latter goods[76]; if we are wholly dependent on others for essential resources, then we live by their permission, and our independence is illusory.[77] Such control of territory and resources is therefore an important element of self-determination.

There are presumably other instrumental arguments that might be proposed, but these suffice for our purposes. What do they imply about the scope of the rights required for a people to be self-determining?

A people must be able to provide the goods highlighted by each argument: to protect and develop its distinctive culture, to the extent this is valuable for persons living therein; to stabilize institutions, politics, and markets to the extent necessary for persons to make meaningful choices about how their lives will be lived; to make and implement choices about the provision of public goods; and to manage the natural resources that provide a material basis for all of the above. To do any of these, a state might plausibly require ETMs. Protecting a valued culture might mean restricting imports of cultural goods. Stabilizing economic expectations might mean temporarily insulating domestic markets. Providing public goods and managing natural resources might mean restricting imports and exports. We thus find a clear basis, in these

---

[73] (Hume, 2000: §3.2.3, esp. §3.2.2.11–14). This view can in turn be traced at least to Aristotle: (Kelly, 1992: 37). On the limits of this view: (Moore, 2012: 85–87, 93–94).

[74] Rawls adopts a version of this view: (Rawls, 1999: 38–39). The connection here is not a necessary one. We can readily imagine collective management schemes for many resources. However, the absence of such schemes at present, and the difficulties of constructing them, justifies emphasizing territorial rights as the principal mechanism for managing scarce resources in the world as it is.

[75] See, on the link between self-determination and sovereignty over resources: (Kratochwil, 1986: 42).

[76] Moore labels this the "standard view" of territorial rights: (Moore, 2012: 85) Cf. (Armstrong, 2013; Kolers, 2012).

[77] This claim is obviously closely linked with the intrinsic argument above. However, it is distinguished by the strong but contingent relation that it identifies between resource control and robust collective, and in turn individual, autonomy.

instrumental arguments, for distinguishing which ETMs can be justified under self-determination, and which cannot.

One potential instrumental argument must be rejected, however. This is the claim that peoples must necessarily judge *for themselves* what measures are required under any of these arguments. This claim to self-judgment is generally advanced in instrumental terms. In its simplest form, it simply restates the strong (Hobbesian) sovereignty objection discussed in Chapter 4[78]: if the values protected by self-determination have overriding importance, then peoples must exercise their powers securely, which requires having the final say on whether they require to be exercised.[79] To the extent this argument depends on international anarchy, it is subject to the same replies advanced there. In most cases, there is little reason to believe, and much reason to doubt, that peoples will be more secure in their self-determination if each claims a privilege to determine for itself what this requires.[80] There is, however, a moderate form of the argument that we can accept. This is the claim that, in many cases, a people is best placed to determine what is required to protect the values underpinning its own self-determination. The specific content of those values will vary across peoples; in a number of cases, that variation is the reason self-determination is valued. In consequence, members of a community have epistemic advantages in determining the relative importance of particular practices, choices, or goods, and the measures required to protect them.[81] This, however, remains compatible with international review of the self-determination justifications that states offer for their policies.

5.6   Integrating Self-Determination Arguments

The intrinsic, expressive, and instrumental arguments each provides a different account of the minimum powers a people requires in order to be self-determining.

The intrinsic argument requires that peoples have a sufficient range of choices to ensure effective self-authorship, but tells us little about the

---

[78] Hobbes himself regards adjudication as an essential element of sovereignty, and the impossibility of alienating it as an argument against limited government: (Hobbes, 1996: 124–125).

[79] Macintyre defends this view.

[80] This does not mean that we must reason from global justice to domestic limits, but only that the limits of self-determination must be defined for the international context. Cf. (Miller, 2000: 167).

[81] (Dietsch, 2011: 2114; Margalit & Raz, 1990: 457).

extent of that range, or its relevance to choices affecting outsiders. It motivates a power of peoples to enter into commitments and attach themselves to shared projects, but without an account of the precontractual baseline against which such commitments are acquired. The expressive argument focuses our attention on inequalities, whether this be one people exercising power over another, or one enjoying effective self-determination while another does not; but it tells us little about what it actually means to enjoy effective self-determination. The instrumental arguments, by contrast, offer a relatively concrete account of the kinds of functions that self-determination plays, and in turn the kinds of specific powers that a people needs to have and exercise in order to be regarded as self-determining, in a valuable sense.

We need not choose between these three approaches. Rather, we might consistently hold that peoples have an intrinsic claim to exercise some powers, expressive claims to others, and instrumental claims to others again.[82] We can therefore integrate the three approaches to construct a composite account of the powers required by self-determining peoples, and thereby to delineate the scope of EGC's self-determination proviso. Doing this suggests two main ways self-determination might qualify EGC.

The first concerns powers essential to the self-determination of the regulating people, and relies primarily on instrumental arguments. The scope of the measures it justifies depends on the scope of those instrumental arguments, but runs at least to measures necessary to protect the various goods noted above. To the extent that a measure, including an ETM, is required for these purposes, it can be justified under self-determination. To the extent it goes further, whether because it pursues another goal, or is unnecessary to the particular goal pursued, it cannot be so justified. We might thus expect that instrumental arguments will do most work in filling in the content of the self-determination proviso; however, the expressive and intrinsic arguments also have work to do, including in particular in circumstances where international developments undermine a people's capacity for effective self-authorship, or measures adopted by one state undermine the self-determination of another.

The second relates to shared goals and standards, and relies primarily on the intrinsic argument. As noted above, the intrinsic argument tells us little about peoples' claims to determine matters affecting others, limiting its role in justifying ETMs. Its principal implication for external polices

[82] (Philpott, 1998: 82).

was in justifying a treaty power or, more generally, a power of peoples to commit themselves to particular goals. This need not take the form of legal commitments: just as promising is wider than contracting, there may be many ways that peoples might commit themselves to shared standards, goals, and projects. However, once made, such commitments provide a plausible basis, grounded in the intrinsic argument, for justifying ETMs in pursuit of such goals and projects. These are justified in terms of the self-determination of both the regulating people and the affected outsiders.

The expressive argument plays a secondary role. Its concern for equal self-determination will support certain measures necessary to protect peoples' domestic choices from international influences; but many of these might equally be justified under either the intrinsic argument, or the instrumental argument from stability. In most cases, therefore, the expressive argument provides an additional justification; but the measures justified are likely mainly to be identified by the intrinsic and instrumental arguments. We thus reason, for example, that it is instrumentally valuable for peoples to be able to stabilize their particular cultures; that some peoples are substantially more constrained in doing this by outside influences; and that there is therefore both an instrumental and an expressive claim on the part of such peoples to adopt measures, including ETMs, required for them to achieve that end.

It is worth clarifying, for the avoidance of doubt, that my claim here is not that states are only justified in adopting measures under these two categories, or indeed that these are the only ways that self-determination is relevant to the justification of measures. Most obviously, in Chapter 3, self-determination was relevant in explaining why we do not demand specific justification for DEMs, which we linked in this chapter to the intrinsic and expressive arguments. Rather, my concern here has been to identify when self-determination might be relevant, not simply as a background justification for DEMs, but as an explicit justification for ETMs not falling under the principal, egalitarian justification emphasized in Chapter 3. And in this capacity, I have argued, it is limited to the two categories outlined above. What this means in practice will be worked out further in subsequent chapters.[83]

---

[83] See in particular Chapters 7 and 8.

5.7   Conclusion

This chapter completes the elaboration and normative defense of EGC. Having set out the positive argument for that principle in Chapter 3, and addressed a range of potential objections in Chapter 4, this chapter has elaborated the reasonable principle of self-determination that, I suggest, qualifies EGC. By examining various arguments for self-determination, I identified the specific considerations that are relevant in determining when the self-determination proviso might apply in practice.

In the next chapter, my focus moves from theory to doctrine. I examine the WTO's rules on border measures and discrimination in light of the normative claims defended in these earlier chapters. Contrasting EGC with dominant economic accounts, I argue that EGC can better serve to both explain and critique those rules. That argument is extended in subsequent chapters to the principal GATT exceptions, and thereafter to the WTO rules on trade remedies and domestic regulation. While at various points in these later chapters I return to the normative claims motivating EGC, these play a secondary role. Justification has been our principal concern up to now. Hereafter, we are more concerned to assess the fit between EGC and the trade regime, and its utility as a critical and interpretive lens. Both elements are required to answer the questions with which Chapter 1 began.

PART III

Law

6

Border Measures, Discrimination, and ETMs

6.1 Introduction

This book began with two questions: first, what does justice demand in the regulation of international trade? And second, to what extent does the existing regime for trade in goods respond to those demands? The first part introduced those questions, explaining both their complexity and their urgency. The second part proposed an answer to the first question, defending the principle of Equality in Global Commerce and its corollary for Domestic Economic Measures. The four chapters that comprise this third part seek to answer the second question, turning from pure theory to the relations between theory and practice.

As outlined in Chapter 2, my goal in these later chapters is both explanatory and critical: I enquire whether the rules in key areas of the trade regime can be understood as expressing EGC; but I also suggest how those rules might be revised in light of that standard. My goal is also, and in consequence, interpretive: I enquire whether and to what extent EGC can guide adjudicators in interpreting and progressively developing these rules, particularly where the agreements themselves are unclear.

I start with the GATT as the historical and conceptual core of the WTO, around which everything else is constructed. The present chapter addresses the GATT rules on border measures and discrimination (the Core Disciplines). The former comprise prohibitions on quantitative restrictions (Article XI), and on tariffs above levels agreed in multilateral negotiations (Article II). The latter comprise prohibitions on discrimination, variously described, whether between foreign countries (Article I – "MFN" or "Most Favored Nation") or between domestic and imported products (Article III – "National Treatment"). Chapter 7 addresses two sets of qualifications to the Core Disciplines: first, various provisions that relax those disciplines in their application to developing countries (the Development Provisions); and second, the General Exceptions in Article XX (the General Exceptions), which permit departures in pursuit of specified goals and subject to specified conditions.

The argument across these two chapters is straightforward. Existing approaches imperfectly explain both the Core Disciplines and the qualifications thereto. While superficially plausible, their explanations fail to track the specific rules, or the distinctions they draw between objectionable and permissible measures: they cannot make sense of the GATT's nondiscrimination rules or their relation with the General Exceptions; they struggle with the specific exceptions in Article XX and the jurisprudence thereunder; and they cannot account of the Development Provisions or the AB's approach thereto. EGC offers an alternative account that, while also imperfect, seems preferable on each point.

In the first half of this chapter, I introduce the dominant economic theories of the trade regime, outlining how each explains key features of the GATT, and contrasting these with explanations suggested by EGC.

From there, I move on to examine specific aspects in more detail. The second half of this chapter addresses discrimination, highlighting the ambiguity of the relevant provisions, the difficulties of existing theories in guiding their interpretation, and the greater capacity of EGC to do so. Chapter 6 turns from disciplines to qualifications, addressing the Development Provisions and the General Exceptions. Among the many qualifications to the Core Disciplines, I focus on these for their breadth of application and their prominence in legal and political practice and academic scholarship.

In each case, I emphasize the ambiguities in the relevant rules, the problems for existing approaches in resolving these, and EGC's potential to better guide interpretation.

6.2   What Are Trade Agreements For? Competing Stories

Various scholars propose economic explanations of the function of trade agreements. Of these, two are most prominent.[1] The first explains trade

---

[1] See e.g. (Dunoff, 1999) (identifying these approaches, together with embedded liberalism, as the dominant accounts of GATT/WTO); (Baldwin, 2012: 30–33; Mavroidis, 2012: 14–24; Regan, 2006, 2014) (addressing variations on these approaches). I focus on theories that purport to explain the structure and purpose of the WTO agreements. There is much more to trade economics than the economics of trade agreements. However, given my goal here is to understand the WTO agreements, the latter is my focus.

agreements as helping to solve a prisoner's dilemma that arises when states use trade restrictions to manipulate their terms of trade (the Terms of Trade Theory, or TTT). The second explains them as restraining recourse by states to inefficient, and hence domestically irrational, protectionism (the Protectionism Theory, or PT). Both purport to resolve the economic puzzle of trade agreements: why, given benefits from unilateral liberalization, do states instead link their own liberalization to that of others?[2] In this section, I introduce these explanations and contrast them with that suggested by EGC, providing a foundation for later discussions.

6.2.1   Terms of Trade: Solving Prisoners' Dilemmas

TTT begins from the observation that tariffs, while affecting prices in the home market, with consequent efficiency effects, also affect world prices, and hence terms of trade.[3] They reduce demand for, and hence real prices of, imported products. Provided the terms of trade gain exceeds the efficiency loss, tariffs increase national welfare.[4] However, if multiple states pursue terms of trade advantages, each partially neutralizes the terms of trade effects of the others' measures. The combined effect may leave world prices unchanged. However, the efficiency losses remain, producing a net loss in national and global welfare. If one state acts, it gains at the other's expense. If all act, all lose against a free trade baseline. This is the terms of trade prisoner's dilemma.[5] TTT claims trade agreements ameliorate this by linking states' policies to those of their trading partners.[6]

The core of the GATT on this view is the iterative process of reciprocal tariff bargaining whereby states move from the inefficient noncooperative equilibrium towards efficient, politically optimal, tariffs.[7] Reciprocity

---

[2] (Krugman, 1997: 113).

[3] (Bagwell & Staiger, 2002: 16–18) citing *inter alia* (Johnson, 1953).

[4] (Krugman et al., 2012c: 231–232).

[5] (Bagwell & Staiger, 2002: 23). As so described, TTT assumes governments are solely motivated by national welfare, an assumption generally thought to be false. Bagwell and Staiger modify TTT to account for this, showing that terms of trade competition impairs global welfare, even assuming governments also use tariffs to pursue domestic distributive goals (Bagwell & Staiger, 2002: 23–27). On this approach, the only inefficiency that trade agreements address is the terms of trade prisoners' dilemma (Bagwell & Staiger, 2002: 25). For an alternative, politically motivated terms of trade model (Grossman & Helpman, 1995).

[6] (Bagwell & Staiger, 2002: 27). For a broadly similar view, albeit expressed in less formal economic terms: (Jackson, 1989b: 15).

[7] (Bagwell & Staiger, 2002: 60).

ensures that liberalization, while reducing the efficiency costs, does not affect terms of trade.[8] It thus focuses liberalization on the specific problem it is intended to solve.[9] Article II (Tariff Binding) is concerned, on this view, to ensure states do not deviate from their bargain. Because quantitative restrictions can have similar terms of trade effects to tariffs, Article XI (Quantitative Restrictions) is similarly explained as protecting that bargain.[10]

The nondiscrimination rules in Articles I (Most Favored Nation) and III (National Treatment) are similarly explained as protecting the terms of trade bargain. Given three or more states, increased liberalization between two can adversely affect the terms of trade of the third. By multilateralizing liberalization, MFN protects against this possibility.[11] Similarly, domestic regulations that restrict imports may have terms of trade effects. While these may result from either discriminatory or nondiscriminatory regulation, national treatment makes it more costly for governments to manipulate terms of trade in this way, because costs cannot be targeted, making the terms of trade bargain more robust.[12]

TTT explains the General Exceptions as addressing measures that, while indirectly affecting a state's terms of trade, in fact pursue some other goal.[13] The prisoner's dilemma identified by TTT arises only when states intentionally manipulate terms of trade. Many measures will affect terms of trade without this being their goal, and their net welfare effect need not be negative.[14] In consequence, TTT does not suggest that such measures be disciplined.[15] However, the difficulties of determining whether a measure pursues a genuine nontrade goal mean that, in

---

[8] Ibid., 59–64. Politically optimal tariffs are only one point on the cooperative Pareto frontier, which includes various joint policies with differing distributive effects.

[9] It is however doubtful whether reciprocity in practice is sufficiently precise to fulfill this role (Jackson, 1989b: 123). Srinavasan suggests reciprocity converges on an inchoate sense of fairness with little relation to the concept identified by Bagwell and Staiger: (Srinavasan, 2005). Finger explicitly denies GATT reciprocity tracks that concept: (Finger, 2005: 33–34).

[10] (Krugman et al., 2012: 236–237).

[11] Without this problem, MFN would constitute an inefficient impediment to cooperation (Bagwell & Staiger, 2002: 71–94, 2010).

[12] (Horn, 2006; Horn & Mavroidis, 2004).

[13] Art. XX can also be explained under an incomplete contracting model. However, that model cannot itself identify why some considerations and not others are included in Art. XX, thus reducing to a form of legal positivism. For a noncategorical, incomplete contracting model: (Bagwell, Mavroidis and Staiger, 2002).

[14] (Bagwell & Staiger, 2002: 125–141; Mavroidis, 2007: 194; Regan, 2006: 959–960).

[15] Some restrictions on such measures may however arise from its understanding of nonviolation complaints.

practice, strict rules on border measures and discrimination may catch some such measures[16]; the General Exceptions mitigate this.

The Development Provisions (most prominently Article XVIII, Part IV, and the Enabling Clause) are potentially troubling for TTT. Historically, these responded to demands couched in terms of equity and development[17]; but such arguments are incompatible with TTT's motivational assumptions.[18] Rather, the Development Provisions are only explicable under TTT if we assume that developing countries constitute an insignificant share of international trade and cannot significantly affect the terms of trade of the major developed economies.[19] Given the centrality of reciprocity in TTT, nonreciprocity and preferential market access are significant deviations,[20] but both are explained by their limited impact on developed countries' terms of trade. This is further entrenched by graduation provisions that withdraw preferences once exporters become internationally competitive.[21]

TTT thus tells a plausible story about Core Disciplines, General Exceptions. and Development Provisions. It has been subject to various criticisms.[22] The most significant is its reliance on the implausible premise that states are significantly motivated by terms of trade.[23] Efforts to translate the language of market access, which clearly is a concern in trade negotiations, into the language of terms of trade are insufficient to avoid this objection.[24] It is similarly insufficient to argue that the externalities from trade policies are mediated through terms of trade effects; to support TTT's explanatory claims policies must be motivated by those effects, as this motivation in turn establishes their inefficiency and

---

[16] I take this point up further in §6.3.3 below.   [17] (Lim, 2012).

[18] TTT assumes states maximize their national welfare subject to domestic distributive concerns, while explaining the development provisions in terms of equity requires assuming developed states are willing to sacrifice their own welfare to realize gains for developing countries.

[19] (Horn et al., 2010: 396). The Development Provisions have not been a focus of TTT theorists; the suggestions in this paragraph therefore combine brief references in the literature with what seems the most logical way to account for these exceptions from this perspective.

[20] For this point, albeit in a less formal model: (Charnovitz, 2002b: 37).

[21] (Mavroidis, 2007: 141).

[22] See generally: (Ethier, 2004; Mavroidis, 2007: 14–18; Regan, 2006).

[23] (Ethier, 2004; Krugman et al., 2012c: 255–256; Regan, 2006: 969–981, 2014: 410–414). Although for a contrasting result: (Broda et al., 2008).

[24] (Bagwell & Staiger, 2002: 28–30; Mavroidis, 2007: 17–18). The biggest problems appear where concerns for terms of trade and market access suggest opposite approaches, including export duties and subsidies.

constitutes the prisoner's dilemma.[25] However, given my focus on fit in this part, I bracket these problems of justification, focusing instead on how TTT explains the provisions of the GATT and the case-law.[26]

6.2.2   Protectionism: Restraining Irrationality

The Protectionism Theory (PT) tells a different story.[27] Whereas TTT emphasizes practices that are locally welfare-enhancing but globally inefficient, PT addresses the domestic inefficiency of restrictive trade policies. It starts from the theory of comparative advantage, which teaches that states gain from liberal trade policies, regardless of whether these are also adopted by others.[28] PT claims that the GATT disciplines restrictive policies that, by inhibiting efficient exchanges and distorting domestic prices, forego these potential gains, and so reduce national welfare.[29]

PT theorists tell various stories about why such welfare impairing policies are adopted, and how trade agreements help prevent them. One shows how the concentration of benefits and dispersal of costs from protectionism lead to an imbalance of political lobbying, explaining trade agreements as tools for balancing the lobbying activities of exporting and import-competing industries.[30] A second highlights governments' difficulties sending credible signals about future economic policy, explaining trade agreements as commitment devices whereby governments bind themselves in respect of future actions.[31] In either case, PT theorists regard protectionism as a political pathology: it is a function of special interests co-opting government to place their interests ahead of national welfare.

---

[25] (Regan, 2006: 954–956).   [26] See generally: §2.6.2 above.

[27] Regan suggests this story reflects the shared self-understanding of trade practitioners: (Regan, 2015).

[28] (Krugman et al., 2012: 54–77). While modern trade models are more complicated than Ricardo's, the basic result remains the same. Monopolistic competition models identify harms from free trade in certain circumstances; however, as Krugman argues, these rarely suffice to justify restrictive policies: (Krugman, 1992). To the extent these models justify unilateral intervention, they may motivate an alternative prisoner's dilemma account of the GATT.

[29] For a classic statement of this view: (Jackson, 1989b: ch. 1). See also (Baldwin, 2012: 32–33; Mavroidis, 2012: 16–18).

[30] (Krugman et al., 2012: 260–266). For reviews of this approach: (Rodrik, 1995; Rogowski, 2006; Trebilcock & Howse, 1999: 16).

[31] E.g. (Maggi & Rodriguez-Clare, 1998; Staiger & Tabellini, 1987).

Regan advances a generalized version of PT, which he labels the "domestic irrationality story."[32] He defines protectionism as "regulation (including taxation) adopted *for the purpose* of improving the competitive position of some domestic economic actors, usually import-competing producers, *vis-à-vis* their foreign competitors."[33] Protectionism, so understood, is fundamentally concerned with the motivation rather than the effect of regulation or taxation.[34] While Regan accepts that states pursue goals other than national welfare, including distributive goals, he argues protectionism is an inefficient tool for these purposes: there are almost always less socially costly alternatives available. PT's objection to protectionism thus becomes a special case of a general principle of efficiency in public policy.[35]

PT explains the Core Disciplines as restricting such inefficient protectionism. Tariffs and quotas are disciplined because they distort domestic prices, with consequent efficiency effects.[36] The nondiscrimination disciplines are similarly explained in terms of domestic efficiency.[37] Thus, MFN avoids efficiency costs where discrimination among countries causes trade diversion, shifting demand to more expensive alternatives.[38] National Treatment addresses specifically protectionist regulations, which treat domestic and imported products differently *in order to* improve competitive conditions for domestic products, with consequent efficiency costs.[39]

Like TTT, PT explains Article XX as protecting measures that, while *prima facie* objectionable, in fact lack the requisite motivation.[40] While recognizing that measures pursuing nonprotectionist goals may be

---

[32] (Regan, 2006: 967–968).   [33] Ibid., 952.

[34] For an alternative effects-based definition, (Neven, 2001). Regan argues that, provided regulations are domestically efficient, they are also internationally efficient, obviating the need to address unintended "protectionist" effects: (Regan, 2002: 452–453).

[35] Ethier combines the two approaches, showing how domestically inefficient protectionism generates international externalities that are in turn addressed through trade agreements. However, by combining international and domestic welfare functions without a common metric, he loses the capacity of both PT and TTT to distinguish between efficient and inefficient externalities, and hence to explain (other than based on revealed preferences) why some measures are disciplined while others are not (Ethier, 2004) (While this is not a novel criticism, I can locate no source for it.).

[36] (Krugman et al., 2012: 229–232).   [37] (Choi, 2003: 3).

[38] (Jackson, 1989b: ch. 6). Trade diversion occurs when differing levels of protection imposed on different exporters lead consumers to prefer products of less efficient exporters over those of more efficient exporters, because the former are subject to lower levels of protection and so are made to appear less expensive or more desirable to consumers.

[39] (Sykes, 1999b; Verhoosel, 2002: 76–78).

[40] Jackson explains Article XX in somewhat different terms, as protecting interests deemed to outweigh the value of free trade (Jackson, 1989b: ch. 9). However, this makes sense only if we understand the WTO as fundamentally deregulatory, which is difficult to reconcile

domestically inefficient, it is only protectionist measures that are *necessarily* so, and hence it is only protectionist measures that require to be disciplined.[41] Measures falling under Article XX are not protectionist, and hence not disciplined.[42] Like TTT, exponents of PT recognize that it may not be possible to distinguish between objectionable and nonobjectionable measures, requiring broader restrictions than the theory otherwise implies. However, theory alone cannot draw this line: rather, it depends on the difficulties of proof and the costs of under- and over-disciplining.[43]

Because PT explains the GATT as disciplining domestically inefficient measures, the Development Provisions cannot be explained simply in terms of equity: we do not help developing countries by freeing them to harm themselves. Rather, to the extent PT explains the Development Provisions, it must show how particular conditions prevailing in developing countries mean that measures are efficient that elsewhere would be inefficient.[44] Thus, for example, market failures may make infant industry protection efficient for developing but not developed countries.[45] Similarly, nonreciprocity, provided it is interpreted narrowly, can be explained as reflecting the rationality of selective protectionism for developing but not for developed countries.[46] Preferential market access is less easily explained, as there is little reason to assume the efficiency costs of tariffs vary significantly depending on whether the exporter is a developed or developing country.[47]

The most common objection to PT is its failure to explain why, if the ill that trade agreements address is domestic inefficiency, international disciplines are necessary or appropriate to treat it.[48] Further, if governments are motivated to benefit vested interests through protectionism, we might wonder why they would want to tie their hands through trade agreements. As noted, existing accounts emphasize the role of trade

---

with more recent practice, and can identify a distinct value in free trade. Certainly, under PT, which addresses Pareto inefficiencies, there can be no question of outweighing.

[41] (Regan, 2006: 986–987). We can imagine other regulatory disciplines motivated by both PT and Regan's extended domestic irrationality view, some of which are discussed in Chapter 9.

[42] (Sykes, 1999b: 32).

[43] For an attempt to assess these latter costs: (Howse & Levy, 2013: 339). I discuss these problems further in §6.3 below.

[44] (Bhagwati, 1988: ch. 5; Lester et al., 2012: 847–848).

[45] (Krugman et al., 2012c: 287–291).   [46] (Ray, 1998: 650–654).

[47] (Panagariya, 2002: 1426). PT can defend targeted preferences based on incentivizing industrialization, but this cannot explain the way the preference system has in fact developed.

[48] (Mavroidis, 2012: 17; Regan, 2006: 966–967).

agreements in stimulating balancing coalitions, offsetting political costs, and constituting credible commitments[49]; but many of these functions could be achieved without international discipline.

In the revised form advanced by Regan, PT faces a second objection. It claims that protectionism is almost always inefficient. In national income terms, this is plausibly the case. However, Regan's domestic irrationality approach accepts that states, like their citizens, pursue diverse goals. Efficiency is therefore understood in terms of regulatory preference satisfaction.[50] Yet there are clearly regulatory preferences that *can* be efficiently pursued through protectionism; most obviously, preferences over production location. If such preferences are admitted, PT's claim of domestic inefficiency fails.[51] Regan avoids this conclusion by assuming that such location-based preferences are a function of political manipulation by protection-seeking industries, and so are invalid.[52] However, as he himself recognizes, many other regulatory preferences may similarly reflect political manipulation. It is only because he regards this as less common that he argues we should accept these latter preferences, but not those supporting protectionism.[53]

More generally, his account lacks any obvious way to distinguish illicit manipulation from the normal operation of political processes. Arrow's theorem teaches that, given relatively trivial assumptions, collective preferences cannot be consistently derived from the aggregation of individual preferences[54]; and in practice, regulatory preferences always express the views of politically motivated groups, whether producers, consumers, or simply particularly concerned pressure groups.[55] Given this, it is not clear how Regan distinguishes between legitimate and illegitimate preferences; but this is essential for PT to justify its prescriptions.

6.2.3   EGC: Expressing Justice

TTT accounts for trade agreements in terms of global efficiency, while PT explains them through local efficiency. Each approach argues that trade

---

[49] (Mavroidis, 2012: 16–17). See text at fn. 30 and 31 above.   [50] (Regan, 2006: 959).

[51] (Regan, 2015: 399–400).   [52] (Regan, 2006: 963, 987–989).

[53] Ibid., 964 Bona fide location-based preferences seem particularly plausible in the context of traditional industries, which are associated with national identity; and agriculture, which substantially shapes physical environments. E.g. (Guy, 2007: 1–9; Jackson, 1989b) Cf. (Risse, 2012: 270), §5.5 above.

[54] (Campbell & Kelly, 2002; Trachtman, 1998: 57–58).

[55] This is the generalized upshot of the collective action problems motivating Regan's argument.

agreements promote national welfare, and that their specific terms protect anticipated welfare gains. Without denying that trade agreements are welfare-enhancing, EGC suggests an alternative hypothesis. It claims that states owe outsiders, whether persons or peoples, justifications for the measures they adopt. To the extent this is the case, we might expect rules governing state action in particular domains to express the conditions under which such action is justified. This, EGC suggests, is a function of WTO law.

Given this suggestion, how does EGC explain these provisions? I provide an overview of EGC's account in this section, developing it further thereafter.

Turning first to border measures and discrimination. As discussed in Chapter 1, such measures, as a rule, pursue their goals specifically through the regulation of international economic activity, and so constitute ETMs.[56] We might therefore account for restrictions on such measures in GATT Articles I, II, III, and XI by reference to the demanding standard by which EGC claims such measures should be judged. It is because they constitute ETMs, EGC suggests, that these measures are disciplined. Tariffs, quotas, and discriminatory domestic taxes and regulations represent, of course, a subset of ETMs; and there might even be a small class of tariffs that do not constitute ETMs. However, these categories constitute an adequate proxy, which is more straightforward to apply in practice than the ETM definition set out in Chapter 1.

In most cases, these measures will not meet the standard prescribed by EGC, and so are properly prohibited. However, in appropriate circumstances, ETMs may be justified under EGC, whether under global equality or self-determination. If the restrictions in Articles I, II, III, and XI are understood as identifying and restraining ETMs, we might in turn understand the Development Provisions and General Exceptions as tracking the conditions for their justification.

We thus understand the Development Provisions as expressing EGC's justification of ETMs pursuing global equality of individual opportunity by improving the position of less-advantaged individuals. Those provisions facilitate developing countries in improving their position, whether by giving them greater freedom to adopt measures that they perceive as advancing their own economic development, or by giving them access to markets on terms that promote that development, despite the costs this imposes on nonpreferred countries.[57] It is not simply that these measures

---

[56] §1.6.1 above. On discrimination, see also §6.3.4 below.   [57] Cf. §3.7 above.

are efficient for developing countries, as PT suggests, or that they impose negligible costs, as TTT assumes, but rather that their use is justified to outsiders subject to them, including in particular, developed countries. This would remain the case regardless of whether their economic effects were identical for developed and developing states, or whether they impose significant terms of trade costs on others.[58]

The General Exceptions can similarly be understood under EGC. EGC anticipates two routes, apart from the primary egalitarian justification, whereby ETMs might be justified. Both fall under self-determination. The first justifies measures that are necessary for a people to become or remain self-determining. The second invokes ends that are, as a matter of contingent fact, shared by those subject to the relevant measures. EGC suggests that each specific Article XX exemption should be understood as expressing one or other, or in some cases both, of these ideas.[59] So, for example, EGC understands Article XX(a), on public morals, as primarily concerned with peoples' protection of the public culture of their own states and secondarily with vindicating internationally shared moral standards.[60]

EGC thus suggests a plausible reconstruction of the Core Disciplines, explaining both the prohibitions and the exceptions. Like TTT and PT, it faces obvious objections, most prominently in its account of tariff binding (Article II). EGC characterizes tariffs as ETMs, and to that extent objectionable. However, the GATT does not prohibit tariffs, instead lowering them through progressive rounds of multilateral negotiations.[61] EGC thus seems not to fit this central aspect of the GATT/WTO system.

A number of responses might be offered. First, we might argue that the GATT expresses a norm of progressive tariff reduction, and current developed country bindings effectively prohibit significantly trade-distorting tariffs in most cases.[62] Second, focusing on reciprocity in negotiations, we might argue that remaining unjustified tariffs reflect a coordination problem

---

[58] This is subject to the obvious caveat that such measures are supported by some plausible economic theory as to their effectiveness for development purposes; I take up this point further in Chapter 7.

[59] Other provisions that I do not examine might be similarly understood in these terms, most obviously Art. XII (Balance of Payments) and Art. XXI (Security Exceptions). The historic exclusion of agriculture from GATT liberalization, and the continuing special regime under the Agreement on Agriculture, might also be explained in this way.

[60] I take this point up further in Chapter 7 and, in more detail, in: (Suttle, 2017).

[61] GATT II.1(a) and XXVIII bis.

[62] (World Trade Organization. et al., 2012). Jackson argues this was the case even before the Uruguay Round (Jackson, 1989b: 117–118). The duty progressively to reduce tariffs is

that can only be solved iteratively.[63] Third, we might enquire whether remaining tariff peaks reflect areas where measures are justified as preserving some important aspect of self-determination.[64] Fourth, and least satisfactorily, we might explain it as the accommodation of normative principle to inhospitable political reality.[65] This last explanation is unsatisfactory because *ad hoc*. Political contingency can be invoked to excuse a multitude of theoretical sins, so we are rightly skeptical of any story that invokes it; but in particular cases, it may be the best explanation.[66]

6.3   The Problem of Discrimination

At this point, there seems little to choose between these approaches. Each tells a story about what trade agreements are for, and why they might include provisions like the Core Disciplines. However, those stories are quite different. Importantly for legal practice, each has different implications for the interpretation and application of those disciplines. To adjudicate between them, we must examine those implications in more detail, in the context of specific interpretive questions. It is to that task that I now turn.

This requires some narrowing of focus. While the previous section addressed the Core Disciplines as a whole, this section looks specifically at nondiscrimination. I make this choice for two reasons.

First, it is in addressing discrimination, more than border measures, that the three approaches diverge. Aspects of the border measures rules might support one approach or the other. The lack of bindings on export taxes, for example, might count against TTT, although it also has implications for PT and EGC.[67] By contrast, the fact that tariffs are bound rather than eliminated

---

reflected in various provisions including, in the GATT, the Preamble, Art. XXVIII, and XXXVI.8; and in the Marrakesh Agreement, the Preamble and Art. III.2.

[63] On the need to solve coordination problems to realize justice, §4.2.2 above. For a moralized variant, albeit lacking an account of relevant moral obligations: (Bird et al., 2009). In fact, these coordination problems are precisely the reason TTT invokes reciprocity and iteration.

[64] See esp. §5.4 above. This seems most plausible for agriculture.

[65] Recall Ruggie's characterization of international authority as "a fusion of power and legitimate social purpose": (Ruggie, 1982: 385). On the risks that normative argument obscures the realities of power in international negotiations: (Jörke, 2013).

[66] Recall the discussion of political constraints on theoretical fit in Chapter 2. We there recognized that failures of fit were less troubling where, as seems plausible here, we can point to narrowly political reasons why practice might not conform to principle.

[67] Thus, Mavroidis, while advancing a version of TTT, invokes domestic political economy to explain the absence of both uses of and constraints on export duties: (Mavroidis, 2012:

might count against PT and EGC, but is hardly conclusive.[68] Article XI's prohibition on export restraints is perhaps less obviously relevant to PT than TTT and EGC; but recent experience with Chinese export duties highlights how far export restraints can serve simple protectionism.[69] These points aside, however, the rules on border measures are largely compatible with each approach. By contrast, EGC's account of nondiscrimination is potentially quite different to the two economic explanations, and therefore provides a useful focus for considering its relative merits.

Second, the nondiscrimination provisions' textual ambiguity makes purposive interpretation inevitable. There simply are not the resources within the texts to support specific conclusions about these rules. They therefore allow us to see most clearly how the competing theories might guide that task.

I first review the relevant obligations to highlight their ambiguity. I then review the AB's jurisprudence on likeness, which I suggest has failed satisfactorily to address this.[70] This, I next suggest, reflects the difficulty of reconciling the nondiscrimination provisions with the prescriptions of either PT or TTT. Finally, I show how EGC can suggest a more satisfactory approach.

---

60) Ethier emphasizes export taxes' continued availability in rejecting TTT: (Ethier, 2004: 304). Cf. (Bagwell et al., 2013: 129–130). While in theory, export taxes can replicate the protective effects to tariffs, in practice using them for this purpose will usually demand prohibitive political and cognitive resources: (Lerner, 1936).

[68] Indeed, it might plausibly be argued that the extent of tariff cuts achieved to date itself undermines TTT. Recall, TTT assumes a trade-off between terms of trade gains and efficiency costs from tariffs; by jointly optimizing these we identify the optimum tariff. Because terms of trade effects are a function of market power, optimum tariffs are small for all but the largest importers. If observed tariff cuts exceed estimated optimum tariffs, this suggests negotiations address more than terms of trade effects. I am not aware of any study comprehensively addressing this issue. A promising starting point might be: (Broda et al., 2008). Bagwell and Staiger argue empirical evidence from accession negotiations supports their position: (Bagwell & Staiger, 2011b).

[69] *China-Rare Earths; China-Raw Materials.* Historically, nonagricultural export duties have been used predominantly by resource-exporting developing countries in the context of industrialization policies (Qin, 2012: 1163). We might thus understand the absence of disciplines as partly reflecting EGC's egalitarian concerns. Export restrictions in agriculture are less readily explicable in these terms, and may better be understood under self-determination: (Karapinar, 2011: 391). Export duty disciplines in developing accession countries, most prominently China, might challenge this account. See (Qin, 2012: 1149–1154). However these, like many other provisions of China's Accession Protocol, can equally be understood as part of a broader effort to balance a rising great power, the one case where Chapter 4 suggested realist arguments might directly challenge EGC: (Qin, 2010: 168). Cf. §4.2.1 above.

[70] (Mavroidis, 2007: 192–193).

6.3.1   The Ambiguity of Discrimination

Nondiscrimination features at various points in the goods regime.[71] As the AB in *EC-Tariff Preferences* recognized, its ordinary meaning is ambiguous, including both the drawing of distinctions *per se*, and the drawing of distinctions on an "improper basis."[72] The principal nondiscrimination obligations in the GATT, Article I (Most Favored Nation) and Article III (National Treatment), do not refer to discrimination. Rather, they refer variously to treating less favorably, or taxing dissimilarly, or extending treatment "immediately and unconditionally," to various classes of products, whether "like" or "directly competitive or substitutable." In each case, they require that we identify two categories of products that stand in some relevant relation, and compare the treatment afforded to each against the relevant standard. However, the same ambiguities appear in each case, whether we focus on the treatment to be accorded, or the categories of products.

This is clear from a cursory inquiry into these terms' ordinary meanings[73]?

What, for example, does it mean for two products to be "like" one another?[74] This is plainly a matter of degree; two products may be more or less like one another.[75] It is also a matter of kind; whether two objects are "like" depends on how we classify them.[76] The concept of likeness has very little intrinsic content.[77] Rather, it seems, asking whether two items are "like" invites the response "in what sense?" and "to what extent?," and indirectly, "for what purpose?."[78] Directly competitive or substitutable is perhaps clearer, emphasizing the market and the uses of products.[79] However, it remains a matter of degree. We must still ask "to what extent?"[80]

---

[71] E.g. GATT Art. I, III, XX, TBT 2.1, SPS 2.3, 5.6, Enabling Clause fn. 3.

[72] *EC-Tariff Preferences*, (AB), §152–153.

[73] As to the relevance of which: *Vienna Convention on the Law of Treaties*, Art. 31(1).

[74] For discussions of this concept: (Choi, 2003; Conrad, 2011: 168–232; Horn & Mavroidis, 2004; Hudec, 1998; Porges & Trachtman, 2003).

[75] *US–Taxes on Automobiles*, (GATT Panel), §5.6.   [76] (Roessler, 1997: 29).

[77] Horn and Mavroidis suggest likeness has "no context-independent 'true' economic meaning": (Horn & Mavroidis, 2004: 42).

[78] For example, Howse and Regan argue: "The real issue is the existence of differences between the products that justify different regulation . . . This is not a recondite interpretation; it is the ordinary meaning of 'like' in this context." (Howse & Regan, 2000: 260–261) Cf. (Regan, 2002: 445–449).

[79] *Korea-Alcoholic Beverages*, (AB), §115. This quality of direct competition or substitution is emphasized in: (Howse & Regan, 2000: 267).

[80] *Korea-Alcoholic Beverages*, (AB), §116.

The comparative standards are similarly open. "Less favorable" seems clearer than "dissimilar," which is in turn clearer than "extended immediately and unconditionally"; but none is especially precise. More problematic, is it relevant why a product is treated as it is?[81] Is sufficiently different treatment enough, or must treatment be accorded to a product *because of* its origin to constitute a breach?[82] "[S]o as to afford protection" might support the latter view, but it also raises further questions.[83]

Applying these rules, then, raises interpretive questions whose answers affect the scope of the rules and policy space allowed to members.[84] Each must be answered individually; but they together pose the question noted above: are we concerned about distinctions between products *per se*, or only distinctions drawn on some improper basis, and if the latter, then which bases are improper? Unfortunately, while the AB's approach has evolved, it has yet to provide a satisfactory answer. As these problems are best illustrated in the likeness jurisprudence, it is here I will focus, before linking the problem back to the theoretical approaches introduced above.[85]

6.3.2   Three Approaches to Likeness

Three distinct approaches appear in the later GATT and WTO jurisprudence on likeness, here labeled Regulatory Likeness, Objective Characteristics, and Competitive Likeness.[86]

The dominant approach in the earlier WTO cases, beginning with *Japan – Alcohol II*, assesses likeness by reference to the "objective characteristics" of

---

[81] (Bagwell et al., 2013: 163–167).

[82] Taxation "in excess of" domestic products is generally understood in the first, stricter, sense: *Argentina-Hides and Leather, (Panel)*, §11.184,11.260; *Japan–Alcohol II*, (AB), p.16. A recent unappealed panel report interprets "unconditionally" under MFN in the latter sense: *US-Poultry (China)*, (Panel), §7.435. The AB's refusal to interpret TBT's concept of "legitimate regulatory distinction" into GATT I and III seems largely to settle the question in favor of the former, stricter, approach: *EC-Seal Products*, (AB), § 5.87–5.117.

[83] On this question (Hudec, 1998: 16; Porges & Trachtman, 2003). For a purely econometric approach (Neven, 2001).

[84] (Choi, 2003: 5).

[85] Lang describes the emergence of these questions, and more generally the problem of delineating states' regulatory autonomy, as the breakdown of an earlier consensus that included shared understandings about legitimate behavior and what was and was not of concern to the trade regime. It was these understandings, much more than the texts themselves, that formerly guided members in bringing complaints, and panelists in resolving them: (Lang, 2011: esp. ch. 7, 8).

[86] The various approaches to likeness described here are identified in a number of existing accounts including: (Conrad, 2011; Hudec, 1998; Verhoosel, 2002).

the relevant products.[87] Originating with the *GATT Working Party on Border Tax Adjustments*, this Objective Characteristics approach examines likeness, on a case-by-case basis, in terms of end uses, consumer tastes and preferences, the product's properties, nature and quality, and tariff classification.[88]

That this test is radically indeterminate should be obvious, given the points made above. It requires addressing likeness divorced from the context and purpose of the question. Assuming any products must have some similarities and some differences, it gives no guidance on which differences matter. Nor does it tell us how to weigh similarities and differences falling under each of the four categories mentioned. The AB has effectively conceded this indeterminacy, describing likeness as "an accordion [that] stretches and squeezes in different places as different provisions of the WTO Agreement are applied," lacking any "precise and absolute" definition.[89] While evocative, this image provides little guidance to members or subsequent panels. Likeness is a case-by-case matter, to be determined having regard to whichever factors adjudicators decide are significant in a particular case. Hudec characterizes this as a "smell test," an empty formula obscuring the real basis for decisions, which he suggests must be something like the GATT "Aims and Effects" test that it purported to replace.[90]

The Aims and Effects test appeared in two leading GATT panels, until rejected in *Japan – Alcohol II*.[91] Those panels recognized that likeness was inherently fluid[92]; that equating likeness with identity would unduly restrict Articles I and III[93]; and that if likeness was not equated with identity, then like products would necessarily share some features, but not others. The practical question was therefore "which differences may form the basis of regulatory distinctions ... [o]r, conversely, which similarities between products prevent regulatory distinctions?"[94] To answer this question, panels adopted a teleological approach, arguing that Article III was fundamentally concerned with protectionism, and served only to prohibit "regulatory distinctions between products applied so as to afford protection to domestic

---

[87] *Japan-Alcohol II*, (AB), p. 20. See also *Canada-Periodicals*, (AB), pp. 21–22. *Japan-Alcohol II* revived a test previously elaborated in *Japan-Alcohol I*, (GATT Panel), §5.6. Cf. *Spain-Unroasted Coffee* (GATT Panel), §4.6–9.

[88] *Border Tax Adjustments*, report of the Working Party adopted December 2, 1970, L/3464, para 18.

[89] Japan-Alcohol II, (AB), p. 21.   [90] (Hudec, 1998).

[91] *US-Autos*, (GATT Panel), §5.5-.10; *US-Malt Beverages*, (GATT Panel), §5.25.

[92] *US-Autos*, §5.9.   [93] Ibid., §5.8.   [94] Ibid., §5.6. Cf. (Trachtman, 1998: 65–67).

production."[95] Where measures drew *bona fide* regulatory distinctions, otherwise than so as to afford protection, products should be regarded as "unlike," simply because they did not share the relevant characteristic.[96] Whether a regulatory distinction was applied so as to afford protection turned on the aims and effects of a challenged measure.[97]

This approach is characterized as Regulatory Likeness.[98] It has the virtues of recognizing the indeterminacy and contextuality of "likeness," and providing a straightforward solution to the problems this poses. Instead of asking whether two products are "like," we consider whether, *given a member's objectives*, the differences between them make them relevantly unlike.

Most recently, the AB has emphasized the competitive relation between products at the expense of the Objective Characteristics approach. Thus, in *EC–Asbestos*, the majority treated the product's objective characteristics as informing a cross-competitiveness test, examining how each affected the competitive relation between products, holding that "[a] determination of 'likeness' . . . is, fundamentally, a determination about the nature and extent of a competitive relationship between and among products."[99]

This approach is labeled Competitive Likeness. In giving competitiveness priority, it brings some coherence to the concept of likeness, explaining how the various criteria fit together. However, as observed by the dissenting AB member in *Asbestos*, emphasizing the economic relation between products to the exclusion of other factors risks ignoring cases where products are clearly unlike, despite any competitive relation.[100]

Notwithstanding these concerns, the AB has since reiterated the fundamentally economic character of likeness, explaining that product characteristics are relevant only in so far as they help identify "the nature and extent of a competitive relationship."[101] Criteria that in *Japan–Alcohol* constituted a test for likeness are now simply "tools . . . for organizing and assessing the evidence relating to the competitive relationship between and among the products."[102] Likeness is explicitly reduced to competitiveness or substitutability, albeit under Article III.2, it requires a very high degree of competitiveness, close to but less than perfect substitutability.[103]

---

[95] Ibid., §5.7.   [96] Ibid., §5.9.   [97] Ibid., §5.10.

[98] For discussions see e.g. (Hudec, 1998; Porges & Trachtman, 2003; Regan, 2003).

[99] *EC-Asbestos*, (AB), §99.   [100] Ibid., §151–154; (Flett, 2010: 28).

[101] *Philippines-Distilled Spirits*, (AB), §119.   [102] Ibid., §153.

[103] It has been suggested the "aims and effects" analysis might be revived at the comparative stage of the analysis, and certain AB dicta support this approach. However, this does not

While the cases advance various justifications for this evolving approach, these are unconvincing. In rejecting the Aims and Effects test, the Panel in *Japan – Alcohol*, in reasoning endorsed by the AB, emphasized its lack of textual support, and the difficulty identifying regulatory purpose in particular cases.[104] The textual argument is weak. Likeness is a fluid concept to which the panels and AB necessarily give content; and the Objective Characteristics approach similarly lacks textual support.[105] The problems of identifying regulatory purpose are similarly overstated; in other areas, including Article XX and protective application under Article III.2, the AB has successfully addressed this question.[106] The move from Objective Characteristics to Competitive Likeness is similarly unmotivated. In *Asbestos*, the AB started from the assumption that Article III seeks to prevent members affecting the competitive relationship between domestic and imported products so as to afford protection to domestic production.[107] From this, it concluded not simply that a competitive relation is a necessary condition for likeness, which seems plausible, but rather that it was a sufficient condition – a clear *non sequitur*[108]. The incoherence of Objective Characteristics might itself constitute a compelling reason to favor Competitive Likeness, but the AB has never acknowledged this failing in its former approach.

6.3.3   The Contradictions of PT and TTT

The AB's own explanations seem insufficient, then, to justify its approach. However, existing theories similarly fail to do so.

In an ideal world, PT and TTT converge in advocating Regulatory Likeness. Each regards Competitive Likeness as too broad, condemning cases where similar products are treated differently on grounds irrelevant to the particular ills those theories identify (protectionism, terms of trade manipulation).[109] However, each can be reconciled with Competitive Likeness in practice. Assuming states have both incentive and capacity

---

resolve the conceptual confusion, at least under the GATT: (Flett, 2013). Further, the AB in *Seals* seems clearly to reject this possibility. See fn. 82, 115, 119. My argument here is limited to the GATT: as the AB has emphasized, discrimination under TBT 2.1 is different, at least in part for the structural reasons emphasized below: *US-Clove Cigarettes*, (AB), §174–175; Cf. § 6.3.5 below.

[104] *Japan-Alcohol II*, (Panel), §6.16.   [105] (Conrad, 2011).
[106] (Horn & Mavroidis, 2004: 48–50, 55–58).   [107] *EC-Asbestos*, (AB), §98.
[108] Ibid., §99.   [109] (Horn & Mavroidis, 2004: 56–57; Regan, 2003: 744).

to conceal their true regulatory purpose, a Regulatory Likeness test will fail in many cases to identify objectionable measures.[110] Competitive Likeness might then provide a satisfactory proxy for Regulatory Likeness; we might more effectively identify protectionism and/or terms of trade manipulation by targeting Competitive Likeness than by directly targeting Regulatory Likeness.[111]

A number of commentators offer qualified defenses of Competitive Likeness on this basis.[112] A benefit of this approach is its straightforward explanation of the function of the General Exceptions in Article XX. If we assume that, by design, the prohibitions in Articles I and III catch many measures that are not in principle objectionable, then we can understand Article XX as exempting some of these "false positives" from those prohibitions.[113] Their combined effect is to more closely track the underlying rationale than either untempered Competitive Likeness, which would be over-inclusive, or direct Regulatory Likeness, which while optimal in theory, would be under-inclusive in practice.

There are however problems with this approach.

First, Article XX provides a closed and restrictive list of purposes.[114] Many policies that states pursue are not protected under Article XX.[115] To the extent such policies distinguish among competitively like products, they could not be defended under Article XX.[116] This implies

---

[110] The AB has recognized this problem in various contexts: *Chile-Alcoholic Beverages*, (AB), §62; *US-Clove Cigarettes*, (AB), §113.

[111] (Lester et al., 2012: 262).

[112] E.g. (Choi, 2003: 8; Horn, 2006). Others advocate using competitive likeness as an initial proxy, subject to rebuttal based on regulatory purpose: (Horn & Mavroidis, 2004; Regan, 2003: 451).

[113] (Horn, 2006; Mavroidis, 2007: 254–258).

[114] (Davies, 2009: 537–538; Horn & Mavroidis, 2004: 56–57).

[115] In *Seals*, the EU raised this concern, albeit unsuccessfully, in the comparative analysis under I.1 and III.4: *EC-Seal Products*, (AB), §5.118. Exactly which policies can and cannot be brought within Article XX will depend on how the specific paragraphs are interpreted, a point I come back to in the next chapter. It suffices here to note two relatively clear examples of excluded policies. First, Regan suggests environmental regulations addressing unpleasant smelling but physically harmless emissions (Regan, 2009). Second, regulations concerned with the appearance of both built and natural environments, of the kind common in planning laws; a rule prohibiting the use of aluminum cladding on buildings, for example, could readily yield a GATT complaint that would be difficult to defend under Art. XX. While these might seem somewhat trivial examples, more obviously significant cases, including environmental concerns generally, are avoided only through a very wide reading of the Art. XX categories, which reading in turn requires to be justified.

[116] (Mavroidis, 2007: 249–253). For this critique, addressing the Objective Characteristics approach: (Mattoo & Subramanian, 1998: 307–308). This creates an understandable

certainty can be purchased only at the cost of restricting states' legitimate discretion.

Second, Article XX itself presupposes that we can determine regulatory purpose by asking whether measures pursue one of the listed goals or constitute "arbitrary or unjustifiable discrimination . . . or a disguised restriction on international trade." Yet if this inquiry is possible under Article XX, it is surely also possible under Articles I and III? There is thus little reason to accept the additional constraints on domestic policy implied by Competitive Likeness.[117]

Such considerations lead others to reject Competitive Likeness for Regulatory Likeness.[118] If, they reason, it is possible to identify regulatory purpose, then, this should be done at the initial stage, not under a subsequent exceptions analysis. This ensures governments pursuing legitimate policies other than those protected under Article XX can do so, provided they do not adopt means prohibited under the Agreements.

However, advocates of Regulatory Likeness struggle to explain the role of Article XX in this account. If, as they suggest, only measures that are in fact protectionist or actively seek to manipulate terms of trade fall under Articles I and III, then the set of measures falling under both Articles I or III and Article XX is empty. Yet the AB has made clear that Article XX does indeed apply to Articles I and III; thus adopting Regulatory Likeness, informed by either PT or TTT, requires rejecting established AB jurisprudence on this point.[119]

---

incentive on the part of the AB to interpret the Article XX list expansively, to a point where the list itself imposes no significant restriction. While this might avoid the objection of unnecessary restrictiveness, it seems clearly at odds with the structure of the agreement, effectively reading out the bulk of the relevant provision.

One way economic approaches might be reconciled to such restrictiveness is by reference to an effects-based, rather than a motivation-based, terms of trade approach; however, while this would suggest restricting states' pursuit of *bona fide* policies in particular circumstances, it would motivate a proportionality analysis, rather than the categorical exceptions in fact found in Article XX.

[117] Opinions vary on whether under- or over-regulation is more problematic in this context: (Howse & Levy, 2013: 339).

[118] E.g. (Mavroidis, 2007; Neven, 2001; Regan, 2003; Verhoosel, 2002).

[119] Mavroidis stands out for his directness in confronting this problem, arguing the AB's case-law is misguided, and that Article XX should rarely apply to Articles I and III: (Mavroidis, 2007: 256–258). The only role he concedes for it is justifying embargoes targeting unrelated concerns: (Mavroidis, 2012: 361–362). The problem is also recognized, albeit less directly, in: (Hudec, 1998). For the view that this was the negotiators' intention: (Irwin et al., 2008: 162–163).

The AB has recognized the importance of Article XX in shaping its interpretation of Articles I and III: *US-Clove Cigarettes*, (AB), §109. A similar point appears in *US-Gasoline*, (AB), p. 18. By contrast, in *EC-Asbestos*, the AB (§115) argued the two should be

Exponents of PT and TTT thus face a dilemma. Assuming, as each does, that Regulatory Likeness is the ideal, Competitive Likeness imposes unnecessary restrictions to solve a nonexistent problem; whereas directly applying Regulatory Likeness is incompatible with the structure of the Agreement and the established AB case-law. Indeed, this might explain the attraction of the Objective Characteristics approach; its incoherence allowed the AB to avoid this dilemma, surreptitiously adopting Regulatory Likeness while ostensibly applying a combination of Objective Characteristics, Competitive Likeness, and General Exceptions to justify its conclusions.[120]

A further problem with Regulatory Likeness informed by PT or TTT is determining what constitutes a legitimate regulatory distinction. This is the essence of any noncompetitive likeness analysis. PT and TTT recommend disciplining only measures that pursue protectionist/terms-of-trade-manipulating goals. However, both the AB and former GATT panels have highlighted regulatory distinctions that, while pursuing *bona fide* nonprotectionist aims, would not prevent products being categorized as "like."[121]

Beyond specific cases, some classes of nonprotectionist distinction seem to raise particular concerns for both members and adjudicators.[122] The most prominent have addressed Non-Product Related Production Processes and Methodologies (NPRPPMs). NPRPPMs are regulations that treat physically identical products differently based on production methods. Particularly prominent are environmental regulations that accord different treatment to products depending on the environmental impact of their production or harvesting.[123] While not unambiguous, GATT Panel and Appellate Body reports, as well as members' practice,

---

interpreted independently, thereby avoiding the need to explain how health considerations could be addressed under both. The approach in *Asbestos* is however implicitly rejected in *Seals* where the AB observes that the existence of Art. XX "weighs heavily against an interpretation of Articles I:1 and III:4 that requires an examination of whether the detrimental impact of a measure on competitive opportunities for like imported products stems exclusively from a legitimate regulatory distinction": *EC-Seal Products*, (AB), §5.125.

[120] For an argument on these lines: (Hudec, 1998).

[121] E.g. *Argentina-Hides and Leather*, (Panel), §11.220, 11.259; *US-Malt Beverages*, (GATT Panel), §5.19.

[122] This is particularly evident in recent TBT cases, which relocate the issue to the comparative analysis. E.g. *EC-Seal Products*, (Panel), §7.290–7.301. Racist preferences and nonprotectionist origin-specific conditions are obvious examples. E.g. *Belgium-Family Allowances* (GATT Panel).

[123] E.g. *US-Tuna (Mexico)* (GATT Panel); *US-Tuna (EEC)* (GATT Panel); *US-Tuna II, (AB)*; *US-Shrimp, (AB)*. Cf. *EC-Seal Products*, (AB).

suggest distinctions based on NPRPPMs cannot distinguish products under Articles I and III.[124] While the leading authorities are unadopted GATT reports, and addressed this question under Article XI rather than Article III, they clearly reject distinctions based on NPRPPMs.[125] The reports' nonadoption reflected unrelated political considerations and, as Conrad notes, "[t]he contracting parties were mostly very appreciative of the outcome" of these disputes[126]. In the leading WTO decision, *US–Shrimp*, the United States didn't deny the *prima facie* violation, instead focusing on Article XX.[127] While references in *Dominican Republic–Cigarettes* to factors unrelated to products' foreign origin raised the possibility some NPRPPMs might be compatible with Article III, further comments in *US-Clove Cigarettes* and, especially, *EC-Seals*, seem to rule this out.[128]

Concerns about such nonprotectionist regulatory distinctions cannot be accommodated under PT or TTT. If we assume that the GATT targets protectionism or terms of trade manipulation, then there is no reason to

---

[124] Such distinctions may suffice under TBT 2.1, insofar as that provision effectively incorporates the Article XX exception analysis into the primary discrimination analysis. *US-Tuna II*, (AB), §2.11.

[125] *US-Tuna (Mexico)* (GATT Panel), §5.14–5.15, 5.24–5.34; *US-Tuna (EEC)* (GATT Panel), §5.8–5.9, 5.26§5.27, 5.36–5.39.

The textual arguments in these decisions have been heavily criticized. The better view is probably that whether NPRPPMs are permissible turns on whether the products among which they distinguish are "like" under Articles I and III. This in turn depends on how we understand likeness for these purposes. A competitive likeness approach, particularly when combined with a "hypothetical like product" analysis of the kind applied in *Canada-Periodicals* and *US-Poultry (China)*, will constitute an effective prohibition on NPRPPMs. Conversely, a regulatory likeness approach informed by PT or TTT will accept such measures.

[126] (Conrad, 2011: 17). While various members expressed concerns that *US–Tuna (Mexico)* would undermine multilateral environmental cooperation, the US "stood virtually alone in its insistence that Article XX allows scope for unilateral trade measures to protect the environment": (Gaines, 2001: 755). Cf. (Bhagwati, 2004: 154–158).

[127] *US-Shrimp*, (Panel), §3.143.

[128] *Dominican Republic-Cigarettes*, (AB), §96; *EC-Seal Products*, (AB), §5.103–105 The focus in these cases is comparison rather than likeness, reflecting the TBT jurisprudence, but this does not affect the overall argument. The Panel in *US-Tuna II* addressed this question under TBT 2.1, applying the "objective characteristics" approach. It suggested NPRPPMs as such could not make products unlike, although they could be indirectly relevant in affecting consumer tastes and preferences. The panel did accept that NPRPPMs could ground legitimate regulatory distinctions under 2.1, but the AB's decision in *Seals* seems to foreclose this possibility under GATT. While some commentators read *Tuna II* as evidence that PPMs are not a distinctive category, its relevance to the GATT can only be under the exceptions analysis: (Howse & Levy, 2013: 358–359).

discipline these measures.[129] This leads proponents of both theories to deny that NPRPPMs raise distinctive problems.[130] In response, opponents of NPRPPMs invoke sovereignty and extraterritoriality to defend their position, arguing that addressing NPRPPMs does not fall within the scope of regulatory freedom protected by Articles I and III.[131] However such arguments, in justifying disciplines otherwise than by reference to protectionism/terms of trade manipulation, clearly contradict PT/TTT.

6.3.4 Reconstructing Nondiscrimination through EGC

Accounting for these concerns, and for the relation between Articles I, III, and XX, requires explaining Articles I and III as tracking something other than protectionism or terms of trade manipulation. Neither PT nor TTT can do this.

EGC, on the other hand, can. Recall, EGC asks whether measures pursue their goals specifically through regulating international economic activity.[132] This will include protectionist and trade manipulating measures, and measures that constitute arbitrary or unjustifiable discrimination, but it will also include measures that pursue other goals, including those mentioned in Article XX, through international trade effects. A Regulatory Likeness test informed by EGC, which enquires whether products can be distinguished from a regulatory perspective that does not constitute the relevant measure as an ETM, could therefore explain Articles I and III, while maintaining their relation with the exceptions in Article XX. This does not yet explain Article XX's role[133]; but it suggests an account of discrimination that need not subsume it.

EGC can also account for the case-law on NPRPPMs by identifying what is problematic about them: they pursue their goals specifically through the regulation of international economic activity. Consider the regulations at issue in *Shrimp*, which required that exporting countries' shrimp fishing fleets adopt devices to protect sea turtles that might otherwise become caught in nets.[134] It was not in dispute in that case that the United States was concerned about turtle mortality arising from

---

[129] Indeed, Regan argues that the language of externalities applies equally to production externalities from NPRPPMs as consumption externalities from conventional regulations. (Regan, 2009: 112).
[130] (Charnovitz, 2002a; Howse & Regan, 2000; Regan, 2009).
[131] (Bartels, 2002; Mavroidis, 2007: 277–285) Cf. (Howse, 2002b: 104).   [132] §1.6.1 above.
[133] As to which see §7.3.2 below.   [134] *US-Shrimp*, (AB), para 2–6.

fishing practices in exporting countries.[135] By those regulations, it sought to incentivize the adoption of practices that result in lower overall turtle mortality.[136] Thus, the regulations pursued their goal, reduced turtle mortality, specifically through their effects on international economic activity. The exporting fishermen were directly subject to those regulations, in the sense that their effects on those fishermen were precisely the mechanism whereby the regulations pursued their goals; they were not side effects, but rather the primary mechanism by which they acted. As such, EGC claims that justification is due to those fishermen in the more stringent terms appropriate to ETMs.[137]

Some commentators deny that NPRPPMs operate in this way. Thus, Regan argues that such regulations, rather than regulating outsiders, simply prevent the citizens of the regulating state themselves promoting the objectionable activity.[138] This reflects an image of importing states as collective consumers, making consumption choices subject to the same moral considerations as individuals.[139] However, this image, by anthropomorphizing the state, elides the moral distinctiveness of institutions, the role of states in structuring the international economy, and the extent to which states, by their domestic regulatory practices, shape the options not only of insiders but also of outsiders.[140] Others focus on whether NPRPPMs coerce outsiders, which misses the point on this view.[141] Many domestic regulations coerce outsiders; what distinguishes NPRPPMs is that they directly and inclusively coerce them, which in turn affects the justifications they evoke. Finally, it is sometimes claimed that NPRPPMs need not aim at changing behavior in exporting jurisdictions; they may simply ensure that citizens of the importing state are not subject to the "moral taint" of being associated

---

[135] There are admittedly suggestions the measures also addressed competitive disadvantages from domestic regulation: *US-Shrimp*, (Panel), §3.212–3.215.

[136] (AB), §138.

[137] It is not relevant, for this analysis, whether there is a "territorial nexus" with the regulating state. This may, however, be relevant to the Article XX analysis. The AB has, to date, avoided pronouncing on the need for such a nexus under Art. XX: *US-Shrimp*, (AB), §133; *EU-Seals*, (AB), §5.173.

[138] (Regan, 2009: 113).   [139] This is expressed as "a refusal to buy": (Regan, 2009: 112).

[140] Indeed, Regan's objection here seems to be simply a claim of sovereignty or, perhaps, that choices fall under the self-determination of peoples. To the extent this is the case, the argument in Chapters 4 and 5 shows its inadequacy. The analogy to individual choice might also suggest an assumption that, provided this freedom is accorded to all, its exercise cannot be objectionable. However, as noted in Chapter 5, this latter assumption is untenable, given states of radically unequal size and influence.

[141] On NPRPPMs and coercion: (Charnovitz, 2002a: 68–69, 100–101; Crosby, 2009: 126); *US-Shrimp*, (AB), §161–167.

with objectionable foreign practices.[142] Three responses occur. First, it is doubtful whether in practice such association, as opposed to direct causation, is a significant reason for regulating.[143] Second, to the extent legislation is motivated by the moral quality of a practice, rather than concern for its effects on some purported good or harm, it conflicts with the liberal principle of legitimacy *vis-à-vis* domestic citizens.[144] Third, to the extent it achieves this goal by targeting imports, as opposed to through undifferentiated measures, it remains an ETM, albeit one that may be justifiable under the self-determination proviso.[145]

How might an EGC-inspired Regulatory Likeness test work? Like the Aims and Effects approach, it recognizes that products can be distinguished on diverse bases, and the key question is which differences justify regulatory distinctions. Further, like that approach, it asks how a particular distinction fits into the challenged measure, and what purpose it serves. The only bases for distinguishing products that it excludes are those that pursue goals specifically through the regulation of international economic activity. This would include distinctions addressing NPRPPMs, as well as origin-specific conditions and many producer-specific conditions. However, it would also include distinctions based on the physical properties, where their rationale lay in the pursuit of a goal through the measure's effects on international economic activity. It would thus deny, for example, that indigenous hunted seals could be distinguished from those commercially hunted; but it would also deny that seal products could be distinguished from, say, mink products, if the rationale for making that distinction was to change the practices of foreign seal-hunters.[146] And EGC's emphasis on constructive interpretation would license looking

---

[142] (Howse & Langille, 2012; Howse & Regan, 2000). This distinction clearly featured in the EU's submissions in Seals: *EC-Seal Products*, (Panel), §7.374.

[143] Certainly there is little suggestion in *Tuna* or *Shrimp* that the purpose of the legislation is other than reducing the incidence of the relevant harms. In *Seals*, the EC does make this claim. However, references to "individual and collective participation ... [in] the economic activity which sustains the market for commercially hunted seal products," seem more concerned with effects on animal welfare than the intrinsic moral quality of products: (AB), §7.375.

[144] Regan argues such measures can be justified on "preference-maximizing grounds," addressing an emotional or moral externality: (Regan, 2009: 114–115). While commendably direct, the principle of political legitimacy invoked is incompatible with contemporary liberalism, under any of its leading interpretations: (Hart, 1963; Kant, 1991: 73–74; Mill, 1989: 15–16, 57; Rawls, 1996: 216–218, 292; Raz, 1986: 421 and ch. 15).

[145] See further §7.3.2 below.

[146] The test proposed relates only to Articles I and III. Whether any measure might be defended under Art. XX is addressed below.

behind measures' stated purposes, to capture cases of disguised discrimination, so understood.

EGC thus provides a plausible account of GATT nondiscrimination rules. It can account more readily than PT or TTT for both the relation between those rules and Article XX, and the distinctiveness of NPRPPMs, and provides a basis for identifying legitimate and illegitimate distinctions among products that more closely tracks practice under the Agreements.

The most likely objection at this point is EGC's lack of textual support. Various responses occur. First, as discussed, the indeterminacy of discrimination means interpreters cannot avoid giving it content. EGC's capacity to account for the relation between Articles I, III, and XX, and for the existing practice, including in particular on NPRPPMs, gives reason to prefer it. Second, references to protectionism, particularly in Article III.1, can be read as supporting this approach. Protectionism has no consensus definition.[147] We might argue Article III.1 refers not to protectionism narrowly conceived, but rather to measures pursuing their goals through effects on international trade, and thorough manipulating trading partners and their interests and incentives. EGC would then explain why protectionism, so understood, was objectionable. Like other such explanations, it has implications for the scope of the concept and the interpretation of provisions addressing it; but rather than supplanting a protectionist Regulatory Likeness test, it would simply clarify it. Third, the argument in Chapter 2 for constructive interpretation of multilateral agreements, together with the arguments for EGC in Chapters 3 through 5, provide direct support for this approach. If the normative argument for EGC is accepted, then understanding nondiscrimination in this way makes these rules the best they can be.

6.3.5 Discrimination and Technical Regulations

Before proceeding, it is worth contrasting the approach to discrimination in the GATT, and the problems it faces, with the way discrimination has been understood under Article 2.1 of the Agreement on Technical Barriers to Trade. Article 2.1 includes language closely modeled on Article III.4 GATT, albeit extending to both MFN and National Treatment. As with the GATT, the AB has understood likeness under Article 2.1 in competitive terms. However, it has approached the

---

[147] Contrast the approaches proposed by Regan and Neven above.

comparative stage of the test quite differently. Under the GATT, it has understood less favorable treatment as capturing any situation where a measure detrimentally impacts conditions of competition for like imported products, regardless of the reasons for this.[148] Under Article 2.1 TBT, by contrast, less favorable treatment includes an additional test, namely whether that impact is a consequence of the origin of the relevant product, or instead stems from a legitimate regulatory distinction drawn by the challenged measure. In the latter circumstance, no discrimination will be found.[149]

The effect of this additional step is to make TBT discrimination sensitive to regulatory purpose. In explaining the different approach, the AB has pointed to the function of the TBT Agreement, whose focus on regulatory measures necessarily imports the drawing of distinctions between products;[150] and the absence of any equivalent of Article XX GATT in the TBT Agreement, which means the balance between nondiscrimination and regulatory autonomy must be struck entirely within Article 2.1.[151]

The upshot is a potentially more flexible nondiscrimination regime than under the GATT. Because Article 2.1 does not contain a closed list of legitimate purposes that can support distinctions, it need not raise the kinds of dilemma for economic approaches outlined above. Rather, its flexibility means it can accommodate whichever approach we prefer. In consequence, while TBT discrimination provides little guidance in choosing between approaches, it again highlights the need for some approach to guide interpretation and give content to what are otherwise largely indeterminate concepts.[152]

6.4   Conclusion

This chapter has marked a turn, from theory to doctrine. Having spent the first half of this book constructing an account of distributive justice in international trade regulation, our focus has shifted to enquire how far the existing positive law of the trade regime can be understood as reflecting that account, and how far in turn that account might help us to resolve questions that arise within that positive law.

---

[148] *EC-Seal Products*, (AB), §5.116–5.117 and, on the analogous question under Art. I.1 GATT, ibid., §5.93.
[149] *US-Clove Cigarettes*, (AB), §175.   [150] Ibid., §169.   [151] Ibid., §109.
[152] I take up further in Chapter 9 the scope of legitimate regulatory purposes under TBT, and the AB's approach thereto.

In the first half of this chapter, I introduced the dominant economic accounts of the GATT, and contrasted these with the explanation suggested by EGC. I suggested that, at a general level, each provided a plausible account of many of the rules, while facing problems of fit on particular details. The second half of the chapter looked in detail at one of those areas, discrimination. It highlighted the problems existing approaches face in accounting for both the content of these rules, and their relation to other elements of the GATT; and showed how EGC could both better explain those rules, and also provide a more plausible guide to their interpretation.

The next chapter continues our focus on the GATT, turning from rules to exceptions, to enquire whether EGC can similarly add value in explaining and interpreting the key qualifications to the Core Disciplines.

Justifying ETMs: Development Provisions and General Exceptions

7.1 Introduction

EGC does not claim that ETMs are never permissible. It makes the more modest claim that they are subject to a more demanding standard of justification than other measures: they are justified if and only if they pursue global equality of individual opportunity, subject to a reasonable principle of self-determination. Because many of the ETMs that we encounter in practice pursue neither equality nor self-determination, they are to that extent unjust. But where a measure does meet this standard, it is unobjectionable.

In Chapter 6, I explained the GATT Core Disciplines' prohibitions as tracking the category of ETMs. Measures caught by Articles I, II, III, and XI are disciplined because they are ETMs; and understanding them in these terms resolves recurring problems in the discrimination jurisprudence in particular. However, the prohibitions in the GATT are only half of the story. To understand the extent of the restrictions the GATT imposes, we must also consider the exceptions and quali-fications. In this chapter, I examine how far these, and in particular the Development Provisions and the General Exceptions, can be understood as expressing the justificatory standards of EGC, exempt-ing measures that meet that standard and that are, in consequence, unobjectionable.

The chapter is divided into two sections.

In the first section, I examine the Development Provisions, which I suggest can be understood as expressing EGC's primary, egalitar-ian, justification. As in Chapter 6, I contrast the explanations sug-gested by Protectionism (PT) and Terms of Trade (TTT) theories with those deriving from EGC, before examining EGC's interpretive implications, and its compatibility with the AB's own approach to these provisions.

In the second section, I examine Article XX, suggesting that it can be understood as expressing the two limbs of EGC's account of self-determination. I argue that EGC can better account for the structure and content of Article XX than either PT or TTT; and that it can also provide a more plausible explanation of the AB's jurisprudence thereunder.

7.2   Development Provisions

A theory of distributive justice in international trade regulation might be expected to make economic development its central concern. Certainly, for global egalitarians, the facts of poverty, underdevelopment, and global inequality are the clearest economic injustices in the contemporary world. As discussed in Chapter 2, when these theorists address the trade regime, it is unsurprising that they make economic development, including Special and Differential Treatment (SDT) for developing countries, a central concern. Indeed, supporting SDT seems to be the only implication that can be reliably derived from such views for the trade regime.

EGC similarly makes economic inequality a key concern, and the primary basis on which it suggests ETMs may be justified. However, a key merit I claim for EGC is that its implications are not limited to inequality, rather covering the full gamut of problems arising in the trade regime. To demonstrate this, the four chapters in this part examine a range of questions across different doctrinal areas. In consequence, I necessarily spend less time on international inequality than might otherwise be expected. This ground is well covered in existing works, so while I need to show how EGC understands development, I spend more time on those areas where problems of distributive justice have been less fully explored to date. This should not be read as implying that economic inequality is unimportant. It is not the whole of global economic justice, so I do not make it my sole concern; but it is a central problem, so it is certainly one I must address.

The claim that inequality is only one problem among many fits well with the history of trade regime, which came rather late to this issue. Developing countries had little influence in the original GATT negotiations: the agreement was negotiated between the developed countries, and its principal concerns were those of the developed countries.[1] Arguably the most significant evolution in the goods regime thereafter

---

[1] (Hudec, 2011: 32; Irwin et al., 2008: 108; Lester et al., 2012: 813; Wilkinson & Scott, 2008: 481).

has been the increasing participation of, and accommodation towards, developing countries.[2] From the 1950s, newly independent developing countries pressed for greater recognition and accommodation of their concerns in the organization of the global economy.[3] Through new international coalitions and a new international organization, the United Nations Conference on Trade and Development, they lobbied for a New International Economic Order (NIEO), which would ensure a more equitable division of the benefits from international economic cooperation.[4] The GATT was an important focus of that lobbying, leading to various amendments and extensions of the agreement, and a suite of related practices collectively termed Special and Differential Treatment (SDT).[5] While talk of the NIEO has faded, SDT remains an important part of the GATT, and has been extended, albeit in limited ways, to the other Covered Agreements.[6] At the same time, development has become a specified goal of the organization; and beyond the legal disciplines, it is the focus of the Committee on Trade and Development and, at least nominally, of the Doha Development Round negotiations.[7]

As they affect the Core Disciplines, the principal SDT measures are: the infant industry and balance of payments provisions in Article XVIII[8]; the nonreciprocity provisions in Article XXXVI(8) GATT and Article 5 Enabling Clause; and the preferential market access provisions in Article 1 Enabling Clause (together, the "Development Provisions.")[9] While only Article XVIII creates enforceable rights and obligations, the permissive and/or hortatory nonreciprocity and preferential market access provisions have substantially shaped developing country participation in the GATT/WTO. Developing countries have not been required to reduce and bind tariffs to the same extent as developed countries,

[2] For three very different perspectives: (Hudec, 2011; Krasner, 1985; Rolland, 2012).

[3] (Hudec, 2011: 51–60).

[4] (Bhagwati, 1988: ch. 5; Hudec, 2011: 51–52; Irwin et al., 2008: 124 et seq; Krasner, 1985: 72–81; Rolland, 2012: 69). On developing countries' use of coalitions in the Uruguay Round: (Narlikar, 2003).

[5] (Hudec, 2011: 41–42, 64–72).   [6] For a comprehensive review: (Rolland, 2012).

[7] WTO Agreement, Preamble, Art. IV.7; Doha Ministerial Declaration 2001.

[8] On the use of Art. XVIII: (World Trade Organization, 2012a: 394–395, 2012b: 292–293).

[9] My focus here is on SDT as it affects the Core Disciplines. I touch on SDT in trade remedies and domestic regulation in later chapters. However, SDT appears at many other points in the trade regime, which I do not examine. Not all will necessarily be explicable in the way I explain the Development Provisions here; different rules in different agreements will have different functions. However, in all cases, EGC hopes to shed light on how the particular SDT rules are and should be understood, albeit in many cases it suggests they are significantly narrower than they should be.

leaving them with greater flexibility to apply tariffs in pursuit of domestic objectives.[10] Preference schemes have been adopted by all of the major developed economies.[11] A number have also created superpreferential schemes for subsets of developing countries.[12] Their combined effect is that developing countries: (a) have not had to reduce tariffs to the same extent as developed countries, leaving them greater flexibility to apply tariffs in pursuing development objectives; (b) can often export to developed countries on terms more favorable than those available to developed country exporters; and (c) have significant freedom to derogate from their commitments for infant industry promotion or balance of payments purposes. The consequence, as various authors observe, is to effectively exempt developing countries from much of the GATT disciplines.[13]

In this section, I examine whether and to what extent each of the approaches discussed can make sense of these Development Provisions and of the AB's case-law thereunder. I first examine the explanations suggested by PT/TTT, suggesting these fail to account for key features of these provisions. I next explore how EGC accounts for these. Finally, I examine the AB's approach to the Development Provisions in *EC–Tariff*

---

[10] (Bagwell & Staiger, 2011a: 2–3). For average applied and bound tariffs of states at various levels of development: (Martin et al., 2011: 6).

[11] UNCTAD: *Generalised System of Preferences: List of Beneficiaries.* Some scholars argue preferences are mandatory, but this seems implausible as a legal, rather than moral, claim: (Onyejekwe, 1994). For a proposal to bind preferences under Art. II GATT: (Bartels & Häberli, 2010).

[12] For a critical review of the EU's current GSP+ scheme: (Bartels, 2007).

[13] (Hudec, 2011: 119). For the smallest and least developed countries this implicit waiver is reinforced by a lack of dispute resolution complaints against them: (Mosoti, 2006; Odell, 2010). While the Uruguay Round broadened and deepened developing countries' tariff commitments, a qualitative difference remains between the breadth and levels of developed and developing country bindings. Thus, while developing countries went from binding 21% to 73% of tariffs, developed countries moved from 78% to 99%; and average bound tariffs for developed countries are 12%, as against 40% for developing countries. This comes through even more clearly for individual countries. India, for example, has bound tariffs on 74.4% of tariff lines, but its average bound tariff level is 48.5%, with over 70% of bound tariffs exceeding a prohibitive 15%. That India's average applied tariff is 13.5%, with less than 20% of applied tariffs exceeding 15% highlights the extent to which this represents an effective absence of multilateral discipline across the bulk of its tariff policy.

Of course, as critics observe, this may simply obscure many ways developing countries are disproportionately burdened, including through limited multilateral liberalization in goods of export interest, including agriculture and textiles. E.g. (Finger, 2001; Trebilcock et al., 2013: 630–633).

Preferences, arguing this is incompatible with PT/TTT, while readily according with EGC.

7.2.1   Explaining the Development Provisions through PT and TTT

What explanation can we offer for the Development Provisions?

PT explains them as reflecting different economic conditions prevailing in developing countries, which mean that policies that would be inefficient in developed countries are rational for developing countries.[14] This reflects the intellectual roots of the NIEO in development economics and dependency theory.[15] Dependency argues that the structure of the international economy poses insuperable obstacles for developing countries.[16] It is only through direct intervention to promote domestic industries that developing countries can hope to improve their long-term position. Dependency need not deny the claims of comparative advantage; rather, it rejects their applicability to developing countries.[17]

Progress has been made in recent years in clarifying how far deviations from free trade benefit developing countries.[18] Development economics' initial focus on import substitution and infant industry is now seen as a special case of capturing positive externalities at early stages of industrialization.[19] However, this is only one of many common market failures in developing countries that mean that socially optimal levels of investment and risk are only achievable through state intervention.[20] Such concerns ground a plausible claim that targeted protectionism of the kind anticipated by nonreciprocity and Article XVIII may be locally efficient. As such, they allow protectionism theorists to explain both restrictions on protectionism generally, and the permissibility of developing country protectionism under a general theory of domestic efficiency.[21]

---

[14] For a sympathetic statement of this view: (Chang, 2005).

[15] (Prebisch, 1964; Rolland, 2012: 16–24).

[16] On variants within dependency theory, and its selective invocation by developing country governments: (Krasner, 1985: 81–85).

[17] On the relation between dependency and the NIEO: (Bhagwati, 1988: ch. 5) (Krasner, 1985: 81 et seq).

[18] (Krugman et al., 2012c: 286–298).   [19] Ibid., 302–303.   [20] (Ray, 1998: 650–654).

[21] Admittedly, most exponents of PT are relatively skeptical of these provisions. E.g. (Bhagwati, 1988: 91–92; Regan, 2006: 963). However, to the extent this is the case, such approaches cannot aid the interpretive task faced by the AB. For a more sympathetic, and in consequence potentially more fruitful, approach: (Rodrik, 2011: 135–184).

It is harder to explain preferential market access on this view. That developing countries benefit from improved market access is plausible, albeit contested.[22] However, developed countries would benefit equally from such access. The gains are simply the efficiency gains from reduced protectionism, and the rents from trade diversion.[23] For importing states, welfare effects are mixed at best.[24] In so far as preferences reduce protectionism, they may yield efficiency gains through trade creation; but these are necessarily less than might be expected from MFN liberalization, and the possibility of trade diversion means there may be efficiency losses. The relation between preferences and welfare is further complicated by the fact that costs often fall on nonpreferred competitors.[25] It thus becomes unclear from whose perspective we should be judging the efficiency of these rules.[26]

A further difficulty is the mixed empirical evidence of the Development Provisions' effectiveness.[27] As noted, nonreciprocity and Article XVIII were intended to facilitate import substitution industrialization. However, the poor performance of countries adopting these policies, both in absolute terms and relative to those pursuing export led growth, caused a general disillusionment with import substitution.[28] Instead of enabling new industries to grow and achieve international competitiveness, ISI has often allowed industries to avoid necessary reforms, remaining uncompetitive by international standards, and surviving purely through sales in the protected home market.[29] Similar objections are raised to preferential market access.[30] At the same time, nonreciprocity has reduced developing countries' influence in negotiations.[31] If policies facilitated by the Development Provisions do not

---

[22] (Grossman & Sykes, 2005: 60–63; Hudec, 2011: 174–185).

[23] (Grossman & Sykes, 2005: 57–60). As originally conceived, preferences were intended to facilitate industrialization, and to that end would be offered to developing countries in limited sectors and for limited periods: (Mavroidis, 2012: 152–155; Prebisch, 1964: 65). However, the systems ultimately adopted failed to reflect this concern, and were more clearly tailored towards protecting developed country interests: (Bartels & Häberli, 2010).

[24] (Bhagwati et al., 1998; Krugman et al., 2012: 275–278).

[25] (Grossman & Sykes, 2005: 64; Rolland, 2012: 160–161).

[26] This is further complicated by the fact costs for developed country consumers often substantially exceed benefits for developing country producers: (Mavroidis, 2007: 145).

[27] For reviews of the evidence: (Grossman & Sykes, 2005; Mavroidis, 2012: 188–192; Panagariya, 2002; Trebilcock et al., 2013: 620–634).

[28] (Bhagwati, 1988: ch. 5, 2004: 60–66; Krugman et al., 2012c: 286–298).

[29] (Bhagwati, 2004: 62; Hudec, 2011: 131).

[30] (Hudec, 2011: 120–121; Panagariya, 2002).

[31] (Hudec, 2011: 158–163; Irwin et al., 2008: 131–132).

actually facilitate domestically efficient outcomes then they cannot be defended under PT.[32]

However, the most serious objection highlights the motivational assumptions of PT. PT views protectionism as reflecting some pathological feature of the political process that leads states, absent trade agreements, to adopt collectively suboptimal policies. If this problem arises for states generally it presumably arises for developing countries in particular.[33] By exempting developing countries, we thus condemn them to the irrational domestic outcomes that trade agreements remedy.[34] We might fashion a narrow set of development exceptions that would avoid this problem; but that certainly has not been the effect of the Development Provisions to date.[35]

We thus find that, despite its superficial attraction, PT cannot account for the Development Provisions in a way consistent with its own assumptions.

TTT suggests a more straightforward, but no more plausible, explanation.[36] Recall, TTT is concerned with measures adopted by states that, because of their economic size, can affect world prices and thereby move terms of trade in their own favor.[37] Because their economies are small, many developing countries – and especially least developed countries – lack the market power to affect world prices. In consequence, they lack any incentive to engage in terms of trade manipulation.[38] They are not in the terms of trade prisoner's dilemma, and so do not need the Core Disciplines to solve it.[39] Further, because developing countries are economically small, developed countries can deviate from MFN in their favor without affecting the terms of trade that they have negotiated among themselves.

There are a number of problems with this account.

---

[32] (Mavroidis, 2007: 145–148; Srinavasan, 2005: 84).

[33] If developing countries were for some reason less vulnerable than developed countries to the special interests, lobbying, and regulatory capture that drive the antiprotectionist account of trade agreements, then this objection would not arise. Unfortunately, the opposite appears more likely in practice. For one example of the ways the different political structures typical of developed and developing countries may make the latter more prone to economic dysfunction: (Khan, 2005).

[34] (Robert E. Hudec, 2011: 131–132).   [35] (Hudec, 2011: 144–150).

[36] I am not aware of any extended treatment of the Development Provisions under TTT; the account offered and criticized here is therefore my best attempt to derive such an account from this theory.

[37] (Bagwell et al., 2013: 108–109).   [38] (Irwin et al., 2008: 131).

[39] For this point, albeit as a criticism of TTT: (Ethier, 2004: 304).

First, the assumption that developing countries are too small to affect world prices is implausible. Most obviously, China, a developing country, is on some measures the largest economy in the world, and four other developing countries appear among the 11 largest national economies.[40] More generally, all countries, developed and developing, have a positive optimum tariff, albeit for most it is relatively low[41]; and evidence suggests that even many smaller developing countries perceive, in some areas at least, significant scope for tariffs improving their terms of trade.[42]

Second, the conclusion that large countries would unilaterally bind themselves vis-à-vis small countries does not follow from TTT. Given the motivational assumption that states optimize terms of trade subject to efficiency costs and domestic politics, we should only expect trade agreements among large states; in relations between large and small states, we should see no agreements, and unrestrained exploitation by large states. This is not what we observe in relation to developing countries – or indeed small developed countries.[43]

Third, TTT cannot explain the form of the Development Provisions. While broad, these are not unrestricted. Both nonreciprocity and Article XVIII express particular economic concerns, whether balance of payments and infant industry protection in Article XVIII, or "development, financial and trade needs" in the Enabling Clause.[44] They do not address terms of trade, and if this was a significant consideration, it is not obvious why they would be structured as they are.[45] Similarly, in

---

[40] Gross Domestic Product 2015, PPP adjusted, *World Bank World Development Indicators Database*. One study suggests the terms of trade component in China's pre-accession tariff was up to 25 percent: (Broda et al., 2008: 2033–2034). Admittedly, by virtue of its Accession Protocol, China is subject to greater restrictions that most developing, or indeed developed, countries. The other four (India, Brazil, Indonesia, and Mexico) enjoy more typical developing country treatment under the GATT, including very high average bound tariff rates (48.5%, 31.4%, 37.1%, and 36.1%, respectively) and high proportions of tariffs bound above 15 percent (71.5%, 96.4%, 90.6%, and 98.7%).

[41] (Krugman et al., 2012c: 283–285).

[42] Thus, terms of trade components appear in tariffs of *inter alia* Bolivia, Paraguay, and Algeria: (Bagwell & Staiger, 2011a: 11–12; Broda et al., 2008: 2033–2034, 2050–2052). GSP schemes' graduation provisions might partly answer this point, but recall these do not apply to nonreciprocity or Art. XVIII.

[43] (Mavroidis, 2012: 21). A response might emphasize the high transaction costs from discriminatory tariffs: (Mavroidis, 2012: 132). An alternative bites the bullet, denying that bindings negotiated between developed countries in any way benefit developing countries: (Bagwell & Staiger, 2011a: 7–9).

[44] Decision L/4903, November 28, 1979.

[45] Again, GSP graduation provisions provide some support for TTT, but have limited scope and effect: (Bartels & Häberli, 2010).

so far as TTT explains the Enabling Clause as acceptable because developing countries are economically small, it cannot explain the restrictions on the form preferential schemes take.[46]

7.2.2   EGC and the Development Provisions

Neither PT nor TTT provide a plausible account of the Development Provisions. We next ask how EGC explains these?

Recall, EGC claims that ETMs are just if and only if they pursue global equality of individual opportunity, through improving the position of less advantaged individuals, subject to a reasonable principle of self-determination. In Chapter 6, I argued EGC could explain the Core Disciplines as addressed to ETMs. If we assume that Articles I, II, III, and XI address ETMs, then we might in turn expect the Development Provisions to express EGC's principal, egalitarian justification. This next section will investigate that hypothesis, considering both how the Development Provisions might be understood in these terms, and EGC's implications for the form of those provisions.

A number of preliminary points merit mention.

First, and most obviously, EGC suggests that the Development Provisions should license measures, whether adopted by more or less advantaged states, that pursue global equality of individual opportunity. As discussed in Chapter 4, there are difficulties with cross-national judgments of individual opportunity, but a principle for a world of states can avoid many of these through adopting state-level economic indicators, such as national income, as proxies. We can thus move very quickly from EGC's underlying concern with equality to the justification of measures pursuing economic development of less advantaged states.

Second, EGC's self-determination proviso, which like the egalitarian justification reflects concern for equal freedom, implies that where possible decisions about policies benefitting the globally least advantaged be made by the communities where those individuals live. The distinction, drawn in Chapter 3, between external and self-authored coercion, provides an initial basis for this preference. Moreover, development economics is not an exact science; and *ceteris paribus* national governments have epistemic and motivational advantages in choosing policies that can

---

[46] This is implicitly recognized in: (Grossman & Sykes, 2005: 64).

best advance their own populations.[47] In consequence, they are entitled to some margin of appreciation in making those decisions. Provided policies *bona fide* pursue global equality, it is not for more advantaged persons or peoples to object that another policy might be more effective to that end. EGC thus avoids the objection, raised against PT above, that many policies adopted under the Development Provisions have yielded little economic benefit.

Third, EGC can only justify measures that in fact pursue global equality of individual opportunity, whether directly or indirectly. It does not suggest exempting developing countries from the GATT entirely. Economic uncertainty is wide, but not unlimited; and EGC cannot justify policies, ostensibly adopted for egalitarian reasons, that cannot advance that goal. This does not imply balancing benefits to less advantaged persons against costs to those more advantaged; but the more advantaged need not accept policies that impair their interests without in fact advantaging others.[48]

Fourth, to the extent measures are required from more advantaged states, these must respect the points above. The egalitarian claims of less advantaged persons cannot justify measures by more advantaged states that in fact pursue collateral goals, or pursue egalitarian goals in ways primarily benefitting those more advantaged states.[49] Where measures reflect such collateral purposes, or ignore the development choices of less advantaged communities, justification will not be possible in these terms. Further, the epistemic and motivational advantages noted above do not apply to more advantaged states; we are therefore justified in more strictly policing the egalitarian justifications more advantaged states offer for their policies.

If EGC is to explain the Development Provisions, then we need to find these ideas reflected in the GATT. How, and to what extent, can we do this?

First, as noted, Article XVIII and nonreciprocity provide broad but limited discretion for developing countries to adopt ETMs necessary for their economic development. While contemporary economic thought is

---

[47] §§3.6, 4.5, and 5.5 above. As noted by the Panel in *Brazil-Aircraft*, (§7.89) "it is the developing country Member itself which is best positioned to identify its development needs." Cited in: (Paliwal, 2011). We might make a link here to both intrinsic and instrumental arguments for self-determination.

[48] These two points are in obvious tension, given the economic uncertainties involved. In consequence, they are best regarded as principles for structuring a conversation about appropriate measures, rather than strict rules appropriate to mechanical application in all circumstances.

[49] See §3.6 above.

skeptical of many policies facilitated by these provisions, they are at least potentially useful for this purpose.[50] In these circumstances, it is not for more advantaged states to object where less advantaged states adopt policies that do not reflect their particular economic ideas.[51] Conversely, measures are justified only to the extent necessary in pursuit of the relevant goal.[52] Whether the line is correctly drawn might be debated.[53] However, the tiered rights in Article XVIII, afforded to different states to differing degrees and subject to differing constraints, highlight the extent to which this provision is concerned with facilitating less advantaged peoples in improving their position, notwithstanding the effects this has on those more advantaged. Nonreciprocity, at least as anticipated in the Enabling Clause and Article XXXVI.8 GATT, is neither a narrowly targeted privilege of the kind suggested by PT, nor an unrestricted exemption of the kind suggested by TTT. Instead, it exempts developing countries from making "contributions which are *inconsistent with their individual development, financial and trade needs.*"[54] The question of what is or is not consistent with those needs is a complex one, which may be the subject of discussions in negotiations, but must ultimately depend on the policies adopted by the relevant developing countries.[55] In practice, admittedly, nonreciprocity has often facilitated indiscriminate protectionism; but this clearly is not its intended purpose.[56] The freedom it protects is broad, reflecting EGC's self-determination proviso, but it is freedom for a specific purpose, namely economic development.

[50] For a full-throated defense: (Chang, 2005). For a more qualified approach: (Hoekman, 2005).

[51] This does not mean, as the AB has recognized, that where different instruments can be used more advantaged states cannot expect that less disruptive ones should be adopted, without restricting states' development policies: *India-Quantitative Restrictions, (AB),* §121–130 esp. §128.

[52] Similar considerations inform the Understanding on the Balance of Payments Provisions of the General Agreement on Tariffs and Trade 1994. The Panel in *India-Quantitative Restrictions* (§5.155–5.156, 5.216–5.223), interpreting Art. XVIII's provisions on balance of payments, recognized the tension between international justification as 'necessary', and domestic choice of development strategy. Similarly in its treatment of adequacy the Panel (§3.373) relied on both international standards provided by the IMF, and domestic standards articulated by the Reserve Bank of India.

[53] The limited use of the infant industry provisions might suggest these are overly restrictive, although this might equally reflect contemporary views on the value of such policies: (World Trade Organization., 2012b: 292).

[54] Enabling Clause, Para 5; GATT, Note Ad Art. XXXVI(8).

[55] The disappointing achievements of the Doha Round are probably best explained by mercantilist self-interest, but arguably also reflect differences on the moral demands of non-reciprocity. Contrast (Cho, 2009: 583–587) with (Lamy & Goldin, 2014).

[56] (Bartels, 2003).

Second, unlike PT and TTT, EGC suggests straightforward explanations of preferences. There are two ways we might describe preference schemes. First, by conceiving preference schemes as regimes combining high tariffs on imports from some sources, with low tariffs on others, we can see them as themselves constituting ETMs that pursue their goals specifically through their (differential) effects on international economic activity. These could be justified under EGC's egalitarian limb. Given the limited executive capacities of shared international institutions, the detailed design of such schemes must be left to donor countries; but as schemes adopted by more advantaged states for the benefit of less advantaged states, they would be subject to stricter scrutiny than the development policies of those less advanced states themselves.[57] Second and alternatively, by focusing only on their treatment of developing countries, we can understand preference schemes as the selective withdrawal by developed countries of unjustifiable ETMs (i.e. tariffs). As noted earlier, reciprocal tariff cuts can be understood as solving a coordination problem among states, each of whom initially imposes unjustified tariffs on the others.[58] However, if we assume that developing countries are asymmetrically justified in imposing tariffs, then developed countries can no longer rely on this logic to justify their tariffs *vis-a-vis* developing countries. Preferences then become simply corollaries of nonreciprocity.[59]

EGC also explains why the Development Provisions are chosen over cheaper and potentially more effective development interventions. The real costs of preferences and nonreciprocity for developed countries may greatly exceed those of direct financial aid, for a given benefit for beneficiaries.[60] If donors and beneficiaries were simply concerned with promoting development, the Development Provisions would offer very poor value. The conventional explanation of their use emphasizes the indirect ways trade measures impose costs on consumers.[61] EGC, by contrast, explains this fact directly, arguing that developing countries have claims in justice to the Development Provisions that may not extend to

---

[57] This explains both GSP schemes' discretionary quality, and disciplines on their use for collateral purposes: (Bartels, 2007). It also explains why much of the language in Part IV and the Enabling Clause is hortatory; these identify considerations to which developed states should have regard in exercising the discretion afforded to them.

[58] §6.2 above. Cf. (Nagel, 2005: 115–118).

[59] For an empirical illustration of this link: (Özden & Reinhardt, 2005).

[60] Those costs may accrue directly, through trade diversion, or indirectly, through impediments to MFN liberalization. On the argument for substituting aid for preferences: (Hoekman & Prowse, 2005).

[61] (Hudec, 2011: 176–177).

alternative, including cheaper and potentially more effective, development interventions.[62]

Readers might object that the Development Provisions, with their crude distinction between developed and developing countries, bear little relation to the hierarchy expressed in EGC.[63] Recall, EGC approves ETMs to the extent they advance global equality of individual opportunity through improving the position of less advantaged individuals. Relations of relative advantage exist between persons at all levels of development. Simply distinguishing developed and developing countries elides this fact. It might be better expressed through Charlton and Stiglitz's proposed recursive preferences, under which each country would afford duty-free quota-free access to imports from all lower income countries, while being free to restrict imports from higher income countries.[64] Certainly, Charlton and Stiglitz's proposals would constitute a plausible interpretation of EGC. However, for various reasons the existing Development Provisions might be preferred. First, as noted above, preference schemes have distributive and efficiency effects between recipient and nonrecipient. Affording preferences to developing countries, but not to lower income developed countries, might therefore be more readily reconciled with EGC than affording them to all lower income countries.[65] Similarly, by maintaining restrictions on the preferences afforded to developing countries generally while offering more extensive preferences to least developed countries a scheme may better express the concerns of EGC.[66] Second, the crude distinction between developing and developed countries obscures a more textured approach in practice. The Enabling Clause specifically provides for additional

---

[62] This argument might be combined with Hudec's, invoking EGC to explain why political and economic assessments of cost diverge. Critics might object that developed countries should be free to "buy off" the obligations arising under EGC through more efficient direct aid payments. Under a purely utilitarian principle, this might be the case. However, insofar as EGC's underlying concern, as outlined in Chapter 3, is to reconcile the inevitable fact of coercion with persons' and peoples' status as free and equal, this objection does not arise. Interestingly, it seems clear that this objection would hold against the strategies that Sangiovanni labels *outweighing* or *compensation*; indeed, those strategies substantially reduce to the idea that we can "buy off" injustice. EGC denies that this is the case.

[63] For this criticism of SDT generally: (Mayeda, 2004: 748–749).

[64] (Stiglitz & Charlton, 2005: 94–95).

[65] This is a special case of preference erosion: (Francois et al., 2006: 205–211).

[66] Recall that the *Bananas* dispute was substantially driven by distributive effects among developing countries: (Salas & Jackson, 2000: 146–152). For similar problems with the EU's EBA initiative: (Page & Hewitt, 2002).

preferences for least developed countries, and the 2005 Hong Kong Ministerial committed to duty-free-quota-free access for all LDCs.[67] The Enabling Clause also affords flexibility to preference donors to further distinguish among beneficiaries to the extent necessary to address specific development, financial and trade needs. A waiver permits preferences from developing to least developed countries;[68] at least seven developing countries, including China and India, have implemented such preferences.[69] Finally, as noted above, Article XVIII distinguishes among countries at different stages of development. The Development Provisions thus reflect much of the variable geometry implicit in EGC. Third, practicability considerations may inhibit schemes including greater variability than the existing Development Provisions. Concerns are frequently voiced that transaction costs from the existing Development Provisions, including in particular compliance with rules of origin, substantially reduce the value of those provisions.[70] Given transnational value chains, additional differentiation between countries exponentially increases these administrative burdens, which may adversely affect their value even for beneficiaries of such additional differentiation.[71] Further, the limited executive capacity of international organizations in this area means that specifics must be decided at the level of donor governments; effective coordination may thus only be possible through adopting relatively crude categories.[72]

A stronger objection to understanding the Development Provisions in terms of EGC is their weakness as legal provisions. Notwithstanding suggestions to the contrary in GATT reports, it is now generally assumed that Part IV GATT creates no significant obligations.[73] Despite the language of nonreciprocity many developing countries, and particularly new members, face demands for greater liberalization.[74] And while the Enabling Clause imposes conditions on the form of preference schemes, there is no obligation to adopt such schemes in the first place. This seems difficult to reconcile with EGC's understanding of these provisions as

---

[67] *Enabling Clause* Art. 3(d); *Hong Kong Ministerial Declaration*, §47. Other special preferences, such as the US *African Growth and Opportunity Act*, operate under specific waivers: Decision WT/l/754 2009.

[68] Decision WT/L/304, 1999.   [69] (World Trade Organization., 2007: 108).

[70] (Brenton & Manchin, 2003: 759–763; Francois et al., 2006: 198–199).

[71] (Augier et al., 2005: 570, 602; Collier & Venables, 2007: 1329–1332).   [72] §4.3.4 above.

[73] A number of GATT panels examining Part IV imply that, without mandating particular actions, it requires giving appropriate consideration: *EEC-Sugar(Brazil)*, §4.30–4.31; *EEC-Restrictions on Imports of Apples from Chile*, §4.23; *EEC-Restrictions on Imports of Dessert Apples(Chile)*, §12.32.

[74] (Charnovitz, 2008; Qin, 2003).

expressing duties of justice. The objection can be answered, at least in part, by highlighting the significance and pervasiveness of schemes adopted under these hortatory and permissive provisions, the coordination problems involved in internationally prescribed preference and nonreciprocity provisions, and the understandable reluctance of developed countries to commit to legally enforceable schemes, political morality notwithstanding.[75] However, this objection might also remind us that EGC is not simply concerned with explanation; it also has a potential role in guiding progressive development, which might include demanding stronger legally binding and enforceable development provisions.

7.2.3   EGC and the AB's Approach to the Development Provisions

The Development Provisions were raised in a number of GATT-era disputes, but the panels avoided any detailed consideration of their scope or purpose.[76] Nor were they examined in the WTO-era *Bananas* decisions, which focused instead on the terms of the applicable waivers.[77] In *EC–Tariff Preferences*, however, the AB did address one of these provisions, the Enabling Clause, directly. At issue was the permissibility of positive conditionality in the EU's former GSP scheme. The AB's reasoning is expressed in largely textual terms. However, as argued by a number of authors, the textual justification is tenuous at best.[78] It is therefore worth considering how far that case can be explained as expressing a view of the function of the Development Provisions.

India challenged provisions in the EU's GSP scheme affording additional preferences to certain developing countries facing problems relating to the production or distribution of illegal narcotics (the Drug

---

[75] It is noteworthy that the only development provision conferring unilaterally exercisable rights (Art. XVIII) addresses policies where coordination problems and third party action are least relevant. The more aspirational provisions in Part IV, by contrast, address areas where there is more scope for disagreement about appropriate policies, and more need for cooperation to implement them.

[76] As well as the disputes at fn. 73 above, these include: *EEC-Member States' Import Regimes for Bananas (Bananas I); EEC-Import Regime for Bananas(Bananas II); Norway-Restrictions on Imports of Certain Textile Products.* Their main implication for the Development Provisions is that Part IV cannot justify departures from express GATT obligations: *Norway-Textiles*, §15; *Bananas I*, §369–372; *Bananas II*, §160–164.

[77] For an overview: (Guth, 2012).

[78] (Kawaharu, 2006: 51–56; Stamberger, 2003). For two analyses of this question in textualist and originalist teleological terms, reaching opposite conclusions: (Bartels, 2003; Howse, 2003). The Panel (§7.78–7.79) recognized the limits of textualism in this case.

Measures).[79] While India was a beneficiary under the EU's general GSP scheme, it was not eligible to benefit from the Drug Measures.

The Panel concluded that the Drug Measures violated Article I GATT, and were not saved under the Enabling Clause, finding that preference donors had no discretion to impose conditions on or draw distinctions within their preference schemes.[80] Schemes must be open to developing countries generally, excepting only additional preferences for LDCs.[81]

The AB qualified that conclusion, finding that donors could afford additional preferences to particular developing countries, provided these were designed to respond positively to the objective development, financial and trade needs of particular developing countries, and that they were available to all developing countries sharing the relevant needs.[82]

In reaching that conclusion, the AB emphasized that one of the goals of the Enabling Clause was eliminating the previously existing special preferences "based on historical and political ties between developed countries and their former colonies."[83] Such nongeneralized preferences may have served the development purposes of their beneficiaries, but their discriminatory nature also reflected the political interests of their donors.[84] However, the AB found that some distinctions between developing countries were permissible, provided they did not discriminate between "similarly situated beneficiaries."[85] This raises the same problem as the likeness analysis discussed in Chapter 6: what does it mean for two countries to be "similarly situated."[86] The AB looked to the Preamble to the WTO Agreement and the text of Article 3(c) Enabling Clause to conclude that similarly situated meant having "the 'development, financial and trade needs' to which the treatment in question is intended to respond."[87] This in turn required the inclusion in the relevant scheme of objective criteria or standards for determining whether countries shared the relevant need. Provisions for LDCs are, on this view, simply a special case of responding to the needs of particular developing countries.[88]

---

[79] On the history of such GSP conditions: (Switzer, 2008: 114–127).

[80] (Panel), §6.61–7.177, esp. §7.116, 7.144.   [81] *ibid*, §7.145–7.147.

[82] (AB), §162–165, 173, 176.   [83] (AB), §155.

[84] This concern is evident at (Panel), §7.102 and (AB), §156.   [85] (AB), §173.

[86] The Panel (§7.104) cited this problem as a reason for its stricter interpretation.

[87] (AB), §168–173.

[88] Ibid., §172. The waiver for preferences from developing to least developed countries (WT/L/304 June 15, 1999, as extended by WT/L/759 May 27, 2009), and the *Hong Kong Ministerial Decision on Measures in Favor of Least Developing Countries* (Annex F, §36, of the *Hong Kong Ministerial Declaration*) can be understood in similar terms.

There is a tension in the AB's decision, between respecting preference donors' choices about the terms of GSP schemes, and preventing their use for collateral (nondevelopment) purposes. This reflects a wider tension around preferences generally. On one hand, preference schemes are often criticized for their arbitrary exclusions and graduation mechanisms, and more generally for the way their discretionary nature undermines predictability for developing countries, in turn reducing their economic value.[89] Developing countries are disempowered, passive beneficiaries, forced to accept what is offered by preference donors. On the other hand, because there is no positive obligation on states to grant preferences, overly strict disciplines on their terms may discourage preference donors from granting any trade preferences at all. The AB has sought to at least partially allay concerns about donors' arbitrary discretion but, by allowing them to determine which "development, financial and trade" needs to target, it arguably also reinforces developing countries roles as passive "rule-takers."[90]

Neither PT nor TTT suggest plausible justifications for the AB's decision. As noted, PT's emphasis on domestic efficiency struggles to account for trade preferences generally. *A fortiori* it cannot explain why preferences should vary across states based on the factors identified by the AB. Rather, to the extent PT identifies trade diversion as a problem for preferences, it is exacerbated where increased preferences are afforded to states facing particular development financial and trade problems, which are likely, *ceteris paribus*, to be less efficient than other developing countries.[91] For TTT discretion within GSP schemes raises the same problem as discretion to implement such schemes, namely adverse terms of trade effects for nonpreferred exporters. This arises regardless of conditions imposed on that discretion.[92]

Some scholars argue the decision reflects concerns that strict nondiscrimination would make preference schemes unattractive for donors[93]; the AB thus adopted the strictest politically feasible position. However, this downplays the genuine constraints imposed on GSP schemes,

---

[89] E.g. (Bartels & Häberli, 2010).

[90] E.g. (Irish, 2007: 692–695) and more generally (Shaffer & Apea, 2005).

[91] This effect aside, the simple fact of according different preferences at different levels to different countries also means there are more distinctions across which trade diversion may occur.

[92] Indeed, it is these diversionary effects that motivated India's complaint. Cf. (Bagwell et al., 2013: 176).

[93] (Bagwell et al., 2013: 176; Grossman & Sykes, 2005: 65–66; Kawaharu, 2006: 65–66).

including implicitly rejecting many of the most politically sensitive conditions for preference donors.[94] It also ignores the fact that nonpreferred developing countries may be better served by the elimination of GSP schemes entirely than by the continuance of conditional schemes.[95] Thus, even allowing for this concern, it is not clear either PT or TTT would pick out anything like the compromise arrived at by the AB.

A better explanation would take seriously the AB's recognition that the positions of developing countries vary, and that those facing particular development challenges may have good claims to have those challenges recognized and addressed through the regulation of international trade. This is the perspective of EGC. Recall, as noted above, EGC's concern to recognize the particular claims of more and less developed countries, subject to the constraints imposed by the existing international system. I identified above a number of aspects of the Development Provisions that can be understood in these terms. Given the voluntary nature of preference schemes, their relation to individual donor countries, and the absence of any international political agent capable of managing such differentiation, the AB's endorsement of conditional donor discretion provides a further mechanism for responding to such needs.[96]

It is not only EGC's concern for differentiation that is expressed in this case, but also its emphasis on justification through ends that those subject to measures themselves have reason to share.[97] Thus, the AB emphasizes the role of international consensus in determining the ends conditional preferences may pursue, tracing the Clause's history, the 1971 GATT

---

[94] (Bartels, 2007: 882; Howse, 2003: 393, 404; Moss, 2005; Turksen, 2009).

[95] Conditional preferences' zero-sum, inter-beneficiary distributive quality is especially evident with tropical products, as evidenced by political challenges bringing the EU banana regime into conformity with WTO rules: (Horn & Mavroidis, 2004: 55).

[96] For a sympathetic reading of the case in these terms: (Paliwal, 2011). For a more critical view, challenging the scope of preference donors' discretion, and the resulting schemes' transparency and coherence: (Kishore, 2011). One problem with this reading is that the particular development, financial and trade needs identified by donors may not track EGC's concern for global equality of individual opportunity. However, the imprecision of equality of opportunity can in turn explain this. In Chapter 4, I argued national income provides a workable proxy for individual opportunity within particular communities. However, there are other proxies that might similarly be adopted; and where these also enjoy a degree of international endorsement, there may be good reason to adopt them to operationalize the underlying individualist concern. Thus, depending on how the requirement to address development, financial and trade needs is understood, it can effectively track EGCs underlying moral concerns.

[97] Scott highlights the importance of external justification in this case, albeit without settling the substantive question: (Scott, 2004a: 15) Cf. (Chalmers, 2006: 368–371).

Waiver, and its roots in negotiations within UNCTAD.[98] While ostensibly an exercise in textual analysis, this could equally express concerns to judge conditionality by international standards promulgated by a body, UNCTAD, with a strong claim to speak for developing countries.[99] The AB's conclusion, emphasizing objective conditions directly relating to specified "development, financial and trade needs," similarly evokes international standards, defining needs by "an objective standard" identifiable *inter alia* through "[b]road-based recognition . . . in the WTO Agreement or in multilateral instruments adopted by international organizations."[100] The ends pursued thus depend as much on international standards as donor choice[101]. Political necessity may require preference donors have discretion to choose whether and how to grant additional preferences[102]; but those choices must express the shared value of economic development, as understood by the states affected.[103] Thus again we see the demand for justification, and specifically egalitarian justification, that EGC expresses. Not all measures that a state adopts require to be justified in these terms: but preference schemes are External Trade Measures, and so it is in accordance with EGC that these fall to be judged.

7.3   General Exceptions

The Development Provisions are the most significant qualifications in terms of human scope, applying to the vast majority of persons and peoples. Indeed, it is arguably developed, not developing, countries that are exceptional in this regard.[104] However, in dispute settlement practice, the Development Provisions pale next to the General Exceptions. Universal in

---

[98] (AB), §107–108, 143–145. Cf. §160–161.

[99] This might seem to confuse the distinction between necessarily and contingently shared ends. However, the complexity of development policy, and the difficulties making international comparisons of opportunity sets mean that shared standards can play an important role in operationalizing equality in particular circumstances.

[100] (AB), §163.

[101] For concerns about whether the EU's subsequent GSP+ scheme meets these standards: (Bartels, 2007).

[102] Although, as the AB accepted in this case, the Enabling Clause clearly encourages the adoption of such measures: §93, 109–111.

[103] For an elaboration of this idea: (Paliwal, 2011: 74–89).

[104] By way of example of how exceptional the "default" treatment is, in 2002 the EU applied MFN treatment to only six states: (Panagariya, 2002: 1418). Subject to ratification of the EU-Canada Comprehensive Economic and Trade Agreement, and the – less likely – completion of the Trans-Atlantic Trade and Investment Partnership, that number may soon fall to four.

scope, Article XX constitutes the default defense to complaints under the Core Disciplines.[105] As such, accounting for Article XX and its interpretation is an important test for any theory.[106]

I begin this section by reviewing problems in PT's and TTT's accounts of the General Exceptions. I next examine EGC's account of these provisions. Finally, I consider the compatibility of both EGC and economic accounts with the AB's Article XX case-law, focusing on the policing of collateral purposes in the necessity and chapeau jurisprudence, and the turn to internationalism in *EC – Shrimp*. In each case, I suggest that EGC can better account for the AB's approach.

I touched on Article XX in Chapter 5. However, it is worth providing a more detailed overview of its content and structure here, before examining how various approaches might account for it.

Article XX comprises two elements. First, an introductory paragraph, referred to as the *chapeau*, which provides that:

> Subject to the requirement that such measures are not applied in a manner which would constitute a means of arbitrary or unjustifiable discrimination between countries where the same conditions prevail, or a disguised restriction on international trade, nothing in this Agreement shall be construed to prevent the adoption or enforcement by any contracting party of measures [falling under any of the subsequent paragraphs].

Second, immediately after this chapeau, ten individual paragraphs describe classes of measures eligible for exemption under Article XX. These refer to a variety of policy areas, including protecting public morals, protecting human animal or plant life or health, import and export of gold and silver, securing compliance with laws and regulations, prison labor, the protection of national treasures, the conservation of exhaustible natural resources, intergovernmental commodity agreements, and supply shortages. Many of these individual paragraphs include additional conditions that must be met to avail of the exception. However, there is also a significant structural difference among them, in terms of the nexus required between a measure and the relevant policy goals: in three cases, the measure must be necessary to that goal; in three it must relate to the relevant area; and in one each it must be imposed for, undertaken in pursuance of, involve, or be essential to the relevant issue.

Article XX thus has a number of features requiring to be explained: not only the list of policies that can justify measures; but also the required

---

[105] (A. Davies, 2009: 507; Gian, 2014: 229–231).
[106] On the negotiating history of this provision: (Irwin et al., 2008: 164–166).

nexus between policy and measure; the particular conditions under individual paragraphs; and the strict policing of arbitrary or unjustifiable discrimination and disguised restrictions under the chapeau.

7.3.1   Explaining Article XX through PT and TTT

I have already touched on PT's and TTT's explanations of the General Exceptions as tempering an overly broad application of the Core Disciplines. If we assume, as both do, that the Core Disciplines address measures intended to protect domestic production or manipulate terms of trade; and further, that it is not practicable to examine regulatory intent directly; then it makes sense to adopt a proxy, such as Competitive Likeness. If, as a result, unobjectionable measures are caught, then limited exemptions can save some of these. The problems defending this account of the relation between the Core Disciplines and the General Exceptions were discussed in Chapter 6. However, assuming, *arguendo*, that it is correct, I here inquire how well the specific content of Article XX fits either PT or TTT.

A number of the General Exceptions are clearly compatible with PT. For example, measures for the *bona fide* protection of public morals (Article XX(a)) or of human, animal and plant life or health (XX(b)) are clearly not protectionist.[107] Others are less clear. Notwithstanding moral glosses in contemporary analyses, Article XX(e) (prison labor) originally addressed straightforwardly protectionist policies: prison factories have obvious advantages over enterprises that have to pay for labor.[108] Restrictions on trade in gold and silver (XX(c)), when combined with exchange controls, may be substantially protectionist.[109] Controls on exports necessary to ensure inputs for domestic processing industries (XX(i)) and to ensure access to products in short supply (XX(j)) raise similar problems. It thus seems that, rather than exempting measures inadvertently caught by over-wide anti-protectionist disciplines, a number of the exceptions cover measures falling squarely within PT's rationale.[110]

TTT similarly struggles to account for the specific exceptions, for two reasons. First, bona fide measures under each of the specific exceptions

---

[107] This does not, of course, mean protectionist and nonprotectionist motivations cannot coexist, or that one cannot disguise the other.

[108] (Bartels, 2002: 355–356; Irwin et al., 2008: 98; Mavroidis, 2012: 344).

[109] (Ruggie, 1982: 390). On the links between monetary and trade policy: (Daunton, 2012). For a recent critique of the monetary/trade policy equivalence: (Staiger & Sykes, 2010: 593–606).

[110] These latter examples, together with analogous economic stability mechanisms in Art. XIX (as to which see further Chapter 8 below), might lead us to prefer embedded liberalism over the more formal economic theories here discussed. See §2.6.2 above.

may also serve to manipulate terms of trade. Second, a number of exceptions in Article XX address measures that directly manipulate terms of trade in favor of the regulating state. Article XX(g), for example (measures relating to the conservation of exhaustible natural resources) originates in concerns about restricting current exploitation of mineral resources (particularly oil) to protect future production.[111] Assuming the regulating state is large, and regardless of whether it concurrently restricts domestic production/consumption, such restrictions necessarily move terms of trade in its favor.[112] Similarly, restrictions on exports of raw materials and intermediate goods to protect inputs for domestic producers must affect terms of trade to the benefit of the regulating state.[113]

Nor can either approach rely on the Article XX chapeau to save their explanations. Protectionist and terms of trade effects are not simply possible side effects of measures of the kinds described, or motivations that might be disguised by reference to the specific paragraphs. Rather, they are central to them. So, for example, controls on the products of prison labor (XX(e)) (at least on the understanding noted above), and measures protecting access to industrial inputs/domestic supplies (XX(i) and (j)) are necessarily protectionist, serving to prefer domestic over foreign exporters: notwithstanding language to the contrary in Article XX(i) and the chapeau, PT can suggest no other way to understand these.[114] Similarly, measures for the bona fide protection of, say, human, animal and plant life, will frequently affect a state's terms of trade; the only necessary difference between such regulations and tariffs is that the terms of trade gain accrues in consumer welfare instead of government revenue.[115] A key focus in the chapeau jurisprudence has been on whether measures purporting to pursue an exempt purpose also pursue secondary, nonexempt, purposes.[116] That approach, however,

---

[111] (Charnovitz, 1991: 45–47; Irwin et al., 2008: 163).

[112] Art. XX(g) would cover OPEC, for example: (Abdallah, 2005). Although whether OPEC quotas are *prima facie* GATT-inconsistent is unclear: (Mavroidis, 2012: 63–64).

[113] This is well illustrated by the invocation of Art. XX(i) in recent challenges to Chinese export duties: *China-Raw Materials; China-Rare Earths.*

[114] For this point in respect of Art. XX(i): (Mavroidis, 2012: 354). For an analysis of the *chapeau* and XX(j): (Sharp, 2010).

[115] (Staiger & Sykes, 2011: 153–155). Strictly speaking this only raises concerns where standards are higher than they would be absent terms of trade effects. This is a fairly abstract distinction. It suffices to note that nothing in Art. XX is adapted to identify it: (Regan, 2006: 960–962).

[116] *US-Gasoline*, (AB), pp.25–28; *Brazil-Tyres*, (AB), §215, 225–227, 232 *EC-Seal Products*, (AB), §5.300, 5.304–5.306, 5.320.

cannot serve in circumstances where the objectionable feature (protectionism, terms of trade manipulation) is in fact central to the protected purpose. A more substantive chapeau review, as applied in *Shrimp* (see further below) might remedy this: but PT/TTT suggests no criteria for such a review.

The fit between PT/TTT and the specific exemptions in Article XX is therefore imperfect at best. It is not only that, as argued in Part III, these theories cannot account for Article XX's relation to the Core Disciplines; the content of Article XX itself raises problems.

Even ignoring these apparent contradictions, there is a further problem relying on these approaches as interpretive guides to Article XX. Recalling a point made in Chapter 6, beyond their core concerns with protectionism and terms of trade manipulation, these approaches say nothing about the boundary between legitimate and illicit regulation. Yet the most obvious feature of Article XX is its delineation of ten categories of regulation that are protected from challenge: if a measure falls within one of these categories, and meets the various other tests in Article XX, it is exempt from challenge: if it falls outside, then it is not. In consequence, a key interpretive challenge raised by Article XX is to identify the scope of these various categories; but PT and TTT are largely mute on this issue.

7.3.2 EGC and the General Exceptions

How might EGC account for these provisions?

EGC interprets Article XX as expressing two aspects of the principle of self-determination, which it understands as in turn expressing its fundamental concern for equal freedom.[117]

First, EGC recognizes that, to be self-determining, peoples require the capacity to make and act on choices about the shared life of their members, and to realize certain essential interests. ETMs may be necessary to protect that capacity and, to that extent, may be justified to outsiders. However, recalling a distinction drawn in Chapter 3, this extends to measures necessary to protect the capacity of peoples to be self-determining; it cannot justify measures adopted in exercise of that capacity. It is therefore limited to the kinds of functions that I suggested, in Chapter 5, are essential to regarding a community as self-determining.

Second, EGC recognizes that self-determination includes a claim to identify and pursue goals, including through cooperation with others.

---

[117] The argument for these two aspects is set out in detail in Chapter 5 above.

This motivates a power on the part of peoples to commit themselves to particular shared goals, standards, or projects. Where particular goals are in fact shared, ETMs in pursuit of these may be justified to outsiders subject thereto, as pursuing ends that those outsiders themselves share.

Both aspects imply limits. Because they justify measures in pursuit of particular objectives, it matters that measures in fact pursue those objectives. The first, protecting the capacity for self-determination, requires a distinction between the consequences of choice and the capacity for choice. The second is limited by the nature and scope of peoples' prior choices in identifying and committing to shared goals. State consent confers at best provisional legitimacy on international norms. As such, the fact that a goal is invoked in an international agreement cannot conclusively demonstrate that it is shared among the parties thereto. Care is required in determining both that affected peoples have in fact adopted the relevant goal, and also that this extends to its pursuit in the relevant way.

How do these two aspects explain Article XX?[118]

Articles XX (a), (b), (c), (d), (f), (i), and (j) can each be understood as expressing, to varying degrees, the first aspect noted above.[119] Consider: if public morals are understood as relating to a community's shared life and public culture, rather than its judgment of outsiders, their protection is a central case of self-determination.[120] The capacity to protect human, animal and plant life is similarly necessary for regarding a people as self-determining.[121] This is clearest for human life. However, protecting animal and plant life, as important parts of the physical and social fabric

---

[118] The constructive interpretive methodology adopted here might also help PT/TTT in avoiding some of the originalist objections raised above. However, doing so concedes the positivist/originalist claims that proponents of PT in particular commonly invoke.

[119] Art. XX is not the only place this aspect is expressed. It features prominently in the analysis of trade remedies in Chapter 8 below.

[120] As in e.g. (Miller, 1995: 24–27). The protection of national treasures is similarly relevant here, as well as to the idea of nations as trans-historical communities: (Gans, 2003: 49–58; Miller, 1995: 23).

This is the sense of public morals addressed in *China-Audiovisual Materials*, (Panel), §7.751–7.763; (AB), §7.759, and *US-Gambling*, (Panel), §6.457, 6.463–6.465, 6.469–6.473; (AB), §296. The settled definition of public morals ("standards of right and wrong conduct maintained by or on behalf of a community or nation," *US-Gambling*, (Panel), §6.465) is ambiguous in this respect. The AB in *Seals* did not distinguish these two senses, but territoriality was explicitly not addressed on appeal ((AB), §5.173), nor was it addressed by the Panel ((Panel), §7.628). The distinction was clearly recognized by the parties, with the EU emphasizing arguments about the community's shared life: (Panel), §7.374–7.375.

[121] See generally: §5.5 above.

of a community, may also be essential to effective self-determination. Alternatively such concerns might fall under the second aspect below, or be considered in purely distributive terms.[122] Controls on the import and export of precious metals and the exploitation of natural resources, price stabilization measures, and controls on trade in essential products in short supply can all be understood as necessary, particularly for smaller and less resilient economies, to maintain effective control over economic development and ensure equitable distribution among domestic constituencies.[123] Finally, the capacity to ensure compliance with domestic laws is a *sine qua non* of political self-determination. If a people cannot effectively implement their collective choices, as expressed through their political process, then self-determination becomes illusory.[124] If domestic choice is pre-empted by international factors, then self-determination implies a claim to insulate the domestic from the international to the extent necessary to make that choice possible.[125] However, care is needed to distinguish between measures protecting domestic choice, and the nature of the choice protected[126]; the latter must properly fall to the regulating state before it can ground a collateral claim to protection from international preemption.[127]

The second aspect is expressed to varying degrees in Articles XX (a), (b), (e), (g), and (h). This list overlaps with that in the previous paragraph. For example, public morals, while reflecting the shared life of a community domestically, can also be understood in global terms, as expressing judgments of right conduct shared by peoples generally.[128] Such "international public morals" differ from those considered above.

---

[122] This tension emerges in the AB jurisprudence, discussed further below.

[123] See §§5.4, 5.5 above. The AB's emphasis on stability under XX(j) fits well with this explanation: *India-Solar Cells* (AB), §5.71. However, in each case the provisos in the relevant paragraphs serve to emphasize that self-determination cannot be purchased at the expense of other peoples. Consider, for example, the AB's suggestion that the proviso to Art. XX(g) expresses a concern for even-handedness: *US-Gasoline*, (AB), p. 21. Cf. *China-Rare Earths*, (AB), §5.123–5.136. A similar concern motivates the AB's skepticism in *Solar Cells* of India's concerns about supply security and reliance on imports: §5.75–5.78.

[124] Recall Miller's image of nations as communities "active in character": (Miller, 1995: 24); §4.3 above.

[125] Note, however, that it is domestic choice, rather than relations with other peoples, that is protected: *Mexico-Soft Drinks*, (AB), §75.

[126] See §3.4 above.

[127] See Chapter 5 generally. The proviso to Art. XX(d) makes this point clearly: *Brazil-Retreaded Tyres*, (Panel), §7.387–7.388.

[128] For an interpretation of public morals in these terms: (Howse, 2002a: 1368).

Domestic public morals might justify ETMs protecting a community's shared life, whereas international public morals express approbation of or demand compliance from outsiders. To the extent that this is the case, they must be grounded in the collective choices of the peoples concerned, or at least a large proportion thereof.[129] The protection of human, animal, and plant life might also be understood in these terms, particularly where states act to protect these values outside their borders. Controls on the products of prison industry might be understood as reflecting a collective recognition of their moral complexity. Finally, the conservation of exhaustible natural resources is the archetypal global common concern.[130] Again, this problem looks different internally and externally. The conservation of a state's own resources is essential to effective self-determination.[131] Concern for natural resources elsewhere, whether in others' territories or the global commons, requires justification in other terms. Global environmental degradation may undermine particular states' capacity for self-determination but this has not been the sole focus of such concerns.[132] Global environmental arguments typically bifurcate into anthropocentric and transcendental claims. The former evoke the value of environmental resources for human persons and peoples; while the latter evoke the inherent value of nature, biodiversity, or particular animal and plant species.[133] To the extent environmental

---

[129] The justificatory distinction between inward and outward oriented public morals is addressed in: (Charnovitz, 1997). For an approach skeptical of such "transnational" public morals, as facilitating unilateralism and protectionism: (Wu, 2008: 240–242). Cf. (Bhagwati, 2004: 155). While *Gambling* and *Seals* are more concerned with domestic public morals, references in both to international norms can be understood in these terms: (*US-Gambling*, (Panel), §6.471–473; *EC-Seal Products*, (Panel), §7.408–409, 7.420). Where a complainant has not themselves formally endorsed the relevant norm, a further question arises as to its evidentiary significance. Measures targeting human rights compliance may also be justifiable under the targeted people's capacity for self-determination. I discuss both aspects of public morals in more detail in: (Suttle, 2017).

[130] On the link between cooperation and international conservation: (Charnovitz, 1991: 52–53). Interestingly, in tracing the move from cooperative to unilateral conservation measures, the examples Charnovitz highlights are cases where the relevant harms (overfishing, ozone depletion) impact the regulating state.

[131] See §5.5 above. On both the relation between natural resources and self-determination, and the inherent limits of this argument: *China-Rare Earths*, (Panel), §7.261–277.

[132] To the extent global commons problems are understood in these terms, response may be justified under the first limb. Compare the "securitization" of environmental discourse: (Trombetta, 2008). Anthropomorphic climate change is the most plausible candidate for this. Whether responses are best justified under the first or second aspects depends on the implications for effective self-determination of both regulating and third states. I do not address this question.

[133] (O'Neill, 1997: 127–129).

measures addressing global commons are anthropocentric, they are also frequently distributive; they protect the value for some of conserving resources, at the expense of the value for others of exploiting them.[134] ETMs pursuing such distributive concerns cannot be justified under the principle of self-determination (although they may be justifiable under the distributive limb of EGC).[135] Conversely, arguments in transcendental terms rely on contestable value claims, which we cannot assume are shared; as such, these similarly cannot directly justify ETMs.[136] However, to the extent conservation reflects a *collective* political choice among relevant peoples, we may justify measures to protect resources in the territories of those peoples, or in the global commons, under this second aspect of self-determination, subject to the concerns noted above about the quality and scope of that choice.[137]

The chapeau plays two roles on this account.

The first, policing the intrusion of extrinsic considerations, has been most prominent in the case-law. In *Gasoline, Tyres* and *Seals*, the chapeau analysis focused on whether discrimination tracked the exempted interest, or instead addressed other, extrinsic, considerations.[138] If, as EGC suggests, ETMs are justified under self-determination only in pursuit of relatively narrow and specified goals, then it matters that they in fact pursue those goals, and are not tailored to advance other interests.

However, the AB in *Shrimp* suggests a more substantive role for the chapeau, "locating and marking out a line of equilibrium between the right of a Member to invoke an exception under Article XX and the rights of the other Members under varying substantive provisions."[139] In that case, particularly in discussing coercion and negotiations, the AB goes beyond whether extrinsic considerations intrude, to inquire whether the manner in which the exempted interest is pursued is itself reasonable, having regard to the claims of outsiders.[140] This is the second function of

---

[134] Ibid., 130–131, 136–137.

[135] See §3.7. It might be objected that this implies a competitive race to the bottom. However, EGC can bite this bullet, explaining why some are entitled to run, and win, that race.

[136] See §3.4, 3.7.

[137] See §5.6. As discussed below, the Art. XX chapeau can be read in these terms: *US-Shrimp*, (AB), §156, 159.

[138] Cf. the references at fn. 116. The analysis of arbitrariness in *Tyres* is particularly expressive of this concern.

[139] *US-Shrimp*, (AB), §159.

[140] See further the discussion of *Shrimp* below. The AB has confirmed that the chapeau may play different roles in different contexts: *US-Shrimp*, (AB), §120.

the chapeau, one that EGC suggests may be most relevant in circumstances where a measure falls under self-determination's second aspect, concerning the pursuit of shared goals: it is thus unsurprising, as I discuss further below, that this more demanding analysis appears in a case, *Shrimp*, that falls squarely under that second aspect.

Understanding Article XX in this way thus offers two key advances over the leading economic approaches. First, it provides a standard for judging what falls within, and what outside, the various categories of measure described in that article. To the extent a measure falls under either limb of self-determination, we can expect it to fall within one of the categories listed. Second, it makes sense of the nexus and *chapeau* requirements by explaining why it matters that we draw a line between exempt and nonexempt measures, and police the intrusion of collateral purposes. If Article XX exempts a limited class of measures under self-determination, then it matters that measures invoking this exception do in fact fall into that class.

7.3.3   EGC in the Article XX Jurisprudence

EGC thus suggests an account of Article XX that avoids anomalies in the PT and TTT accounts. We next ask whether this can help understand the existing jurisprudence, and guide its progressive development. I consider two issues. While the first, constraints on accommodating unlisted objectives under Article XX, is relevant to both limbs of EGC's self-determination proviso, I focus on the first, inward, aspect. The second, the emphasis on internationalism in *Shrimp*, reflects the second, outward, aspect.

7.3.3.1   Policing Collateral Purposes

A key distinction between PT/TTT and EGC is in their understanding of the specific goals and functions listed in Article XX: for PT/TTT, these are simply proxies for nonprotectionist purposes; whereas EGC understands them as tracking the (limited) circumstances wherein ETMs may be justified under self-determination. In consequence, EGC suggests strictly policing the goals that measures pursue, whereas PT/TTT counsel a more relaxed approach. This issue arises at two points: the "nexus" language in the individual paragraphs ("necessary," "relating to," etc.); and the chapeau. How these are interpreted will determine how readily states can avail of the General Exceptions and, in turn, how far these reflect each of the approaches examined.[141] The issue is clearest in paragraphs invoking necessity (XX(a), (b), and (d)), so it is on these that I focus; but similar issues arise under other paragraphs.[142]

In *Korea-Beef* the AB addressed necessity, against the backdrop of GATT jurisprudence equating necessity with "least GATT-inconsistent alternative."[143] It first noted that necessary was not the same as indispensable.[144] A measure may be necessary to achieving a goal, even if it the relevant goal could be achieved by other means. Where a measure is not indispensable, the AB suggested weighing and balancing *inter alia* the contribution made by the measure, the importance of the common interest or values protected, and the impact of the measure on imports or exports.[145] The greater the contribution a measure makes, and the more important the common interest or values, the easier it is to justify it; while a greater impact on imports or exports makes justification harder.

This approach has been adopted in a number of subsequent cases.[146] However, as various commentators observe, taken at face value the language of balancing is incompatible with members' right to determine their own standards and levels of enforcement, which the AB has elsewhere endorsed.[147] If balancing meant weighing the benefits of a measure, in terms of its contribution to the relevant nontrade goal, against the costs, in terms of trade restrictiveness, inquiring whether the costs were proportionate to the benefits, then it would necessarily mean substituting the AB's judgment about appropriate standards for that of the member state. The AB's references to balancing must therefore go, not to the proportionality of the measure, but to whether the least trade restrictive alternative is

---

[141] (Kapterian, 2010: 92).

[142] Each requires a "sufficient nexus" between measure and interest: *China-Rare Earths*, (AB), §5.87–5.90. I offer no explanation for the different language in each paragraph. In *US-Gasoline*, the AB placed significant emphasis on the different nexus language in different paragraphs, arguing that these must imply different requirements. However, given the interpretation of XX(g) in *Rare Earths*, and the chapeau in *Tyres*, it is unclear how much practical difference this makes.

[143] *US-Section 337*, (GATT Panel), §5.26. Cf. *US–Gasoline*, (Panel), §6.24–6.28.

[144] *Korea-Beef*, (AB), §161.   [145] Ibid., §164.

[146] Most prominently, *EC-Asbestos*, (AB), §171; *Brazil-Tyres*, (AB), §178–182, *EC-Seals*, (AB), §5.214.

[147] *Korea-Beef*, (AB), §176; (Regan, 2007) Cf. (Kapterian, 2010: 119; Neumann & Turk, 2003: 208–209; Shaffer & Trachtman, 2011: 140–144; Weiler, 2009: 140). The same point arises under other paragraphs. States' discretion to determine their level of protection has been affirmed under: XX(a)(public morals) *China-Audiovisual Services*, (AB), §318; XX(b)(human health) *EC-Asbestos*, (AB), §168, *Brazil-Tyres*, (AB), §140; XX(g) (natural resources): *US-Gasoline*, *(AB)*, p.30. Cf. (Kapterian, 2010: 100).

adopted.[148] The importance of the goal pursued would then go to the standard or level of enforcement chosen, or the appropriate margin of appreciation.[149] A respondent's claim to pursue a high standard or level of enforcement will be more plausible if the goal pursued is one to which *that member* attaches significant value.[150] Conversely, where the ostensible goal is comparatively unimportant *from the perspective of the regulating state*, a claim to pursue high standards may be implausible.[151] Alternatively, importance might affect the margin of appreciation, allowing more leeway to members in identifying appropriate measures in pursuit of more important common interests or values.[152] This may involve an element of balancing; but what is balanced is the enforcement, transaction, and political costs of adopting one response over another, rather than the response itself.

This rejection of substantive balancing accords with PT and TTT. Because both see Article XX as exempting nontrade motivations, they deny that balancing trade and nontrade values has any role to play.[153] If measures genuinely pursue nontrade goals then, on these approaches, they are unobjectionable; Article XX simply identifies such measures.[154] An overly demanding application thereof risks unjustifiable policy restrictions.[155]

However, while less objectionable than a strong proportionality approach, the interpretations sketched above remain problematic for PT/TTT. Using importance to assess members' preferred standards will inevitably restrict regulatory choice.[156] Further, because it deduces the chosen standard from the measure challenged, it risks ignoring political and practical constraints.[157] PT/TTT characterize such constraints as

---

[148] Cf. (Osiro, 2002).

[149] Cf. (McGrady, 2009: 163). Regan argues (in 2007) that none of the decided cases in fact engages in substantive balancing, notwithstanding the AB's language. That remains the case today.

[150] For an interpretation in these terms: (Osiro, 2002: 138–139).

[151] (Weiler, 2009: 144).

[152] For this interpretation: (Neumann & Turk, 2003: 211; Trebilcock et al., 2013: 682).

[153] Regan's "domestic rationality" extension might afford some role for balancing, although its focus on local efficiency suggests political, not judicial, organs should make this judgment: (Regan, 2006: 987–988; Trachtman, 1998: 34). Motivating strong balancing under an economic approach requires something like Trachtman's property rights analysis. (Trachtman, 2007; Trachtman, 2008) Cf. (Bown & Trachtman, 2009). However, even then, strong balancing requires according a degree of political authority to central decision-makers that is less plausible in the WTO than in the federal and quasi-federal systems that Trachtman elsewhere analyses: (Trachtman, 1998) Cf. (Howse & Nicolaidis, 2001: 239–240).

[154] (Kapterian, 2010: 90).   [155] (Neumann & Turk, 2003: 208).

[156] (Kapterian, 2010: 108).   [157] (Howse & Langille, 2012: 418–419).

valid grounds for regulation, so counsel against any approach that does not give them full weight. The margin of appreciation interpretation is problematic for similar reasons. Margins of appreciation provide space to accommodate those political and practical considerations. Provided these do not disguise a trade motivation, PT/TTT suggest states be allowed to have regard to them, to whatever extent they deem appropriate. Balancing then seems unjustifiably restrictive.[158]

EGC, by contrast, can readily accommodate these interpretations.

Like PT/TTT, it rejects strong balancing: if we understand Article XX as protecting measures necessary for members to be self-determining, then there can be no question of balancing these against trade effects, subject to the DEM proviso.[159]

However, EGC regards such measures as justified only to the extent actually necessary to vindicate members' self-determination. This is distinct from vindicating the particular political choice reflected in a measure.[160] EGC therefore suggests reviewing members' asserted choice of standard to identify what vindicating self-determination in fact requires in the particular case. The importance of a particular goal, from the relevant member's perspective, can play a role in this analysis, in so far as protecting and expressing a people's distinctive values is an important aspect of self-determination.[161] However, it is the underlying value, rather than the political choice, that requires to be protected. Respecting self-determination means respecting local conceptions of that value; but this is not necessarily incompatible with reviewing political interpretations of those conceptions, or the ways they are expressed in particular instances.

EGC's restrictive account of permissible purposes similarly explains margin of appreciation balancing. Unlike PT/TTT, EGC does not assume that the various political and practical considerations shaping regulation can be invoked to justify it to outsiders. The first aspect of self-determination cannot justify ETMs beyond the *minimum* required to give effect to that value; to the extent measures go beyond that minimum, they must be justified in some other terms. Balancing, based on a shared objective

---

[158] Apart entirely from the question of balancing, the AB's approach to reasonable availability arguably imposes too high a standard, given PT/TTT's accounts of this test: *Brazil-Tyres*, (AB), §156, quoting *US-Gambling*, (AB), §308. Cf. (Kapterian, 2010: 121).

[159] See §5.6 above. The limited constraint implied by the proviso can in turn be picked up under the *chapeau*, as to which see further below.

[160] See §3.4 above.

[161] See §5.5 above. See also Chapter 9 below on self-determination in SPS and TBT.

conception of value, might play a role here without undermining the importance for self-determination of respecting local conceptions of value in the choice of goals and levels of protection.[162]

The second place where accommodating nonexempt goals is policed is the chapeau's prohibition on arbitrary and unjustifiable discrimination. The AB has confirmed that arbitrariness here is not limited to "capricious or unpredictable reasons"[163]: rather, it arises wherever there is no "rational connection" between discrimination and the relevant Article XX goal.[164] As in *Brazil-Tyres*, this may include discrimination reflecting political or legal constraints on the regulating state. Proponents of PT/TTT criticize this conclusion, as unduly restricting states' regulatory autonomy[165]: but EGC makes sense of it, as preventing states tailoring ETMs in pursuit of ends that are not shared by those directly subject to them.

The underlying problem for PT/TTT is that they draw no principled distinction between matters listed in Article XX and other considerations. They therefore see no difficulty with such other considerations shaping regulations, provided they are nonprotectionist. Standards review and margin of appreciation balancing, and a rigorous application of the chapeau, necessarily restrict members accommodating such considerations, and therefore raise concerns under PT/TTT. EGC, by contrast, provides a principled defense of that distinction, explaining why such other considerations cannot directly justify ETMs, and hence why we strictly police such collateral considerations, both under the individual paragraphs and the chapeau.

7.3.3.2   Policing Shared Goals

The second limb of EGC's self-determination proviso, emphasizing the pursuit of contingently shared goals, appears most clearly in the AB's analysis in *Shrimp*. I highlight below the extent to which this analysis contrasts with that in other Article XX cases, and then suggest how EGC might explain this.

This dispute concerned US regulations on shrimp imports from countries permitting fishing practices likely to increase sea turtle mortality. The US did not deny that the regulations violated Article XI,[166] but

---

[162] The fact that such balancing is admissible does not mean it is straightforward. The demanding standard for nonavailability in *Tyres* reflects continued suspicion of allowing domestic interests to shape ETMs. Nor need it imply that consideration of relative costs is permissible: Cf. *US-Gasoline*, (AB), p. 28.

[163] *Brazil-Tyres*, (AB), §217, 232.   [164] Ibid, §227; *EC-Seals*, (AB), §5.300, 5.306.

[165] E.g. (Trebilcock et al., 2013: 684).

[166] In fact, on the argument in Chapter 6, the regulations at issue in *Shrimp* would fall under Articles I and III, and would be discriminatory under the modified aims and effects approach advocated there.

argued they fell under, *inter alia*, Article XX(g), as measures "relating to the conservation of exhaustible natural resources [...] made effective in conjunction with restrictions on domestic production or consumption."

The AB began its Article XX analysis by noting that "the domestic policies embodied in [measures covered by Article XX] have been recognized as important and legitimate in character."[167] In consequence, it reasoned, we cannot assume that measures conditioning market access on the adoption of particular policies are *a priori* unjustifiable.[168] This emphasis on policies "recognized as important and legitimate in character" seems at odds with the focus in other cases on the priority of national choice.[169] Rather than addressing policies *collectively* recognized as important, those other cases seem more concerned to protect members' capacity to themselves decide what is important and legitimate, within the constraints of a categorical approach.[170]

They next addressed the scope of Article XX (g). This involved a wide-ranging internationally focused inquiry, examining how natural resources were understood when the GATT was negotiated, but also how they were currently understood, in light of the "contemporary concerns of the community of nations,"[171] adopting an "evolutionary" approach and considering wider international environmental law and practice to conclude that sea turtles constituted an exhaustible natural resource.[172] Again, it seems that global rather than local standards are prioritized: it is irrelevant whether the United States values protecting sea turtles if the contracting parties, or indeed the international community as a whole, do not.

The contrast is not only with the approach under other paragraphs of Article XX, but also with other XX(g) cases including *Gasoline* and *Raw Materials*.[173] The key distinction is that these cases concerned natural resources within the regulating state's territory, whereas *Shrimp* addresses the protection of resources internationally.[174] In the former

---

[167] *US-Shrimp*, (AB), §121.   [168] Ibid.

[169] As noted, this concern for domestic choice is not limited to Art. XX(d). See the cases cited at fn. 147 above. While domestic choice is not denied in *Shrimp*, it is less prominent.

[170] See the cases at fn. 147.   [171] (AB), §129.   [172] Ibid., §130–134.

[173] E.g. *US-Gasoline*, (AB), pp. 30–31 (on levels of protection); *China-Raw Materials*, (Panel), §7.380–7.381 (on the broad discretion implicit in sovereignty over natural resources).

[174] The AB did not explicitly address the jurisdictional limits of XX(g), relying on sea-turtles' migratory nature and presence in US waters to sidestep this issue: *US-Shrimp*, (AB), §131 Cf. the approach to XX(b) in *EC-Tariff Preferences*, (Panel), §7.203–7.206.

case, resources are regarded as primarily a concern, and indeed a value, for the regulating state. Making choices about these, managing them responsibly, and ultimately profiting from them, are core aspects of self-determination.[175] In the latter case, the relation is quite different.

This emphasis on shared goals continues in the AB's interpretation of relatedness, noting that protecting sea turtles was a policy shared by all participants in the case, and indeed "the vast majority of the nations of the world."[176] While ostensibly considering whether the US measure was reasonably related to the relevant ends,[177] this suggests looking further, at whether those ends are shared by the relevant parties.

The AB also adopts a more demanding approach to the chapeau than in previous or subsequent cases. In *Gasoline*, the chapeau was explained as preventing abuse of the exceptions, and ensuring these were not applied to frustrate legal obligations.[178] By contrast, in *Shrimp* the need to "maintain a balance of rights and obligations"[179] imposed substantive limits on the measures adopted. In particular, the US requirement that the same policy be adopted in all exporting countries, regardless of local conditions, was judged unreasonable, and hence unjustifiable.[180] Instead, before imposing restrictions it was incumbent on the US to engage exporting nations in "serious, across the board negotiation" in pursuit of bilateral or multilateral conservation agreements.[181] This was based in part on the preference for negotiations in international environmental law generally.[182] Criticism of the *soi disant* coercive nature of the measures at issue similarly implies

---

[175] This is particularly clear in *China-Raw Materials*, (Panel), §7.381 Cf. the emphasis on even-handedness:§7.404–7.406. The Panel in *China-Rare Earths* was similarly concerned (§7.261–7.270) to emphasize both the role of national choice in conserving territorial natural resources, and the connection between resources and self-determination.

[176] *US-Shrimp*, (AB), p. 135.   [177] Ibid., §141, following *US-Gasoline*, (AB), p. 19.

[178] *US-Gasoline*, (AB), p. 22.

[179] *US-Shrimp*, (AB), §156. While not discussed here, the emphasis on a balance of rights in *Shrimp* suggests the chapeau might also give effect to EGC's DEM proviso as regards measures justified under the first, inward-looking, limb of self-determination.

[180] Ibid., §164.   [181] Ibid., §166.

[182] Ibid., §168. The AB was also concerned that agreements were pursued with some countries and not others, but the duty to negotiate is clearly freestanding, independent of discrimination: §168, 170. Cf. (Scott, 2004b: 336–337). While negotiations were also suggested in *Gasoline*, this related to information and verification requirements not, as in *Shrimp*, the design of the underlying measures. (Contrast *Gasoline*, p. 27 ("appropriate procedures ... to mitigate the administrative problems pleaded") with *Shrimp*, §172 ("negotiations for establishing consensual means of protection and conservation ... policies ... are all shaped by the Department of State, without the participation of the exporting Members.").)

This conclusion is not affected by the AB's subsequent clarification that a duty to negotiate in good faith did not imply a duty to reach agreement; the duty to negotiate,

substantive limits on the extent to which members can pursue their preferred policies[183]: a state may restrict imports to manipulate the incentives of private parties, but it may not dictate the regulatory choices of other states.[184]

At each point, the approach in *Shrimp* seems distinct from that in those Article XX cases, including *Beef, Gasoline,* and *Tyres,* that express the first limb of EGC's self-determination proviso.[185] Whereas these emphasize domestic choice, *Shrimp* consistently invokes international standards.[186] Further, to find these it looks beyond the WTO Agreements to international law and practice more generally.[187] Ostensibly, this serves to interpret the language of the GATT; but the AB seems equally concerned to examine how far goals are shared among the international community, and how far that community considers appropriate the means adopted.

Like the strict policing of collateral purposes, this outward-looking interpretation of both Article XX(g) and the chapeau conflicts with PT/ TTT. If our concern is with protectionism and terms of trade manipulation, then whether the nontrade goals pursued by a measure are shared internationally is simply irrelevant.[188]

EGC, by contrast, makes sense of this approach. The protection of migratory sea turtles clearly does not constitute a prerequisite to US self-determination, in the way that the protection of the health of its citizens or the conservation of its own natural resources does. It thus cannot

---

and the invocation of shared values, emphasize the international structure of the required justification. *US-Shrimp (Art. 21.5-Malaysia),* (AB), §122–124.

[183] *US-Shrimp,* (AB), §161. Cf. (Gaines, 2001: 786–789).

[184] For an account accepting this conclusion, but denying that it constitutes a departure from the *Korea-Beef* approach: (Neumann & Turk, 2003: 229–230). Cf. (Osiro, 2002: 139–140) The AB arguably relaxes this restriction in *US-Shrimp (Article 21.5-Malaysia),* (AB), §143–144, 147.

The substantive restrictions in *Shrimp* similarly contrast with *Brazil-Tyres,* where the chapeau analysis focused on whether discrimination bore a "rational connection to the objective falling within the purview of a paragraph of Article XX, or would go against that objective": (AB), §226–227. Cf. §228, 232, 246–247. On the relation between these analyses: (A. Davies, 2009: 518–521). While criticized by exponents of PT/TTT as unduly restrictive, the *Tyres* approach is closer to those approaches than *Shrimp.* A similar approach appears in *Seals,* (AB), §5.299–5.300, 5.306. However, aspects of *Shrimp* are also evident in e.g. §5.320. This arguably reflects the difficulty, noted above, of classifying *Seals* under the approach adopted here. See fn. 120 above.

[185] The differences in emphasis cannot be explained solely through the different provisions addressed, given that a number of the cases contrasted address the identical provisions. E.g. *US-Gasoline, China-Raw Materials, China-Rare Earths* on XX(g), *US-Gasoline, Brazil-Tyres, EC-Seals* on the chapeau.

[186] On *Shrimp* as external accountability: (Scott, 2004a: 15–20).

[187] (Howse & Nicolaidis, 2001: 244–245).

[188] For this point, arguing against a territoriality requirement: (Trebilcock et al., 2013: 676).

plausibly fall under the first limb of EGC's self-determination proviso. Given this, the second aspect of EGC's self-determination proviso suggests ETMs pursuing that goal will be justified only where that goal is in fact shared by those outsiders who are subject to them. This, I suggest, is precisely what the AB's approach in *Shrimp* tracks.[189]

EGC thus explains both the content of Article XX, and the AB's approach to it, including the differing emphases in various cases. Further, it seems better than either PT or TTT at explaining these.

7.4   Conclusion

Chapter 5 showed how EGC understands the GATT's Core Disciplines on border measures and discrimination as tracking the category of External Trade Measures. ETMs are subject to a demanding justificatory standard, which they will not usually meet. In consequence, we would expect most such measures to be prohibited. This, I suggested, was the function of the Core Disciplines.

This chapter finished that story, examining how far the exceptions and qualifications to the Core Disciplines can be understood as tracking the justifications that EGC suggests apply to ETMs. It focused on two sets of rules: the Development Provisions in Article XVIII, Part IV, and the Enabling Clause; and the General Exceptions in Article XX. These, I suggested, can be understood as expressing EGC's egalitarian and self-determination limbs respectively. In each case, I showed the difficulties existing approaches have accounting for the relevant rules, the explanations suggested by EGC for these, and the extent to which EGC, more than existing approaches, can provide both justification and clarification for the AB's existing jurisprudence thereunder.

In the next chapter, this approach is extended to disciplines on trade remedies. The prominence of trade remedies in dispute settlement practice and the confusion in existing theoretical accounts of their function make them an important test of EGC's relevance to diverse and contested disciplines. Chapter 9 extends the approach further, to disciplines on domestic regulation in the SPS and TBT Agreements.

---

[189] It might be objected that explaining much of Art. XX through shared goals is incompatible with its role in justifying unilateral action. However, the agency problems discussed in Chapter 4, and invoked in explaining the Enabling Clause, are equally relevant here: (Gaines, 2001: 809–811). There is no contradiction in permitting unilateral action in pursuit of shared ends, particularly given international disciplines policing that action.

8

Trade Remedies and Fairness in International Trade Regulation

8.1 Introduction

Trade remedies generate a disproportionate share of WTO disputes. Of 501 disputes between 1995 and 2015, 105 addressed the Subsidies and Countervailing Measures Agreement (SCM), 112 the Anti-Dumping Agreement (ADA), and 48 the Safeguards Agreement (SA).[1] The GATT aside, the SCM and ADA are easily the most cited Annex 1A agreements, with the SA a respectable fifth.[2] Any general theory of WTO law must therefore account for trade remedies. This chapter aims to do this.

Despite this prominence in disputes, and in the practice of many states,[3] there is little consensus about the function that trade remedies can and should play.[4] Howse and Neven, for example, explain the lack of preambles to the ADA and SCM as reflecting a lack of consensus among negotiators on the underlying goals of either agreement[5]; Diamond similarly characterizes the SCM's consensus on subsidies as "more apparent than real"[6]; Grossman and Mavroidis characterize the SA, somewhat euphemistically, as "opaque about its intended objectives"[7]; while Finger dismisses anti-dumping arguments as incoherent rhetoric, and anti-dumping practice as "ordinary protectionism with a good public relations program."[8]

---

[1] (Leitner & Lester, 2016: 294).

[2] One estimate suggests 30 percent of disputes between 2001 and 2008 concerned dumping or CVDs: (Bown & Prusa, 2011: 361).

[3] On the increasing use of anti-dumping in particular: (Niels, 2000: 469–471; Prusa, 2005: 684–693; Zanardi, 2004).

[4] (Jackson, 1997: 281; Zheng, 2012: 154–155).

[5] (Howse & Neven, 2003: 155–157) Cf. *US-ADCVD (China)*, (AB), §301.

[6] (Diamond, 2008: 649–650).   [7] (Grossman & Mavroidis, 2005b: 115).

[8] (Finger, 1992: 121) Cf. (Bown & Sykes, 2008: 129). For a nineteenth century forerunner of this view: (Rodrik, 2011: 31).

This dissensus goes beyond states' and negotiators' intentions, reflecting a deeper concern that the WTO's trade remedy rules lack any coherent rationale. While the former raises problems for originalist treaty interpretation, the latter poses a more serious challenge, both to the legitimacy of the agreements, and to their interpretation in other than a narrowly textualist manner.[9] When combined with often obscure, confusing, or contradictory treaty language, and an incomplete and conflicting negotiating history, the lack of a coherent rationale poses near-insurmountable barriers to consistent interpretation.[10]

I suggest that the absence of a consensus theory of trade remedies reflects a reluctance to take seriously the idea of fairness. Fairness is a recurring feature in trade remedies discourse, including before the AB.[11] However, it has generally evoked skepticism among scholars.[12] Given differences in competitive conditions across countries, which are themselves essential for trade, there is no obvious baseline against which to define fairness.[13] Indeed, fairness itself is a problematic concept for the economics-dominated literature in this area.[14] Instead, theoretically minded scholars have concentrated on more tractable concepts like efficiency, while empiricists emphasize the priority of imports, regardless of fairness, in stimulating recourse to trade remedies.[15] The result has been skepticism about the current regime, leading to calls for its abolition, reform, or at best toleration as a politically necessary evil.[16]

I argue an appropriate conception of fairness can explain the distinctive shape of the rules in this area, and offer useful guidance on their interpretation and application in hard cases. In particular, I argue that the conception of fairness implicit in EGC can serve this purpose.

The challenge is to identify and delineate the problems to which these disciplines respond. What exactly is wrong with subsidies and dumping, that means we need mechanisms for responding to them? Why are safeguards an appropriate response to some kinds of economic dislocation, but not to others? In each case, the answer presumably has

---

[9] On the limits of textualism: (Horn & Weiler, 2005: 251–253). On interpretive challenges of theoretical dissensus: (Howse & Neven, 2003: 157–159).

[10] On relating theory to object and purpose: (Mavroidis, 2007: 6–20). Cf. in the SA context: (Grossman & Mavroidis, 2005b: 109–115).

[11] E.g. *US-Line Pipe*, (AB), §80 Cf. (Lindsey, 1999: 3–4; Wauters, 2010: 334–336).

[12] E.g. (Abbott, 1996: 442–450; Barceló, 1991; Cass & Boltuck, 1996: 351–354; Prusa, 2005: 694; Stegemann, 1991: 382).

[13] (Lowenfeld, 1980: 219).   [14] (Sykes, 2003a: 11).

[15] (Finger, 1992: 141; Lowenfeld, 1980: 214).

[16] E.g. (Finger & Artis, 1993; Stegemann, 1991: 395–401; Voon, 2010: 626; Zheng, 2012).

something to do with imports, as imports are what these remedies primarily target.[17] However, while economics can identify harms from imports in certain circumstances, the trade remedies rules don't map well onto those circumstances. By focusing instead on fairness, and in turn on justification, we find an alternative basis for distinguishing. It is not that the effects addressed are necessarily different, in degree or kind, from those suffered in other circumstances; but they are unjustifiable, having regard to their source and the relation between their authors and those on whom they are imposed.

The argument proceeds in three parts. In Section 8.2, I review a number of existing approaches to trade remedies, highlighting their deficiencies. Section 8.3 develops my own account, derived from EGC, and shows how it explains these disciplines. Finally, Section 8.4 considers a number of problems in trade remedies case-law, suggesting EGC can illuminate and potentially resolve these.

The strategy is similar to Chapters 6 and 7: I contrast EGC's approach with leading economic and political explanations, arguing EGC achieves a better fit. Many of these existing explanations reflect aspects of the Protectionist and Terms of Trade approaches. However, the diversity of arguments makes this typology less helpful here.

The general economic skepticism of trade remedies raises a methodological challenge. As noted, many theorists are less concerned to explain or defend trade remedies than they are to criticize and reform them. These may regard the positions criticized here as straw-men. Certainly, I do not claim that I am challenging consensus economic explanations. Nor do I claim the objections discussed in Section 8.2 are especially novel; economic criticism of trade remedies is well established. However, in so far as EGC is here advanced as both explanation and justification, the appropriate contrast is with existing explanatory and/or justificatory, rather than purely critical, approaches. I have tried to represent these fairly.

What are the key features requiring explanation? In the case of subsidies, I focus on the definitions of prohibited and actionable subsidies. While distinct, the SCM constitutes an effective prohibition on trade-affecting subsidies in either category. We must therefore explain what is distinctive and objectionable about such measures, as distinct from others affecting the international economy, such as to justify both a prohibition, and a right for states to impose countervailing duties

---

[17] Subsidies are also multilaterally disciplined. I return to this point below.

(CVDs) on subsidized imports. In the case of dumping, the focus is similarly on explaining what is problematic about the pricing practices (price discrimination and below-cost selling) to which anti-dumping responds, as distinct from other commercial practices, such as to justify imposing anti-dumping duties (ADDs). In the case of safeguards the problem is to explain why trade-restricting safeguards are an appropriate response to injury in some circumstances but not others. Each of countervailing duties, anti-dumping duties, and safeguards constitute limited exemptions from the disciplines on border measures in GATT Articles II and XI, so any account must also explain why an exemption is appropriate for these, but not other, measures.

8.2   Economic Approaches to Trade Remedies

The leading justifications of trade remedies draw on economics and political economy to explain the functions these rules serve.[18] This section reviews those accounts, and the challenges they face.

8.2.1   Subsidies

The most common argument against subsidies highlights their price-distorting effects as reducing market efficiency.[19] Subsidies induce inefficient over-production, divert resources from more efficient uses, and reduce national and global welfare.[20] If the WTO promotes locally and globally efficient production, then it makes sense to target subsidies.[21]

As an explanation of the WTO rules, however, this has a number of flaws. First, given market failures, positive externalities, and public goods, subsidies can promote efficiency by assuring producers the full social value of production.[22] Subsidies are frequently the first best response to market failures.[23] Their availability is also necessary to demonstrate

---

[18]   For subsidies and dumping, this involves two questions. First, what is objectionable about the practice? And second, why are CVDs/ADDs the appropriate response (Finger & Artis, 1993: 69; Sykes, 2003a: 24).

[19]   (Howse, 2010: 92–93; Lester et al., 2012; Mavroidis, 2007: 179; Rubini, 2009: 40; Sykes, 2003a, 2010: 475). The argument is analogous to PT.

[20]   (Schwartz & Clements, 1999: 129–130).

[21]   For a variation emphasizing commitment problems: (Brou & Ruta, 2012).

[22]   (Howse, 2010: 94–97; Mavroidis, 2007: 180; Sykes, 2010: 476).

[23]   (Bhagwati & Ramaswami, 1963) Cf. (Bagwell & Staiger, 2006; Lester, 2011: 370–372; Mavroidis et al., 2008: 294). For recent analyses linking this problem to various interpretive questions: (Pal, 2014; Rubini, 2012).

protectionism's inefficiency.[24] Without subsidies, the case for free trade is weakened; yet with the expiry of the non-actionable subsidies provisions, no non-agricultural subsidies are above challenge.[25] Further, the efficiency argument ignores the ways pervasive government activity affects costs and prices in contemporary economies.[26] The SCM disciplines only "specific" production subsidies, as well as export and import-substitution subsidies[27]; but there is little reason to think specific subsidies are more or less distorting than broad based government programs in areas like health, education, welfare, and employment assistance, that are firmly outside the scope of the SCM.[28] This argument thus fails to explain why we target these measures and not others.

A second approach explains regulation as solving a competitive subsidization prisoner's dilemma.[29] Where two governments subsidize competing industries, each incurs costs without affording any competitive advantage to either. Both will be better off by reducing their subsidies, but neither can do so without coordinating with the other.[30] This argument is most commonly applied to export subsidies, but can apply to production subsidies where these are granted with a view to the international competitive position of supported industries.[31] The political problem is identical to TTT, but the economic mechanism runs through imperfect competition not terms of trade.[32]

This argument only justifies disciplining subsidies where such prisoner's dilemmas arise.[33] However, those circumstances are relatively narrow.[34]

---

[24] (Mavroidis, 2007: 179) Cf. §6.2.2 above.   [25] (Howse, 2010: 86; Mavroidis, 2012: 566).

[26] (Horn & Mavroidis, 2005: 233–245; Sykes, 2010: 501–503) Contrast: (Bigdeli, 2011: 15). Some scholars explain this on pragmatic grounds: (Jackson, 1997: 297; Rubini, 2009: 364–367).

[27] SCM Art. 1.2 and 3.1. Cf. Part 3 below.

[28] (Sykes, 2003a: 8, 2010: 511–515; Wouters & Coppens, 2009: 29–30). For a review of the positions: (Rubini, 2009: 360–364). This contradicts a common assumption in legal scholarship. E.g. (Howse, 2010: 92–93; Lester et al., 2012: 429).

[29] (Bagwell et al., 2013: 182–191; Barceló, 1991: 320; Mavroidis, 2007: 180; Mavroidis et al., 2008; Sykes, 2010: 475, 499) Cf. (Hufbauer & Erb, 1984: 8–9).

[30] (Sykes, 2003a: 9).   [31] This raises definitional questions, addressed at fn. 125 below.

[32] (Krugman et al., 2012: 302–309).

[33] (Mavroidis, 2007: 180). While subsidies on exports in general adversely affect states' terms of trade, and hence national welfare, given specific market conditions they may confer first mover advantages and/or act as commitment devices allowing producers to deter competitors, acquire greater market share, and earn supra-normal profits, which might suffice to offset the national welfare loss from subsidization. This will only hold in very specific market conditions, which, perhaps unsurprisingly, are likely to include the market for large civilian aircraft.

[34] (Green & Trebilcock, 2010: 117; Sykes, 2003a: 12, 24). Bagwell and Staiger expand this model by politically weighting export industries. The result, while formally an export

Further, there are suggestions strict subsidies disciplines, by limiting the ways states can benefit industries, make it harder to solve the terms of trade prisoner's dilemma.[35] Some export subsidies may also be both locally and globally efficient, where they offset existing distortions that would otherwise lead to suboptimal trade.[36] Thus, again, this argument fails to explain why we focus on the particular measures disciplined.

A third argument characterizes subsidies disciplines as protecting market access commitments made under the GATT.[37]

Certainly, subsidies can impede market access, and tariffs can be replicated with taxes and subsidies.[38] On this approach, specificity is sometimes explained as a proxy for protectionism, albeit a poor one.[39] However, while this may justify disciplining some subsidies, it cannot support SCM's extensive disciplines, or the imposition of CVDs.[40] Two problems stand out. First, SCM disciplines are not limited to products where market access commitments have been made[41]; and second, because export subsidies, and many production subsidies, negatively affect terms of trade, this approach is incompatible with national welfare accounts of trade agreements.[42]

Further, to the extent any of these arguments justify disciplining subsidies, they do not extend to CVDs.[43] CVDs are imposed on imports

oriented prisoner's dilemma, is closer in structure to Ethier's political externalities model, and might be better understood in terms of locally inefficient protectionism than strategic trade policy: (Bagwell & Staiger, 2001). For an application: (Horn & Mavroidis, 2005).

[35] (Bagwell & Staiger, 2006; Sykes, 2010: 476).

[36] (Bagwell et al., 2013: 179–182; Panagariya, 2000: 5–7).

[37] (Bagwell & Staiger, 2006: 877; Howse, 2010; Rubini, 2009: 37; Sykes, 2010: 495).

[38] (Sykes, 2010: 492–495).

[39] The main problem being that specificity is frequently essential to socially efficient subsidies: (Sykes, 2010: 513–514).

[40] (Bagwell & Staiger, 2006; Sykes, 2003a: 17–18, 2010: 495–498).

[41] Bagwell and Staiger argue non-violation complaints can more efficiently discipline measures, including subsidies, undermining market access commitments; although given the AB's demanding approach to non-violation, it may be insufficiently flexible for this purpose.

[42] (Green & Trebilcock, 2010: 119–120; Krugman et al., 2012). By contrast, import-substitution and production subsidies displacing imports from domestic markets can improve terms of trade.

[43] This leads some scholars to reject economic justifications in favor of an "entitlement" account, which assumes that "firms are entitled to that domestic market outcome which would have resulted from a 'fair' competitive process, by which is meant one which has not been 'manipulated' by foreign government subsidization": (Goetz et al., 1986, 18–19). Cf. (Diamond, 1988). In rejecting economic justifications, and emphasizing manipulation, this approach has much in common with EGC. However, its focus on producer entitlement is unmotivated: (Jackson, 1989a, 742–746). EGC thus provides a more consistent and plausible rationale.

into the home territory. They do nothing to address distortions or competitive dynamics, merely diverting their effects to other markets.[44] Nor can they be supported on market access grounds, as countervailed sales happen in the imposing state's own market.[45] It is not clear what distinctive harm a state suffers in consequence of subsidized imports.[46] The SCM emphasizes harm to competitors; but this is no different to that from similarly cheap unsubsidized imports.[47] The argument for free trade teaches that states gain by importing goods cheaper than they can be produced domestically; it is irrelevant why imports are cheaper.[48] Aside from very rare cases where international subsidization can be plausibly regarded as predatory,[49] subsidized imports are as beneficial as unsubsidized ones, and the appropriate response by an importing state is to "send a thank-you note to the embassy."[50]

None of these arguments, then, provide satisfactory explanations of the SCM disciplines or the reasons for applying CVDs.

8.2.2 Safeguards

Turning next to safeguards, we find two economic and two political arguments commonly advanced to explain these rules.

First, it is argued that safeguards provide a mechanism for compensating those who lose out from trade liberalization.[51] The economic argument for free trade claims that it maximizes aggregate welfare, while recognizing that some groups lose out from the move to free trade.[52] It

---

[44] (Sykes, 1989, 227–229).

[45] We might reconstruct TTT to account for this. However this highlights again subsidies' mixed effects on terms of trade. Further, the tests for applying CVDs will not track when such an argument applies: (Sykes, 1989: 215–226). A market access explanation of CVDs might explain them as a mechanism for maintaining the pro-trade balancing coalition described in anti-protectionist theories. Foreign subsidies can be expected to reduce support for trade in the affected industries. CVDs provide a mechanism for paying off affected industries, thereby maintaining the pro-trade political coalition. The difficulty with this explanation is that CVDs' focus on imports means they will frequently be unavailable, to or fail meaningfully to benefit, relevant export constituencies.

[46] (Trebilcock et al., 2013: 395).   [47] (Panagariya, 2000: 3–5; Sykes, 1989: 210–211).

[48] (Jackson, 1997: 282; Sykes, 2003a: 11). CVD proponents might reject free trade, but if so, the implication is protectionism *simpliciter*, not CVDs.

[49] (Sykes, 1989, 238–239, 241–250, 2003a: 11).

[50] (Sykes, 2003a: 11). To the extent arguments for subsidies disciplines succeed, we might justify CVDs as enforcement measures. However, given these only address imports, and not effects in home or third markets, this argument is weak.

[51] (Dunoff, 2010, 403–404; Grossman & Mavroidis, 2005b: 109–110; Sykes, 1991: 269–270).

[52] (Krugman et al., 2012: 34).

may be desirable, ethically or politically, to compensate these groups. On this view, the injury test in the SA identifies constituencies adversely affected by liberalization, and safeguards compensate them.[53]

Second, it is argued safeguards facilitate adjustment.[54] The move to free trade stimulates factors of production to move from less efficient to more efficient applications.[55] Adjustment costs are incurred in this process.[56] Safeguards give an industry breathing space to more effectively manage this transition.[57] They may also avoid adjustment costs incurred where a temporary cost or price shock undermines the short-term profitability of an industry; safeguards allow the industry to ride out the shock and get back on its feet.[58]

Both arguments have similar problems. First, protectionism is an inefficient tool for these purposes.[59] If the goal is compensating workers, for example, then direct payments are more efficient than protecting an entire industry.[60] If we want to sustain an industry temporarily, whether to facilitate managed wind-down or a medium-term return to profitability, then production subsidies are more efficient than safeguards.[61] More generally, the costs of moving from one equilibrium to another are more easily addressed through, for example, targeted worker training programs, than by sustaining, even temporarily, a failing industry.[62]

---

[53] This reflects safeguards' historical rationale in the GATT and the US Reciprocal Trade Agreements Act. However subsequent evolutions, including the AB's attenuation of the link from liberalization to harm, limit its contemporary relevance. (Zampetti, 2006: 100–103).

[54] (Crowley, 2010: 386–387; Dunoff, 2010: 404–407; Grossman & Mavroidis, 2005b: 111–114; Hizon, 1994: 108; Jackson, 1997: 176; Sykes, 1991: 263–264).

[55] (Ray, 1998: 648–650).

[56] (Sykes, 1991: 265–267). This is especially relevant for developing countries with incomplete or inflexible markets.

[57] (Sykes, 1991: 263–264).   [58] (Grossman & Mavroidis, 2005b: 112).

[59] Ibid., 113–114 (Sykes, 1991: 264–265, 272). The adjustment argument must also assume imperfect markets or externalization of adjustment costs to explain why the necessary costs are not met through markets: (Sykes, 1991: 264). While these are not bad assumptions, their emphasis risks challenging the economic justifications of liberal trade generally.

[60] (Krugman et al., 2012: 236–237; Sykes, 1989: 267–268; Zheng, 2012: 163).

[61] (Jackson, 1997: 177; Sykes, 1989: 264).

[62] (Sykes, 1991: 268). An objection here might highlight the non-pecuniary benefits of employment for workers, including skills-maintenance, socialization, and self-worth. However, the former can be achieved through subsidization. It seems plausible that the latter, in so far as it depends on workers' sense that they are making a valuable contribution, might be undermined by explicit subsidization. However, given protectionism is simply disguised subsidization, its advocacy on this basis fails the test of publicity: a state

Both also fail to explain why either compensation or adjustment assistance are appropriate for losses from trade liberalization, but not other causes.[63] Businesses suffer temporary and permanent declines for many reasons. It is not obvious why losses from liberalization should be treated differently to those from other changes, whether geographic, economic, or political. One explanation highlights the extent to which these losses result from a conscious government policy to liberalize trade, imposing losses on some for the benefit of the community as a whole;[64] but many other government policies will equally have this quality. Another explanation invokes moral hazard, suggesting that focusing on losses from imports ensures states take responsibility for economic developments within their control.[65] However, this cannot explain why safeguards are unavailable for unforeseeable and unavoidable domestic shocks.

Political arguments emphasize safeguards' role as "escape clauses," allowing states to suspend obligations where political costs of compliance are higher than expected.[66] They suggest two rationales. First, states will agree to greater liberalization *ex ante* if they know they can defect from commitments if costs are too high *ex post*[67]; and second, by allowing temporary, limited protectionism when politically necessary, states can more readily sustain long-term liberalization.[68]

Both arguments contain elements of truth, but each has problems. First, there is little reason to assume the SA will pick out the politically salient cases these arguments invoke.[69] Where the rules are over-inclusive, authorizing action when not necessary, domestic decision-making processes provide an additional fail-safe. However, it is equally likely they will be under-inclusive, preventing action in politically critical cases. Further, the safeguard rules focus on injury from imports, but (depending on how

---

cannot act on this basis without misleading at least some of its citizens (i.e. the relevant workers) as to the basis on which it is acting.

[63] (Dunoff, 2010: 404; Grossman & Mavroidis, 2005b: 110; Jackson, 1997: 176; Sykes, 1991: 270–271).

[64] (Jackson, 1989b: 16).   [65] (Horn & Mavroidis, 2003: 80–82).

[66] For an overview: (Crowley, 2010; Dunoff, 2010).

[67] (Crowley, 2010: 383–384; Saggi, 2010: 375; Sykes, 1989: 277–280).

[68] (Bagwell & Staiger, 1990; Dunoff, 2010: 406; Jackson, 1997: 177; Jones, 2004; Posner & Sykes, 2011: 259–260). Wauters uses these arguments to link safeguards to GATT Art. XX and XXI: (Wauters, 2010, 337). Sykes argues safeguards make it harder to resist protectionism: (Sykes, 1989: 273–274) Cf. (Grossman & Mavroidis, 2005b: 114–115). The AB invoked a version of the political argument in *US-Line Pipe*, §83. Embedded liberalism explains safeguards on his logic: (Howse, 2002b: 95).

[69] (Saggi, 2010, 377–378).

this concept is interpreted[70]) injury from domestic sources can also undermine support for free trade.[71] There is no mechanism in the SA for a decision maker, whether domestic or international, to consider the political issues canvassed by these arguments.

For lawyers these approaches have a further weakness; they provide no guidance in interpreting the rules.[72] A quasi-judicial body applying a legal text cannot plausibly assess the political pressures on governments. Knowing that the SA is designed to relieve political pressures tells us nothing about the (nonpolitical) tests expressed therein. At most, it cautions against interpreting those tests inflexibly, so that legal technicalities not restrict politically necessary actions.[73] How much flexibility, however, turns on how the underlying provisions are understood. But to answer this question the political economy arguments can only refer back to the text, no wiser as to how it should be interpreted.[74]

8.2.3   Dumping

Notwithstanding the problems explaining the subsidies and safeguards rules, anti-dumping remains the most problematic trade remedy from a theoretical perspective.[75] The central problem is that price discrimination by enterprises is often economically rational, and causes no distinctive harm to other market participants.[76] Equilibrium prices will vary across partially integrated markets.[77] Where prices are higher in a producer's home market than in an overseas market, given plausible assumptions about market power and demand elasticity, it makes sense

---

[70] Cf. §8.4.2 below.

[71] There is presumably a link between the perceived source of injury and associated political costs. However, given the limited understanding of international economics in public discourse, there is no necessary connection between the actual sources of injury and how these are publicly perceived.

[72] (Grossman & Mavroidis, 2005b: 115).

[73] For a similar point, albeit addressing the ADA: (Howse & Neven, 2003: 158–159).

[74] This is implicitly recognized in (Bown & Sykes, 2008: 131), and more explicitly in (Horn & Mavroidis, 2003: 404). This highlights one disadvantage of the formal legalized WTO dispute system, as compared with more flexible, diplomatic, and hence politically aware, GATT system.

[75] For an overview: (Niels, 2000). I do not address concerns about protectionist abuses of anti-dumping. Many rules are subject to abuses, and to the extent they are, may require revision. My concern is the prior question of whether there is a reason to have these rules. In answering that question, some idealizing of practice seems reasonable.

[76] (Jackson, 1997: 249–250; Niels, 2000: 474–475).   [77] (Krugman et al., 2012: 225).

to sell goods overseas at lower prices.[78] To the extent this results in cheaper goods in the export market, it confers the same consumer benefits as undumped exports.[79] Reiterating a point made earlier, gains from trade accrue regardless of why cheap goods are available on international markets.

Various arguments seek to distinguish dumping as harmful. The most common grounds anti-dumping in antitrust, claiming both protect conditions of competition.[80] While reflecting the historical position in the United States, this argument has little contemporary relevance.[81] Whereas antitrust protects conditions of competition for consumers' benefit, anti-dumping protects competitors.[82] The tests for predatory pricing in antitrust are significantly more demanding than those in anti-dumping[83]; and as an empirical matter, the conditions for effective predation rarely hold in anti-dumping cases.[84]

Another approach links dumping to the existence of protected home markets in which a producer enjoys artificially high prices.[85] Certainly, in the case of sustained dumping, a protected home market is an important factor, both in maintaining price differences and preventing reimports.[86] However, this does not identify any problem with dumping per se. Rather, dumping is a symptom of protectionism in the "sanctuary" home market; it is protectionism that is objectionable.[87] Further, if the real problem is protectionism, this argument fails to show why anti-dumping is a sensible response.[88] Rather, like CVDs, anti-dumping simply redirects the distortive effects of protectionism into other markets.

A third approach sees anti-dumping as responding to strategic or mercantilist trade policies seeking to drive domestic production out of a

---

[78] (Jackson, 1997: 252–253; Zheng, 2012: 160–161).   [79] (Zheng, 2012: 162–163).

[80] E.g. (Jackson, 1997: 253–254; Lester et al., 2012: 473–474; Mavroidis, 2007: 362–363).

[81] (Barceló, 1991: 314–315; Finger, 1992: 133; Niels, 2000: 468–469, 481–483; Stegemann, 1991: 383; Zanardi, 2004: 303–304). Howse and Neven go further, denying there is any conceptual reason for extending anti-trust principles globally: (Howse & Neven, 2003: 156).

[82] (Finger, 1992: 141; Finger & Artis, 1993: 50; Niels, 2000: 478; Stegemann, 1991: 383).

[83] (Finger, 1992: 141; Finger et al., 2001: 7; Kovavic, 2010: 266–268; Prusa, 2005: 683–684, 695–696).

[84] (Mavroidis, 2007: 362 fn. 94; Stegemann, 1991: 384). Strategic dumping is similarly rare: (Niels, 2000: 475–476).

[85] E.g. (Mavroidis, 2007: 361–362; Niels, 2000: 477, 483).

[86] (Mastel, 1998: 43; Mavroidis, 2007: 362).   [87] (Mavroidis, 2007: 362).

[88] Bhagwati highlights "systemic" effects of unanswered dumping: (Bhagwati, 1988: 35). Broude's analysis of dumping in global welfare and strategic terms, however, undermines that approach, confirming that the problem, if one exists, is simply protectionism: (Broude, 2003).

target market.[89] Unlike the antitrust argument, it emphasizes the interests of producers, and more generally of states, in maintaining productive capacity in particular industries.[90] States are threatened by the loss of those industries, and dumping may be a mechanism whereby those losses occur. However, to the extent it is accepted, this approach is too broad to explain anti-dumping. The key harm identified is the loss of domestic production in particular sectors.[91] But this results as easily from undumped imports from a lower cost producer as from dumped imports[92]; it is an argument for protectionism *simpliciter*.[93] Further, it only applies to a narrow set of markets where strategic trade is relevant.[94]

Other arguments against dumping exist, but they largely reduce to some variation on the foregoing.[95]

In general, the economic arguments are either under-inclusive, justifying action in only a small subset of the cases defined as dumping, and not obviously because it is dumping; or over-inclusive, justifying action in many cases where no dumping occurs.

This recalls Lowenfeld's suggestion, that market penetration, rather than dumping or subsidization, is the actual cause of complaint in most cases.[96] It also recalls the political argument for safeguards, which we find advanced with minor modifications to explain and justify anti-dumping.[97] In its simplest form, it is the same argument, and open to the same objections, with the additional concern that the dumping regime is even less suited to identifying politically salient cases, and lacks in most cases an additional political check before anti-dumping duties are applied.[98]

---

[89] (Mastel, 1998: passim; Mavroidis, 2007: 363–364).

[90] (Mastel, 1998: 99). This argument is linked to the strategic trade literature, touched on above. Mastel seeks to extend the argument by emphasizing how mercantilist policies affect location decisions: (Mastel, 1998: 16–17, 68–72, 75).

[91] (Mastel, 1998: 70–71).

[92] (Finger & Artis, 1993: 42; Lowenfeld, 1980: 210, 219). For an unsuccessful attempt to identify particular harms from dumping: (Mastel, 1998: 65–98).

[93] This arguably reflects the origins of anti-dumping in straightforward demands for protectionism: (Finger, 1992: 123–124).

[94] (Niels, 2000: 475–476). While Mastel recognizes his argument's dependence on the strategic trade literature, he denies that its conclusions are necessarily limited to strategic industries, for reasons of administrative efficiency and inter-industry fairness: (Mastel, 1998: 66).

[95] For reviews: (Broude, 2003: 308–312; Jackson, 1997: 253–255; Mavroidis, 2012: 408–422).

[96] (Lowenfeld, 1980: 210) Cf. (Hathaway et al., 2003: 821, 823; Prusa, 2005).

[97] See e.g. (Howse & Neven, 2003: 156–157; Zheng, 2012: 163–167).

[98] (Finger & Artis, 1993: 69; Finger et al., 2001: 9–10; Jackson, 1997: 255; Mavroidis, 2007: 364–365; Zheng, 2012: 167–168). Public interest tests in domestic anti-dumping rules may alleviate this, at least as regards over-inclusiveness. See (Bronckers, 1996: 19–21) However, their practical effectiveness is doubtful: (Davis, 2009: 5–10). On the need for

A more sophisticated political argument suggests that anti-dumping responds to cases where political concerns about *unfair* trade might undermine support for a trade agreement.[99] It is certainly plausible that both workers and owners who suffer as a result of trade practices that are perceived as unfair would be more likely than others to object, and thereby undermine political support for free trade. On this view, it is more important, for instrumental political reasons, to respond to trade practices that are perceived as unfair than it is to address similar harms resulting from ostensibly fair trading.[100] Finger's characterization of dumping as protectionism with "good public relations" captures something important: there is something about both dumping and subsidization that makes politicians and electorates more susceptible to protectionist responses. Unlike the conventional political argument, this approach might offer some guidance on how the ADA should be interpreted. It suggests that, whereas the object of the rules is political efficiency, they must also track some suitable conception of fairness. However, it does not tell us what the appropriate sense of fairness is. It is to this question that I turn in the next part.

8.3   Fairness, EGC, and Trade Remedies

Existing approaches, then, cannot account for key features of the trade remedies regime. Further, to the extent they do explain it, they provide little guidance for interpreters. I suggested earlier that this reflected a reluctance to take seriously the idea of fairness. However, what fairness means for these purposes is not obvious.[101] In this section, I argue an appropriate account of fair and unfair trade can be derived from EGC, and that existing trade remedy rules can be understood on this basis. I begin with some preliminary points, rejecting an alternative conception of competitive fairness. I then consider each category of trade remedy separately, showing how the WTO disciplines can be derived from EGC.

8.3.1   Competitive Fairness

There is a sense of fairness that is central to market allocation. This is competitive fairness, akin to pure procedural justice or formal equality of

---

more political (including democratic) oversight of anti-dumping: (Zheng, 2012: 176–179).

[99] (Bhagwati, 1988: 34–35; Mastel, 1998: 17). Stegeman criticizes this as encouraging protectionism: (Stegemann, 1991: 382, 390). Cf. (Zheng, 2012: 180).

[100] For an analogous account of subsidies: (Sykes, 2003a: 25).

[101] See generally: (Cass & Boltuck, 1996).

opportunity.[102] It is the fairness of the "level playing field," emphasizing the conditions under which competitors interact, concerned that neither enjoy any illicit advantage over the other.[103] Provided competitive conditions are fair, it relies on competition and interaction in the market to determine a fair outcome. One recent exponent labels this conception "market fairness."[104]

However, competitive fairness cannot identify the distinctive unfairness of subsidization and dumping. Competitive fairness expresses an ideal of self-authorship and, in its most intuitively plausible form, requires equalizing external competitive conditions.[105] However, this cannot be a goal in international trade.[106] Rather, relative efficiencies lead countries to specialize in activities where they enjoy comparative advantages.[107] A textile manufacturer in a low-wage low-skill economy will, by that fact, enjoy an insurmountable advantage over a competitor in an economy with more skilled labor and higher wages. The competitive success of the former need not reflect greater commercial skill, industry, or any other quality intrinsic to the competitors; the deck was stacked in his favor from the start. From the perspective of the latter, this

---

[102] As formal equality of individual opportunity, this sense of fairness features in most liberal theories. E.g. (Rawls, 1971: 65). It is also expressed in the idea of "pure procedural justice": (Rawls, 1996: 72–73). Between persons, it is explicable as expressing basic equality. It is less obviously explicable between firms or peoples. Some defenses of "market freedoms" might have this implication. E.g. (Tomasi, 2012: 237–247). The libertarian principle of entitlement implies something like this view: (Nozick, 1974: 150–153). However, many market conditions that we might identify as unfair are likely compatible with libertarian entitlement and, to a lesser extent, with market freedoms. Confusingly, many liberals also value competition instrumentally, as promoting efficiency. E.g. (Hayek, 1944: 37–41). However, given my argument that efficiency cannot explain trade remedies rules, these are not relevant.

[103] On the sporting analogy: (Cass & Boltuck, 1996: 355–360). Cf. (Hudec, 1999: 231–232; Jackson, 1997: 247–248). On the expansion of this ill-defined concept: (Jackson, 1997: 274–277). A similar view motivates the "entitlement" approach: (Goetz et al., 1986: 17–19).

[104] (Tomasi, 2012: 176–196). Tomasi's view is broader, incorporating a comprehensive account of social and economic justice under market democracy. However, it incorporates at least part of the level playing field image.

[105] We cannot equalize competitors' intrinsic characteristics without denying self-authorship and reducing fairness to distributive equality.

[106] Zampetti links this conception of fairness to pre-GATT US protectionism: (Zampetti, 2006: 46–55) Cf. (Lim, 2012: 145–146).

[107] (Krugman et al., 2012: 71). This may not hold in intra-industry trade but, even here, economies of scale, and particularly external economies, make a level playing field undesirable: (Krugman et al., 2012: 174–178).

may seem unfair; but it is not a sense of unfairness the trade regime can admit.[108]

A weaker sense of market fairness takes natural and economic facts as given, equalizing only those advantages afforded by institutions and public authorities.[109] This is the sense of fairness invoked when scholars define subsidies against a baseline of an undistorted market.[110] However, again, it is not the sense of fairness underpinning trade remedies. As noted, general government programs can be as distortive as specific subsidies, but it is only the latter that are identified as unfair.[111] Indeed, many of the factors determining comparative advantage are affected by government action.[112] A state with comprehensive public education will enjoy a comparative advantage in industries requiring skilled labor[113]; while a country with strong institutions might enjoy comparative advantage in legal and financial services.[114] In each case, producers are advantaged and disadvantaged by public institutions. However, despite occasional claims of "social dumping" and unfair competition by low-wage economies, WTO law does not treat competition between such producers as unfair.[115]

Thus for our purposes competitive fairness seems incomplete at best, as it cannot specify *which* advantages are fair or unfair.[116] For this, we need a substantive account of justice in international economic regulation. For the reasons identified in Chapter 2, it seems unlikely existing accounts can serve this purpose. I therefore examine in the next sections how EGC answers this question, and thereby explains trade remedies disciplines.

8.3.2 Subsidies

If EGC is to explain the subsidies disciplines, then it must be on the basis that the subsidies disciplined, whether prohibited or actionable, constitute

---

[108] On the poor fit between competitive fairness and AD/CVD practice: (Hudec, 1999: 272–278).

[109] E.g. (Cass & Boltuck, 1996: 358; Hudec, 1999: 272–278).

[110] (Goetz et al., 1986: 18; Rubini, 2009: 204–205; Sykes, 2003a: 3). See further the discussion of benefit definition below.

[111] (Sykes, 2003b: 19–21) Cf. (Rubini, 2009: 20–21). Indeed, subsidies rules seem more concerned with fairness between enterprises in the same country: (Wouters & Coppens, 2009: 30–32).

[112] (Jackson, 1997: 18–19; Rubini, 2009: 361).   [113] (Sykes, 2003b: 4–6).

[114] On the relation between institutions, financial services, and comparative advantage: (Ju & Wei, 2011).

[115] (Howse, 1999: 163–164). For an overview: (Hudec & Bhagwati, 1996) Cf. (Hudec, 1999: 257–272; Mayeda, 2004: 740–742).

[116] Cf., in respect of IPRs: (Spence, 2001: 275–276).

ETMs. To the extent this is the case, they are subject to the justificatory standards appropriate to such measures; and if they do not meet those standards, are unjust or, in trade remedies discourse, unfair, and so appropriately disciplined.

Subsidies are clearly the kinds of measures that EGC is concerned to evaluate, namely aspects of nonvoluntary institutions that distribute fundamental rights and duties and determine the division of advantages from social cooperation.[117] To the extent they alter conditions of competition, they determine the division of advantages. They are nonvoluntary in two senses: first, they are an exercise of public authority,[118] whether in disbursing funds appropriated through the coercive tax system,[119] according beneficiaries the use of public assets or credit,[120] or refraining from some coercively imposed tax[121]; and second, the affected outsider has no choice but to accept the new market conditions constituted thereby.[122] Recall, from market participants' perspectives, a subsidy can be practically indistinguishable from a tax, regulation, or other more obviously coercive measure.[123]

But are subsidies ETMs?

Once we accept that subsidies are nonvoluntary, it is straightforward to show that prohibited subsidies are ETMs. An export subsidy is one that is "contingent, in law or in fact, ... upon export performance."[124] If we assume, which seems reasonable, that a subsidy pursues its goal by making some activity more attractive than it would otherwise be, then export subsidies *ipso facto* pursue their goals by regulating international economic activity.[125] Regardless of the goals pursued, the means adopted

---

[117] §3.4 above.

[118] The AB has emphasized the importance of public authority in the definition of "public body" in SCM 1.1(a) (1): *US-ADCVD (China)*, (AB), §284, 290, 317–318.

[119] SCM 1.1(a) (1) (i).   [120] SCM 1.1(a) (1) (i) and (iii).   [121] SCM 1.1(a) (1) (ii).

[122] The adverse effects test in Art. 5 can be understood in these terms. See further below. We might object here that private action can similarly constitute new market conditions, which others participants experience as non-voluntary. In certain circumstances, this is indeed the case, a point picked up further in fn. 203 below.

[123] Cf. fn. 37, 38 above.   [124] SCM 3.1(a).

[125] The tests for export contingency reflect this. In particular the fact that subsidies to "enterprises which export" are not *ipso facto* export subsidies reflects the need for an appropriate intentional nexus between subsidy and international economic activity: SCM, fn. 4; *Canada-Aircraft*, (AB), §170. Mavroidis reads *Canada-Aircraft* as incorporating an implicit intention test: (Mavroidis, 2012: 571). However *EC-Aircraft* rejects this, focusing instead on "design, structure and modalities of operation," to determine *inter alia* whether the subsidy "provides an incentive to skew anticipated sales towards exports": *EC-Aircraft*, (AB), §1047. This approach, emphasizing objective characteristics and the way a subsidy pursues its goals, is readily reconcilable with EGC. Admittedly, the

act directly on international trade. A similar argument applies to local content subsidies. Such subsidies, being "contingent . . . upon the use of domestic over imported goods,"[126] incentivize a shift from imported to domestic products, altering the conditions of competition for imported goods, and thereby regulating international economic activity.[127] Constructive interpretation commits us to making sense of the measures that states adopt; and neither export nor import-substitution subsidies make sense except as ETMs.[128]

It is less obvious that production subsidies constitute ETMs. They may pursue various goals, many unrelated to international economic activity. Production subsidies on untraded products are unlikely to constitute ETMs. They may have indirect effects on foreigners, but they do not address international trade in the required way.[129] Even for traded products, as discussed, we cannot assume production subsidies are protectionist.[130]

However, ETMs do not reduce to protectionism, and closer examination suggests production subsidies on traded goods are necessarily ETMs. The archetypal production subsidy increases returns from economic activity in order to promote or maintain that activity, for some social goal.[131] It might offset costs imposed by other public measures, or internalize some positive externality. In either case, it pursues its goal by increasing returns to producers. However, an account of the means by which it pursues its goal must also include the market into which that producer sells, and the other participants therein. If price elasticity of demand is low then increased production (whether against historical or

---

fact that exports are merely anticipated may frequently indicate the required attitude; but this can be addressed under the actionable subsidies category.

[126] SCM 3.1(a).

[127] The AB in *Canada-Autos* (§123, 143) held that the *Canada-Aircraft* contingency analysis applied under 3.1(b). To the extent *EC-Aircraft* modifies that analysis, it presumably also applies.

[128] Cf. fn. 131 below.

[129] An apparent subsidy to non-traded products might of course implicitly subsidize downstream producers. Cf. *US-Softwood Lumber IV*, (AB), §139–147. Similarly, local content subsidies in non-traded industries may address international trade in relevant inputs: e. g. *Canada-FIT*.

[130] Cf. §5.2.1 above.

[131] There are of course subsidies that simply confer rents. However, I assume this is not the ideal case, by reference to which such measures generally should be understood. The most prominent exception is developed country agricultural subsidies. Indeed, it is presumably for this reason that the Agreement on Agriculture (Annex 2, §1 and 6) seeks to delink agricultural subsidies and production: if subsidies are simply about supporting farmers then they need not affect agricultural production.

counterfactual baselines) can only come at the expense of competitors. Even where elasticity is high, effects on competitors will still be part of the means/ends story. Moreover, these are not simply side effects. Rather, the subsidy pursues its goal by shifting the balance between costs, prices, competitors, and consumers. For internationally traded products, that necessarily includes both insiders and outsiders.[132]

It is not simply that production subsidies necessarily affect foreign producers and consumers. Many DEMs will have such effects. What is distinctive about ETMs is that they pursue their goals specifically through the regulation of international economic activity.[133] A production subsidy seeks not only to change behavior, but to adjust the balance between market participants. This implies an intentional stance towards both recipients and nonrecipients. The target is a particular market balance that, in an internationally traded sector, necessarily accords some role, positive or negative, to outsiders, whether as producers or consumers. Production subsidies, when so understood, cannot but express the requisite intentional attitude; there is no other way to understand them.[134]

EGC thus tells a story about production subsidies as ETMs. How well does that story fit the SCM?

Two features of the agreement seem particularly relevant.

The first, specificity, requires that actionable subsidies be "specific to an enterprise or industry or group of enterprises or industries."[135] This implies that a measure is targeted, whether at particular enterprises or industries. As noted, economic approaches struggle to explain specificity.[136] It is a poor proxy for market distortion or protectionism. It may, however, be effective for identifying ETMs. Specificity means that, to be actionable, a production subsidy must be addressed to a particular market and the specific competitors and consumers therein.[137] This

---

[132] It might here be objected that this applies equally to Pigouvian taxes, which are substantially symmetrical with subsidies. However this ignores the ease with which outsiders can offset the relative effects of such taxes. This might suggest that Pigouvian taxes, while potentially constituting ETMs, do not require disciplining; or we might derive from this an argument for disciplining such taxes.

[133] §1.6.1 above.

[134] The position may be different in non-market economies, where pervasive manipulation of price mechanisms makes specificity insufficient to identify ETMs. This point was reflected in pre-2006 US subsidies policies: (Ahn & Lee, 2011: 10).

[135] SCM 2.1.   [136] §5.2.1 above.

[137] The exact scope of specificity has proved difficult to define. Whereas "entreprise" is readily definable, "industry" is more difficult, and "group" of enterprises or industries invites a broad exercise of discretion. The Panel in US-Upland Cotton (§7.1142) recognized the unavoidable imprecision involved.

implies some proximity between subsidy and foreign competitors and consumers; they form a definable group on whom the subsidy acts.[138] They are, in the language of EGC, directly subject to the relevant measure.[139]

The second is the adverse effects test under Article 5.

A recurring challenge for economic approaches is to identify some distinctive harm from subsidization, and to account for the focus on harm to competitors without considering benefits to consumers. EGC avoids this by understanding adverse effects as concerned less with harm than with identifying whether measures in fact constitute ETMs. As noted above, in the case of export and import-substitution subsidies this is necessarily the case. Production subsidies, by contrast, are identified as ETMs because they address competitors in the relevant market, making them an intentional focus of the relevant measure. If no outsider is affected by a subsidy, they cannot be subject to it, and so no justification is owed to them. The adverse effects test identifies whether this is the case. Absent adverse effects, a production subsidy is not an ETM.

This also explains why benefits to consumers play no role.[140] If we assume these provisions identify whether measures address outsiders in the required way, then it is irrelevant whether losses for one group (competitors) are offset by gains for another (consumers).[141] Trading

---

[138] That specificity doesn't require deliberately limiting access doesn't change this. As elsewhere, the question is not what the government seeks to do, but rather what it in fact does. Subsidized access to a good of exclusive interest to a particular industry remains a subsidy addressed to that industry: *US-Softwood Lumber IV*, (Panel), §7.116–7.117. The need to assess specificity in terms of how a measure addresses agents is similarly evident in the focus on availability rather than actual use: *US-ADCVD* (China), (AB), §368. See also the analysis of de-facto specificity: *EC-Aircraft*, (Panel), §7.961–7.964.

[139] This also explains the emphasis on like products in Arts. 5, 6, and 16, notwithstanding subsidies may adversely affect upstream or downstream producers. Cf. the analysis under the SA in *US-Lamb*, (AB), §77–96, applied under the SCM in *Mexico-Olive Oil*, (Panel), §7.195–7.196 (Mavroidis, 2012: 583–584).

Specificity might also distinguish subsidies pursuing their goals through effects on production from those whose goal is limited to benefiting recipients, in so far as it invites the question why subsidies are not generally available. The most plausible answer will often be that the relevant subsidy, through its effects on production, advances the interests of the subsidizing people generally.

[140] Art. 5.1(a) and (c), 6.3. Art. 5.1(b) ("nullification or impairment of benefits") is not necessarily limited to competitors, although in practice they are likely to be its focus. While the Panel in *Korea-Commercial Vessels* (§7.577–7.578) distinguished between injury to *domestic industry* and prejudice to the *interests of another Member*, it is clear that the latter is not a holistic inquiry: the focus remains on identifying impacts on a member's "*trade interests* in respect of a product."

[141] This objection also arises from human rights approaches: (Petersmann, 1992: 26; Petersmann, 2002: 629–630).

off gains and losses is an important function of the political process, but it is the preserve of the relevant political community; outsiders cannot justify their ETMs by purporting themselves to engage in that process.[142] The upshot is something like the "entitlement" approach, which understands subsidies disciplines as protecting firms' entitlement to a particular market outcome, not manipulated by foreign government subsidization.[143] However, EGC, by characterizing that market outcome as an entitlement of peoples rather than firms, and linking it to a wider normative theory, avoids the objection that this entitlement is unmotivated.[144]

Contingency, specificity, and adverse effects are all thus explained by EGC. Benefit and financial contribution can be similarly explained as elements identifying subsidies with nonvoluntary institutions of the kind identified by EGC as subject to justification. As noted above, financial contribution picks out subsidies as exercises of public power. Benefit, by contrast, tracks the way subsidies impact market participants, thus determining the distribution of benefits from international economic cooperation.[145]

EGC thus explains both prohibited and actionable subsidies, explaining why they are disciplined, and why the categories are defined as they are.

EGC also provides a distinctive account of when subsidies are justified. The subsidies regime is frequently criticized as too restrictive, prohibiting efficient and socially desirable subsidies.[146] With the expiry of non-actionable subsidies, no nonagricultural subsidy is above challenge

---

[142] See §3.6 above. Recall, we identified the capacity to implement socio-economic justice as falling under the instrumental argument for self-determination. Buchanan labels this capacity "distributional autonomy": (Buchanan, 2000: 705). Of course an importing state might conclude that the benefits of cheap imports outweigh the harm to producers and on that basis refrain from imposing CVDs or initiating a WTO dispute. Nothing in the SCM prevents this. However it is for the importer, not the subsidizing state, to make this judgement.

[143] (Goetz et al., 1986: 18–19).   [144] See discussion at fn. 43 above.

[145] EGC thus implies an economic rather than an accounting definition of benefit. On this distinction: (Diamond, 2008; Grossman & Mavroidis, 2003: 186–189, 196–197, 2005a: 83–87). The AB has equivocated on this point. Its market benchmark approach suggests an accounting definition: *Canada-Aircraft*, (AB), §157,158. A similar implication arises from the jurisprudence on change of ownership: *US-Lead Bismuth*, (Panel), §6.82, *EC-Aircraft*, (AB), §718–749. By contrast, the concept of continuing benefit implies a more economically oriented test: *US-Lead Bismuth*, (AB), §62. Diamond suggests causation requirements obviate the need for an economic definition: (Diamond, 2008: 667–669). However, his approach seems then to render benefit superfluous: (Diamond, 2008: 667–669). I discuss the implications of EGC for defining benefit further below.

[146] See fn. 22–26 above. Also (Mavroidis, 2012: 664–665; Rubini, 2009: 255).

under the SCM.[147] Subsidies pursuing innocuous and non-protectionist goals (e.g. environmental protection and rural development) are open to challenge. This, critics argue, makes the rules over-broad. EGC, however, defends this status quo by emphasizing how even socially efficient subsidies must be justified to outsiders. Further, it identifies limited grounds on which such subsidies may be justified. The mere fact that a goal is valued by the state adopting it is insufficient. One state might value particular environmental goals, for example, but this cannot justify ETMs to outsiders that do not value them in the same way.[148] EGC thus provides a clearer rationale for subjecting socially optimal subsidies to international disciplines.

This does not mean subsidies are never justifiable, but only that they must meet the justificatory standard appropriate to ETMs. The implications of that standard were discussed in detail in Chapter 7. Where goals are in fact shared, subsidies in pursuit of them may be justified. The former non-actionable subsidies might be understood in these terms, although this is contestable.[149] Further, to the extent that Art. XX GATT is understood in these terms, EGC suggests it be read as an exemption, not only from the GATT, but from the Covered Agreements generally, and from the subsidies disciplines in particular.[150]

EGC also suggests some subsidies are justifiable on egalitarian grounds. While there is some recognition of this in SCM Article 27, this falls short of EGC's prescriptions. EGC implies developing country subsidies should not generally be open to challenge or countervailing by developed countries.[151] Such subsidies, to the extent they pursue economic development, are

---

[147] Art. 8 and 31 SCM; Art. 21.1 AoA.   [148] See §3.4 above.

[149] These provisions were never invoked during the five years they were in force. The main obstacle to their extension was opposition from developing countries who perceived them as biased toward developed countries, and as failing to address subsidies of particular development interest: (Bigdeli, 2011: 4–10).

[150] For an ambivalent analysis of the applicability of Article XX to subsidies: (Rubini, 2012: 558–570). The AB's approach in *China-Rare Earths* (§5.55–5.57) suggests this is at least possible. For the view that Article XX is not applicable, and that members should therefore negotiate a specific environmental subsidies carve-out: (Shadikhodjaev, 2014). On the AB's efforts in *Canada-FIT* to accommodate concerns falling under Art. XX, without explicit reliance thereon: (Charnovitz & Fischer, 2015: 207).

[151] There is some recognition of this in the *Doha Ministerial Decision on Implementation-Related Issues and Concerns*, §10.2. However, development subsidies have not played a significant role in the negotiations: (Gallagher, 2007: 77). Development subsidies have been the subject of complaints under the SCM, for example *Brazil-Aircraft*, and the SCM substantially restricts developing countries freedom to implement proven pro-development subsidy policies: (Gallagher, 2007: 70–71).

justified under EGC's primary egalitarian limb. There are, of course, other reasons, including many of the economic arguments canvassed above, why less developed countries might be better to restrict their use of subsidies. However, the justification for such restrictions must derive from their own interests, or potentially those of other less developed countries, and not from their impact on the more developed.

In respect of both self-determination and economic equality, then, EGC offers both explanation and critique. It makes sense of features that we find in the agreements, but it also suggests a direction for progressive reform.

Finally, EGC suggests a distinctive role for CVDs. Recall, economic approaches, to the extent they identify harms from subsidization, cannot explain why CVDs are an appropriate response. EGC explains CVDs as protecting self-determination, and specifically a state's capacity to pursue its preferred economic path in the face of others' unjustified ETMs. As noted above, CVDs do not eliminate the effects of subsidies, merely diverting them to other markets. However, they do allow a state to insulate its home market from those effects, to the extent it deems necessary. As discussed in Chapters 5 and 7, while self-determination is exercised both internally and externally, each makes different demands. The effects of ETMs in states' home markets are plausibly more serious threats than their effects internationally. While international market effects necessarily address a state's producers, home market effects similarly coopt consumers.[152] International effects might certainly undermine a state's capacity to manage its domestic economy, falling under the instrumental arguments in Chapter 5; but domestic market effects more clearly involve one state acting on, and exercising power over, another, implicating the expressive and indeed intrinsic arguments.[153] Further, unlike international market effects, home market effects can be addressed in a relatively targeted manner through CVDs.[154] While CVDs are themselves ETMs, they can be justified to those subject to them, namely

---

[152] This might explain why some agricultural subsidies are countervailable but not subject to multilateral discipline: *US-Upland Cotton*, (AB), §531–533.

[153] The role of expressive and intrinsic arguments explains the lower injury threshold for CVDs and ADDs, as against safeguards.

[154] The symmetry between subsidies and CVDs explains why subsidies, but not other ETMs, are countervailable. While not straightforward, identifying the subsidy component in an import is more tractable than other ETMs. We can understand anti-dumping as an analogous remedy for non-subsidy ETMs. The emphasis on responding to others' unjustified ETMs means this account of CVDs and ADDs includes elements of corrective, as well as distributive, justice.

subsidized exporters and the subsidizing state itself, as doing no more than neutralizing the effects of prior unjustifiable subsidies.[155] CVDs are thus understood as justifiable auxiliary measures, allowing a state to act unilaterally to protect a central aspect of its self-determination, while relying on the multilateral process to restrain the underlying objectionable behavior.[156]

8.3.3 Safeguards

EGC thus accounts for subsidies disciplines on the basis that subsidies constitute ETMs; they are in consequence subject to the higher justificatory standards appropriate to ETMs; and to the extent they are not so justified, are properly subject to multilateral discipline and unilateral countervailing.

We need a different story to account for safeguards, which address injury from "fair" trade. To do this, we focus again on the role of self-determination in EGC, but without any intervening reference to unjustified ETMs.

The SA affords members some discretion on the form safeguards take.[157] However, regardless of form, their function means safeguards will necessarily constitute ETMs. They are permitted in response to injury from imports, and to address that injury they target the imports that are its source.[158] As such, they necessarily pursue their goal specifically through regulating international economic activity, and must be justified in terms appropriate to ETMs.[159] How might we do this?

As argued in Chapters 3, 4, and 5, peoples must take the international economy as they find it, and exercise self-determination within the

---

[155] This explains both the duty to limit CVDs to the amount of any subsidization, and preference for limiting them to redressing injury: SCM Art. 19.2 and 19.4. Neither makes sense if CVDs serve to deter or neutralize subsidies generally.

[156] This might seem to contradict EGC's sufficientarian account of self-determination, particularly given CVDs' moderate injury threshold. See generally: (Mavroidis, 2012: 577–584). However, the distinction between sufficiency of options and options subject to the will of another, found in sufficientarian accounts of autonomy and EGC's account of self-determination, explains this difference. See §§3.4, 5.4 above.

[157] (Mavroidis, 2012: 170) GATT Art. XIX (1) (a), SA Art. 1.

[158] SA Art. 2.1, 2.2, 5.1. *Argentina Footwear (EC)*, (AB), §113, *US-Wheat Gluten*, (AB), §96 (both concluding that safeguards must be applied to all of the products whose import have been identified as causing injury).

[159] The argument that safeguards necessarily constitute ETMs might alternatively invoke their function as exceptions from the GATT disciplines, and the argument in Chapter 4 that those disciplines are themselves addressed to ETMs.

constraints it imposes. Provided they have the minimum capacities discussed in Chapter 5, their exposure to the international economy will not prevent their being self-determining, nor can they complain about injuries suffered in consequence of that exposure.[160] However, there may be circumstances when developments in the international economy undermine states' capacities effectively to make economic choices or pursue their chosen paths to development, below the minimum required for effective self-determination. In these circumstances a people might justifiably adopt measures, including ETMs, to ameliorate the effects of those international developments. This, EGC suggests, is the function of safeguards.[161]

How far can this story explain the features of the SA?

EGC assumes that safeguards protect self-determination, understood as *inter alia* a minimum level of control over a people's economic course.[162] If this is the case, then we should find it reflected in the conditions for their use.

Safeguards are available where imports "cause or threaten to cause serious injury to the domestic industry that produces like or directly competitive products."[163] Note, first, the "serious injury" threshold, contrasting with "material injury" in SCM and ADA.[164] This fits EGC's account. If safeguards were justified directly under self-determination then we would expect a more demanding test than for measures responding to those wrongfully adopted by others[165]; we are here concerned with self-determination as sufficiency, rather than as equality with or exclusion of others. Serious injury is in turn defined as "a significant overall impairment in the position of a domestic industry."[166] The AB has emphasized the "very high" and "exacting" standard this implies, which is "much higher" than the material injury standard in the SCM and ADA.[167] Art 4.2(a) lists a number of factors relevant to this inquiry, including rates of increase and market share of imports, "changes in level

---

[160] This follows from the terms in which the two principles are stated in Chapter 1. To the extent the effects of exposure to the international economy are a function of others' DEMs, there is no injustice provided they do not impair the relevant state's capacity to become or remain well ordered. To the extent that they are a function of ETMs, by contrast, they are an appropriate object of complaint unless justified in the terms of EGC.

[161] For the avoidance of doubt, the argument here is not about the permissibility or appropriateness of redistributive policies generally. As a matter of domestic social justice, such policies will likely be required, regardless of the causes of economic dislocation. The argument here relates only to using ETMs for this purpose.

[162] See §5.5, 5.6 above.   [163] Art. 2.1.   [164] SCM Art. 15 fn. 45; ADA Art. 3 fn. 9.

[165] Cf. fn. 153, 156 above.   [166] Art. 4.1(a).   [167] US-Lamb, (AB), §124.

of sales, production, productivity, capacity utilization, profits and losses, and employment." While it is not necessary that an industry be declining on all of these measures, each must be taken into account in making the assessment of significant overall impairment[168]

Safeguards do not serve, then, to protect domestic industries from all injury from imports, but only from very serious, verging on existential, threats.[169] The economic approaches cannot explain this. Equity and adjustment arguments apply equally to all injuries suffered as a result of liberalization. The political arguments might explain the serious injury test; but equally, an industry facing lesser injury might be more influential, and hence pose a greater political threat than one in real trouble, as required by the SA.

EGC tells a more straightforward story. States are not entitled to adopt ETMs in response to any and all adverse effects from trade, but only where this is necessary to protect their capacity for effective economic self-determination. Material injury is not a threat to self-determination. Significant overall impairment, however, adversely affects not only the affected industry, but also a people's capacity to pursue their preferred economic path, and persons' capacities to form and act on life plans in the economic sphere. To the extent these are important aspects of self-determination, EGC regards ETMs protecting them as justified.[170]

Whether safeguards are justified, and the conditions attaching to their use, turn on the conception of self-determination adopted. I understand self-determination as in large part sufficientarian; provided peoples have a minimum level of autonomy and are not subject to unjustified external constraint, they can be regarded as self-determining.[171] Above this threshold, self-determination need not co-vary with economic development: a relatively wealthy people might find its self-determination threatened in circumstances where a less advantaged people is secure.[172] In particular, insofar as self-determination is understood to include distributive

---

[168] *Argentina-Footwear*, (AB), §139.

[169] The AB has characterized safeguards as "extraordinary and temporary relief" available in "an extraordinary emergency situation": *US-Line Pipe* (AB), §80–83. Cf. (Zheng, 2012: 125) (arguing, given the ADA's economic incoherence, it should incorporate this same injury test).

[170] See §5.5 above.   [171] See §3.4 and Chapter 5 generally.

[172] Stable democracy, for example, appears possible only above a certain income threshold: (Collier & Rohner, 2008; Grzymala-Busse & Jones Luong, 2006: 657–658). But recent work suggests national income is only weakly correlated with democracy, and there is reason to believe the causal relation may run from democratic stability to wealth: (Acemoglu et al., 2008) Cf. (Rawls, 1999: 106–107).

autonomy, a state's capacity to determine the distribution of resources under its control is distinct from the absolute size of that bundle of resources.[173] Self-determination can thus justify more advantaged peoples applying ETMs against those less advantaged. That said, egalitarian concerns, and the possibility that ETMs defending the self-determination of some might undermine that of others, give reason for caution in considering such measures.

This is reflected in the SA, which, without tying the use of safeguards to economic development, provides some leeway for developing countries, both as users and targets. It seeks, where possible, to displace the distributive effects of safeguards from developing to developed countries,[174] and to relax time limits on the developing countries' use of safeguards, without relaxing the injury standard,[175] The latter reflects a plausible assumption that developing countries may be more exposed, and less able to respond to developments in the international economy.[176]

A number of other features of the SA are also explicable on this basis.

As discussed, economic approaches cannot explain why safeguards are not available where injury results from causes other than imports.[177] EGC's emphasis on self-determination explains this. In part, it reflects an ideal of national responsibility that is a necessary corollary of self-determination; at least above a minimum threshold, self-determination cannot justify a state externalizing the costs of its own choices. The negative economic consequences of domestic policy cannot be understood as undermining self-determination; rather, they are its (albeit unfortunate) expression.[178] However, it also reflects self-determination's limits in justifying exclusive rather than inclusive ETMs[179]; where a development in the international economy causes injury to domestic industry, the effect of a

---

[173] See §5.5 above.

[174] Art. 9.1. In *US-Line Pipe* (§132) the AB identified a positive obligation to take "all reasonable steps" to ensure *de minimis* imports from developing countries are not subject to safeguards. The drafting history of Part IV GATT suggests an intention to exempt developing country trade from safeguards absent compelling contrary reasons: (World Trade Organization., 2012a: 1045).

[175] Art. 9.2.

[176] Recall the discussion of equal self-determination and the expressive argument in §5.4 above.

[177] I discuss further in §8.4.2 below the difficulties with causation in safeguards jurisprudence, suggesting that EGC can contribute to resolving these.

[178] See §4.5.2, 5.3, 5.5. Recall, we are here concerned to protect peoples' capacity to implement their preferred economic–including distributive–policies. The upshots of those policies may be unexpected, but they remain theirs.

[179] §3.5 above.

safeguard is to buffer the domestic from the international. Further, that international effect is itself in part a function of measures adopted by other peoples, albeit these may be DEMs or otherwise justifiable ETMs.[180] Conversely, where injury results from domestic developments, even those (e.g. natural disasters) outside the scope of national responsibility, safeguards displace the resulting instability from domestic to international, the epitome of an inclusive measure. This might be permissible on egalitarian grounds, but it cannot be justified under self-determination.[181]

The link to self-determination also explains why safeguards are available only in response to unforeseen developments.[182] Self-determination implies national responsibility, for what a state does, but also for responding appropriately to outside developments. Where developments are foreseeable, this must include preparing appropriately.[183] Thus, a safeguard regime justified under self-determination would be limited to unforeseen developments that cause or threaten serious injury to domestic industries.[184]

EGC also explains time limits in the SA.[185] Recall, self-determination can more readily justify exclusive than inclusive measures.[186] It thus provides grounds for suspending cooperation in a particular field, not

---

[180] Recall that DEMs will not be justified where their effect is to undermine the self-determination of others.

[181] Among the many claims made in this book, this is the one in which I have least confidence. It seems to imply, for example, that the economic effects of a freak hurricane in a foreign country could justify safeguards, while those of a hurricane at home could not. But this surely fetishizes the relationship between people and territory. The two cases might however be distinguished by the fact that, in the former, the adverse effects translate directly from nature to domestic economy, while the latter involves an intervening role for other peoples. Both are cases of brute luck, but this latter feature may distinguish them as regards self-determination.

[182] GATT Art. XIX (1) (a).

[183] This has similar implications to moral hazard arguments noted above. However, while these value responsibility instrumentally, self-determination gives it intrinsic significance.

[184] The AB's resurrection of foreseeability has been criticized as contradicting the SA's intent, and as incoherent given these rules' indefinite duration: E.g. (Lee, 2001: 1239–1242; Sykes, 2003b: 277–278, 2004: 540) Cf. (Mueller, 2003: 1139–1141; Ormonde Driscoll, 2005). However it makes sense under EGC, as does the AB's effective deletion of the requirement that injury result from "obligations incurred by a Member": *Argentina-Footwear(EC)* (AB), §91, (Sykes, 2004: 540). Admittedly the AB's application of the foreseeability test from the time an obligation was incurred runs contrary to this account, being more readily explained under the *ex ante* political argument: *Korea-Dairy*, (AB), §86; *Argentina-Footwear(EC)*, (AB), §96. I discuss further below EGC's implications for foreseeability.

[185] SA Art. 7. Admittedly, economic approaches can similarly account for these, as neither equity nor adjustment arguments would justify indefinite safeguards. Limits are less obviously appropriate under political arguments, but certainly do not contradict them.

[186] See §3.5 above.

for inclusively coercing others and manipulating the terms of that cooperation. Time-limited safeguards provide a breathing space for countries, while assuring others that over the medium term their success will turn on their own productive capacities. Even short-term measures will have some inclusive effects, but together with the other constraints canvassed above the potential for abuse is limited to the extent possible.[187]

8.3.4 Dumping

EGC thus provides a straightforward explanation of safeguards and subsidies disciplines. What of anti-dumping? In this section, I suggest that an anti-dumping regime is similarly explicable under EGC.

Dumping and subsidies are together categorized as "unfair" trade practices.[188] We earlier explained the unfairness of subsidies in terms of their status as ETMs. However, we cannot so readily identify dumping with ETMs, because dumping, in contrast with other WTO disciplined practices, is a practice of market participants, often private parties.[189] It is defined as exporting goods at less than normal value, in turn understood as a price below that charged in the home market, or below the average cost of production.[190] This may reflect explicit or implicit subsidization, but that is not part of its definition.[191] How, then, can we make the link from EGC to the "unfairness" of dumping?

One approach recalls the "sanctuary market" concept discussed above.[192] Whereas the exact links between dumping and sanctuary markets are contested, there is certainly reason to believe that sustained dumping is only possible when a home market is protected from competition and/or re-importation of dumped products.[193] A state can benefit its own producers in various ways, but for price discrimination to be rational and sustainable, some market segregation is a prerequisite.[194]

---

[187] This is reflected in the provisions on safeguards and developing countries, which, as noted above, seek to separate self-determination needs and economic distributive effects. The link to responsibility provides a further basis for explaining time limits, analogous to that sketched above in respect of foreseeability.

[188] *US-Line Pipe*, (AB), §80.   [189] (Mavroidis, 2012: 409).   [190] ADA, Art. 2.1.

[191] GATT Art. VI (5) both recognizes this potential relationship, and prohibits the pursuit of double remedies in such situations. This does not prevent the concurrent application of ADDs and CVDs, but only protects against double-counting: *US-ADCVD (China)*, (AB), §541. We must therefore account for the anti-dumping rules without invoking, at least directly, the assumption that dumped products are also subsidized.

[192] §8.2.3 above.   [193] (Jackson, 1997: 254; Mastel, 1998: 41–44).

[194] (Mastel, 1998: 43).

Further, that market segregation commonly reflects ETMs adopted by the exporting state.[195] In these circumstances, the injury suffered by competitors is a function not simply of the dumping practiced by market participants, but also of the ETMs sustaining the closed home market.[196] However, unlike the conventional sanctuary market argument, I do not suggest that anti-dumping serves to discipline those ETMs,[197] or that the closed home market necessarily makes competition between market participants unfair. Rather, the argument parallels that relating to CVDs above. The *effects* of unjustified ETMs on a people's domestic economy constitute a challenge to their economic self-determination; and ETMs, in the form of anti-dumping duties, that address this threat can thus be justified to those subject to them. Like CVDs, ADDs are explained as protecting peoples' economic self-determination, and are only indirectly concerned with injury to, or competitive fairness between, market participants. There is no suggestion that the economic effects of dumped imports are different to those resulting from low priced non-dumped sales[198]; rather, what distinguishes dumped sales is that those effects cannot be justified to those subject to them.[199]

This explains one curious feature of the ADA; while it authorizes ADDs, it does not directly discipline dumping. In this it contrasts with the SCM, which provides for both multilateral discipline and unilateral countervailing; and with the rest of the Covered Agreements, which

---

[195] There may be circumstances where market segregation results from measures other than ETMs, including the actions of private parties: (Mastel, 1998: 48–50). To the extent this is the case, the argument is weakened. That said, in circumstances of oligopoly where private actors can effectively close a market, the arguments for focusing on public measures under EGC may extend to such dominant market players. I do not pursue this point. Market segregation resulting from regulatory differences and geography may also pose problems for this view.

[196] Admittedly this is only the case where export sales are below home prices, and may not hold where a constructed normal value is applied. However restrictions on when this is permissible mean that, even in the latter case, sustained dumping will usually depend to some extent on measures adopted by exporting states. To the extent this is not the case, it suggests stricter constraints on using constructed prices.

[197] As with CVDs, the conditions for imposing ADDs make deterrence implausible: ADA 9.1. Rather, we look to the other provisions of the Covered Agreements for the relevant disciplines.

[198] This is reflected in the ADA's adoption of the same material injury standard discussed above under the SCM: ADA Art. 3 fn. 9.

[199] As with subsidies and CVDs, importing peoples may prefer to benefit from cheap imports rather than protecting domestic producers. The ADA is permissive in this regard. The injury inquiry does not purport to assess welfare effects of dumping: (Mavroidis, 2012: 441).

emphasize multilateral disciplines. EGC explains that, because dumping is not itself unjust, it is not directly disciplined. We focus instead on defining circumstances where others may respond to it; while relying on other provisions of the Covered Agreements to discipline the underlying ETMs. Anti-dumping thus stands in the same relation to the other Covered Agreements as CVDs do to the multilateral subsidies disciplines.[200]

A second approach links dumping to action (or inaction) by the exporting state. It begins from the claim that sustained price discrimination or underselling require market power in the domestic market, whether sustained by ETMs, legal monopoly, or otherwise. It is not then simply the action of commercial enterprises: rather, it expresses a synergy of commercial enterprise with market power and the (at least tacit) public authority of the exporting state. In these circumstances, the actions of exporters can be to some extent attributed to the state; and their pursuit of private ends through a specific focus on, and action towards, the international economy constitute something like an ETM.[201] Dumping from nonmarket economies in particular can be understood in these terms: where the exporting enterprise is a public monopoly, or otherwise an instrument of the state, its actions can be directly assimilated to exercises of public authority and, to the extent that they act specifically on the international economy, including through differential pricing, constitute ETMs.[202] Even in the case of market economies, however, this approach highlights the extent to which private enterprises with market dominance are effectively insulated from market disciplines, giving them power analogous to that of states, and hence potentially subject to demands for justification of a similar kind.[203] This

---

[200] Understanding AD in this way also explains why Article 15 prescribes restraint in applying anti-dumping measures towards developing countries. To the extent their ETMs may be justified, there may correspondingly be no grounds for imposing AD duties to redress these.

[201] This recalls Mastel's characterization of dumping as, in some cases, "a de facto element of national industrial policy": (Mastel, 1998: 44).

[202] We can thus explain both specific provisions for non-market economy treatment, and the use of constructed (including third-country) baselines in such circumstances. E.g. Second Note Ad Art. VI.1 GATT; Art. 15 China Accession Protocol. Cf. *EC-Fasteners* (AB), §285–290 Elsewhere the AB in that case recognized (§376) that state influence on different enterprises' pricing and output decisions in NMEs might lead to these being considered together for anti-dumping purposes.

[203] I do not suggest that all actions by private enterprises are subject to such demands, which would seem quickly to imply the abolition of the market system. However, there is a qualitative difference between the interaction of enterprises, including those of quite

approach differs from the antitrust arguments discussed above because it highlights the role of international price discrimination and underselling into export markets, and the consequent intentional orientation towards outsiders, in constituting the exercise of market power as an ETM.[204] The mere absence of effective antitrust rules need not be objectionable. Again, anti-dumping is seen on this view as insulating the domestic economy from ETMs imposed by others; but the objectionable practice is the dumping itself, rather than the institutional context that facilitates it.[205]

These approaches emphasize different aspects of anti-dumping. The first is more concerned with discriminatory pricing between home and export markets. The second more clearly implicates below-cost selling and price discrimination between export markets. In either case, they suggest, the purpose of identifying normal value and comparing it with import price is to determine whether, and to what extent, export behavior is referable to exporting state ETMs or analogous quasi-private measures.[206]

EGC thus provides a plausible account of anti-dumping, and hence constitutes an advance on existing approaches. However, are there specific features of the ADA that support this explanation?

The most obvious is the ADA's emphasis on fair comparison between export price and normal value.[207] Because economic approaches can identify no distinctive problem with price discrimination, *a fortiori*

---

different scales, in a relatively competitive market, and the capacity of dominant enterprises to unilaterally determine conditions of competition. Relative symmetry goes a long way towards justifying agents' actions in the former case, but not the latter. Obviously, in both cases, there will be concurrent questions about the justification of the background institutions. However, this is one case where the primary focus on the state, for which I argued in earlier chapters, is not justified.

[204] The AB's emphasis on regularity and intelligibility of a pattern in the context of targeted dumping can similarly be understood in this way: *US-Washing Machines* (AB), §5.25.

[205] This last point goes some way towards rebutting the likely objection that this constitutes an argument for international anti-trust rather than anti-dumping. It suggests that anti-competitive situations and practices are not, in themselves, necessarily objectionable. It is only when dominant enterprises adopt the appropriate international orientation that problems arise. However, there is certainly room here to argue for some limited form of international anti-trust to address such cases.

[206] It might be objected that this ignores the way constructed normal values lead to findings of dumping without price discrimination or below costs selling. See (Lindsey, 1999). However, we can certainly understand Art. 2 as attempting (albeit imperfectly, especially in the treatment of costs in 2.2.1) to track the two approaches described here. That much unjustifiable protectionism takes place under cover of anti-dumping is not denied: my claim here relates to the rules' aspirations, not their practical failings.

[207] ADA Art. 2.4.

they cannot explain ADA's rules for identifying such discrimination. That there should be such rules may be explained by the need to minimize abuse; but this begs the question of why price comparison is the appropriate technique.[208] EGC identifies acting on distinct markets as objectionable, regardless of predation or injury to particular industries; and whereas price discrimination and below-cost selling are poor proxies for the latter, they accurately pick out the former.[209]

EGC also explains why, while dumping affects individual market participants, it is both assessed and addressed at the level of products and members. Thus, the AB has emphasized that dumping relates to a product as a whole, and not to individual transactions.[210] Further, injury is assessed by reference to the importing industry as a whole, those who are suffering and those doing well.[211] If anti-dumping protected competitors then neither position would make sense: individual competitors may be affected by sporadic low priced imports, and for those suffering injury it will be irrelevant that others are doing well.[212] By contrast, if we understand anti-dumping as protecting the economic self-determination of peoples, both features make sense.[213]

EGC does not identify dumping itself as necessarily objectionable, but rather as symptomatic of other unjustified practices. It shows how anti-dumping duties can be justified as measures protecting self-determination without implying they remedy the underlying practices. In this, it parallels the trade regime's ambivalent treatment of dumping, explaining both why anti-dumping duties are permissible, and why there is no general prohibition on dumping as a practice. While necessarily tentative, EGC hopes thereby to provide a coherent account of the anti-dumping regime.[214]

---

[208] Cf. (Zheng, 2012: 182–183) (arguing, based on economic approaches, that this element should be dropped). The provision in Art. 2.4.2 for alternative methods of price comparison, which will frequently yield different results, and among which states are free to choose at their discretion, highlights the arbitrariness of comparison in the absence of a justification therefor.

[209] I discuss further in §8.4.3 EGC's implications for the form of the price comparison exercise.

[210] *US-Softwood Lumber V*, (AB), §92–96.

[211] ADA Art. 3.1 and 4.1; *US-Hot Rolled Steel*, (AB), §190,204–206.

[212] This contrasts with the usual practice in civil anti-trust suits, where individual enterprises can pursue claims.

[213] This approach can also explain AD by NMEs, where the idea of producer entitlements makes little sense.

[214] I concede EGC's account of dumping is less clear than other trade remedies, and on particular details may be more critical than explanatory.

8.4   EGC and Interpretation of Trade Remedies Rules

EGC, then, can explain the main features of the WTO trade remedies rules. To that extent, it represents an advance on existing approaches. However, it can also serve a valuable interpretive role. By accounting for the object and purpose of these rules, it can contribute to their consistent elaboration and application. To demonstrate this I next examine a number of recurring definitional problems in each area, showing how EGC can guide their resolution.

8.4.1   Subsidies and Benefit

Disciplined subsidies are defined by four criteria[215]: contingency (on export performance or the use of domestic over imported goods)[216]; specificity[217]; financial contribution[218]; and benefit.[219] The AB generally treats these separately.[220] Given the prevailing theoretical landscape, this seems unsurprising. A holistic approach would require an account of the purpose the category of disciplined subsidies serves. The consequence, however, has been a puzzling and incoherent jurisprudence.[221] The difficulties are clearest in the case of benefit under Art 1.1(b), so it is here that I focus.

The SCM does not define benefit.[222] The AB has consistently understood it counterfactually, asking whether a "'financial contribution' makes the recipient 'better off' than it would otherwise have been, absent that contribution."[223] The relevant counterfactual is the terms a recipient would have received in the market.[224] This raises the question how this market baseline is constructed. Does it refer to the market absent the relevant financial contribution, or to a hypothetical perfectly competitive

---

[215] See generally: (Mavroidis, 2012: 532–575; Rubini, 2009; Wouters & Coppens, 2009).

[216] SCM Art. 3.   [217] SCM Art. 2.   [218] SCM Art. 1.1(a).   [219] SCM Art. 1.1(b).

[220] E.g. *US-ADCVD (China)*, (AB), §446 (examining benefit without reference to specificity); *Canada-FIT*, (AB), §5.159–5.166 (examining benefit without reference to contingency); *US-FSC*, (AB), §91 (examining financial contribution without reference to specificity). There is some recognition of the parallels in the analysis of general infrastructure in *EC-Aircraft*, but the issues are still examined separately. The distinction in *US-Carbon Steel (India)* between the challenged financial contribution and other government prices suggested the possibility of interpreting benefit together with financial contribution, but the AB's subsequent endorsement of a market baseline precludes this.

[221] A similar point appears in: (Diamond, 2008).

[222] SCM Art. 1.1(b). Art. 14 does provide relevant context, touched on further below.

[223] *Canada-Aircraft*, (AB), §157.   [224] Ibid.

market without significant government intervention?[225] While earlier cases left this question open, more recent decisions have focused on the latter, competitive market, model.[226]

This competitive market baseline has no explicit textual basis. The AB's justification for it is that any other approach risks circularity.[227] However, the alleged circularity arises not from the agreement but rather from the way the AB has posed the question. If the question asked is whether a government has conferred a benefit on a recipient then it seems necessary to construct a counterfactual without government intervention. By contrast, if we ask whether (i) a financial contribution (ii) confers a benefit that is (iii) specific to a group of enterprises or industries or (iv) contingent on exports or domestic content, then we have many more options to construct the counterfactual. The fact of government distortion need not render a comparison circular once we distinguish between distortion from the relevant measure and other background distortion. Alternatively, we might emphasize the link between benefit, specificity, and contingency, asking whether a measure confers benefits on one group but not another.[228] Again, this avoids the need to construct a competitive market baseline. Either is compatible with the language of the SCM.[229] However, in so far as either demands an account of how the elements of the subsidy definition fit together, and in turn of the function that definition plays, they are unavailable to an AB that has declined to engage with these questions.

---

[225] Market access and competitive subsidization explanations suggest the former, while trade-distortion implies the latter.

[226] The leading case on constructed baselines, *US-Softwood Lumber IV*, is ambiguous on this point: (AB), §93, 99–102. *US-ADCVD (China)* clearly prefers an undistorted competitive market baseline: (AB), §446,500–509. The AB in *US-Carbon Steel (India)* (§4.167–4.170), while recognizing that government prices other than the financial contribution at issue might be relevant to establishing the relevant benchmark, emphasized that such government prices must be market-based rather than policy-based, thus reinforcing the competitive market baseline. Cf. *Ibid*, § 4.151–4.156. The Panel in *Canada-FIT* (§7.275) distinguishes between a market that is "'perfectly competitive' in the sense of economic theory" and one where "there is effective competition, in the sense that prices for the purchased good must be established through the operation of unconstrained forces of supply and demand", suggesting the latter as the appropriate standard. (The AB does not address this point.). For an account celebrating this jurisprudence's incoherence: (Lang, 2014) Cf. *US-Countervailing Duties (China)* (AB), para 4.50–4.53, 4.59.

[227] *US-Softwood Lumber IV*, (AB), §93.

[228] Rubini highlights the importance of such intra-state distributive questions to the definition of a subsidy: (Rubini, 2009: 21–23).

[229] Indeed, they arguably better reflect the language of Art. 14.

Lack of textual support is not the only problem with the AB's approach, however. A bigger concern is how that approach breaks down in cases where no counterfactual competitive market baseline can be identified. This was the case in *Canada-FIT*, which addressed preferential pricing schemes for renewable electricity generators. It was accepted in that case that, without government intervention, there would be no market for renewable electricity. There was thus no counterfactual competitive market against which to compare the prices offered under the challenged scheme. The AB's response was to distinguish between government interventions that create markets, and those that intervene in existing markets.[230] The role of the government as market creator cannot be excluded; but taking that role as given, the benefit comparison should be conducted by reference to the resulting (hypothetical) competitive market.[231] We thus hold fixed government interventions creating markets, while excluding interventions that distort them.

This, however, raises the question of what it means for a government to create a market, as opposed to distorting an existing one.[232] In *Canada-FIT*, for example, it was not the case that there were no potential buyers for renewable electricity; rather, it could not compete with cheaper and more reliable nonrenewable sources. However if this is enough to escape a benefit analysis the subsidies disciplines would be largely frustrated. We might look to the legitimate public policy objectives pursued by the relevant measures, but the AB emphasizes that questions of definition and justifiability should be kept separate.[233]

An objective market definition methodology might alleviate this concern.[234] However, the AB, while invoking economic language, effectively deferred to government policy in defining the relevant market.[235] Indeed, it is difficult to see how else they could proceed. Government action creates (and eliminates) markets in infinite ways. No market can be defined apart entirely from government action.[236] If the goal is counterfactual comparison

---

[230] *Canada-FIT* (AB), §5.188.   [231] Ibid., §5.190.

[232] (Rubini, 2014: 914–916). It also, separately, raises the question of why these should be subject to such different disciplines. It is not enough to say, as some have suggested, that we can leave the effects of market creation to be disciplined by other rules, as those other rules will, by assumption, have different requirements, which differences in turn require explanation.

[233] §5.185. On the difficulties this poses: (Charnovitz & Fischer, 2015: 203–207; Pal, 2014).

[234] Such an objective methodology was adopted in *EC-Aircraft* in defining the relevant domestic industry: (AB), §1117–1123.

[235] §5.169–5.177. For criticism of the market definition methodology more generally: (Rubini, 2014: 910–914).

[236] This point is made, albeit to another purpose, in: (Lang, 2014: 13).

of benefit, and we cannot interrogate the reasons a market has been constituted as it has, then there is no choice but to work from the baseline that public policy has created.

The AB's approach to constructing counterfactual baselines, however, provides no more critical purchase. It examines how much a government would have to offer to procure the particular energy supply mix desired, taking account of the economic realities of producers or potential producers.[237] But this is the essence of an efficient subsidy, offsetting enough of the costs of production to incentivize socially optimal production. Defining benefit in terms of production costs thus means such subsidies escape review.

The problems with *Canada-FIT* result from addressing benefit as a discrete component, unrelated to the other criteria defining subsidies, or to an account of their function. Because existing approaches cannot explain those criteria, they similarly cannot suggest an alternative approach.

How can EGC resolve these problems?

As discussed above, EGC identifies objectionable subsidies with ETMs, and understands the criteria in the SCM as steps towards operationalizing that concept. By understanding them in this way, we can apply those criteria as an interrelated whole, rather than approaching each separately. By examining benefit together with specificity, contingency, and financial contribution, we escape both the circularity the AB has sought to avoid, and the unrealism into which it has instead fallen.

Recall, we earlier explained contingency and specificity as expressing ETMs' focus on international economic activity. By making these latter concepts our starting point, the benefit inquiry becomes more tractable. We are then concerned to identify whether a benefit is conferred on a *specific* industry etc., or *contingent* on exports/local content. The most obvious comparison then becomes, not the terms available in some hypothetical market, whether competitive or otherwise, but rather the terms available absent the specific or contingent intervention. Government measures affect markets and market participants in many ways. To the extent these are neither specific nor contingent, they are not ETMs, and are not disciplined under the SCM. An appropriate counterfactual, then, holds fixed all aspects of the market except those that are specific or contingent in the required sense. We are still engaged in a counterfactual comparison, but the comparison is also in part

---

[237] *Canada-FIT* (AB), §5.228–5.234.

interpersonal: it inquires how another producer, falling outside the relevant category, would fare *in the market as it is*. This will not solve every problem with defining benefit. Cases like *Softwood Lumber*, in particular, where the nature of a good limits beneficiaries, may still require comparative or hypothetical market counterfactuals.[238] However, even here, EGC suggests we focus not on an ideal market, but rather on a market that is as close as possible to the actual market, distorted as it may be by government involvement. By giving an account of what this exercise aims to do, however, EGC can guide the necessary interpretive choices.[239]

8.4.2   Safeguards, Foreseeability, and Causation

The AB has faced various challenges in defining the conditions for applying safeguards.[240] I here focus on two, foreseeability, and causation.

Art XIX (1) (a) GATT requires, as a precondition to applying safeguards, that increased imports result from "unforeseen developments." While largely ignored in pre-WTO GATT practice, and omitted from the SA, the AB resurrected this condition, relying on narrowly textual arguments and with little guidance on the function of the test.[241] While foreseeability is a familiar legal concept, Art XIX does not indicate when or by whom developments must be unforeseen.[242] Panels and the AB have focused on whether developments were or should or could have been foreseen by the adopting state at the time commitments were undertaken.[243] Under the GATT, conceived as a temporary regime, that interpretation made sense. Under the WTO, now over two decades

---

[238] *US-Softwood Lumber IV*, (Panel), §7.116.

[239] Baseline problems similarly arise in identifying financial contributions, especially in respect of foregone revenues under Art. 1.1(a) (1) (ii). Existing approaches, looking to a "defined normative benchmark" (*US-FSC*, (AB), §90) or "legitimately comparable income" (*US-FSC (Article 21.5-EC)*, (AB), §91, 98), are substantially indeterminate. EGC can guide this inquiry by explaining its goal: identifying treatment privileging specific or contingently defined recipients. Thus, a relevant factor in identifying financial contribution is whether treatment is afforded only to specific enterprises or industries. Cf. *US-Aircraft* (2nd complaint), (Panel), §7.133.

[240] For an overview: (Grossman & Mavroidis, 2005b: 106–109; Sykes, 2003b).

[241] *Argentina-Footwear (EC)*, *(AB)*, §89. See further the discussion at fn. 184 above. On the history of this requirement: (Messenger, 2016: 97–111).

[242] (Grossman & Sykes, 2007: 91–92).

[243] *US-Steel Safeguards*, (Panel), §10.39, 10.41–10.43, *Argentina-Preserved Peaches*, (Panel), §7.25–7.28, *Argentina-Footwear (EC)*, *(AB)*, §96, *Korea-Dairy*, (AB), §86.

old, it is rapidly losing relevance,[244] suggesting the AB must eventually dispense with foreseeability, or adopt a dynamic test, considering foreseeability on a rolling basis.

Neither text nor existing theories offer clear guidance on this question.[245] The *ex ante* political argument favors the present foreseeability test, but this seems impracticable going forward. The other economic and political arguments either see no role for foreseeability or, at most, accord it instrumental value in minimizing moral hazard.[246] Yet, having resurrected foreseeability, it seems unlikely the AB will drop it again. EGC, by contrast, strongly favors retaining a foreseeability requirement, albeit applied dynamically. EGC explains safeguards as protecting self-determination, which includes responsibility for managing the domestic economy and responding appropriately to international developments.[247] Safeguards cannot, on this view, be justified to address developments that could have been subject to appropriate preventive action. Foreseeability therefore should track the capacity and responsibility of national authorities to anticipate developments in time to take appropriate action. This need not imply a fixed period; rather, when developments must be unforeseen will depend on the responses available, and how long these take to implement.[248]

Foreseeability, then, requires a choice between alternatives, and EGC seems best placed to guide that choice.

Causation, by contrast, poses a deeper problem of attributing any coherent meaning to the test set out in the agreements.

The causation requirement is expressed in similar language in GATT Art. XIX and the SA: "any product is being imported . . . in such increased quantities and under such conditions as to *cause or threaten* serious injury to domestic producers."[249] Unfortunately, as various scholars observe, standard economic theory teaches that in a market system imports cannot cause anything, including injury to producers.[250] Imports are a function of relative demand and costs of production in

---

[244] (Grossman & Sykes, 2007: 92; Lee, 2006b: 387–399; Sykes, 2004: 526–527).
[245] (Saggi, 2010).   [246] For the latter view, (Horn & Mavroidis, 2003: 408–409).
[247] §4.5.2, 5.3–5.
[248] A long-stop of 8 years might be implied from the SA's maximum safeguard duration. If we assume any adjustment facilitated by safeguards can be implemented within that time, then presumably any developments foreseeable eight years earlier could already have been addressed.
[249] GATT Art. XIX.1 (a). Cf. SA Art. 4.2.
[250] (Grossman & Mavroidis, 2005b: 123; Grossman & Sykes, 2007: 113; Horn & Mavroidis, 2003: 412–416; Saggi, 2010: 376–377; Sykes, 2004: 528–529, 2006a).

the home and foreign markets.[251] An increase in domestic demand or production costs, or a drop in foreign demand or costs will lead to increased imports, whether by raising the home price, or lowering the foreign one. It is price changes that cause increased imports; and it is relative prices that cause of injury to domestic industry. Imports are part of the story, but they cannot be its cause.[252]

This problem is amplified by the non-attribution requirement, under which adjudicators must distinguish between injury from increased imports and that from other factors[253]; safeguards may only respond to the former. Imports, however, are themselves necessarily a function of other factors affecting relative prices. Further, it is through price effects that almost any "other factor" harming an industry must act. The question then becomes how to distinguish developments whose effects, mediated through relative prices, are regarded as *caused by* increased imports, and those that constitute "other factors," whose effects on prices are not so attributable.[254]

There is nothing in the texts to answer this question.[255] Further, the AB, while addressing these issues in a number of decisions, has provided no clear guidance. As various critics highlight, on causation, it has adopted a straightforward correlation test without addressing the correlation / causation distinction; while candidate "other factors" identified by parties are generally accepted without criticism.[256] While this allows

---

[251] (Krugman et al., 2012: 58–59).

[252] For a contrary view, arguing for the autonomy of legal and economic approaches: (Lee, 2006a, 2006b: 398–403). A similar argument is advanced in: (Messenger, 2013). As Messenger acknowledges, the challenge for such approaches is to explain the basis for an autonomous legal account of causation. This must in turn depend on an account of what this test is for, the question that EGC here answers.

[253] Safeguards Agreement, Art. 4.2(b).

[254] (Sykes, 2004: 984–986). The need for a non-attribution analysis seems similarly to undermine the proposal to understand safeguards causation in INUS terms: (Ahn & Moon, 2010: 1049 et seq.).

[255] (Grossman & Mavroidis, 2005b: 122).

[256] See generally: (Sykes, 2004: 543–560). On the substitution of correlation for causation: (Ahn & Moon, 2010: 1039–1041; Grossman & Sykes, 2007: 100, 111–112). For examples: *Argentina-Footwear, (AB)*, §144, *US-Steel Safeguards*, (Panel), §10.301–10.302. While a "conditions of competition" test supplements the correlation analysis, it does not remedy the conceptual uncertainty: *US-Steel Safeguards, (Panel)*, §10.313–10.317. On previous US practice: (Sykes, 2004: 531–532) On non-attribution: (Grossman & Sykes, 2007: 101–102); *US-Wheat Gluten*, (AB), §69–70; *US-Line Pipe*, (AB), §200–222. For examples of "other factors" accepted uncritically: *Argentina-Footwear, (Panel)*, §8.269, 8.278, *US-Wheat Gluten*, (AB), §91. For a critical overview (Wauters, 2010).

the AB to decide disputes, it tells us little about how future cases might be decided, or indeed, why past cases were decided as they were.[257]

Faced with textual incoherence, theory might suggest principled interpretations. However, existing theories offer little guidance.[258] As discussed, none identifies a clear reason for treating injury from imports differently from other causes; in consequence, they say nothing about the subsequent question of how to distinguish between them.

EGC, by contrast, offers a clear answer. By identifying safeguards with self-determination, it focuses on developments in the international economy, to the exclusion of domestic factors. It thus suggests interpreting injury from increased imports as referring to injury consequent on international price shocks, whether from falling demand or production costs.[259] Where increased imports result from domestic price shocks, EGC identifies self-determination, and specifically national responsibility, as a compelling reason to restrain safeguards from externalizing adjustment costs properly falling on the community responsible; such domestic developments, it suggests, should properly constitute "other factors."[260]

8.4.3   Dumping and Zeroing

While ADA disputes have addressed various aspects of anti-dumping methodology, unquestionably the most contentious have related to zeroing. While generating less public debate than disputes around environmental and human health issues, after 36 reports in 19 separate disputes, zeroing is perhaps the most litigated issue in the WTO.[261] While recent changes in US practice have reduced its relevance,[262] the resistance the AB's conclusions on zeroing provoked from the US, and its inability to

---

[257] (Grossman & Sykes, 2007: 114–116).   [258] (Sykes, 2004: 534).

[259] For this approach in prior US practice: (Sykes, 2004: 533–535). On the popularity of this approach: (Sykes, 2006a: 982). EGC however explains why this is the appropriate interpretation, something that Sykes recognizes existing approaches have failed to do: (Sykes, 2006a: 983).

[260] EGC thus suggests a coherent role for non-attribution.

[261] "WTO, Disputes by Subject": www.wto.org (retrieved October 6, 2016). For an overview: (Ahn & Messerlin, 2014: 274). Between 1998 and 2010, US zeroing disputes constituted 13 percent of all Panel and 20 percent of all Appellate Body reports: (Martin et al., 2011: 3).

[262] On changes in US policy to comply with previous AB reports on zeroing: (Cho, 2012). However, this has not prevented the subsequent litigation of a further case, US-Washing Machines, on targeted zeroing.

offer a convincing defense of those conclusions, have tested the AB's authority to near breaking point.[263] Accounting for zeroing thus seems an important task of any theory of anti-dumping.

Zeroing is a method of calculating an overall dumping margin for a product by aggregating individual margins, which may reflect specific models, transactions, or time periods. Individual margins may be positive (export price below normal value) or negative (export price above normal value). If these are simply averaged then individual negative margins will partially offset positive margins, leading to a lower overall margin or, if negative margins exceed positive, a negative dumping finding. Where zeroing is applied, however, negative margins are simply ignored ("zeroed"), leading to a higher overall dumping margin.[264] While zeroing was an accepted practice during the Uruguay Round,[265] and is not explicitly prohibited in the ADA,[266] the AB has consistently found it impermissible, a view that the US in particular has vigorously disputed.

The zeroing conflict can be understood as one between textualism and teleology. The US, defending zeroing, focused on the language of the ADA and the absence of an express prohibition on the practice.[267] The AB similarly provided textual justification for its view that zeroing is impermissible.[268] However, in the absence of clear treaty language, the permissive standard of review mandated by Article 17.6 seems to undermine the AB's position.[269] The consequence has been a series of decisions limiting the weight of Article 17.6 to make it compatible with the AB's position on zeroing.[270]

---

[263] (Langland, 2008: 569; Spaulding, 2006: 424–427) Cf. *US-Stainless Steel (Mexico)* (AB), §160–162. Most recently, the United States' 2016 blocking of the reappointment of AB Member Seung Wha Chang was widely attributed to dissatisfaction with the zeroing jurisprudence: (Shaffer, 2016).

[264] For a detailed description: (Mavroidis, 2012: 438–440).

[265] (Alford, 2006: 209; Spaulding, 2006: 395–398). For an overview of both pre-Uruguay Round practice and the ADA's drafting history: (Kim, 2002: 39–50).

[266] Although for an argument that the strengthened fair comparison requirement in the ADA justifies this move: (Kim, 2002: 50–56). A more permissive attitude towards zeroing was suggested as part of the Doha Round negotiations: (Lester, 2008: 840; Voon, 2007: 229–230). However, as of March 2010 there was no convergence on this issue: (Negotiating Group on Rules, *Report by the Chairman*, March 22, 2010, TN/RL/24). It is unclear whether this issue will be taken up if the rules negotiations are resumed, which itself is unclear: (Negotiating Group on Rules, *Report by the Chairman*, March 14, 2014, TN/RL/W/255).

[267] (Bown & Sykes, 2008: 129). E.g. *US-Softwood Lumber V*, (Panel), §7.192.

[268] E.g. *US-Softwood Lumber V (Article 21.5)*, (AB), §87–109.

[269] (Bown & Sykes, 2008: 131–132) On the weakness of these AB's arguments: (Voon, 2007).

[270] Most prominently, *US-Softwood Lumber V, Art. 21.5*, (AB), §39, 123; *US-Continued Zeroing* 269–275, 317; but also e.g. *US-Zeroing*, (AB), §189; *US-Stainless Steel (Mexico)*

This ignores the most obvious explanation of the AB's position, namely that zeroing is incompatible with *any* principled account of the *function* of anti-dumping.[271] Zeroing systematically overestimates dumping margins compared with other calculation methods.[272] However, this only constitutes an objection if there is reason to prefer those other methods of calculation. Where the text does not settle the issue, it can only be answered through an account of what anti-dumping practice is about.[273] For example, some defenders of zeroing analogize dumping to driving above a speed limit: it is no defense to a speeding charge that my *average* speed is below the speed limit.[274] If dumping is like speeding, then there is no problem with zeroing. We thus need to know what exactly is wrong with dumping, and hence what anti-dumping practice is for, before we can say whether and why zeroing is objectionable. This, however, existing approaches cannot explain.

EGC answers this question by reference to the relationship between ETMs and dumping. As such, it identifies objectionable dumping with export practices that effectively constitute, or that could only be adopted in the presence of, such ETMs, namely *sustained* selling by an exporter at less than normal value. Neither intermittent sales below normal value, nor sales at different prices to different importers, necessarily reflect any privileged position enjoyed by the exporter in its home market; provided the average export price over a reasonable period is equal to normal value, variations may simply reflect rational pricing given market fluctuations.[275] Zeroing is therefore problematic because it identifies as dumping practices to which EGC suggests no objection.[276]

(AB), §76, 136; *US-Zeroing (Japan)* (AB), §189; *US-Zeroing (EC)* (AB), §134. Cf. (Tarullo, 2002) (suggesting these Art. 17.6 interpretations reflect skepticism about anti-dumping generally); (Alford, 2006) (highlighting the weakness of the AB's approach).

[271] This is reflected in AB's reliance on the ADA's fair comparison requirements, albeit without a substantive account of fairness: *US-Softwood Lumber V (Article 21.5-Canada)*, (AB), §142.

[272] (Crowley, 2008) Cf. *US-Zeroing (Japan)*, (AB), §123.

[273] Voon suggests such an account has been implicitly advanced by reference to the role of average pricing in the ADA: (Voon, 2007: 219). Cf. *US-Softwood Lumber V*, (Panel), §9.19.

[274] In US practice, this often translates into concern for "masked" dumping: (Alford, 2006: 207–208; Spaulding, 2006: 396).

[275] As discussed, EGC's two accounts of the problem of dumping point to different ways of calculating normal value. Another upshot of this view is an argument to revise Art. 2.2.2 ADA to preclude constructed normal values above fixed costs.

[276] The shift in US practice to emphasize "targeted dumping" is potentially problematic on this view. (Porter & Bidlingmaier, 2013: 495–496). However, the second explanation of

Why can't existing approaches advance this explanation? As discussed, those approaches cannot identify what is wrong with dumping in general. In consequence, they see zeroing as merely a particularly flagrant case of a generally disreputable practice, providing no basis for distinguishing the permissible from the illicit.[277] By contrast EGC, by offering a principled defense of anti-dumping generally, allows us to distinguish elements that can be justified from those, such as zeroing, that cannot. It thus provides a more plausible principled defense of the AB's position than those other approaches.

8.5 Conclusion

EGC tells a story about the justification of measures regulating the economy, both domestically and internationally.

This chapter has applied that story as an explanatory and interpretive lens for trade remedies. It has argued that EGC provides a better explanation than competing theories for key features of the trade remedies rules, and can serve as an interpretive aid, potentially informing teleological interpretation of those rules. It has done this in two ways: first, by showing how key features of the trade remedies rules can be derived from EGC; and second, by identifying responses EGC suggests to persistent problems in the case-law.

Chapter 9 extends this approach to the WTO's rules on domestic regulation. This requires a shift in emphasis, from ETMs to DEMs. It also requires a more constructive, and indeed creative, stance, as EGC is applied less to explain the treaties and case-law, and more to illuminate alternative paths we might follow to bring greater consistency to domestic regulation jurisprudence.

---

antidumping above, emphasizing the intentional relation between dominant exporter and export market, suggests a solution; and, as noted above, the emphasis on regularity and intelligibility in the AB's approach in *Washing Machines* fits well with this approach.

[277] E.g. (Spaulding, 2006: 389–395). One former Appellate Body member has suggested in conversation that the zeroing cases were motivated by a sense that zeroing led to anti-dumping duties that were "simply too high"; but this can only make sense if we know what the "right" level of duty is, something we cannot learn from views that condemn all anti-dumping duties.

Domestic Regulation, Self-Determination, and DEMs

9.1 Introduction

The disciplines discussed in Chapters 5 through 8 address trade policy, narrowly understood. Border measures, discrimination, and trade remedies are the traditional preoccupations of the trade regime.[1] While clarified and extended in the Uruguay Round, most of these rules were at least foreshadowed in GATT 1947.

Other Uruguay Round agreements went further, constituting genuine innovations.[2] This chapter addresses two of these, the Agreement on Sanitary and Phytosanitary Measures (SPS), and the Agreement on Technical Barriers to Trade (TBT) (together, the Regulation Agreements). Both address domestic regulation. Both go beyond discrimination, imposing procedural and substantive restrictions on regulations affecting goods trade.[3] While foreshadowed in the Tokyo Round Standards Code, this was the first time that the multilateral regime reached so deeply into the domestic affairs of members, a "dramatic shift in focus"[4] leading one commentator to announce the birth of "post-discriminatory" trade law,[5] while others compare the revolutionary implications to the postwar prohibition on the use of force.[6] More directly than earlier disciplines, they raise conflicts between trade and sovereignty.[7] Further, in seeming to mandate cost–benefit analysis, they go beyond the security of mutual advantage to address internationally conflicting interests.[8] Various

---

[1] (Trachtman, 2007: 632–633).
[2] For an overview: (Dunoff, 2006b; Heiskanen Veijo, 2004).
[3] For an overview of their relation to GATT disciplines: (Marceau & Trachtman, 2002).
[4] (Trebilcock & Howse, 2005: 202).   [5] (Hudec, 2003) Cf. (Buthe, 2008: 227–230).
[6] (Horn & Weiler, 2005: 251).   [7] (Trebilcock & Howse, 2005: 202–204).
[8] (Howse, 2000: 2330–2333).

commentators highlighted the risks here, which if not navigated cautiously could undermine the WTO's legitimacy.[9]

As in previous chapters, I ask how we should understand these disciplines and, in particular, whether they can fruitfully be understood in terms of EGC. In doing so, I focus on those aspects of the Regulation Agreements that are at once novel, going beyond GATT disciplines; and relevant, potentially challenging or supporting EGC's account of trade regulation. Novelty explains why I don't focus on nondiscrimination: both agreements include nondiscrimination obligations, but SPS nondiscrimination (Article 2.3) largely tracks the Article XX chapeau,[10] while recent AB jurisprudence has effectively equated TBT nondiscrimination (Article 2.1) with GATT nondiscrimination.[11] Relevance explains why I don't address transparency and monitoring,[12] inspection and conformity assessment,[13] committees,[14] equivalence,[15] or institutional aspects of harmonization.[16] Many of these, while innovative and potentially transformative, are concerned more with procedure than substantive rights[17]; while others are explicable under various approaches, and so cannot adjudicate the value of EGC.

This leads me to focus, in TBT, on Article 2.2's requirement that measures be no more trade restrictive than necessary to fulfill a legitimate objective, and Article 2.4's invocation of international standards; and in SPS, on scientific justification and risk assessment in Articles 2.2, 3.3, and 5, and the promotion of international harmonization in Article 3. Their combined effect is that domestic regulations, regardless of GATT compliance, require justification in terms of "legitimate objectives" (TBT) or "scientific principles" (SPS); and where international standards exist, states are incentivized to follow these in their domestic regulation, and departures therefrom require specific justification. These requirements, more than any others, go beyond disciplining how states do regulation, to

---

[9] (Du, 2011; Howse & Levy, 2013: 350) Cf. (Echols, 2001: 149; Shaffer, 2008: 22–24). The AB has acknowledged this challenge, and the need to respect the agreements' delicate balance: *EC-Hormones* (AB), §177.

[10] While *Australia–Salmon (21.5)* found SPS discrimination included dissimilar products (Panel, §7.112), that interpretation is reconcilable with EGC, albeit probably not with the *Seals* AB's chapeau analysis (§5.201). SPS does introduce a novel nondiscrimination provision (Art. 5.5) addressing discrimination between risks. While I do not have space to address this provision in detail, the biggest issues it raises relate to the authority of science and its relation to risk, discussed in §9.4 below.

[11] (Marceau, 2013: 6–13). See the discussion in §6.3.5 above.

[12] TBT Art. 2.5, 2.6, 2.9; SPS 5.8, 7, Annex B.   [13] SPS Art. 8, Annex C.

[14] SPS Art. 12 (Lang & Scott, 2009a; Naiki, 2009).   [15] TBT Art. 2.7, 2.8, SPS 4.

[16] TBT Art. 2.5, 2.6, SPS Art. 3.1, 3.4, 3.5, 12.4. Cf. fn. 85 below.   [17] See §2.6.2 above.

address what regulation states can do.[18] I argue EGC can account for these innovations, and provide guidance on their interpretation and application.

Like previous chapters, I contrast explanations from various approaches. However, the argument here is both more tentative and more constructive: more tentative, because these agreements are less fully explored[19]; more constructive, because this uncertainty means interpretation leans more on justification than fit.[20]

Section 9.2 reviews competing accounts. These express variants on local and global efficiency, but concerns for sovereignty and democracy are also prominent. Many of the theoretical frameworks drawn on here are familiar from earlier chapters, but they require modification or extension to make sense of the more intrusive disciplines in the Regulation Agreements.

Section 9.2 also outlines EGC's account of these disciplines, which emphasizes two ideas: first, the need to police domestic economic measures, albeit against the less demanding justificatory standards applicable thereto; and second, the need to discipline nondiscriminatory ETMs that are not otherwise picked up by the GATT Core Disciplines.

Sections 9.3, 9.4, and 9.5 examine specific issues under the agreements, enquiring how far these fit with, or are illuminated by, the various theoretical approaches discussed.

Section 9.3 focuses on "legitimate objective[s]" in TBT's key "post-discriminatory" provisions, Articles 2.2 and 2.4, arguing existing theories struggle to explain its function, and hence guide its interpretation. EGC, by contrast, can do so, while also reconciling conflicting approaches in the case-law.

Section 9.4 examines SPS's emphasis on science, and the problems this raises. It suggests that, compared with existing approaches, EGC better justifies both SPS's invocation of science, and the AB's approach thereto.

Section 9.5 examines international standards under both agreements, highlighting the balance the agreements seek to strike between promoting harmonization and respecting regulatory autonomy. Again, it argues that these rules are better understood through EGC that competing approaches.

---

[18] (Jackson, 1997: 223–224; Scott, 2002: 372).
[19] This is particular true of TBT, applied in only five disputes, four since 2011.
[20] See §2.6.2 above.

9.2   Explaining the Domestic Regulation Agreements

Existing approaches explain these agreements from local and global perspectives.[21] It is in this order that I address them. Local perspectives include anti-protectionism, regulatory efficiency, and deliberative democracy. Global perspectives include terms of trade and market fragmentation.

9.2.1   Domestic Approaches

The most prominent approach explains these agreements as targeting domestically inefficient protectionism.[22]

Recall, nondiscriminatory regulations can be protectionist, increasing compliance costs for foreign producers.[23] These may not violate Article III GATT because they impose identical restrictions on imported and like domestic products.[24] However, in many circumstances their trade effects will be identical, conferring an advantage on domestic over foreign producers;[25] while unnecessary compliance costs can actually make them more wasteful then either border measures or discriminatory regulations.[26]

This view reads the agreements' requirements as proxies for protectionism.[27] As such, and to avoid unnecessarily restricting regulatory freedom, it emphasizes procedural over substantive requirements, and counsels against unduly strict interpretations.[28]

---

[21] Protecting human, animal and plant life and health, and indeed other regulatory goals, are obviously important considerations in these agreements but they are not the goals they pursue. Rather, they are qualifications on those goals, e.g. they pursue efficiency subject to public health, anti-protectionism subject to legitimate regulation etc.: (Charnovitz, 1999: 276) Cf. (Gruszczynski, 2010: 3).

[22] See e.g. (Howse & Levy, 2013; Roberts, 1998: 377–379, 384–385; Van den Bossche & Zdouc, 2013: 895–896).

[23] This approach ties SPS to agriculture liberalization in the Uruguay Round: (Jaiswal, 2003; Maruyama, 1998: 662).

[24] See §6.2.2, 6.3.1.

[25] Admittedly, under the competitive conception of discrimination in the GATT, such regulations may actually be deemed to be discriminatory, making it less surprising that the AB has focused more heavily on TBT's nondiscrimination requirements than its rational regulation rules.

[26] (Sykes, 1999a: 60–61, 1999b).

[27] (Green & Epps, 2007: 300, 303; Mavroidis, 2012: 669; Scott, 2007: 3). Rigod, while advancing a terms of trade argument, explains much of SPS as tracking protectionism: (Rigod, 2013: 525–528) Cf. (Shaffer, 2008: 24–25).

[28] (Green & Epps, 2007: 303–305; Perdikis et al., 2001: 384; Trebilcock & Howse, 2005: 230–231). For this approach to procedural review: (Shaffer & Trachtman, 2011: 149–152).

It reads Article 2.2 TBT as imposing a least trade restrictive alternative test, while according unfettered discretion to members in defining both their objectives, and standards of fulfillment.[29] It reads Article 2.2's references to "legitimate objective" as meaning "non-protectionist," downplaying the "illustrative list" of legitimate objectives in that Article.[30] It similarly downplays the disciplines on international standards, emphasizing their application only where suitable to members' goals.[31]

It reads SPS's invocation of science as requiring at most a rational basis for measures, denying that either SPS, or science generally, can define what risks states should accept.[32] It emphasizes members' rights to define appropriate levels of protection.[33] It reads risk assessment as purely procedural, emphasizing states' regulatory autonomy.[34] And it emphasizes states' freedom, under Article 3.3 SPS, to depart from the international standards and avoid Article 3.1's harmonization obligation, ensuring international standards respect regulatory freedom.[35]

On this view, these agreements police whether regulations are protectionist, without otherwise restricting their justification. They express a model of minimally restrictive rational regulation, but only as a heuristic for identifying protectionism.[36] They should not restrict states' *bona fide* regulatory preferences. Means may be reviewed, but with care to respect goals.[37] Further, this view leaves no room for balancing.[38] Costs to outsiders play no role.[39]

If we understand WTO law generally as disciplining protectionism, this is an obvious interpretation.[40] However, it fits imperfectly. It effectively reads out TBT's "legitimate objective" requirement, and Article 2.2's illustrative list thereof. While open, that list suggests legitimate objectives are not unlimited.[41] Similarly, SPS's science and risk provisions seem inevitably

---

[29] (Howse, 2002e; Mavroidis, 2012: 693–694). For a fuller discussion of the requirements of Article 2. 2 and its explanation under this and other approaches, see section III below.

[30] E.g. (Howse, 2002e: 253). This view is implicit in: (Howse & Levy, 2013: 370–374). On the illustrative list in such approaches: (Mavroidis & Saggi, 2014: 307).

[31] E.g. (Du, 2007: 302; Howse, 2002e: 248; Naiki, 2009).

[32] (Echols, 2001: 5–6; Mavroidis, 2012: 722–723).

[33] SPS Art. 2.1 Cf. (Scott, 2007: 35–40).   [34] (Epps, 2008; Guzman, 2004a; Shaffer, 2010).

[35] E.g. (Quick & Blüthner, 1999: 610–615).

[36] (Hoekman & Trachtman, 2010: 173–174).   [37] (Mavroidis, 2012: 693).

[38] (Hoekman & Trachtman, 2010: 155).   [39] (Regan, 2006: 984).   [40] See §6.2.2 above.

[41] For this reading: (Desmedt, 2001: 458–459). Du, writing before the recent cases, reads both "legitimate objective" and "risks of nonfulfillment" as affecting margin of appreciation, reflecting Art. XX case-law: (Du, 2007: 297–301).

to restrict some non-protectionist measures. Given a robust commitment to scientific rationality we might think measures without scientific basis were *ipso facto* irrational; but this doesn't make them protectionist.[42] This approach's downplaying of international harmonization might also be queried; while the AB has taken care to limit the implications of those provisions, they surely impose more constraint than the anti-protectionist interpretation suggests.[43]

Turning next to regulatory rationality, introduced in Chapter 4.[44] Recall, this view understands trade agreements as disciplining trade-affecting policies that are domestically inefficient.[45] It recognizes that regulations may be domestically inefficient without being protectionist.[46] National welfare suffers when regulation fails accurately to track citizens' regulatory preferences.[47] Causes include political pressure from affected (but not necessarily protectionist) groups, regulatory agencies' limited capacities, and incomplete information about effects and alternatives.[48] Whatever the cause, the result is domestically suboptimal regulation.[49]

On this interpretation, SPS and TBT ameliorate the worst excesses of such inefficient regulation by imposing a model of rational regulation, and requiring states to justify departures therefrom. This is clearest in SPS's emphasis on science and risk assessment.[50] Assuming risks to human animal and plant life and health are best assessed in scientific terms, requiring scientific justification restrains irrational prejudice, hysteria, and superstition.[51] TBT is less prescriptive, but its references to necessity, legitimate objectives and risks of nonfulfillment are explicable in these terms.[52] Legitimate objectives are, then, objectives that accurately track community preferences, as against "illegitimate" politically motivated preferences.[53] Harmonization and transparency are explained as facilitating exchange of regulatory knowledge and minimizing regulatory costs.[54] Equivalence,

---

[42] (Victor, 1999: 922).
[43] *EC-Hormones*, *(AB)*, §169–177. On protectionism and harmonization: (Howse, 2000: 235–236).
[44] (Regan, 2006); §6.2.2 above.   [45] (Regan, 2006: 968).   [46] Ibid., 968.
[47] (Hoekman & Trachtman, 2010: 155–156, 174–175).
[48] Ibid., 155–156; Sykes, 1999b: 18–19.   [49] (Regan, 2006: 968).   [50] SPS Art. 2.2, 3.3, 5.
[51] (Green & Epps, 2007: 302–303; Howse, 2000; Trebilcock & Soloway, 2002: 546–550). Regan sees only qualified support for risk assessment on this approach: (Regan, 2006: 968).
[52] TBT Art. 2.2. See: (Regan, 2006: 968).
[53] This raises the same aggregation problems identified in §4.2.2 above.
[54] (Du, 2007: 301–302; Scott, 2007: 193). It is possible international harmonization might be less efficient than domestic regulation, due to *inter alia* the risk of international regulatory

consultations, and dispute settlement inform states about the costs regulations impose, and about potential alternatives.[55] Consistency requirements link specific policies to underlying social risk profiles.[56]

Howse proposes a variation on this approach, suggesting SPS's risk and science requirements facilitate robust deliberative democracy.[57] (While addressed to SPS, similar arguments might extend to TBT.) SPS, Howse argues, can be understood as "enhancing the quality of rational democratic deliberation about risk and its control."[58] The requirements of transparency, risk assessment, and scientific evidence protect the conditions for deliberative reason, and thus promote democratic legitimacy.[59] However, against such deliberative concerns, Howse weighs the need to respect "citizens' real choices, even where these seem irrational as measured against . . . a perfectly rational deliberative process."[60] Democracy demands deliberation, taking account of the claims of others and relying as far as possible on sound information and reasoning; but decisions must ultimately rest on citizens' choices, regardless of their apparent rationality.[61]

The two approaches are distinct: the former sees SPS correcting democratic failures; the latter integrates it into a conception of democracy in deliberative rather than preference-aggregation terms.[62] Risk assessment ensures decisions are made on the best available evidence, in terms citizens can accept. Transparency and scientific evidence allow citizens to understand and challenge decisions, making them more democratic.[63] However, to ensure deliberation not disguise elite prescription, citizens must remain free to disregard scientific or other opinion.[64] Procedural requirements should therefore be robustly enforced, while respecting democratic choice on substantive questions. Science is necessary to

---

capture: (Dunoff, 2006b: 164–165). Open standard setting processes are advocated to address this risk: (Wijkström & McDaniels, 2013: 1035–1036).

[55] (Hoekman & Trachtman, 2010: 156; Scott, 2007: 162–179).

[56] Regan, in discussion, has advanced a similar view, albeit addressing TBT and *Clove Cigarettes*. Contrast: (Howse, 2000: 2350–2353).

[57] (Howse, 2000).   [58] Ibid., 1330.   [59] Ibid., 2334.   [60] Ibid., 2335.

[61] Cf. (Du, 2011). This contrasts with Petersmann's account of the WTO's constitutional functions, which demands restricting majoritarian decision-making, more closely approximating regulatory rationality. See §2.6.2 above.

[62] For an approach seeking to extend this democratic ideal to the WTO generally: (Atik, 1998). Cf. (Hudec, 1992).

[63] While also invoking democratic claims of outsiders, Howse's emphasis on citizens' choices precludes understanding his approach in global terms: (Howse, 2000: 2356–2357). Cf. Scott's global judicial review interpretation, fn. 84 below.

[64] (Howse, 2000: 2337). On regulation's doubtful democratic credentials: (Fisher, 2006).

this process, but cannot be decisive.[65] Instead, this view emphasizes members' freedom to politically determine their appropriate level of protection, counseling restraint in applying necessity and restrictiveness tests, to ensure these not force states to compromise their goals.[66]

We might query the normative attraction of both approaches. As well as invoking a questionable account of collective preferences,[67] regulatory rationality is unavoidably paternalistic, denying polities the freedom to harm themselves through policies that they have freely chosen.[68] Yet Howse's approach faces the opposite challenge: by ultimately accepting majoritarian choice over deliberative reason, it concedes its own aspiration towards universal justifiability in favor of imposing on minorities the *ex hypothesi* unjustifiable preferences of majorities.[69]

The more obvious problem for both is their awkward fit. Both suggest explanations of "legitimate objective," but neither can explain the illustrative list. Each gives scientific requirements different emphasis: deliberative democracy reads these as procedural, while regulatory rationality suggests a substantive role.[70] Both recognize the diversity of bases for regulation, and so counsel caution in finding violations.[71] Each tells a story about international harmonization, as potentially improving the quality of domestic decisions; but neither gives it great weight.

More generally, because both are inward looking, they must explain why SPS and TBT provide no remedies for citizens of regulating states.[72] Protectionist theories face similar objections; but it is at least plausible that protectionism will stimulate outsiders to complain, in turn remedying domestic failures. That relation does not hold for domestic regulation generally. Further, both approaches recognize under- and overregulation as equally problematic[73]; but the agreements only address the former.[74] Consistency requirements may occasionally highlight under-regulation,

---

[65] (Howse, 2000: 2342).

[66] Ibid., 2353–2356 Cf. (Regan, 2006: 987–988). Many approaches balancing trade and other goals fit here. Those advocating a particular balance or methodology (e.g. cost–benefit analysis) fall under regulatory rationality. Those emphasizing political choices approximate Howse's approach, e.g. (Flett, 2010: 23–25; 2013).

[67] (Howse, 2000: 2333).

[68] Regan questions its extension in the Regulation Agreements, albeit for epistemic not democratic reasons: (Regan, 2006: 986–987).

[69] On this tension in theories of global deliberative democracy: (Scheuerman, 2006).

[70] Although contrast the views at fn. 51 above.

[71] Regulatory costs also undermine regulatory rationality approaches, particularly with regard to risk assessment: (Dunoff, 2006b: 173–174) Cf. (Regan, 2006: 987).

[72] Cf. Petersmann's arguments for an individual complaint mechanism: §2.6.2 above.

[73] (Galeotti & Kemfert, 2004).   [74] (Charnovitz, 1999: 276).

but the combination of trade restrictiveness tests, safe harbors under international standards, and the incentive structures of foreign complainants mean under-regulation will generally escape review.[75]

9.2.2   Global Approaches

A second group of theories explain SPS and TBT in terms of global efficiency, emphasizing how adverse effects on outsiders can exceed their benefits for insiders. There are two ways this may be the case.

The first is the terms of trade prisoner's dilemma, discussed in Chapter 6.[76] Regulating states may impose standards that would be inefficient in the absence of terms of trade effects, knowing some of the cost is borne by foreign exporters. The problems with this approach, including in particular the practical relevance of terms of trade effects in trade agreements, have been discussed in Chapter 6.[77] Its account of SPS and TBT broadly tracks the protectionist approaches discussed above.

The second is through fragmentation from uncoordinated domestic policy-making.[78] Variations in domestic standards impose costs on producers who must either comply with multiple standards, or produce different products for each market, or accept exclusion from one or more potential markets.[79] These problems become particularly prominent in the context of transnational value chains, where production involves multiple enterprises across multiple jurisdictions. While domestic efficiency accounts emphasize tradeoffs between costs and benefits domestically, this approach emphasizes costs for outsiders, whose interests are not counted in domestic politics.[80]

---

[75] This deregulatory tendency is emphasized in (Du, 2010). On the possibility international standards might "ratchet up" regulations: (Charnovitz, 1999: 284–285; Scott, 2007: 261–266).

[76] E.g. (Mavroidis, 2012: 677; Rigod, 2013: 520–529; Weiler & Neven, 2005: 314–315).

[77] §6.2.1.

[78] (Dunoff, 2006b: 164; Scott, 2007: 41–44; Thomas, 1999: 491; Van den Bossche & Zdouc, 2013: 851–852). This concern partly motivates Trachtman's "constitutional economics" approach: (Trachtman, 2006: 632–634, 638–640, 2007: 639–651). For a variation emphasizing participation and broad deliberation: (Shaffer, 2008). Cf. Jackson's "power allocation" approach: (Jackson, 2003: 797–800).

[79] On the various costs involved: (Sykes, 1999a: 52–57). Cf. (Du, 2010; Mayeda, 2004: 742; McDonald, 2005: 251). For an econometric analysis of the costs imposed by developed country regulations on developing country producers in particular: (Maskus et al., 2005).

[80] (Green & Epps, 2007: 289) Cf. (Bagwell et al., 2002: 60–61; Hoekman & Trachtman, 2010: 155–156). It is not unusual for scholars to move between local and global accounts without acknowledging this. E.g. (Chang, 2003: 764–766; Perdikis et al., 2001: 385–386; Trebilcock & Howse, 2005: 202; Trebilcock & Soloway, 2002).

Where regulation imposes significant costs on outsiders to achieve limited gains for insiders, it will be globally inefficient, even if locally efficient.[81] This generates a second prisoner's dilemma that depends on uncoordinated domestic regulation not terms of trade manipulation.[82] This might alternatively be understood as an impure coordination game, where mutual coordination is preferable, but states disagree on the coordination point.[83]

The problem is solved through a combination of international harmonization, and global cost–benefit constraints.[84] This view therefore emphasizes the Regulation Agreements' harmonization provisions, counseling strictly policing departures from international standards.[85] It suggests reviewing regulations for *bona fides* and unnecessary restrictiveness, but also for whether benefits for regulating states outweigh costs for outsiders.[86] It suggests interpreting science and risk provisions strictly, to ensure outsiders are not sacrificed to address remote or

---

[81] Regan suggests this is economically incoherent because any international inefficiency is internalized through price changes: (Regan, 2006; 2007: 958). For a similar view: (Sykes, 1999a). I do not need to resolve this point. It suffices that both scholars and policy-makers understand these agreements as addressing such inefficiencies. We can examine their fit without adjudicating economic coherence.

[82] (Reid, 2010). On the range of possible responses to regulatory conflict: (Sykes, 1999a: 61–70, 2000). Note that the problem here is distinct from the regulatory race-to-the-bottom. While this latter problem may or may not be real, there is no plausible reading of the Regulation Agreements that suggests they can solve it.

[83] For an account of regulatory harmonization in these terms: (Drezner, 2007: ch. 3–4). Divergent preferences over coordination points may be particularly relevant given differing levels of development: (Mayeda, 2004: 751–754). Of course, states may frequently prefer to maintain their own regulatory standards than coordinate on any other, making harmonization suboptimal: (Sykes, 1999a: 68–70).

[84] (Buthe, 2008: 232, 244–247; Trachtman, 2007). Scott's account of WTO law as judicial review, improving the democratic credentials of legislation by offering accountability to affected outsiders, falls under this approach. However, her largely procedural approach does not resolve how the interests of outsiders should feature in decision-making: (Scott, 2004a: 19–21).

[85] (McDonald, 2005: 266; Thomas, 1999: 514–516; Wijkström & McDaniels, 2013: 1014, 1017). Scott emphasizes the SPS Committee as a tool of regulatory coordination: (Scott, 2007: 45–48). Cf. (Lang & Scott, 2009a). The delegation of standard-setting to specialized organizations supports the view of regulation as an impure coordination game: (Buthe, 2008: 247–250). On the various interactions with international standard-setting bodies: (Howse, 2006; Livermore, 2006; Scott, 2004b; Stewart & Johanson, 1998; Winickoff & Bushey, 2010). A potential competitive fairness argument for harmonization parallels that considered in respect of trade remedies, and can be dismissed for similar reasons: (Gruszczynski, 2010: 77–78).

[86] This gives sense, for example, to the "risks nonfulfillment" language in TBT 2.2. Cf. (Desmedt, 2001: 459–460; Du, 2011: 276–277). Mavroidis, reading TBT as largely anti-protectionist, welcomes the AB's rejection of this interpretation: (Mavroidis, 2013: 522).

speculative risks.[87] It emphasizes equivalence obligations and performance requirements as minimizing unnecessary market fragmentation.[88]

While no doubt reflecting an important motivation for these agreements, global efficiency also faces problems of fit. Most obviously, both agreements' emphasis on states' freedom to determine levels of protection undermines calls for cost–benefit balancing.[89] Further, harmonization rules seem too weak for this account[90]; if states can freely depart from standards that do not achieve their goals, then it is hard to see what additional efficiencies these disciplines achieve.[91]

9.2.3   Equality in Global Commerce

EGC understands the Regulation Agreements as primarily disciplining Domestic Economic Measures; and secondarily disciplining ETMs not addressed elsewhere.

Explaining these agreements under EGC requires first distinguishing how the measures they address map onto EGC's categories. Three points arise.

First, SPS serves both to discipline measures complying with GATT, and to clarify an existing exception thereto.[92] In consequence, whereas technical regulations are reviewed under both GATT and TBT, SPS measures are only reviewed under SPS.[93] SPS must therefore deal comprehensively with both ETMs and DEMs. By contrast, many non-SPS ETMs will also be disciplined under GATT, as discussed in Chapter 4.[94]

---

[87] For the tradeoff between strict review, domestic autonomy, and trade benefits: (Peel, 2012: 431).

[88] (Donahue, 2000: 371–373).

[89] There are suggestions of balancing in some SPS cases but the better view is that balancing is not required. Similarly while there are suggestions of balancing under TBT, particularly in *COOL*, these are by no means clear: (Marceau, 2013: 21, 28).

[90] (Motaal, 2004; Scott, 2004b: 327–329; Victor, 1999: 871–872, 926–929). *US-Chickens (China)*, (Panel), §7.465–7.483.

[91] A weaker global efficiency approach would apply only necessity or least restrictive alternative tests. Elements of this appear in: (Scott, 2004a). However, absent balancing, costs to outsiders are unnecessary to motivate this approach, which fits more readily under regulatory rationality.

[92] (Andemariam, 2006: 525–526; Scott, 2007: 9–10).

[93] SPS Art. 2.4. Cf. (Scott, 2007: 29–30); *US-Poultry (China)*, (Panel), §7.465–7.483.

[94] This might seem backwards given recent AB practice of addressing TBT before GATT. However the AB's interpreting TBT 2.1 in light of GATT Art. I, III, and XX supports this view. See e.g. *US-Clove Cigarettes*, (AB), §109; *EC-Seal Products*, (AB), §5.121–5.126. Similarly, while SPS measures are reviewable under GATT, the combination of 2.4 SPS and the interpretation in *US-Poultry (China)* means SPS will generally be determinative.

Second, while measures disciplined under GATT can be understood as ETMs,[95] not all ETMs are disciplined under GATT. Not all ETMs will be either border measures or discriminatory regulations, even applying the modified aims and effects approach suggested in Chapter 6. Such non-GATT ETMs may be addressed under these agreements.

Third, SPS measures are defined by their purpose, protecting human animal and plant life within the regulating Member State.[96] This constitutes an important aspect of self-determination, as that concept was elaborated in Chapter 5; a people that cannot protect these interests lacks effective self-determination. SPS measures constituting ETMs are therefore potentially justifiable under EGC's self-determination proviso.[97] They remain distinct, however, from SPS measures constituting DEMs, which are justified as exercises of, rather than necessarily measures protecting, self-determination.

The first function that EGC suggests the Regulation Agreements serve is as a discipline on DEMs.

Recall, EGC regards DEMs as justified under self-determination, provided they do not impair the basic rights of outsiders, or their capacity to become or remain well ordered. Subject to that proviso, outsiders cannot object to such measures, regardless of their distributive effects. However, we might still inquire whether effects on outsiders are a necessary consequence of that self-determination. In many cases, they may not be, at least in any valuable sense. The failures of regulatory rationality or discursive democracy highlighted above will be relevant here. However, the point is not limited to these cases. There may be many situations where costs are imposed on outsiders for no gain for insiders. To the extent outsiders bear costs, not in consequence of a people's pursuit of valued goals, but simply due to shortsightedness, irrationality, or regulatory capture, this may not be justified.[98] This claim remains distinct from regulatory rationality and discursive democracy, however, in seeing outsiders' claims as having independent moral standing, rather than being proxies for domestic interests. However, these are not claims to have their interests weighed against those of insiders, as advocates of global cost–benefit analysis suggest; but only to be protected from being sacrificed without this serving any meaningful purpose.

---

[95] See §6.2.3 above.   [96] SPS Annex A. Cf. (Scott, 2007: 17–25).

[97] This assumes the territorial scope of SPS measures mirrors that of the state, the most obvious reading of Annex. A. For some doubts on this: (Scott, 2007: 11–12).

[98] Recall, even in respect of DEMs, justification is due, albeit mutual recognition of the value of self-determination makes that justification relatively straightforward. See §3.4 above.

This implies only limited disciplines. It suggests procedural requirements that improve the regulatory process without restricting goals pursued or means adopted.[99] It suggests transparency requirements so outsiders can assess measures' justification.[100] It supports equivalence, necessity, and restrictiveness tests, but with substantial deference to regulatory choice.[101] Importantly for later discussion, it suggests legitimate objectives in TBT be understood in broad terms, as the permissible goals of DEMs are not restricted in the way those of ETMs are. Further, it suggests acknowledging the full range of objectives measures pursue, including minimizing regulatory costs.[102]

A second function is disciplining ETMs not caught by GATT Core Disciplines.

Not all ETMs are border measures or discriminatory regulations.[103] The EU Seal regime, for example, pursues its animal welfare goals by reducing the international demand for seal products, and thus the incentives for foreign hunters to engage in seal hunting. So understood, it clearly constitutes an ETM, but not necessarily a discriminatory one.[104] TBT in particular can address such measures.

This second function implies more extensive and intrusive disciplines than the first. In TBT, it implies legitimate objectives be read as justifiable, in the terms appropriate to ETMS, as discussed in Chapter 7. This suggests a function for the illustrative list in Article 2.2, identifying objectives that may be legitimate for these purposes.[105] A more restrictive approach is similarly implied in policing ETMs pursuing these legitimate objectives; whereas with DEMs the permissibility of diverse objectives suggests according wide discretion to regulating states, for ETMs the range of legitimate objectives is narrower, so we must carefully ensure measures are not tailored to advance other, illegitimate, ones.[106] Similarly, the need

---

[99] E.g. SPS 5; TBT 2.2, 5–8.   [100] E.g. SPS 7; TBT 2.5, 2.9.

[101] E.g. SPS 2.2, 4; TBT 2.2, 2.7, 2.8.

[102] Necessity is thus understood less strictly than under Art. XX GATT. The provisions' different wording, the contrast between closed and open lists of objectives, and their different roles as rule and exception, provide adequate justification.

[103] See §1.6.1 above.

[104] *EC-Seal Products*, (Panel), §7.374. The alternative public morals explanation might constitute the regime as a DEM; this possibility is discussed in Chapters 1 and 7 above. While *Seals* included discrimination complaints, this point applies regardless of these. The AB's restrictive interpretation of technical regulation in *Seals* (§5.25–5.46) does pose a potential objection, albeit one whose impact remains to be seen.

[105] See §5.6, 7.3.2 above.

[106] The analysis here is similar to that under the Art. XX chapeau.

for and effectiveness of ETMs, including their scientific basis, might be more strictly policed than DEMs.[107] A more demanding approach to harmonization, and justifying departures therefrom, is also suggested, in line with the Article XX approach outlined in Chapter 7.

A third function, served specifically by SPS, is to clarify when ETMs protecting human animal and plant life are justified.

SPS in part constitutes a gloss on XX (b) GATT; and the considerations EGC makes relevant to Article XX are potentially relevant here also.[108] This function is served by procedural requirements in SPS, and by its emphasis on science.[109] To the extent SPS addresses ETMs, it must require their justification not simply in the democratic terms appropriate to DEMs, but rather in shared terms acceptable to outsiders directly subject to them. Science plays a key role here. However, SPS also applies to DEMs. To the extent the justificatory demands of these two classes differ, EGC suggests different emphases in applying SPS disciplines to each.[110]

A fourth function is to police, albeit weakly, EGC's DEM Proviso protecting the basic rights of outsiders and their capacity to become or remain well ordered.[111]

We find some recognition of this in provisions for SDT and technical assistance.[112] While largely hortatory, these recognize both that developed countries' regulations may negatively impact developing countries, and that there is a duty to ameliorate those impacts, whether by taking account of them in designing regulations, or minimizing them through technical assistance.[113] The hortatory quality of these obligations can be explained by the sufficientarian nature of the underlying duty. The mere fact that DEMs have negative effects on outsiders does not make them unjust, provided they do not impair basic rights or self-determination[114];

---

[107] This reflects the different structures of justification for each. Transparency and least restrictive alternative tests are similarly relevant here.

[108] See especially §5.5, 7.3.2, 7.3.3.1 above.   [109] I.e. Art. 2.2, 3.3 and 5.

[110] Cf. fn. 227 below.   [111] See §1.6.3, 3.5, 3.7.

[112] TBT 11, 13; SPS 9, 10. Without explicitly addressing the "development dimension," these agreements' disciplines generally might also serve this purpose by promoting rational regulation and thus minimizing unnecessary impacts: (Scott, 2007: 282–284). Prevost distinguishes between concerns for developing countries' capacities to implement the SPS disciplines, and their capacity to comply with SPS measures adopted by others. This paragraph focuses on the latter: (Prevost, 2005: 88).

[113] On the limited effectiveness of both, and proposals under the Doha negotiations: (Scott, 2007: 284–302) Cf. (Jaiswal, 2003: 4378–4379; Mayeda, 2004: 759–761; Prevost, 2005: 90–102). Such provisions are particularly difficult to explain under domestic efficiency accounts: they are more readily reconcilable with global efficiency approaches.

[114] §1.6.3 above.

but the causal complexity this latter standard implies makes a strict rule unworkable. As with SDT under GATT, this implies legal discretion obscures moral obligation.[115]

9.2.4   Adjudicating the Approaches

EGC thus offers a plausible account of the Regulation Agreements. However, existing theories similarly account for many of the key features. Each faces problems of fit, but none is fatal. Adjudicating whether EGC can add to our understanding of these agreements, or guide their interpretation, therefore requires looking in greater detail at specific issues, and the case-law thereunder. Three areas where the various approaches most clearly diverge are in their understanding of legitimate objectives in Article 2.2 TBT, of science and risk under SPS, and of international harmonization under both. It is therefore on these that I focus.

9.3   TBT and Legitimate Objectives

The concept of "legitimate objective" is central to EGC's account of TBT. In this it differs from other approaches discussed above.

Article 2.2 TBT's least trade restrictive alternative test refers to fulfillment of "a legitimate objective." Regulation is permitted only to the extent necessary to fulfill such objectives. Discrimination and unnecessary restrictiveness arise only once a legitimate objective is identified.[116] Legitimate objectives are similarly prerequisites for departing from international standards,[117] and explaining the justification of trade restrictive regulations to outsiders.[118] The scope of legitimate objectives is therefore crucial to TBT.

Yet TBT does not define legitimate objectives. While Article 2.2 provides an "illustrative list,"[119] the AB has emphasized this list is open: not all legitimate objectives are listed.[120] The question therefore arises how we identify such objectives.

Two approaches appear in the case-law.

---

[115] See §7.2.2–3 above.   [116] (Mavroidis & Saggi, 2014: 315).   [117] Art. 2.4.
[118] Art. 2.5.
[119] The third sentence of Article 2.2 TBT provides: "Such legitimate objectives are, *inter alia*: national security requirements; the prevention of deceptive practices; protection of human health or safety, animal or plant life or health, or the environment" (emphasis in original).
[120] *US-Tuna II*, (AB), §313.

The question was first addressed by the panel in *EC-Sardines*, which accorded broad discretion to states in identifying legitimate objectives. It first noted that the list in Article 2.2 was open, also referring to the preamble's recognition of other objectives and its emphasis on nondiscrimination and members' right to determine their appropriate level of protection.[121] From these it concluded that "it is up to the Members to decide which policy objectives they wish to pursue and the levels at which they wish to pursue them," distinguishing TBT's deference on goals from its stricter policing of means.[122] Panels must still determine whether a member's goals are legitimate[123]; but the content of that inquiry seemed to focus on their genuineness, as supported by "*relevant public policies or other social norms*".[124]

The panel in *US-COOL* addressed more directly whether an objective – providing consumers with country of origin information – was legitimate. Having recited the *Sardines* Panel's approach,[125] it examined the text of Article 2.2, concluding from "[t]he type of objectives explicitly listed" that "the legitimacy of a given objective must be found in the 'genuine nature' of the objective, which is 'justifiable' and 'supported by relevant public policies or other social norms'."[126] As the list is open, the panel reasoned, "a wide range of objectives could potentially fall within the scope of legitimate objectives" and there is no "explicit requirement" that objectives be linked in nature to those explicitly listed.[127]

Canada in that case denied that consumers had any interest in receiving the relevant information.[128] However, given evidence of the widespread practice among WTO members of mandatory country of origin labeling, the panel concluded that such consumer information objectives were considered legitimate by a large proportion of WTO members.[129] It further noted the inclusion of consumer protection as a legitimate objective under the Accountancy Disciplines.[130] Finally, the panel considered evidence of US consumer attitudes to country of origin information.[131] While recognizing the risks of relying on such evidence, the panel found it, together with evidence of practice in other states, demonstrated that

---

[121] *EC-Sardines*, (Panel), §7.118–7.119.   [122] Ibid., §7.120.

[123] Howse highlights this claim in criticizing this case: (Howse, 2002e: 253) Cf. (Mathis, 2002: 342).

[124] *EC-Sardines*, (Panel), §7.121 quoting *Canada-Pharmaceutical Patents* (Panel). Cf. (AB), §286.

[125] *US-COOL*, (Panel), §7.631.   [126] Ibid., §7.632.   [127] Ibid., §7.634.

[128] Ibid., §7.633.   [129] Ibid., §7.638.   [130] Ibid., §7.639.   [131] Ibid., §7.645–7.649.

"consumers generally are interested in having information on the origin of the products they purchase."[132]

In concluding, the panel observed that "whether an objective is legitimate cannot be determined in a vacuum, but must be assessed in the context of the world in which we live. Social norms must be accorded due weight."[133] The objective at issue was "in keeping with the requirements of current social norms in a considerable part of the WTO Membership," and hence legitimate.[134]

A different approach appears in the *US-Tuna II* panel, and the *Tuna* and *COOL* AB reports.

In *Tuna*, the legitimacy of the objectives pursued was explicitly challenged.[135] The panel confirmed that legitimacy was an independent requirement, prior to trade restrictiveness.[136] Having noted that it was for the panel to determine objectives' legitimacy,[137] it concluded that the objectives at issue fell under categories mentioned in Article 2.2, the prevention of deceptive practices, and the protection of animal or plant life or health, or the environment.[138] The latter objectives, as expressed there, did not include any express or implied restriction to endangered species, or link to broader conservation objectives.[139] Further, the objectives "relate[d] to genuine concerns in relation to the protection of the life or health of dolphins and deception of consumers in this respect."[140] Finally, the panel emphasized states' right to determine the policies they wish to pursue.[141]

The *Tuna* AB offered some more general comments on this question. Working from dictionary definitions of "legitimate" and "objective," it found that "a 'legitimate objective' is an aim or target that is lawful, justifiable or proper."[142] It further observed that the list in Article 2.2 was open, constituting "a reference point for which other objectives may be considered to be legitimate."[143] Finally, it referred interpreters to the recitals to TBT, and to "objectives recognized in the provisions of other Covered Agreements [which] may provide guidance for, or may inform,

---

[132] Ibid., §7.650.   [133] Ibid.   [134] Ibid, §7.650.   [135] *US-Tuna II*, (Panel), §7.380.
[136] Ibid., §7.387–7.388. Cf. §7.406.   [137] Ibid., §7.393.
[138] The *US-Clove Cigarettes* Panel had previously found (§7.347), on an uncontested point, that mention of the objective in Art. 2.2 settled its legitimacy.
[139] *US-Tuna II*, (Panel), Ibid., §7.437.   [140] Ibid., §7.438.   [141] Ibid., §7.441–442.
[142] *US-Tuna II*, (AB), §313. There is an ambiguity here. "Lawful" presumably requires only compatibility with the Covered Agreements, while "justifiable" and "proper" suggest a broader examination, and more demanding test.
[143] Ibid.

the analysis of what might be considered a legitimate objective under Article 2.2."[144] It also showed less deference than the *Sardines* panel in identifying the objective pursued.[145]

The *COOL* AB, while endorsing the panel's conclusions, rejected its reasoning in favor of that applied in *Tuna*, first parsing Article 2.2, and then referring to the recitals and the other provisions of the Covered Agreements to determine the objectives' legitimacy.[146] It linked the consumer information objective at issue to preventing deceptive practices, mentioned in Articles 2.2 TBT and XX (d) GATT, and protecting marks of origin, mentioned in Article IX GATT.[147]

It also criticized the panel's reasoning. It queried the basis on which the panel concluded consumers generally are interested in receiving information of the relevant kind.[148] It also queried on what basis the panel linked the objective at issue to consumer protection in the Accountancy Disciplines.[149] Finally, it expressed "some difficulties" understanding the relationship in the panel's reasoning between "the practice in a considerable proportion of WTO Members" and "social norms," and the role these factors played in its analysis.[150]

The *Seals* Panel closely followed the AB in *Tuna* and *COOL*. As public morals are not mentioned in Article 2.2, it looked to the other sources suggested: the recitals to TBT, and objectives recognized elsewhere in the Covered Agreements.[151] Given public morals appear in Article XX (a) GATT and Article XIV (a) GATS, the panel held they constituted a legitimate objective under TBT.[152]

The panel next considered whether addressing public moral concerns about seal welfare fell under this legitimate objective. Referring to GATT/GATS case-law, it noted that "*public morals* is a relative term which needs to be defined based on the standard of right and wrong in a given society."[153] Given the established fact of concern for seal welfare in the EU, the panel found addressing such concerns constituted a legitimate objective.[154] It further noted evidence of practices in other states and international instruments on animal welfare, suggesting "that animal welfare is a globally recognized issue," further supporting its conclusion that addressing such public moral concerns was a legitimate objective.[155]

---

[144] Ibid.   [145] Ibid., §314.   [146] *US-Cool*, (AB), §444.   [147] Ibid. §445.
[148] Ibid., §450.   [149] Ibid., §451.
[150] Ibid., §448,452. The subsequent Art. 21.5 Panel (§7.332–7.333) did not discuss this issue.
[151] *EC-Seals*, (Panel), §7.416.   [152] Ibid., §7.418.   [153] Ibid., §7.419.   [154] Ibid.
[155] Ibid., §7.420.

There is a clear evolution in these cases, from a permissive approach in the *Sardines* and *COOL* panels, to a more demanding test in *Tuna II* and, most clearly, the *COOL* AB and *Seals* Panel.[156]

Both *Sardines* and the *COOL* Panel identify "legitimate" with "genuine," and accord substantial deference to states to determine the objectives their regulations pursue. A legitimate objective is an objective that the regulating state in fact has, supported by "relevant public policies or other social norms." This in turn suggests nonlegitimate reduces to protectionism or disguised special interests, reflecting the anti-protectionist and regulatory rationality approaches discussed in Part I.

The more recent approach assumes an external standard against which legitimacy is judged. It looks to the Covered Agreements for an "illustration and reference point" in determining that standard. It is the agreements, not the regulating state's *bona fides*, that identify legitimate objectives. How that test works remains unclear. In *Tuna* and *Seals*, the objectives were mentioned in the agreements; while in *COOL* the AB reasoned by analogy from a mentioned objective. This approach clearly implies that there is a category of legitimate objectives, definable apart from the preferences of members or their populations. Such an external standard, implying states may have to compromise their regulatory objectives, accords better with global efficiency accounts of the agreement.

This move from an internal to an external standard poses a challenge. How can the AB draw the line between legitimate and illegitimate objectives in a way that is both practicable and politically defensible?[157]

It might have limited legitimate objectives to those mentioned in Article 2.2 or, more plausibly, the Covered Agreements as a whole. This would at least have provided clear guidance; but it would do so by constituting a closed list, albeit one longer than that in Article 2.2. It would thus raise the same concerns for regulatory autonomy as Article XX[158]; *a fortiori*, because TBT disciplines nondiscriminatory regulation.

Having rejected that approach, however, the AB has not elaborated an alternative. In COOL, it reasoned by analogy from objectives mentioned in the agreements to those at issue in that case, recognizing that consumer information "bears some relation" to the prevention of deceptive

---

[156] Mavroidis adopts a contrary view, identifying a consistently deferential attitude in these cases: (Mavroidis, 2013: 514–515). However, the passages he cites don't support his view. Cf. (Marceau, 2013: 16–17).

[157] On the political concerns this question raises: (Goh, 2006; Markus, 2001). Mavroidis raises the same concern against balancing under TBT 2.2: (Mavroidis, 2013: 522).

[158] See §6.3.3 above.

practices, which is mentioned; and noting that origin marking is mentioned in Article XI, albeit in the form of a restriction rather than a permission.[159] The approach is formalistic. There is no account of the kind of relation that is required. Objectives cannot be required to fall under those mentioned without reducing to a closed list. However, the AB expressly rejected an *esjudem generis* approach, instead referring to the listed objectives as "an illustration and reference point."[160] Without more, determining whether a relation to an existing objective is sufficient must appear arbitrary, providing neither justification nor guidance to Members.[161]

A third possibility, hinted at in the *COOL* and *Seals* Panels, is to adopt an evolutionary approach, looking to members' practices as a whole to determine what constitutes a legitimate objective. References to international instruments and other members' practices can be understood in these terms. However, as noted, the *COOL* AB was skeptical of invocations of international practices.

Lacking clear guidance from either the text or the case-law, we might next ask how the various theoretical approaches might answer this question.

As noted, domestic efficiency approaches converge on some version of the permissive approach of the *Sardines* and *COOL* Panels.[162] To the extent that approach is rejected in the more recent cases, they can offer no guidance in identifying an alternative. The external standard implicit in recent cases seems more compatible with global efficiency accounts. However, while these imply an external standard, their emphasis on domestic benefits and foreign costs support strong balancing, not the categorical approach adopted by the AB. A domestic regulation may be globally inefficient regardless of the objective it pursues. Without strong balancing, restricting objectives achieves little; while with it, such restrictions become superfluous.[163]

EGC, by contrast, can provide an account of legitimacy that reconciles the text of the Agreement and the approaches in the case-law.

---

[159] *US-COOL*, (AB), §445.   [160] Ibid., § 443.
[161] On this omission in COOL: (Mavroidis & Saggi, 2014: 307).
[162] See e.g. (Mavroidis, 2012: 693–694).
[163] We might explain a categorical approach through a hypothetical welfare maximizing the bargain/jurisdictional transaction. Trachtman's constitutional economics is suggestive in this regard. See fn. 78 above. It is however implausible that the AB has the informational resources or political legitimacy to identify new categories in this way.

EGC suggests that legitimacy imports two ideas: first, the permissive standard of justification appropriate to DEMs; and second, the more demanding standard appropriate to ETMs.[164] As regards DEMs, objectives are legitimate to the extent they constitute genuine objectives of the relevant people, reflecting the permissive approach of the *Sardines* and *COOL* panels. As regards ETMs, objectives are legitimate to the extent they reflect ends outsiders have reason to share, reflecting the external standards of *COOL* and *Seals*, complemented by an analysis analogous to that suggested in Chapter 7 in respect of Article XX.

Thus, for example, in considering whether the protection of animal life constitutes a legitimate objective in a given case it suggests going beyond the formalistic observation that animal life is mentioned in Article 2.2, to consider whether and to what extent a measure is justifiable to those on whom it is imposed. For DEMs not subject to SPS, this would require only considering whether it pursued a genuine objective of concern to the regulating member. For ETMs, however, legitimacy would turn, first, on the relation between that objective and the capacity of the regulating state for effective self-determination; and, second, on the extent to which protection of the relevant animal life constituted a shared goal among the relevant states. This latter analysis is familiar from the discussion of *Shrimp* in Chapter 7.[165]

This obviously represents both a revision of, and a development on, the existing jurisprudence. In requiring interrogating objectives mentioned in 2.2, it constitutes a revision[166]. In defining the boundaries of "legitimate objective," it constitutes a development. However, given both the confusion in the existing jurisprudence, and the inability of alternative theoretical approaches to address this issue, EGC offers the most plausible route towards a satisfactory resolution. There is nothing here that is entirely novel: both permissive and restrictive standards appear in the case-law; and the Article 2.2 illustrative list, together with the established analogy to Article XX GATT, provide adequate textual basis. EGC simply gives coherence to these disparate approaches.

---

[164] §9.2.3 above.

[165] A further advantage is that this approach avoids substantive moral or policy questions that the AB is ill qualified to consider. The inquiry is a largely positive one, albeit guided by EGC's normative premises. It is quite different to one examining whether, for example, seal hunting is morally or otherwise objectionable, all things considered.

[166] This implies no violence to the text. Rather, it requires interpreting the objectives mentioned in the same way as under Art. XX. It would admittedly involve revisiting the AB's treatment of 'coercive objectives' in *Tuna II* (§334–339).

9.4   SPS and the Authority of Science

SPS might be read as simply elaborating TBT's obligations in the specific context of SPS measures.[167] Legitimate objectives play no role here because SPS measures are defined by their objectives, and these – protecting human, animal, and plant life within the territory of the regulating state – are self-evidently legitimate.[168] We do, however, find nondiscrimination, least trade restrictiveness, international harmonization, and evidence-based regulation. These are specified in greater detail, but this we might expect given SPS's narrower subject matter.[169]

One aspect of SPS that *is* unique, however, is its commitment to science as a benchmark for regulation. Science is explicitly invoked in Articles 2.2, 3.3, 5.2, and 5.7, and implicitly in 4.1("objectively demonstrates"), and 5.1 ("risk assessment"). SPS measures must be "based on scientific principles," and supported by "sufficient scientific evidence"; members may only depart from international standards with "scientific justification"; they must accept the equivalence of other members' SPS measures where objectively demonstrated, presumably by scientific evidence; they must base SPS measures on a risk assessment taking into account available scientific evidence; and where scientific evidence is insufficient they must seek to obtain it. Science thus constitutes an all-purpose threshold of justifiability.

This privileged role for science raises two prominent concerns.

The first, and most obvious, is that science cannot determine the desirability or otherwise of regulation.[170] Science might identify and, ideally, quantify a risk. It might also estimate the effectiveness of responses, and associated costs and benefits. However it provides no mechanism for weighing those costs and benefits to determine whether a risk merits response.[171] That is necessarily a political question, reflecting a society's risk appetite or social welfare function.[172] Scientific authority thus has limited scope. It might estimate the risk to human health from hormone treated beef, or to native apples from fire blight; but it cannot determine whether that risk is worth taking, given associated

---

[167] E.g. (Hoekman & Kostecki, 2009: 252; Van den Bossche & Zdouc, 2013: 895).
[168] SPS, Annex A.1. Cf. TBT 2.2, GATT XX (b), §5.5, 7.3.2 above.   [169] (Motaal, 2004).
[170] (Atik, 1996: 737).
[171] (Peel, 2010; Reid, 2012: 536). An analogous point, albeit in respect of TBT, appears in (Howse & Levy, 2013).
[172] (Cheyne, 2006; Howse, 2000: 2342; Perez, 2007). On the implications of culture and risk for cost–benefit analysis: (Kahan et al., 2006). For a more skeptical response: (Sunstein, 2006).

benefits.[173] However, if science cannot answer this question, some query the substantive significance of these obligations.[174]

The second is less obvious but more fundamental. It challenges the ostensible objectivity of science.[175] Drawing on critical perspectives in the philosophy and sociology of science, it emphasizes the provisional nature of scientific knowledge, and the political nature of scientific consensus.[176] It denies that science can express objective reason, and in consequence denies scientific claims universal validity.[177] To the extent it is accepted, it undermines even those purposes the first concern suggests science might play. If science cannot reliably describe an objective reality, then there is little reason to privilege scientific risk assessments over purely political or democratic ones.[178] Thus, in one version, this concern is expressed as SPS unjustifiably privileging "scientific rationality" over an equally valid "social rationality."[179]

How these concerns are answered turns on the function these disciplines serve.[180]

If we assume SPS addresses protectionism or regulatory rationality we will want to distinguish between political and scientific roles, as suggested by the first concern, and to ensure that the latter not impinge on the former. The absence of scientific evidence might imply that regulations are protectionist or otherwise irrational; but overly demanding evidence requirements risk unnecessarily restricting regulatory autonomy.[181]

---

[173] Advocates of cost–benefit analysis might dispute this.   [174] (Sykes, 2002: 266–268).

[175] For an overview: (Peel, 2010: ch. 3, 2012: 440–446; Reid, 2012: 541; Scott, 2007: 77–80).

[176] (Peel, 2010: 94–96); Perez, 2007; Motaal, 2004).

[177] (Atik, 1996: 746–751; Green & Epps, 2007: 304–306; Kahan et al., 2006: 1092–1094; Peel, 2010: 96–98).

[178] (Davies, 2007; Howse & Horn, 2009; Peel, 2010: 85–88). This objection shades into a related point about social construction of risk perceptions. The two issues are distinct: the latter is more concerned with political value than epistemology; but both motivate a move from scientific to social risk assessment: (Peel, 2010: 104–107).

[179] (Footer, 2007; Isaac & Kerr, 2003). For an account contrasting scientific and cultural responses to food safety: (Echols, 2001).

[180] For a review of the alternatives: (Shaffer, 2008: 34–35). Cf. (Gruszczynski, 2010: 148–153). I do not address purely procedural aspects of risk assessments, as these seem equally compatible with each of the approaches considered.

[181] (Guzman, 2004a: 11–15; Howse, 2000: 2341; Quintillhn, 1999; Sykes, 2002; Trebilcock & Soloway, 2002: 541–543). For the view that science requirements reflect anti-protectionist concerns: (Peel, 2010: 177). Purely domestic theories are not, of course, committed to a precautionary approach. Many polities might, for purely domestic reasons, prefer a more demanding standard for regulations. However, this is neither a necessary condition for regulation to be non-protectionist/rational, nor a choice that such views mandate being made internationally (Chang, 2003: 750–758; Howse, 2000: 2337).

Domestic efficiency approaches might also concede the second challenge. If science is itself political then its authority must be subject to political – and preferably democratic – control.[182] If a democratic polity concludes, absent scientific evidence, that a risk exists, then neither protectionism nor regulatory rationality accounts require overriding that conclusion.[183]

Global efficiency approaches, by contrast, are likely to reject both concerns as overstated. If we want to weigh regulations' benefits for insiders against costs for outsiders, substantive scientific evidence requirements can help police that balance.[184] Maximizing global rather than local welfare implies both the need for proportionality between risk and response, and that this proportionality is an appropriate object of international concern.[185] Global efficiency approaches must be similarly skeptical of challenges to scientific objectivity. They can accept this critique in principle, while denying that social rationality, understood in domestic terms, provides an attractive alternative. Insiders might have reason to prefer political assessments of risk, but for outsiders science retains a more plausible epistemic authority than the potentially capricious preferences of another polity.[186] Further, there is little reason on this approach to defer to the scientific views of the regulating state, which can only reflect the social rationality that science serves to displace.[187]

EGC suggests a more qualified response.

---

[182] (Howse, 2000: 2243; Kahan et al., 2006: 1106–1108).

[183] (Chang, 2003: 756–758; Echols, 2001: 152; Howse, 2000; Howse & Levy, 2013). As Scott observes, democratic responses to risk may play different roles, whether justifying regulation or explaining inconsistency: (Scott, 2007: 149–151). Obviously advocates of domestic approaches might also favor science-based regulation for purely domestic reasons, and domestic legal systems may require it: (Atik, 1996: 736). To the extent they do, they must answer critics of science on their own terms, explaining why epistemically limited scientific claims should trump an otherwise valid political preference. This is the 'cryptically elitist' position that Howse rejects: (Howse, 2000: 2337). Dunoff reaches similar conclusions under Embedded Liberalism: (Dunoff, 2006b: 172). For a mixed approach, combining scientific objectivity, value judgment and political choice: (Biber-Klemm et al., 2011: 302–310).

[184] (Thomas, 1999: 515–517).

[185] E.g. (Shaffer, 2008: 32–33, 38–41; Thomas, 1999: 590–491). On the informational demands implicit in global efficiency accounts, albeit in a domestic balancing model: (Bown & Trachtman, 2009).

[186] See e.g. (Shaffer & Trachtman, 2011: 147–149). Peel, examining international law as a vertical legitimacy problem, highlights science's role as a stand-in for democratic legitimacy: (Peel, 2010: 49–55).

[187] Both points emerge, albeit as corollaries, in: (Atik, 1996). For an analogous point: (Wijkström & McDaniels, 2013: 1036–1038).

On the first challenge, and the distinction between science and politics, it agrees with the domestic efficiency approach. At least as regards DEMs, overly demanding scientific evidence requirements risk undermining self-determination. Science may be valuable in assuring outsiders that measures pursue some minimally rational objective, and are not either disguised ETMs, or wholly irrational exercises imposing costs on outsiders without any benefit to insiders. But this requires only minimal scientific basis.

To fulfill this role, however, science must constitute a shared standard against which insiders and outsiders can judge a measure. EGC thus shares global efficiency theorists' skepticism of challenges to scientific rationality. Even if less sophisticated advocates overstate its claims, scientific assessment remains more accessible to outsiders than purely political judgments.

However, the different structures of justification prescribed by EGC and global efficiency mean objectivity can be relaxed slightly here. To the extent global efficiency approaches balance costs and benefits, they require a strong commitment to objectivity to quantify both. EGC, by contrast, can more readily accommodate uncertainty because it is concerned not to quantify risks, but only confirm their plausibility. This is especially so when considering DEMs; with regard to ETMs, a less deferential attitude may be appropriate.

While SPS's core scientific evidence provisions (Articles 2.2 and 5.2) give little indication which conception of science to prefer,[188] other provisions suggest a role closer to EGC's prescriptions. The emphasis on states' rights to determine their appropriate level of protection supports the distinction, drawn by both domestic efficiency and EGC, between (scientific) assessment of risk and (political) response. The contingent role of international standards similarly suggests the link from science to regulation runs through political choice.[189] However, the emphasis on science, on internationally recognized methods of risk assessment, and on consistency in evaluating and responding to risks, suggest science is understood as objective, in terms preferred by global efficiency and EGC.[190] Finally, Article 5.7, permitting regulation under uncertainty, while compatible with each approach, is more readily reconcilable with EGC's model of sufficient justification than either domestic rationality's concern for *bona fides* or global efficiency's cost–benefit balancing.

---

[188] On the indeterminacy of SPS's account of science: (Peel, 2010: 181–185).
[189] SPS 3.3 See further §9.5 below.   [190] SPS 4.1, 5.1, 5.5, 5.8.

The AB's approach is similarly more readily reconciled with EGC than competing theories.[191]

Consider first the question how far science, divorced from policy, can determine the justifiability of regulation. The AB has addressed this most directly under Articles 2.2, 3.3, and 5.1. Its express statements suggest some ambivalence between requiring proportionality between evidence, risk and response, and requiring only some plausible evidence of a risk that is not wholly speculative. However in practice it applies the latter, less demanding standard, upholding complaints only after comprehensively reviewing and dismissing all plausible scientific bases for particular regulations.[192]

Hormones exemplifies the more permissive view. The AB, discussing the precautionary principle, emphasized both members' right to establish their appropriate level of protection, and the role of "prudence and precaution" in dealing with irreversible risks.[193] It later rejected the suggestion Article 5.1 required evidence of a "minimum magnitude of risk," accepting only that there must be something more than "theoretical uncertainty."[194] It read the requirement that measures be based on a risk assessment as demanding only "a certain objective relationship" between evidence evaluated and measure challenged, later suggesting that "the results of the risk assessment must sufficiently warrant – that is to say, reasonably support – the SPS measure at stake."[195] SPS demands neither a particular threshold of risk, nor a particular weight of evidence, provided there is some evidence to suggest that the risk exists.[196] Thus, where scientific opinion diverges, members may rely on minority or "divergent" opinions.[197] In such cases, by assumption, the weight of evidence will be *against* the existence of the relevant risk. It was the lack of *any* evidence supporting the risk at issue that led both panel and AB to find for the complainants in that case.[198]

The AB in *Continued Suspension* emphasized the rational relationship between evidence, risk and measure, as opposed to a minimum

---

[191] On the AB's treatment of 'appropriate level of protection': (Scott, 2007: 35–40).
[192] On the difficulty holding these questions separate, (Weiler & Neven, 2005: 320–322).
[193] *EC-Hormones*, (AB), §124.
[194] Ibid., §186. There is admittedly a minimal threshold here, given a theoretical risk is greater than zero risk. However, this goes more to science's epistemic authority than its policy domain.
[195] Ibid., §193.
[196] For an interpretation in these terms: (Davey, 2006: 131). For an interpretation reading the case as more demanding: (Sykes, 2002: 266–267).
[197] *EC-Hormones*, (AB), §194.   [198] Ibid., §205–209.

magnitude of risk.[199] These cases' acceptance of a zero-risk ALOP and their treatment of the risk assessment/risk management distinction similarly express a concern to ensure that science does not preempt political choice.[200]

Japan-Apples, by contrast, is sometimes cited as requiring proportionality between risk and regulation.[201] The panel's conclusion, accepted by the AB, that the measures at issue were "clearly disproportionate to the risk identified by the scientific evidence" implies such a relationship.[202] The evidence there suggested that the risk at issue was "negligible," a threshold acknowledged as higher than a merely "theoretical" risk.[203] The treatment of "small" or "debatable" risks in assigning the burden of proof seems similarly to suggest a role for proportionality.[204]

The view that sufficiency implies a substantive threshold also finds some support in the AB's view, in *Varietals*, that Article 2.2 is not restricted to situations where evidence is "patently" insufficient, instead inquiring whether there was "a rational or objective relationship between the SPS measure and the scientific evidence."[205] In so far as this suggests some evidence of risk is insufficient, it similarly implies some proportionality element.[206]

Finally, the AB's approach in *Salmon*, emphasizing the need to go beyond identifying the possibility of adverse effects to evaluate their likelihood or probability, arguably implies a more demanding approach.[207] However, the AB in that case also cited with approval its observations in *Hormones* that likelihood need not be evaluated in quantitative terms, and that there was no requirement to establish a certain magnitude or threshold of risk.[208]

Notwithstanding these ambiguous observations, in each of *Apples*, *Hormones*, and *Varietals* the AB upheld adverse findings only after concluding there was no plausible scientific evidence supporting challenged measures[209]; and in *Continued Suspension*, it overturned an adverse panel

---

[199] *US-Continued Suspension*, (AB), §569.   [200] Ibid., §534–543.

[201] E.g. (Gruszczynski, 2006: 375, 394–395; Mavroidis, 2012: 722–723; Scott, 2007: 90–91).

[202] *Japan-Apples*, (Panel), §163.

[203] *Japan-Apples*, (AB), §239–242 Cf. (Mavroidis, 2012: 723).

[204] *Japan-Apples*, (AB), §160.   [205] *Japan-Varietals*, (AB), §82–84.

[206] For a contrary reading: (Howse, 2000: 2349).   [207] *Australia-Salmon*, (AB), §123.

[208] Ibid., §124.

[209] Notwithstanding the language in *Japan-Apples*, the AB's review of the evidence suggests that it was insufficient even by the *Hormones* standard. This is most obvious in its discussion (§186–188) of historical and practical experience.

finding because there was such a plausible basis.[210] It thus seems that, in practice, scientific evidence is a threshold matter: provided there is some plausible evidence of risk, measures can be justified. Science is a gatekeeper, but cannot dictate the levels of risk members accept.

On the second challenge, to the objectivity and authority of science, the AB's approach again accords more readily with EGC than competing explanations. The democratic skepticism that this concern suggests domestic rationality theorists should hold has been explicitly rejected by the AB. However, the commitment to scientific certainty and objectivity implicit in global efficiency is similarly rejected. Instead we find a moderate position, in line with EGC.

The authority of science was directly challenged in *Hormones*. The EC argued that, notwithstanding scientific consensus on the safety of the relevant substances, the evidence could not prove this beyond doubt.[211] While in part relating to proportionality, this argument also raised the more fundamental question: if science cannot deliver certainty, how can it deny a state's right to regulate? This implication was clearly recognized by the panel. It accepted a key element of the critique of scientific rationality, observing that "science can never provide certainty."[212] However, it proceeded, the risks raised by the EC "are only the consequences of science not being capable of assuring that no risks will ever arise from a substance."[213] If such risks could justify regulation, then scientific evidence and risk assessment requirements would become moot. To give meaning and effect to these provisions, the authority of science, while contingent, must be defended. The AB agreed, observing that "the uncertainty that theoretically always remains since science can never provide absolute certainty . . . is not the kind of risk which, under Article 5.1, is to be assessed."[214]

This point was reiterated in *Continued Suspension*, where the AB distinguished between "ascertainable risk" and "theoretical uncertainty."[215] Risks must be identified within the shared enterprise of objective scientific inquiry.[216] The residual risk from the limits of science cannot ground justification.[217]

---

[210] *US-Continued Suspension*, (AB), §599–616.
[211] *EC-Hormones*, (Panel), §8.149–8.150.   [212] Ibid., §8.152.   [213] Ibid., §8.153.
[214] *EC-Hormones*, (AB), §186.   [215] *US-Continued Suspension*, (AB), §569, 572.
[216] Ibid., §591 on "reputable" and "legitimate" science, and the need for a "qualified and respected source."
[217] (Scott, 2000: 155).

However, the AB in *Hormones* was also concerned to reject any suggestion that science must offer certainty, or even consensus. It thus emphasized the broad scope of scientific enquiry, understood as "systematic, disciplined and objective enquiry and analysis, that is, a mode of studying and sorting facts and opinions." Risk assessment requires looking "not only to risk ascertainable in a science laboratory operating under strictly controlled conditions, but also risk in human societies as they actually exist."[218] Elsewhere, it criticized the panel's distinguishing of scientific examination (risk assessment) and democratic choice (risk management); rather, it suggested, risk assessment implies a more holistic enterprise.[219] The AB also addressed circumstances where respectable scientific opinion diverges, acknowledging regulation might rely on minority science.[220] While references to "mainstream" and "divergent" views might suggest a concession of objectivity, the simultaneous demand that views come from "qualified and respected sources" reaffirms that science, not politics, acts as epistemic gatekeeper.[221] Political choice plays a role in risk assessment, but that choice is exercised within a context constituted by scientific enquiry. As the AB confirms in *Continued Suspension*, panels and AB must ensure that choice is based on "reputable science."[222] The AB's treatment in *Continued Suspension* of scientific evolution similarly recognizes that uncertainty is part of, and internal to, everyday science, not limited to moments of crisis and revolution.[223]

The AB's approach to the relationship between science and politics thus more clearly reflects the implications of EGC than alternative theories.

Two further points merit mention.

First, various authors, drawing on variants of local efficiency, advocate a greater role for public opinion in risk assessment and management.[224]

---

[218] *EC-Hormones*, (AB), §187.

[219] Ibid., §181 Cf. *US-Continued Suspension*. (AB), §542. See also the AB's discussion in *Continued Suspension* (§534, 685) of the relation between sufficiency of scientific information for the purposes of Art. 5.1 and 5.7, and the politically determined adequate level of protection.

[220] *EC-Hormones*, (AB), §194.

[221] Howse, by contrast, reads *Hormones* as authorizing purely democratic determinations of what constitutes science, which seems irreconcilable with the AB's emphasis on the scientific authority of such divergent sources: (Howse, 2000: 2342–2343).

[222] *US-Continued Suspension*, *(AB)*, § 591, 592, 597–598. On the relation between uncertainty and insufficiency under SPS 5.7: Ibid., §677, 703.

[223] Ibid., §702–707.

[224] See e.g. (Chang, 2003: 772–774; Howse, 2000: 2337–2338; Perdikis et al., 2001: 392–397; Reid, 2012: 542–543) Cf. (Foster, 2009).

Notwithstanding an absence of scientific evidence, they argue public disquiet alone suffices to justify regulation.[225] EGC does not deny that public concerns can justify regulation. However, where those concerns reflect only subjective political sentiments, it denies ETMs are justifiable thereunder. Recalling, as noted above, that SPS constitutes an exemption from GATT, which EGC explains on grounds that SPS measures *ipso facto* pursue shared goals, permitting such subjective preferences to ground SPS measures would mean ETMs pursuing subjective preferences avoiding the disciplines in both GATT and TBT. Where an ostensible SPS measure is grounded in public opinion rather than scientific evidence, EGC suggests it should be considered not as an SPS measure, but rather as a non-SPS border restriction or technical regulation, subject to GATT and TBT.[226]

Second, recall that SPS governs both ETMs and DEMs in pursuit of SPS goals. Because SPS goals are *ipso facto* shared, the distinction between these categories is less significant than elsewhere. However, a higher degree of scrutiny may still be appropriate in respect of ETMs than DEMs pursuing SPS goals. This is picked up primarily in the requirements in Article 2.3 that SPS measures not arbitrarily or unjustifiably discriminate or constitute disguised restrictions on trade. However, it may also be relevant to the questions of scientific evidence and risk assessment. We might more strictly police these requirements in respect of ETMs than DEMs, given the different structures of the justification applicable to each. It is therefore worth noting that the cases where a more demanding approach is suggested, *Varietals*, *Apples*, and *Salmon*, are each concerned with border restrictions, whereas the strongest statements of the less demanding approach, *Hormones* and *Continued Suspension*, address SPS-motivated DEMs. While the AB has not elaborated distinct standards for these two categories, the distinction may explain its seemingly conflicting comments.[227]

---

[225] See in particular (Davies, 2007).

[226] For suggestions along these lines: (Scott, 2000: 159–160). On the problem of dual purpose measures generally: (Shapiro, 2007).

[227] Gruszczynski, discussing standards of review, suggests the AB distinguishes cases involving threats to human health from those involving the spread of pests: (Gruszczynski, 2011: 114). However, as Peel highlights, this distinction breaks down in practice, as does any linking standard of review to the importance of a particular SPS goal: (Peel, 2012: 451–455). We might alternatively distinguish cases falling under the first and second clauses of the risk assessment definition, the former relating to the spread of pests and disease, and the latter to contaminants: (Gruszczynski, 2006: 382). In practice, this latter

9.5   International Standards

Legitimate purposes and scientific justification address the bases on which states regulate. Even without international trade, there are good reasons why regulation should have due regard to each. Other innovations in the Regulation Agreements, by contrast, are more closely tied to the nature of international trade as involving economic activity that spans multiple regulatory spaces. These include rules on transparency, equivalence and, most prominently, international standards, which I consider in this section.[228]

While international standards and harmonization are addressed in slightly different terms in the two agreements, the provisions share an underlying structure around which we can build our analysis. In each case, the agreements do three things: first, they provide a mechanism for identifying what constitutes an international standard; second, they specify one or more relationships that a domestic measure may have to such a standard; and third, they attach particular legal consequences, positive or negative, to those relationships.

Identifying international standards in SPS is straightforward: the agreement specifies three organizations – the Codex Alimentarius Commission, the secretariat of the International Plant Protection Convention, and the International Office for Epizootics – whose standards, guidelines, and recommendations are recognized within their respective areas of competence.[229] The identity of international standards in TBT is less clear. This is perhaps unsurprising: while SPS governs a narrow range of objectives, TBT applies regardless of policy area, precluding a simple list of bodies that might promulgate international standards. Given limited guidance in the agreement, the Appellate Body has relied, *inter alia*, on a decision of the TBT Committee to interpret international standards for these purposes as meaning standards adopted by bodies that are open to all WTO members, and that have recognized activities relevant to standardization.[230]

SPS and TBT also use slightly different language to specify the various ways that a measure may be related to an international standard. Article 2.4 TBT refers to members "us[ing] them, or relevant parts of them, as a

---

distinction should map reasonably onto that between ETMs and DEMs, providing textual basis for this approach.

[228] For this point in respect of common standards: (Bacchus, 2014: 11–12).

[229] SPS Annex A.3. The agreement provides for the SPS Committee to identify further organizations, but none have been identified to date.

[230] *US-Tuna II*, (AB), §359.

basis for their technical regulations," a relation very similar to the requirement in Article 3.1 SPS that members "base their [SPS] measures on international standards, guidelines or recommendations, where they exist."[231] The former has been interpreted as requiring that a measure be founded or built upon, or supported by, the relevant international standard, while the latter is read as requiring that the international standard be the principal constituent or fundamental principle of the measure.[232] These are distinct from "conform to," in Article 3.2 SPS, which requires effective identity between domestic measure and international standard.[233] In the absence of panel or AB guidance, we can assume Article 2.5 TBT's reference to measures being "in accordance with relevant international standards" imports a similarly strict requirement.

Finally, as to the consequences of these various relations. Article 2.4 TBT requires members use international standards, unless they would be "an ineffective or inappropriate means for the fulfillment of the legitimate objectives pursued." Article 3.1 SPS requires that members base their measures on international standards, unless (per Article 3.3) "there is a scientific justification, or as a consequence of the level of sanitary or phytosanitary protection a Member determines to be appropriate." Article 2.5 TBT provides *inter alia* that, where a regulation is adopted for one of the legitimate purposes explicitly mentioned in Article 2.2, and is in accordance with relevant international standards, it is rebuttably presumed not to create an unnecessary obstacle to international trade (and in consequence, to comply with the requirements of Article 2.2). Article 3.2 SPS provides that SPS measures that conform to international standards, guidelines, or recommendations "shall be deemed to be necessary to protect human, animal or plant life or health, and presumed to be consistent with the relevant provisions of [the SPS] Agreement and of the GATT 1994."[234]

The upshot, then, is that members are required to base domestic regulations on international standards unless conditions for departing from these are met. Those conditions are not themselves especially onerous, enquiring whether the international standard would achieve the member's goals, whether described in terms of legitimate objectives or appropriate levels of protection. But there is also an incentive toward harmonization: where members go further and conform to/regulate in

---

[231] While not explicitly stated, this is the clear implication from *EC-Sardines* (AB) §242–243.
[232] *EC-Hormones*, (AB), §163; *EC-Sardines*, (AB), §243.
[233] *EC-Hormones*, (AB), §165, 170.
[234] The presumption here is rebuttable: *EC-Hormones*, (AB), §170.

accordance with international standards, they benefit from deemed or presumed compliance with other obligations in the relevant agreements.

What should we make of these provisions?

First, recall that each of the approaches discussed in Part II could identify some role for international standards. How closely do the provisions in the agreements track those approaches?

Turning first to the domestic approaches, whether narrowly anti-protectionist, or broader domestic efficiency or deliberative democracy accounts. These, recall, recommend minimal restrictions on states' freedom to depart from international standards where these do not fit their domestic goals. While the extent of states' freedom to depart from international standards depends on our interpretations of legitimate objectives and scientific evidence, it is certainly plausible that the relatively low thresholds in Articles 2.4 TBT and 3.3 SPS reflect the prescriptions of these domestic approaches.

However, in their identification of international standards, the rules are less easily reconciled with domestic views. Because domestic approaches understand international standards as potential proxies for non-protectionist regulation, examples of best practice, or potential coordination points, they suggest an inclusive definition, admitting a wide range of potential standards. If international standards are merely examples, rather than authorities, then strictly policing what counts as an international standard risks excluding potentially valuable options. The closed list in SPS, and the AB's relatively demanding approach under TBT, seem too strict on this view.

Domestic approaches also struggle to explain the incentives to conform to international standards. If those standards are simply potentially useful models, then there is little reason to incentivize their adoption. Doing so reduces the capacity of other disciplines to police protectionist or otherwise inefficient regulation, and may lead states to adopt standards that fail accurately to track their regulatory preferences, in order to benefit from these safe-harbor provisions.

International approaches are more successful in explaining both safe-harbor provisions, and limitations on identifying international standards. As to the former, because these approaches emphasize benefits that accrue to all members when regulation is harmonized, in the form of less fragmented markets and attendant economies of scale and transnational value chains, they see reasons to incentivize harmonization, even where standards imperfectly track domestic policy preferences. Further, because they give greater weight to international standards, they suggest carefully policing what counts as such. If we want to minimize market fragmentation, we must ensure there is one and only one point on which standards will converge. If we worry that regulation imposes costs on unrepresented outsiders, we must ensure that only those standards in whose preparation outsiders could participate are granted this privileged status.

However, international approaches struggle in explaining the limited restrictions international standards impose. Realizing the efficiencies these accounts anticipate requires meaningful obligations to conform to international standards, subject to only limited exceptions. But Articles 2.4 TBT and 3.3 SPS permit states to depart from international standards wherever this is necessary to achieve their domestic objectives, a degree of discretion incompatible with global efficiency approaches.

EGC suggests a potentially more plausible explanation. We have already seen how Article 2.2's invocation of legitimate objectives and SPS's focus on scientific evidence can be explained as particular instances of EGC's general concern that regulation be justifiable to those on whom it is imposed: in the case of legitimate objectives, this appealed to the self-determination of the regulating state; in the case of scientific evidence, to jointly recognized expertise. In the case of international standards, this same function is fulfilled by appealing to the social authority of international consensus or shared international political processes.

We have already encountered, in the context of Article XX GATT, the idea that we can appeal to politically shared standards to justify regulation. However, as discussed above, in the context of SPS and TBT, we will frequently be concerned with DEMs rather than ETMs. In consequence, the appropriate justificatory threshold is lower, and the role of international standards differs accordingly. Whereas under Article XX our concern was whether goals were shared, we are here more concerned with whether regulations constitute appropriate means towards particular ends that states adopt for themselves in exercise of their self-determination. Sections 9.3 and 9.4 addressed provisions that, at least in part, address this question directly; appeals to international standards do so indirectly.

By invoking international standards we can demonstrate to outsiders that regulations do in fact pursue a legitimate objective, and that they do so in a way that is reasonably tailored to that objective. However, this is not the only way we can do this. In consequence, we would expect significant leeway to depart from international standards, provided states demonstrate in some other way that their regulation, and its impact on outsiders, is a rational expression of their self-determination. This is precisely what Article 2.4 TBT's reference to effective or appropriate means, and Article 3.3 SPS's invocation science and appropriate levels of protection, do.

Understanding international standards as justificatory in this way explains the demanding tests for recognition of international standards. In appealing to international standards we claim that our approach is one that affected outsiders should respect, whether because they have themselves endorsed it, or because they had the opportunity to participate in its selection. It therefore matters that the standard was adopted by a sufficiently open and inclusive process. A standard adopted by a small number of states, through an exclusive process, cannot fulfill this justificatory function.[235]

Further, this approach makes sense of the safe-harbor provisions, which in each case displace (rebuttably or otherwise) other, independent, requirements in the agreements. Recall, at least as regards DEMs, EGC suggests that policing means/ends relations is a large part of these agreements' function. But where a measure conforms to/is in accordance with a relevant international standard, both means and end have been internationally endorsed as appropriate. In consequence, once we accept that appeals to shared standards have justificatory value, and where a regulating state has not simply had regard to, but actually adopted, a relevant international standard, it makes sense to presume compliance with relevant requirements of those agreements.[236]

This can also make sense of a genuine puzzle in the harmonization provisions. As noted above, the obligations in each agreement to base regulations on international standards are subject to qualifications that in turn track independent obligations elsewhere in the agreements. Thus, the Appellate Body characterized Articles 3.1 and 3.3 SPS as giving states a choice: either regulate based on international standards, or regulate to achieve a higher level of protection, provided there is sufficient scientific basis for doing so.[237] However, if states regulate based on – but not conforming to – international standards, then they are still required,

---

[235] Provided the procedure is open and inclusive, this need not require consensus. Cf. *US-Tuna II*, AB, §353. The barriers to participation for developing countries may be particularly troubling in this regard: (Mayeda, 2004: 751–753).

[236] As regards ETMs, EGC suggests that these agreements impose a more demanding standard. However, limiting the presumption in Article 2.5 to measures pursuing goals specifically listed in Article 2.2 accommodates this concern.

[237] *EC-Hormones*, (AB), §169–172.

under Article 2.2 SPS, to ensure that regulation is based on scientific principles, and is not maintained without sufficient scientific evidence; and under Article 5.6, to ensure their regulations are not more trade restrictive than required to achieve their desired level of protection. Yet these are precisely the tests they must meet in order to depart from international standards under Article 3.3. It is thus difficult to see what additional obligation the requirement to regulate based on international standards imports.[238]

EGC, by emphasizing the justificatory function of international standards, legitimate objectives and scientific evidence, suggests a potential solution. Instead of a binary alternative, between domestic choice and international harmonization, it suggests that international standards can play a greater or lesser role in the justification of a measure, depending on the specifics of a case. It might be, for example, that some elements of an international standard are appropriate for a member's purpose, while others are not.[239] We might then expect the member to draw on international standards to the extent practical, and explain its departures by reference to the alternative justificatory tools in the agreements. In practice, justification is rarely a matter of straightforward deduction. Rather, states will appeal to various grounds to fully explain the approach chosen. Seeing the provisions on international standards in this way allows us to recognize states' freedom to depart from them, without rendering the obligations entirely illusory.

9.6   Conclusion

In this chapter, I have advanced an account of SPS and TBT in terms of EGC. I first provided a general account of both agreements in terms of EGC, contrasting this with competing approaches. I then considered three specific issues in the case-law; TBT's concern for legitimate objectives; SPS's reliance on science; and both agreements' invocation of international standards. I argued in each case that the relevant rules, and the approach adopted by the AB, was more readily reconcilable with EGC, albeit requiring further development in the case-law.

---

[238] While it has not been the subject of such explicit analysis by the Appellate Body, a similar point can be made about Article 2.4 TBT, and its relation to Article 2.2.

[239] This makes sense of the AB's interpretation of "based on" as referring to a situation where a member takes some elements, but not others, from an international standard, an interpretation that does little to promote meaningful harmonization: *EC-Hormones*, (AB), §163.

This is the last of four chapters in which I have sought to link EGC with existing WTO doctrines, showing both that it provides a plausible account of those doctrines, and that it can help to resolve recurring problems and guide the progressive development of the case-law. I have examined four main areas of goods regime: the core disciplines in the GATT; the exceptions and qualifications thereto; the rules on trade remedies and subsidies; and, in this chapter, those on domestic regulations in SPS and TBT. In the next, concluding, chapter, I bring these discussions together, linking them back to the normative argument in earlier chapters, and suggesting some implications of my approach for the future directions of the trade regime as a political, rather than purely legal, enterprise.

PART IV

Progress

10

Conclusion: Where to from Here?

The last four chapters analyzed WTO law in terms of the principles of global economic justice that I label Equality in Global Commerce. They showed how the existing rules can be understood as expressing EGC, and how EGC might in turn guide those rules' interpretation and progressive development, making possible a more direct engagement between political theory and international economic law than has previously existed.

At various points, I have advocated new interpretations or amendments. However, by focusing on the existing WTO agreements, I have also rendered static a regime that is in fact constantly, if unevenly, evolving, while my emphasis on explanation and interpretation has risked importing a conservative tendency to an otherwise critical set of principles. To remedy this, in this final chapter, I want briefly to address the changing nature of the trade regime, and to ask what EGC can say about its future direction, before offering some final thoughts on how this study might be extended, and the research agenda that it suggests.

10.1 Where Do We Go from Here? From Deadlock to Variable Geometry

As an institution, the WTO has three aspects: first, a body of rules; second, a dispute settlement system; and third, a negotiating forum.[1] The first two aspects, which were our focus in the last four chapters, have been largely successful. WTO rules have underpinned a period of unprecedented economic globalization and, with the dispute settlement system, helped weather the Great Recession without – so far – a significant retreat to protectionism. While recurrent protectionist rhetoric warns against

[1] *WTO Agreement*, Art. III.

undue complacency, as a body of rules and a dispute settlement mechanism, the WTO has been at least a qualified success.

Its third aspect, as a negotiating forum, is a different story.

Before 1994, eight successful GATT negotiating rounds were completed, progressively reducing tariffs, adopting new agreements, and expanding the trade regime's membership from 23 in 1948, to 123 in 1994. The 1994 Marrakesh Agreement establishing the WTO included a "built-in agenda" for further negotiations, including most prominently on services and agriculture, and provided for biennial Ministerial Conferences to maintain negotiating momentum. While a product of negotiations, the WTO was thus assumed from the start to also be a venue where further negotiations could take place. Even before the first Ministerial Conference in Singapore in 1996, work began on identifying issues to be addressed in the next negotiating round, to be launched at the third Ministerial in Seattle in 1999. However, the Seattle Ministerial ultimately broke down without consensus, against a backdrop of protests in the streets around the conference venue. Instead, the ninth round of multilateral trade negotiations was launched two years later, at the Doha Ministerial in November 2001, as the Doha Development Round or Doha Development Agenda.

It seems fair to say that the Doha Round has not been a success. Following the breakdown of negotiations at the Cancún Ministerial in 2003, contentious items on investment, competition, and government procurement were dropped from the negotiating agenda, leaving trade facilitation as the principal new area of rules negotiation.[2] At the time of writing, almost exactly 15 years after the Doha Ministerial, the resulting Trade Facilitation Agreement, aiming to streamline various procedural impediments to trade, together with the Nairobi Ministerial Decision to eliminate agricultural export subsidies, constitute the most significant liberalizing outputs from the round.[3] It has also yielded what we might describe as various corrective outputs, addressing specific concerns under existing agreements. These include, for example, clarifying the treatment of developing country compulsory licensing of essential medicines under the TRIPS Agreement,[4] and agreeing not to challenge certain developing

---

[2] *General Council Decision on the Doha Work Programme*, 2004.

[3] *Nairobi Ministerial Decision on Export Competition*, 2015. The *Hong Kong Ministerial Decision on Measures in Favor of Least Developing Countries* probably also merits mention here.

[4] *Declaration on the TRIPS Agreement and Public Health*, 2001; *General Council Decision on Implementation of Paragraph 6 of the Doha Declaration on the TRIPS Agreement and Public Health*, 2003.

country food security measures as potential subsidies.[5] However, the round has yielded little by way of progressive liberalization, whether in services, agriculture, or manufactured goods. And indeed, it seems clear following the Nairobi Ministerial that many members have effectively given up on the Doha Round, a fact reflected in the Ministerial declaration.[6]

Many causes might be suggested for the round's poor record.

First, and most obviously, membership is larger and more diverse than during any previous round. With the accession of Afghanistan in July 2016, WTO membership reached 164. This, together with consensus decision-making and the single undertaking, makes for formidable coordination problems.[7] Each of the previous eight rounds took longer than the last, and included a larger number of members. The struggles of the Doha Round might be simply the natural continuation of this trend. Further, it is not simply a matter of numbers. GATT negotiations took place largely within the Western alliance, under the leadership of the United States, and with only two or three real veto players. Since 1994, however, the accession of China and the growth of the larger developing countries have meant more states can effectively block consensus, whether alone or in coalition. It is no longer enough to build consensus between Washington, Brussels, and Tokyo, and then bring the rest of the membership along.

Second, echoing a story told during the Tokyo and Uruguay Rounds, the success of previous rounds means that the issues remaining to be addressed are more contentious, both domestically and internationally, making agreement more difficult. All of the low-hanging fruit have been picked. Over eight rounds of negotiations, most developed country tariffs have been reduced to negligible levels. Further progress on tariffs thus requires tackling those sensitive industries that have been protected from earlier liberalization. Beyond tariffs, nondiscrimination – at least in goods – is well established: so further liberalization requires deeper intervention into domestic policy. In the Doha context, this prominently includes services regulation; elsewhere, it includes competition policy and cross-border investment.

A third explanation, however, is more interesting for our purposes. In a speech in 2013, then Director-General Pascal Lamy attributed the Doha deadlock to one question: whether China – and presumably countries

---

[5] *Bali Ministerial Decision on Public Stockholding for Food Security Purposes*, 2013.

[6] *Nairobi Ministerial Declaration*, 2015, para 32.

[7] A 23 state multilateral negotiation includes 253 unique pairs of negotiating countries. With 164 states, that number becomes 13,366.

like it – was "[a] rich county with many poor? Or a poor country with many rich?" On this turned the practical question of "the appropriate balance of rights and obligations between advanced economies and emerging countries."[8] As discussed in Chapter 7, the idea that different commitments can be expected from developed and developing countries was well established in GATT practice, while the Uruguay Round is often explained as a "Grand Bargain" between developing and developed members. Yet, despite its ostensible character as a Development Round, the question of how commitments should be shared between developing and developed members generally, and between individual countries in particular, has been a prominent fault line in the Doha negotiations. In part, this reflects the politically self-interested character of many trade negotiations. However, it also reflects the difficulties of operationalizing vague commitments to equity in the context of distributive conflict and normative disagreement, and ultimately a lack of consensus on what a fair trade regime looks like. As I have argued throughout this book, trade governance – including trade negotiation – inevitably engages distributive justice. A clearer sense of what distributive justice means in this domain might thus help to make sense of, and build consensus around, the various positions at play in negotiations.

What, then, can EGC tell us about how this balance should be struck and, more generally, about the kinds of problems that should occupy negotiators in the Doha Round, or whatever may take its place?

First, and most obviously, it suggests terms in which further liberalization, whether of goods or services, might be discussed. To the extent that the main cleavage is North/South, EGC's answer is clear. The bulk of protectionist measures still maintained by developed countries are simply unjust *vis-à-vis* developing countries.[9] There are certainly exceptions. As discussed in Chapters 5 and 6, there are grounds relating to self-determination in particular that might justify measures protecting particular industries that are closely connected with the character and shared life of particular communities. However, in many other cases, it suggests developed countries should be withdrawing protectionist measures without necessarily expecting any reciprocal concessions on the part of developing members, regardless of the overall size or competitiveness of those developing members. The fact that China

---

[8] (Lamy, 2013).

[9] While EGC suggests they are also unjust *vis-à-vis* other developed countries, the reasons for reciprocal liberalization noted in Chapter 6 complicate this claim.

is – on some measures – the largest economy in the world does not mean that its citizens are not entitled to demand justification from those more advantaged for the trade-restrictive measures they adopt, and to expect the withdrawal of those that cannot be justified. More generally, EGC's concerns for both self-determination and economic inequality suggest a mandate for assessing further reforms to the trade regime from a pro-development perspective, subject to the various considerations and constraints canvassed in Chapter 7.

Second, as regards other current or potential issues for negotiation, including domestic regulation of goods and services, intellectual property, investment, competition, and revisions to existing rules generally, it suggests caution. EGC does not suggest that all measures that impede market access require to be eliminated. Rather, it emphasizes the justifiability of many choices that states make, notwithstanding their impacts on trade and, in turn, on the interests of outsiders. This implies that states should be free to maintain many measures that restrict trade, provided they are not ETMs, without thereby forfeiting their right to expect others should withdraw their own unjustifiable measures. Not all issues that might be negotiated through the WTO are subject to bargaining in the same terms.

This in turn suggests the need to revise WTO negotiating practices. WTO negotiations take place under a single undertaking rule, with all members subscribing to all disciplines, and nothing agreed until everything is agreed.[10] This has obvious attractions in simplifying negotiations and facilitating issue linkages. However, it also makes it more difficult for states to resist disciplines that they do not see as in their interest; membership of the WTO, itself a *sine qua non* for participation in the global economy, becomes contingent on accepting all disciplines negotiated under its umbrella. Single undertaking rules are thus effectively compulsory for participants in the global economy. This, EGC suggests, significantly limits the kinds of obligations that should be included under the single undertaking. Only those that we can reasonably expect all countries to accept should be included. These will be limited to rules tracking EGC's conception of distributive justice: rules limiting recourse to ETMs except where these are justifiable; and rules disciplining DEMs that fall below the lower threshold appropriate to them. In short, rules like those we have been examining in previous chapters.

---

[10] There are a small number of exceptions to this, including most prominently the Agreement on Government Procurement, which was negotiated and adopted on a plurilateral basis.

But of course, many states will want to go further, reaping economic and other benefits through mutually undertaking additional commitments; and EGC's account of self-determination, as including a capacity to participate in and bind ourselves to shared projects, suggests this should be permissible. However, the fact that some wish to go further cannot license their requiring others to follow. Such additional commitments are therefore not appropriate objects for the single undertaking. The implication, then, is that we should be open to initiatives including some, but not all, of the membership, whether on a plurilateral or a regional basis.

EGC thus endorses variable geometry in trade governance. However, it also implies limits on such variability. In particular, the claim among two or more states to pursue greater openness or stricter disciplines among themselves cannot license their adopting ETMs, including discriminatory measures, towards nonparticipants. The upshot may be that, in many cases, participation may be limited but access to benefits may not. (The WTO Information Technology Agreement provides an example of this approach.) Of course, some initiatives, most obviously harmonization, are effectively self-limiting: to benefit from harmonization a member must itself adopt a relevant standard. But others, like equivalence, have no such limit; a state can benefit from another's equivalence regime without adopting one of its own. Clearly, this conclusion risks creating precisely the kinds of coordination and free-rider problems that single undertaking was intended to solve. It may reduce the benefits that participants can achieve from such initiatives. However, it is the necessary implication of taking seriously the justice claims of nonparticipants. If it makes such initiatives less attractive, then so much the worse for such initiatives.

In fact, the trade regime has already seen a shift towards variable geometry, as deadlock in multilateral negotiations stimulates moves towards plurilateralism and regionalism. On the plurilateral side, the most prominent initiative has been the Trade in Services Agreement (TiSA), promising substantially greater services liberalization than is provided for under the General Agreement on Trade in Services (GATS), or has been realistically in prospect in the Doha negotiations. On the regional side, we have seen two major developments: first, the proliferation of regional trade agreements (RTAs), with 283 currently in force, and new agreements notified at a rate of around 20 per year[11]; and

---

[11] "Regional Trade Agreements: Facts and Figures," www.wto.org (last accessed November 7, 2016).

second, the move from "shallow" integration agreements, focused on tariffs, to "deep" agreements, covering such issues as services, domestic regulation, subsidies, investment, government procurement, intellectual property, competition, labor, environment, and sector-specific rules for, *inter alia*, financial services, telecommunications, and e-commerce.[12] Regional trade agreements have thus evolved from mechanisms for tariff liberalization, to independent loci of international rule-making.

Regionalism seems especially to raise concerns about the relation between participants and nonparticipants. Article XXIV.5 GATT provides an exception for regional trade agreements, which would otherwise violate the MFN obligation. Whereas plurilateral initiatives may in principle be open to all, regional initiatives are almost by definition exclusive to some subset. This exclusivity might reflect one of two quite different scenarios. First, it might express a genuine commitment, on the part of a number of states, to pursue greater integration, whether economic or political. The European Union is the archetype of this model, but it is also evident – albeit to a lesser degree – in MERCOSUR, ASEAN, and at least some African integration initiatives, including the EAC and ECOWAS. Alternatively, it might simply express a desire for preferential market access at the expense of third states, without any aspiration towards deeper or more permanent relations. This latter model captures well such "long-distance" agreements as the EU-Korea or US-Colombia agreements. There are also intermediate cases, like the various EU-ACP Economic Partnership Agreements, which are driven on one side by market access, and on the other by a mix of political, historical, and perhaps even ethical concerns. So-called megaregional agreements, including the TPP, TTIP, and RCEP, may also constitute intermediate cases, although probably closer to the latter, preferential market access model.

What does EGC suggest about these various developments?

First, and most obviously, it is skeptical of regional trade agreements divorced from any wider political or social project. Such agreements license discrimination, and little else. Whether they are more objectionable than the protectionist barriers that they remove is an open question. However, while EGC recognizes that protectionism may be justified in certain circumstances, it seems unlikely those circumstances would apply to justify protectionism generally, while also admitting market liberalization towards

---

[12] These examples are taken from the recently concluded *EU-Canada Comprehensive Economic and Trade Agreement*.

one or more preferred trading partners.[13] EGC thus suggests particular skepticism towards such agreements.

However, the situation is more complicated in the case of genuine integration projects. Again, self-determination seems relevant here. To the extent peoples choose to integrate with other polities, EGC raises no objection. However, constructing the kinds of economic and political links required to sustain such initiatives may require greater liberalization towards regional partners than is achievable multilaterally. Most obviously, the European Communities, as a project of European peace, required mutual liberalization of Franco-German heavy industry precisely in order to realize that underlying political goal. The difference between the two cases is that, in the former, discrimination is the purpose of the initiative, while in the latter, it is a necessary tool towards realizing a goal that is not itself defined by discrimination. There are still ETMs here that require to be justified; but where they pursue *bona fide* integration, there may be grounds for that justification.

Of course, distinguishing *bona fide* integration projects from discriminatory liberalization is not straightforward. The rough sketch above certainly does not do so. Rather, it seems likely that this will require political judgment, reflecting on a large variety of factors, and that even participants themselves may be unsure of the nature of their projects. (The disagreements about the nature of the European project, expressed most clearly in the recent Brexit vote, highlight this.) This uncertainty might explain both why Article XXIV makes no serious attempt to police this line, requiring only that participants liberalize "substantially all trade" between them, and also why the (political) Committee on Regional Trade Agreements is tasked with reviewing their compatibility with WTO rules. It is not that all RTAs meeting Article XXIV's requirements are permissible; rather, EGC suggests that, within the legal space afforded by Article XXIV, states should examine how far agreements are justifiable in the terms expressed by EGC. This is thus one of those areas, noted in Chapter 2, where answering the question "is this permissible legally?" goes only part way towards answering the more salient question, "is this permissible, all things considered?"

The evolution of RTAs from liberalization to rule-making raises further concerns about exclusion, this time from the processes whereby collective decisions are made. One way that the questions of distributive

---

[13] The obvious exception here is South-South FTAs, whose discriminatory elements might be justified under EGC's primary egalitarian limb.

justice that have been my focus overlap with questions of process and legitimacy is in the demand that international rules to which states adhere, beyond the minimum implied by EGC, should reflect a genuine exercise of self-determination, rather than disguised coercion of the weak by the strong. Where rules are made among a subset of members, and intended only to govern relations among those members, this can have implications for subsequent multilateral rule-making. Earlier bilateral, regional, or plurilateral agreements can provide templates for later multilateral rules, pre-empting serious consideration of alternatives that might be preferred by those joining at the later stage. The upshot is that – even absent the single undertaking – many states' adherence to such rules may not express any genuine exercise of self-determination.

Of course, in the context of negotiations generally, and in particular negotiations among states of very different sizes and levels of economic development, agreements will necessarily reflect compromises among the preferences of different groups. The threshold for regarding an agreement as an expression of self-determination cannot, therefore, be that it perfectly tracks a given people's preferences, even if that were a meaningful concept. However, we can certainly identify cases that are nearer or farther from that ideal, and such path-dependent multilateralism seems very far from it.

I offer no general solution to this problem here. However, one implication might be – following a point made above – that rule-making in new areas should be open – emphasizing mutual recognition and equivalence rather than strict regulation or harmonization – in order to facilitate ongoing regulatory conversations among states preferring different solutions to the problems these rules address. The constraint against plurilateral or regional initiatives licensing discrimination against outsiders may also alleviate concerns that these will be unduly pressured to endorse solutions agreed among an initially narrower group.

Bringing these various strands together, EGC gives us a sense of what a "finished" international trade regime might look like: first, a suite of multilateral rules disciplining both ETMs and DEMs in accordance with the justificatory considerations relevant to each; second, a variety of open regional and plurilateral initiatives to innovate rules, solve problems and reap gains above the multilateral baseline; and third, various – closed or open – regional integration initiatives that go beyond rule-making to constitute new units that will themselves fall under the multilateral and plurilateral rules of the first two limbs. We might expect, in this scenario, a high degree of fluidity in the second, and perhaps the third, limbs, against a baseline of relative stability in the first. And that in turn implies that, while we are not there yet, there will come a time when we must reimagine the WTO, from being a venue for political negotiation and action in pursuit of progressive liberalization, to a stable, and indeed static, locus of dispute settlement and administration of rules that are no longer subject to significant amendment, any more than are the background rules of individual states.

10.2   Where Do I Go from Here? Extending the Argument

There is only so much that can be done in a single book. Elements are always omitted that, if included, could make an argument stronger. This book is no different.

Most obviously, as noted in Chapter 2, my argument operates *within* liberal political theory. It extends the liberal theory of socioeconomic justice to international economic regulation, showing why those who are committed to liberal equality domestically should accept EGC internationally. This seemed a reasonable starting point. At least within Anglophone political philosophy, liberalism remains the high ground, upon or against which competing views are built. And, despite recent challenges, it continues to inform the basic concepts and values of the public political cultures of many states, and of much international political practice. However, it remains one position among many, both in the Western tradition and, more significantly, in the pluralist context of global politics. I have not sought, except in passing, to defend liberalism as the appropriate basis for thinking about global justice. However, without that defense the argument can be challenged, as articulating a liberal ideal without any warrant for pursuing that ideal in pluralist political practice.

We can distinguish two challenges here.

The first asks how, within liberalism, liberals should act towards nonliberal societies. Rawls's retreat to political liberalism is one answer. Tan's defense of comprehensive liberalism is another. While doubting that a choice is required, I noted in Chapter 2 my reasons for preferring the latter.

The second asks how we might find agreement with nonliberal peoples, and to what extent we should compromise distinctively liberal principles to achieve political stability. It is here that pragmatic international lawyers and scholars of *realpolitik* counsel caution, highlighting the risk that pursuing contentious ideals of economic justice threatens the peace and stability of the international order.

When posed in these general terms, these challenges have implications far beyond the present project, and are better addressed in their own right, rather than as extensions of this work. However, given the narrower scope of the principles defended here, it may be possible to avoid these challenges without answering them. EGC addresses economic regulation. It only indirectly engages contentious questions about democracy, individual rights, or domestic social justice that are the main focus of pluralist, communitarian, and relativist challenges. Its accommodation with self-determination means it accords significant leeway to communities to organize their own shared lives. It might thus represent an overlapping consensus among a broader set of views than more full-throated individualist accounts of liberal global justice. Exploring the compatibility of EGC with such nonliberal views, and in turn its relevance to communities espousing those views, seems an appropriate next step.

This book has also been limited in its doctrinal scope, focusing on key issues within the WTO goods regime. Readers might accept the claims made herein, but wonder how far the argument applies to other areas of WTO law, and international economic law more generally. The distinction between ETMs and DEMs, on which EGC depends, maps relatively well onto measures affecting trade in goods. It is less clear how it would apply to services, investment, or intellectual property. The movement of factors across borders challenges the distinctions EGC draws, both between classes of measures, and between insiders and outsiders. Is the relation between a product safety regulation and a foreign manufacturer analogous to that between a workplace safety regulation and a migrant worker? How does EGC's emphasis on distributing gains from international cooperation apply to the expropriation of capital that an investor has brought into the expropriating jurisdiction?[14] I am inclined to think that a focus on the justification of coercion, and on the disparate relations between regulator and regulated, can answer these questions. However, the required analysis may be different to that advanced here.

A comprehensive account of justice in international economic regulation would also go beyond my largely doctrinal focus to examine the multilevel domestic and international political discourses on these issues. I have argued that the texts of the agreements and the approaches of adjudicators can be understood in terms of EGC. I have not examined how far this reflects the views actually held by relevant political agents, or the reasons

---

[14] I offer some initial thoughts on this question in: (Suttle, 2016).

why these agreements were adopted. These historical and sociological questions are relevant to positivist treaty interpretation; but they are also relevant to the constructive approach that I outlined in Chapter 2. Stability limits how far principled interpretation can depart from existing political consensus. The benefits of a stable, legalized trade regime may lead states to comply with rules even if these do not perfectly reflect their interests and normative understandings; but if the law fails to roughly track those interests and understandings, it is unlikely to attract compliance or remain practically relevant. This is the practical upshot of the pluralist challenge noted above. It does not mean that interpretation is limited by any existing or historic political consensus. Interpreters, whether adjudicators or scholars, participate in political discourse, albeit in specialized roles, and may themselves contribute to its progressive development. However, this is only possible if their interpretations are recognizably part of, or at least compatible with, those discourses' structures. I have touched on these concerns at various points. However, a fuller examination could both support the arguments advanced herein, and offer valuable additional perspectives on the questions addressed.

10.3   Where Do You Go from Here? On the Value of Interdisciplinarity

I return, finally, to a point I took up in the introduction. This book is motivated by practical problems, but also by an intellectual disquiet about the limited engagement between international economic law and global political theory. Each discipline uses its own tools and techniques, but their objects of concern overlap. Each should be able to look to the other, whether for novel insights into their characteristic concerns, or for interesting new problems to which their methods might fruitfully be applied. That there is so little dialogue between them is not simply a matter of disciplinary chauvinism; both have drawn freely on economics and political science, for example, in advancing their agendas. Rather, as I suggested in Chapter 1, the most plausible explanation is the lack of fit between the prescriptions of political philosophers and the practical problems of economic governance preoccupying international economic lawyers. Demonstrating that this gap could be bridged, and that there could be value in interdisciplinary engagement between IEL and political theory, was an important goal of this project.

This points towards a broader research agenda that seeks to identify other fruitful linkages between these disciplines, and to promote a greater engagement with each by practitioners of the other. Some problems that might benefit from interdisciplinary examination have already been touched on. For example, I explained the conception of fairness in trade remedies in terms of EGC; but this, and in particular the inchoate conception of competitive fairness, might benefit from further work by theorists on the libertarian and liberal right. I explained SDT in egalitarian terms, but theorists emphasizing self-determination, human needs, or capabilities might suggest different functions for these rules. Elsewhere, there is a lively philosophical debate on the justification of migration controls from egalitarian, communitarian, and libertarian perspectives; the WTO's understanding of migrants as factors of production might add value to those debates. Investment protection raises problems of obvious interest to theorists of property and contract; but it also potentially raises the conflict between equality and incentives in left-liberalism.

This necessarily poses challenges for scholars. Engaging with another discipline means becoming familiar with its methods and debates. A working knowledge of economics and political science, both domestic and international, is already a prerequisite for much IEL scholarship. It is not realistic that rapidly evolving debates in political philosophy be added to the standard reading list as well. However, to the extent that scholars do take this step, and produce studies bringing these disciplines together in a form recognizable and digestible to scholars of both, they can potentially provide a valuable additional perspective on debates in both disciplines. It is as a contribution towards that goal that the present study is offered.

BIBLIOGRAPHY

Abbott, K. W. (1996). "Defensive Unfairness: The Normative Structure of Section 301," in J. Bhagwati & R. E. Hudec (Eds.), *Fair Trade and Harmonization: Prerequisites for Free Trade? Volume 2 Legal Analysis*: MIT Press.

Abdallah, H. (2005). "Oil Exports under GATT and the WTO," *OPEC Review*, 29(4), 267–294.

Abizadeh, A. (2007). "Cooperation, Pervasive Impact, and Coercion: On the Scope (not Site) of Distributive Justice," *Philosophy & Public Affairs*, 35(4), 318–358.

(2008). "Democratic Theory and Border Coercion," *Political Theory*, 36(1), 37–65.

Acemoglu, D., Johnson, S., Robinson, J. A., & Yared, P. (2008). "Income and Democracy," *The American Economic Review*, 98(3), 808–842.

Acemoglu, D., & Robinson, J. (2012). *Why Nations Fail: Origins of Power, Poverty and Prosperity*: Crown Publishers (Random House).

Ahn, D., & Lee, J. (2011). "Countervailing Duty against China: Opening a Pandora's Box in the WTO System?" *Journal of International Economic Law*, 14(2), 329–368.

Ahn, D., & Messerlin, P. (2014). "United States–Anti-Dumping Measures on Certain Shrimp and Diamond Sawblades from China: Never Ending Zeroing in the WTO?" *World Trade Review*, 13(02), 267–279.

Ahn, D., & Moon, W. J. (2010). "Alternative Approach to Causation Analysis in Trade Remedy Investigations: 'Cost of Production' Test," *Journal of World Trade*, 44, 1032.

Albin, C. (2001). *Justice and Fairness in International Negotiation*: Cambridge University Press.

Alexander, L. A. (1983). "Zimmerman on Coercive Wage Offers," *Philosophy & Public Affairs*, 12(2), 160–164.

Alford, R. P. (2006). "Reflections on US-Zeroing: A Study in Judicial Overreaching by the WTO Appellate Body," *Columbia Journal of Transnational Law*, 45, 196.

Alston, P. (2002). "Resisting the Merger and Acquisition of Human Rights by Trade Law: A Reply to Petersmann," *European Journal of International Law*, 13(4), 815–844.

Andemariam, S. W. (2006) "Can (Should) Article XX (b) GATT Be a Defense against Inconsistencies with the SPS and TBT Agreements," *Journal of World Investment and Trade*, 7(4), 519–544.

Anderson, E. S. (1999). "What Is the Point of Equality?" *Ethics*, 109(2), 287–337.

Anderson, S. (2011). "Coercion," in E. N. Zalta (Ed.), *Stanford Encyclopedia of Philosophy* (Winter 2011 ed.): Stanford University.

Anscombe, G. E. M. (1963). "War and Murder," in W. Stein (Ed.), *Nuclear Weapons: A Catholic Response*: Burns & Oates/Cardinal Books.

Armingeon, K., Milewicz, K., Peter, S., & Peters, A. (2011). "The Constitutionalisation of International Trade Law," in T. Cottier & P. Delimatsis (Eds.), *The Prospects of International Trade Regulation: From Fragmentation to Coherence*: Cambridge University Press.

Armstrong, C. (2009). "Coercion, Reciprocity, and Equality beyond the State," *Journal of Social Philosophy*, 40(3), 297–316.

(2013). "Resources, Rights and Global Justice: A Response to Kolers," *Political Studies*, 62(1), 216–222.

Arneson, R. J. (2005). "Do Patriotic Ties Limit Global Justice Duties?" *The Journal of Ethics*, 9(1–2), 127–150.

Atik, J. (1996). "Science and International Regulatory Convergence," *Northwestern Journal of International Law & Business*, 17, 736.

(1998). "Identifying Antidemocratic Outcomes: Authenticity, Self-Sacrifice, and International Trade," *University of Pennsylvania Journal of International Economic Law*, 19, 229.

Augier, P., Gasiorek, M., & Lai Tong, C. (2005). "The Impact of Rules of Origin on Trade Flows," *Economic Policy*, 20(43), 567–624.

Axelrod, R. M. (1984). *The Evolution of Cooperation*: Basic Books.

Bacchus, J. (2005). "From the Trenches," *World Trade Review*, 4(03), 499–523.

(2014). "A Common Gauge: Harmonization and International Law," *Boston College International and Comparative Law Review*, 37, 1.

Bagnoli, C. (2011). "Constructivism in Metaethics," in E. N. Zalta (Ed.), *The Stanford Encyclopedia of Philosophy* (Winter 2014 ed.): Stanford University.

Bagwell, K., Mavroidis, P. C., & Staiger, R. W. (2002). "It's a Question of Market Access," *The American Journal of International Law*, 96(1), 56–76.

Bagwell, K., & Staiger, R. W. (1990). "A Theory of Managed Trade," *The American Economic Review*, 80(4), 779–795.

(2001). "Strategic Trade, Competitive Industries and Agricultural Trade Disputes," *Economics & Politics*, 13(2), 113–128.

(2002). *The Economics of the World Trading System*: MIT Press.

(2006). "Will International Rules on Subsidies Disrupt the World Trading System?" *The American Economic Review*, 96(3), 877–895.

(2010). "Backward Stealing and Forward Manipulation in the WTO," *Journal of International Economics*, 82(1), 49–62.

(2011a). *Can the Doha Round be a Development Round? Setting a Place at the Table*: National Bureau of Economic Research.

(2011b). "What Do Trade Negotiators Negotiate About? Empirical Evidence from the World Trade Organization," *The American Economic Review, 101*, 1238–1273.

Bagwell, K., Staiger, R. W., & Sykes, A. O. (2013). "Border Instruments," in H. Horn & P. C. Mavroidis (Eds.), *Legal and Economic Principles of World Trade Law*: Cambridge University Press.

Baldwin, R. E. (2012). "The Case for a Multilateral Trade Organization," in A. Narlikar, M. Daunton, & R. M. Stern (Eds.), *The Oxford Handbook on the World Trade Organization*: Oxford University Press.

Barceló, J. J. (1991). "A History of GATT Unfair Trade Remedy Law – Confusion of Purposes," *World Economy, 14*(3), 311–333.

Barnett, R. E. (1991). "Some Problems with Contract as Promise," *Cornell Law Review, 77*, 1022.

Barry, B. (1973). *The Liberal Theory of Justice: A Critical Examination of the Principal Doctrines in* A Theory of Justice *by John Rawls*: Clarendon Press.

(1982). "Humanity and Justice in Global Perspective," in J. R. Pennock & J. W. Chapman (Eds.), *Nomox XXIV: Ethics, Economics and the Law*: New York University Press.

(1989). *Theories of Justice* (Vol. 1): University of California Press.

Barry, C., & Valentini, L. (2009). "Egalitarian Challenges to Global Egalitarianism: A Critique," *Review of International Studies, 35*(03), 485–512.

Bartels, L. (2002). "Article XX of GATT and the Problem of Extraterritorial Jurisdiction: The Case of Trade Measures for the Protection of Human Rights," *Journal of World Trade, 36*(2), 353–403.

(2003). "The WTO Enabling Clause and Positive Conditionality in the European Community's GSP Program," *Journal of International Economic Law, 6*(2), 507–532.

(2004). "The Separation of Powers in the WTO: How to Avoid Judicial Activism," *International & Comparative Law Quarterly, 53*(04), 861–895.

(2007). "The WTO Legality of the EU's GSP+ Arrangement," *Journal of International Economic Law, 10*(4), 869–886.

Bartels, L., & Häberli, C. (2010). "Binding Tariff Preferences for Developing Countries under Article II GATT," *Journal of International Economic Law, 13*(4), 969–995.

Bartels, L., & Ortino, F. (2006). *Regional Trade Agreements and the WTO Legal System*: Oxford University Press.

Beckett, J. A. (2001). "Behind Relative Normativity: Rules and Process as Prerequisites of Law," *European Journal of International Law, 12*(4), 627–650.

Beitz, C. R. (1979). *Political Theory and International Relations*: Princeton University Press.

(1983). "Cosmopolitan Ideals and National Sentiment," *The Journal of Philosophy*, *80*(10), 591–600.

(1999). *Political Theory and International Relations* (Revised ed.), Princeton, NJ: Princeton University Press.

(2000). "Rawls's Law of Peoples," *Ethics, 110*(4), 669–696.

Bennett, J. F. (1995). *The Act Itself*: Clarendon Press.

Benvenisti, E. (2013). "Sovereigns as Trustees of Humanity: On the Accountability of States to Foreign Stakeholders," *The American Journal of International Law, 107*(2), 295–333.

Berlin, I. (1997). *The Proper Study of Mankind: An Anthology of Essays*: Chatto & Windus.

Besson, S. (2013). "The Allocation of Anti-poverty Rights Duties: Our Rights, but Whose Duties?" in K. N. Schefer (Ed.), *Poverty and the International Economic Legal System: Duties to the World's Poor*: Cambridge University Press.

Bhagwati, J. (1988). *Protectionism*: MIT Press.

(2002). "Afterword: The Question of Linkage," *The American Journal of International Law, 96*(1), 126–134.

(2004). *In Defense of Globalization*: Oxford University Press.

Bhagwati, J., Greenaway, D., & Panagariya, A. (1998). "Trading Preferentially: Theory and Policy," *The Economic Journal, 108*(449), 1128–1148.

Bhagwati, J., & Ramaswami, V. K. (1963). "Domestic Distortions, Tariffs and the Theory of Optimum Subsidy," *Journal of Political Economy, 71*(1), 44–50.

Bhala, R., & Keating, S. B. (2014). "Diversity within Unity: Import Laws of Islamic Countries on Haram (Forbidden) Products," *47*(3), *The International Lawyer*, 343.

Biber-Klemm, S., Burkard, M., Cottier, T., Jusoh, S., & Temmerman, M. (2011). "Challenges of Biotechnology in International Trade Regulation," in T. Cottier & P. Delimatsis (Eds.), *The Prospects of International Trade Regulation: From Fragmentation to Coherence*: Cambridge University Press.

Bienen, D., & Mihretu, M. E. (2010). *The Principle of Fairness and WTO Accession – An Appraisal and Assessment of Consequences*. Paper presented at the Society of International Economic Law (SIEL), Second Biennial Global Conference, University of Barcelona.

Bigdeli, S. Z. (2011). "Resurrecting the Dead – The Expired Non-Actionable Subsidies and the Lingering Question of Green Space," *Manchester Journal of International Economic Law, 8*, 2.

Bird, F., Vance, T., & Woolstencroft, P. (2009). "Fairness in International Trade and Investment: North American Perspectives," *Journal of Business Ethics, 84*(3), 405–425.

Blake, M. (2001). "Distributive Justice, State Coercion, and Autonomy," *Philosophy & Public Affairs, 30*(3), 257–296.

(2013). *Justice and Foreign Policy*: Oxford University Press.

Blake, M., & Smith, P. T. (2015). "International Distributive Justice," in E. N. Zalta (Ed.), *Stanford Encyclopedia of Philosophy* (Spring 2015 ed.): Stanford University.

Borgen, C. J. (2009). "The Language of Law and the Practice of Politics: Great Powers and the Rhetoric of Self-Determination in the Cases of Kosovo and South Ossetia," *Chicago Journal of International Law, 10*, 1.

Bown, C. P. (2011). "Developing Countries and Monitoring WTO Commitments in Response to the Global Economic Crisis," in T. Cottier & M. Elsig (Eds.), *Governing the World Trade Organization: Past, Present and Beyond Doha*: Cambridge University Press.

Bown, C. P., & Prusa, T. J. (2011). "US Anti-Dumping: Much Ado about Zeroing," in M. Martin & A. Mattoo (Eds.), *Unfinished Business? The WTO's Doha Agenda*: Centre for Economic Policy Research/World Bank.

Bown, C. P., & Sykes, A. O. (2008). "The Zeroing Issue: A Critical Analysis of Softwood V," in H. Horn & P. C. Mavroidis (Eds.), *The WTO Case Law of 2004–5: Legal and Economic Analysis*: Cambridge University Press.

Bown, C. P., & Trachtman, J. P. (2009). "Brazil – Measures Affecting Imports of Retreaded Tyres: A Balancing Act," *World Trade Review, 8*(01), 85–135.

Brenton, P., & Manchin, M. (2003). "Making EU Trade Agreements Work: The Role of Rules of Origin," *World Economy, 26*(5), 755–769.

Brilmayer, L. (1989). *Justifying International Acts*: Cornell University Press.

Brock, G. (2009). *Global Justice: A Cosmopolitan Account*: Oxford University Press. (2015). "Global Justice," in E. N. Zalta (Ed.), *Stanford Encyclopedia of Philosophy* (Spring 2015 ed.): Stanford University.

Broda, C., Limão, N., & Weinstein, D. E. (2008). "Optimal Tariffs and Market Power: The Evidence," *The American Economic Review, 98*(5), 2032–2065.

Bronckers, M. C. (1996). "Rehabilitating Antidumping and Other Trade Remedies through Cost-Benefit Analyses," *Journal of World Trade, 30*(2), 5–37.

Brou, D., & Ruta, M. (2012). "A Commitment Theory of Subsidy Agreements," *The B.E. Journal of Economic Analysis & Policy, 13*(1), 239–270.

Broude, T. (2003). "An Anti-Dumping 'To Be or Not To Be' in Five Acts: A New Agenda for Research and Reform," *Journal of World Trade, 37*(2), 305–328. (2010). "The WTO/GATS Mode 4, International Labor Migration Regimes and Global Justice," in R. Pierik & W. Werner (Eds.), *Cosmopolitanism in Context: Perspectives from International Law and Political Theory*: Cambridge University Press.

Brown, A., & Stern, R. M. (2011). "Fairness in the WTO Trading System," *Goldman School of Public Policy Working Paper* No. GSPP11–001.

Brownlie, I. (2008). *Principles of Public International Law* (7th ed.): Oxford University Press.

Buchanan, A. (1990). "Justice as Reciprocity versus Subject-Centered Justice," *Philosophy and Public Affairs 19*(3), 227–252.

Buchanan, A. (2000). "Rawls's Law of Peoples: Rules for a Vanished Westphalian World," *Ethics, 110*(4), 697–721.

(2004). *Justice, Legitimacy, and Self-determination: Moral Foundations for International Law.* Oxford University Press.

Bull, H. (1977). *The Anarchical Society: A Study of Order in World Politics*: Macmillan.

Buthe, T. (2008). "The Globalization of Health and Safety Standards: Delegation of Regulatory Authority in the SPS Agreement of the 1994 Agreement Establishing the World Trade Organization," *Law and Contemporary Problems, 71*, 219.

Butt, D. (2012). "Global Equality of Opportunity as an Institutional Standard of Distributive Justice," in C. Carmody, F. Garcia, & J. Linarelli (Eds.), *Global Justice and International Economic Law: Opportunities and Prospects*: Oxford University Press.

Çali, B. (2009). "On Interpretivism and International Law," *European Journal of International Law, 20*(3), 805–822.

Campbell, D. E., & Kelly, J. S. (2002). "Chapter 1 Impossibility Theorems in the Arrovian Framework," in K. J. Arrow, A. K. Sen & S. Kotaro (Eds.), *Handbook of Social Choice and Welfare*: Elsevier.

Caney, S. (2005). *Justice beyond Borders: A Global Political Theory*: Oxford University Press.

(2008). "Global Distributive Justice and the State," *Political Studies, 56*(3), 487–518.

(2011). "Humanity, Associations and Global Justice: A Defence of Humanity-centred Cosmopolitan Egalitarianism," *The Monist, 94*(4), 506–534.

Cappelen, A. W., Hagen, R. J., & Tungodden, B. (2007). "National Responsibility and the Just Distribution of Debt Relief," *Ethics & International Affairs, 21*(1), 69–83.

Carmody, C. (2008). "A Theory of WTO Law," *Journal of International Economic Law, 11*(3), 527–557.

Carmody, C., Garcia, F., & Linarelli, J. (Eds.). (2012). *Global Justice and International Economic Law*: Cambridge University Press.

Carr, E. H. (1946). *The Twenty Years' Crisis, 1919–1939: An Introduction to the Study of International Relations* (2nd ed.): Macmillan.

Cass, D. Z. (2001). "The 'Constitutionalization' of International Trade Law: Judicial Norm-Generation as the Engine of Constitutional Development in International Trade," *European Journal of International Law, 12*(1), 39–75.

(2005). *The Constitutionalization of the World Trade Organization: Legitimacy, Democracy, and Community in the International Trading System*: Oxford University Press.

Cass, R. A., & Boltuck, R. D. (1996). "Antidumping and Countervailing-Duty Law: The Mirage of Equitable International Competition," in J. Bhagwati & R. E. Hudec (Eds.), *Fair Trade and Harmonization: Prerequisites for Free Trade? Volume 2 Legal Analysis*: MIT Press.

Cassese, A. (1995). *Self-Determination of Peoples: A Legal Reappraisal*: Cambridge University Press.

Cavallero, E. (2010). "Coercion, Inequality and the International Property Regime," *Journal of Political Philosophy, 18*(1), 16–31.

Cedro, R. R., & Vieira, B. F. (2010). "John Rawls' Justice as Fairness and the WTO: A Critical Analysis on the Initial Position of the Multilateral Agricultural Negotiation," *The Law and Development Review, 3*(2), 122–140.

Chalmers, D. (2006). "Administrative Globalisation and Curbing the Excesses of the State," in C. Joerges & E.-U. Petersmann (Eds.), *Constitutionalism, Multilevel Trade Governance and Social Regulation*: Hart.

Chang, H. F. (2003). "Risk Regulation, Endogenous Public Concerns, and the Hormones Dispute: Nothing to Fear but Fear Itself," *Southern California Law Review, 77*, 743.

Chang, H.-J. (2005). *Why Developing Countries Need Tariffs?: How WTO NAMA Negotiations Could Deny Developing Countries' Right to a Future*: South Centre.

Charnovitz, S. (1991). "Exploring the Environmental Exceptions in GATT Article XX," *Journal of World Trade, 25*(5), 37–55.

(1997). "The Moral Exception in Trade Policy," *Virginia Journal of International Law, 38*, 689.

(1999). "The Supervision of Health and Biosafety Regulation by World Trade Rules," *Tulane Environmental Law Journal, 13*, 271.

(2002a). "The Law of Environmental PPMs in the WTO: Debunking the Myth of Illegality," *Yale Journal of International Law, 27*, 59.

(2002b). "Triangulating the World Trade Organization," *The American Journal of International Law, 96*(1), 28–55.

(2008). "Mapping the Law of WTO Accession," in M. E. Janow, V. Donaldson, & A. Yanovich (Eds.), *WTO at Ten: Governance, Dispute Settlement and Developing Countries*: Juris Publishing.

Charnovitz, S., & Fischer, C. (2015). "Canada – Renewable Energy: Implications for WTO Law on Green and Not-So-Green Subsidies," *World Trade Review, 14*(2), 177–210.

Chayes, A., & Chayes, A. H. (1995). *The New Sovereignty: Compliance with International Regulatory Agreements*: Harvard University Press.

(2005). "The New Sovereignty," in O. A. Hathaway & H. H. Koh (Eds.), *Foundations of International Law*: Foundation Press.

Cheyne, I. (2006). "Risk and Precaution in World Trade Organization Law," *Journal of World Trade, 40*(5), 837–864.

Cho, S. (2004). "The WTO's Gemeinschaft," *Alabama Law Review, 56*, 483.

(2009). "The Demise of Development in the Doha Round Negotiations," *Texas International Law Journal, 45*, 573.

(2012). "No More Zeroing?: The United States Changes Its Antidumping Policy to Comply with the WTO," *American Society of International Law Insights*, *16*(8) (March 9, 2012), 1.

(2015). *The Social Foundations of World Trade: Norms, Community and Constitution*: Cambridge University Press.

Choi, W.-M. (2003). *"Like Products" in International Trade Law: Towards a Consistent GATT/WTO Jurisprudence*: Oxford University Press.

Choudhury, B., Gehne, K., Heri, S., Humbert, F., Kaufmann, C., & Schefer, K. N. (2011). "A Call for a WTO Ministerial Decision on Trade and Human Rights," in T. Cottier & P. Delimatsis (Eds.), *The Prospects of International Trade Regulation: From Fragmentation to Coherence*: Cambridge University Press.

Christiano, T. (2015). "Democracy," in E. N. Zalta (Ed.), *Stanford Encyclopedia of Philosophy* (Spring 2015 ed.): Stanford University.

Clements, P. (2013). "Multilateral Development Banks and the International Monetary Fund," in J. Linarelli (Ed.), *Research Handbook on Global Justice and International Economic Law*: Edward Elgar.

Cohen, G. A. (1997). "Where the Action Is: On the Site of Distributive Justice," *Philosophy & Public Affairs*, *26*(1), 3–30.

(2006). "Casting the First Stone: Who Can, and Who Can't, Condemn the Terrorists?" *Royal Institute of Philosophy Supplements*, *58*, 113–136.

(2008). *Rescuing Justice and Equality*: Harvard University Press.

Cohen, J., & Sabel, C. (2006). "Extra Rempublicam Nulla Justitia?" *Philosophy & Public Affairs*, *34*(2), 147–175.

Coleman, J. (1979). "Efficiency, Utility, and Wealth Maximization," *Hofstra Law Review*, *8*, 509.

Coleman, J., & Mendlow, G. (2010). "Theories of Tort Law," in E. N. Zalta (Ed.), *Stanford Encyclopedia of Philosophy* (Fall 2010 ed.): Stanford University.

Collier, P., & Rohner, D. (2008). "Democracy, Development, and Conflict," *Journal of the European Economic Association*, *6*(2–3), 531–540.

Collier, P., & Venables, A. J. (2007). "Rethinking Trade Preferences: How Africa Can Diversify Its Exports," *World Economy*, *30*(8), 1326–1345.

Conrad, C. R. (2011). *Processes and Production Methods (PPMs) in WTO Law: Interfacing Trade and Social Goals*: Cambridge University Press.

Copp, D. (1997). "Democracy and Communal Self-Determination," in R. McKim & J. McMahan (Eds.), *The Morality of Nationalism*: Oxford University Press.

Cottier, T. (2002). "Trade and Human Rights: A Relationship to Discover," *Journal of International Economic Law*, *5*(1), 111–132.

(2013). "Poverty, Redistribution, and International Trade Regulation," in K. N. Schefer (Ed.), *Poverty and the International Economic Legal System: Duties to the World's Poor*: Cambridge University Press.

Cottier, T., & Jackson, J. H. (2000). "Limits to International Trade: The Constitutional Challenge," *American Society of International Law Proceedings of the Annual Meeting, 94*, 220–224.

Cottier, T., Pauwelyn, J., & Bürgi Bonanomi, E. (2005). *Human Rights and International Trade*: Oxford University Press.

Crawford, N. (2002). *Argument and Change in World Politics Ethics, Decolonization, and Humanitarian Intervention*: Cambridge University Press.

Crosby, D. C. (2009). "Tilting at Conventional WTO Wisdom," in T. Cottier, O. Nartova, & S. Z. Bigdeli (Eds.), *International Trade Regulation and the Mitigation of Climate Change*: Cambridge University Press.

Crowley, M. A. (2008). "Comment," in H. Horn & P. C. Mavroidis (Eds.), *The WTO Case Law of 2004-5: Legal and Economic Analysis*: Cambridge University Press.

(2010). "Why are Safeguards Needed in a Trade Agreement," in K. Bagwell, G. A. Bermann, & P. C. Mavroidis (Eds.), *Law and Economics of Contingent Protection in International Trade*: Cambridge University Press.

Cudd, A. (2012). "Contractarianism," in E. N. Zalta (Ed.), *Stanford Encyclopedia of Philosophy* (Fall 2012 ed.): Stanford University.

Daunton, M. (2012). "The Inconsistent Quartet: Free Trade versus Competing Goals," in A. Narlikar, M. Daunton, & R. M. Stern (Eds.), *The Oxford Handbook of the World Trade Organization*: Oxford University Press.

Davey, W. J. (2006). "Reflections on the Appellate Body Decision in the *Hormones* Case and the Meaning of the SPS Agreement," in G. A. Bermann & P. C. Mavroidis (Eds.), *Trade and Human Health and Safety*: Cambridge University Press.

Davies, A. (2009). "Interpreting the Chapeau of GATT Article XX in Light of the 'New' Approach in Brazil-Tyres," *Journal of World Trade, 43*(3), 507–539.

Davies, G. (2007). "Morality Clauses and Decision Making in Situations of Scientific Uncertainty: The Case of GMOs," *World Trade Review, 6*(2), 249–263.

Davis, L. (2009). "Anti-Dumping Investigation in the EU: How Does It Work?" *European Centre for International Political Economy, 4*, 23.

Deardoff, A. V. (2001). "Market Access for Developing Countries," in R. B. Porter, P. Sauve, A. Subramanian, & A. B. Zampetti (Eds.), *Efficiency, Equity and Legitimacy: The Multilateral Trading System at the Millennium*: Brookings.

Desmedt, A. (2001). "Proportionality in WTO Law," *Journal of International Economic Law, 4*(3), 441–480.

Diamond, R. (1988). "Economic Foundations of Countervailing Duty Law," *Virginia Journal of International Law, 29*, 767.

(2008). "Privatization and The Definition of Subsidy: A Critical Study of Appellate Body Texturalism," *Journal of International Economic Law, 11*(3), 649–678.

Dietsch, P. (2011). "Rethinking Sovereignty in International Fiscal Policy," *Review of International Studies, 37*(05), 2107–2120.

Donahue, A. M. (2000). "Equivalence: Not Quite Close Enough for the International Harmonization of Environmental Standards," *Environmental Law, 30*, 363.

Donnelly, J. (2008). "The Ethics of Realism," in C. Reus-Smit & D. Snidal (Eds.), *The Oxford Handbook of International Relations*: Oxford University Press.

Douglas, A. I., Mavroidis, P. C., & Sykes, A. O. (2008). *The Genesis of the GATT*: Cambridge University Press.

Drezner, D. W. (2007). *All Politics is Global: Explaining International Regulatory Regimes*: Princeton University Press.

Du, M. M. (2007). "Domestic Regulatory Autonomy under the TBT Agreement: From Non-Discrimination to Harmonization," *Chinese Journal of International Law, 6*(2), 269–306.

(2010). "Reducing Product Standards Heterogeneity through International Standards in the WTO: How Far across the River?" *Journal of World Trade, 44*(2), 295–318.

(2011). "The Rise of National Regulatory Autonomy in the GATT/WTO Regime," *Journal of International Economic Law, 14*(3), 639–675.

Dufek, P. (2013). "Why Strong Moral Cosmopolitanism Requires a World-State," *International Theory, 5*(2), 177–212.

Dunne, T., Kurki, M., & Smith, S. (2007). *International Relations Theories: Discipline and Diversity*: Oxford University Press.

Dunoff, J. L. (1999). "The Death of the Trade Regime," *European Journal of International Law, 10*(4), 733–762.

(2006a). "Constitutional Conceits: The WTO's 'Constitution' and the Discipline of International Law," *European Journal of International Law, 17*(3), 647–675.

(2006b). "Lotus Eaters: Reflections on the Varietals Dispute, the SPS Agreement, and WTO Dispute Resolution," in G. A. Bermann & P. C. Mavroidis (Eds.), *Health Trade and Human Health and Safety*: Cambridge University Press.

(2010). "How *Not* to Think about Safeguards," in K. W. Bagwell, G. A. Bermann, & P. C. Mavroidis (Eds.), *Law and Economics of Contingent Protection in International Trade*: Cambridge University Press.

Dunoff, J. L., & Trachtman, J. P. (1999). "Economic Analysis of International Law," *Yale Journal of International Law, 24*, 1.

Dworkin, R. (1980). "Is Wealth a Value?" *The Journal of Legal Studies, 9*(2), 191–226.

(1986). *Law's Empire*: Belknap Press of Harvard University Press.

(2002). *Sovereign Virtue: The Theory and Practice of Equality*: Harvard University Press.

(2006). *Justice in Robes*: Belknap Press of Harvard University Press.

(2013). "A New Philosophy for International Law," *Philosophy & Public Affairs*, *41*(1), 2–30.

Eagleton-Pierce, M. (2013). *Symbolic Power in the World Trade Organization*: Oxford University Press.

Echols, M. A. (2001). *Food Safety and the WTO: The Interplay of Culture, Science and Technology*: Kluwer Law International.

Emerton, P. (2009). "International Economic Justice: Is a Principled Liberalism Possible," in S. Joseph, D. Kinley, & J. Waincymer (Eds.), *The World Trade Organization and Human Rights: Interdisciplinary Perspectives*: Edward Elgar.

Endicott, T. (2010). "The Logic of Freedom and Power," in S. Besson & J. Tasioulas (Eds.), *The Philosophy of International Law*: Oxford University Press.

Epps, T. (2008). "Reconciling Public Opinion and WTO Rules under the SPS Agreement," *World Trade Review*, *7*(2), 359–392.

Epps, T., & Green, A. (2010). *Reconciling Trade and Climate: How the WTO Can Help Address Climate Change*: Edward Elgar.

Eskelinen, T. (2011). "Global Basic Structure and Institutions: The WTO as a Practical Example," *Journal of Global Ethics*, *7*(1), 47–58.

Ethier, W. J. (2004). "Political Externalities, Nondiscrimination, and a Multilateral World," *Review of International Economics*, *12*(3), 303–320.

Evenett, S. J., & Hoekman, B. M. (2006). *Economic Development and Multilateral Trade Cooperation*: Palgrave Macmillan/World Bank.

Fine, S. (2010). "Freedom of Association Is Not the Answer," *Ethics*, *120*(2), 338–356.

Finger, J. M. (1992). "Dumping and Antidumping: The Rhetoric and the Reality of Protection in Industrial Countries," *The World Bank Research Observer*, *7*(2), 121–144.

(2001). "Implementing the Uruguay Round Agreements: Problems for Developing Countries," *The World Economy*, *24*(9), 1097–1108.

(2005). "A Diplomat's Economics: Reciprocity in the Uruguay Round Negotiations," *World Trade Review*, *4*(01), 27–40.

Finger, J. M., & Artis, N. T. (1993). *Antidumping: How It Works and Who Gets Hurt*: University of Michigan Press.

Finger, J. M., Ng, F., & Wangchuk, S. (2001). *Antidumping as Safeguard Policy* (Vol. 2730): World Bank Development Research Group.

Fischer, J. M., Ravizza, M., & Copp, D. (1993). "Quinn on Double Effect: The Problem of 'Closeness'," *Ethics*, *103*(4), 707–725.

Fisher, E. (2006). "Beyond the Science/Democracy Dichotomy: The World Trade Organisaton Santiary and Phytosanitary Agreement and Administrative Constitutionalism," in C. Joerges & E.-U. Petersmann (Eds.), *Constitutionalism, Multilevel Trade Governance and Social Regulation*: Hart.

FitzPatrick, W. J. (2003). "Acts, Intentions, and Moral Permissibility: In Defence of the Doctrine of Double Effect," *Analysis*, *63*(280), 317–321.

Flett, J. (2010). "If in Doubt, Leave It Out – EU Precaution in WTO Regulatory Space," *European Journal of Risk Regulation*, *1*, 20.

(2013). "WTO Space for National Regulation: Requiem for a Diagonal Vector Test," *Journal of International Economic Law*, *16*(1), 37–90.

Follesdal, A. (2011). "The Distributive Justice of a Global Basic Structure: A Category Mistake?" *Politics, Philosophy & Economics*, *10*(1), 46–65.

Foot, P. (1994). "The Problem of Abortion and the Doctrine of Double Effect," in B. Steinbock & A. Norcross (Eds.), *Killing and Letting Die*: Fordham University Press.

Footer, M. E. (2007). "Post-Normal Science in the Multilateral Trading System: Social Science Expertise and the *EC-Biotech* Panel," *World Trade Review*, *6* (2), 281–297.

Foster, C. E. (2009). "Public Opinion and the Interpretation of the World Trade Organisation's Agreement on Sanitary and Phytosanitary Measures," in S. Joseph, D. Kinley, & J. Waincymer (Eds.), *The World Trade Organization and Human Rights: Interdisciplinary Perspectives*: Edward Elgar.

Francioni, F. (Ed.). (2001). *Environment, Human Rights and International Trade*: Hart.

Franck, T. M. (1990). *The Power of Legitimacy among Nations*: Oxford University Press.

(1995). *Fairness in International Law and Institutions*: Clarendon Press.

Francois, J., Hoekman, B., & Manchin, M. (2006). "Preference Erosion and Multilateral Trade Liberalization," *The World Bank Economic Review*, *20*(2), 197–216.

Freeman, S. (2001). "Illiberal Libertarians: Why Libertarianism Is Not a Liberal View," *Philosophy & Public Affairs*, *30*(2), 105–151.

(2007). *Justice and the Social Contract: Essays on Rawlsian Political Philosophy*: Oxford University Press.

Fried, C. (1981). *Contract as Promise: A Theory of Contractual Obligation*: Harvard University Press.

Gaines, S. (2001). "The WTO's Reading of the GATT Article XX Chapeau: A Disguised Restriction on Environmental Measures," *University of Pennsylvania Journal of International Economic Law*, *22*, 739.

Galeotti, M., & Kemfert, C. (2004). "Interactions between Climate and Trade Policies: A Survey," *Journal of World Trade*, *38*(4), 701–724.

Gallagher, K. P. (2007). "Understanding Developing Country Resistance to the Doha Round," *Review of International Political Economy*, *15*(1), 62–85.

Gans, C. (2003). *The Limits of Nationalism*: Cambridge University Press.

Garcia, F. (2000). "Trade and Inequality: Economic Justice and the Developing World," *Michigan Journal of International Law*, *21*, 975–1049.

Garcia, F. (2003). *Trade, Inequality, and Justice: Towards a Liberal Theory of Just Trade*: Transnational Publishers.

(2004). "Beyond Special and Differential Treatment," *Boston College International and Comparative Law Review, 27*, 291.

(2006). "Why Trade Law Needs a Theory of Justice," *American Society of International Law Proceedings of the Annual Meeting, 100*, 376–380.

(2013). *Global Justice and International Economic Law: Three Takes*: Cambridge University Press.

Gaus, G. (2010). "Coercion, Ownership and the Redistributive State: Justificatory Liberalism's Classical Tilt," *Social Philosophy and Policy, 27*(01), 233–275.

Gauthier, D. P. (1986). *Morals by Agreement*: Clarendon Press.

Gian, W. (2014). "How General Should the General Exceptions Be?: A Critique of the 'Common Intention' Approach of Treaty Interpretation," *Journal of World Trade, 48*(2), 219.

Gilpin, R. (1971). "The Politics of Transnational Economic Relations," *International Organization, 25*(03), 398–419.

Goetz, C. J., Granet, L., & Schwartz, W. F. (1986). "The Meaning of 'Subsidy' and 'Injury' in the Countervailing Duty Law," *International Review of Law and Economics, 6*(1), 17–32.

Goh, G. (2006). "Tipping the Apple Cart: The Limits of Science and Law in the SPS Agreement after Japan – Apples," *Journal of World Trade, 40*(4), 655–686.

Goldsmith, J. L., & Posner, E. A. (2005). *The Limits of International Law*: Oxford University Press.

Goodin, R. E. (1988). "What Is So Special about Our Fellow Countrymen?" *Ethics, 98*(4), 663–686.

Gosepath, S. (2011). "Equality," in E. N. Zalta (Ed.), *The Stanford Encyclopedia of Philosophy* (Spring 2011 ed.): Stanford University.

Graeber, D. (2011). *Debt: The First 5,000 Years*: Melville House.

Green, A., & Epps, T. (2007). "The WTO, Science, and the Environment: Moving towards Consistency," *Journal of International Economic Law, 10*(2), 285–316.

Green, A., & Trebilcock, M. (2010). "The Enduring Problem of World Trade Organization Export Subsidies Rules," in K. Bagwell, G. A. Bermann, & P. C. Mavroidis (Eds.), *Law and Economics of Contingent Protection in International Trade*: Cambridge University Press.

Grossman, G. M., & Helpman, E. (1995). "Trade Wars and Trade Talks," *Journal of Political Economy, 103*(4), 675–708.

Grossman, G. M., & Mavroidis, P. C. (2003). "US-Lead and Bismuth II United States – Imposition of Countervailing Duties on Certain Hot-Rolled Lead and Bismuth Carbon Steel Products Originating in the United Kingdom: Here

Today, Gone Tomorrow? Privatization and the Injury Caused by Non-Recurring Subsidies," in H. Horn & P. C. Mavroidis (Eds.), *The WTO Case Law of 2001*: Cambridge University Press.

(2005a). "United States – Countervailing Measures concerning Certain Products from the European communities (WTO Doc. WT/DS212/AB/R): Recurring Misunderstanding of Non-Recurring Subsidies," in H. Horn & P. C. Mavroidis (Eds.), *The WTO Case Law of 2002*: Cambridge University Press.

(2005b). "United States – Definitive Safeguard Measures on Imports of Circular Welded Carbon Quality Line Pipe from Korea (WT/DS202; DSR 2002:IV, 1403; DSR 2002:IV, 1473; DSR 2002:V, 2061) Not for Attribution," in H. Horn & P. C. Mavroidis (Eds.), *The WTO Case Law of 2002: The American Law Institute Reporters' Studies*: Cambridge University Press.

Grossman, G. M., & Sykes, A. O. (2005). "A Preference for Development: The Law and Economics of GSP," *World Trade Review*, 4(1), 41–67.

(2007). "WTO Case Law: The American Law Institute Reporter's Studies United States – Definitive Safeguard Measures on Imports of Certain Steel Products," *World Trade Review*, 6(01), 89–122.

Gruszczynski, L. (2006). "Science in the Process of Risk Regulation under the WTO Agreement on Sanitary and Phytosanitary Measures," *German Law Journal*, 7, 371.

(2010). *Regulating Health and Environmental Risks under WTO Law: A Critical Analysis of the SPS Agreement*: Oxford University Press.

(2011). "How Deep Should We Go? Searching for an Appropriate Standard of Review in the SPS Cases," *European Journal of Risk Regulation*, 1, 111.

Grzymala-Busse, A., & Jones Luong, P. (2006). "Democratization: Post-Communist Implications," in B. R. Weingast & D. A. Wittman (Eds.), *The Oxford Handbook of Political Economy*: Oxford University Press.

Guth, E. (2012). "The End of the Bananas Saga," *Journal of World Trade*, 46(1), 1–32.

Guy, K. M. (2007). *When Champagne Became French: Wine and the Making of a National Identity*: Johns Hopkins University Press.

Guzman, A. T. (2004a). "Food Fears: Health and Safety at the WTO," *Virginia Journal of International Law*, 45, 1.

(2004b). "Global Governance and the WTO," *Harvard International Law Journal*, 45, 303.

Harrison, J. (2007). *The Human Rights Impact of the World Trade Organization*: Hart.

Hart, H. L. A. (1955). "Are There Any Natural Rights?" *The Philosophical Review*, 64(2), 175–191.

(1958). "Positivism and the Separation of Law and Morals," *Harvard Law Review*, 71(4), 593–629.

(1963). *Law, Liberty and Morality*: Stanford University Press.

Hasenclever, A., Mayer, P., & Rittberger, V. (1997). *Theories of International Regimes*: Cambridge University Press.

Hathaway, C. M., Horlick, G., Stewart, T., Ellard, A., & Mastel, G. (2003). "Antidumping, Countervailing Duties and Trade Remedies: Let's Make a Deal?" *The International Lawyer, 37*, 821.

Hayek, F. A. v. (1944). *The Road to Serfdom*: G. Routledge & Sons.

Heiskanen Veijo, A. (2004). "The Regulatory Philosophy of International Trade Law," *Journal of World Trade, 38*, 1–36.

Hizon, E. M. (1994). "The Safeguard Measure/VER Dilemma: The Jekyll and Hyde of Trade Protection," *Northwestern Journal of International Law and Business, 15*, 105.

Hobbes, T. (1996). *Leviathan* (1651) (Rev. ed., R. Tuck ed.): Cambridge University Press.

Hoekman, B. (2005). "Operationalizing the Concept of Policy Space in the WTO: Beyond Special and Differential Treatment," *Journal of International Economic Law, 8*(2), 405–424.

Hoekman, B., & Kostecki, M. M. (2009). *The Political Economy of the World Trading System: The WTO and Beyond* (3rd ed.): Oxford University Press.

Hoekman, B., & Prowse, S. (2005). "Economic Policy Responses to Preference Erosion: From Trade as Aid to Aid for Trade," *World Bank Policy Research Working Paper*, 3721.

Hoekman, B., & Trachtman, J. (2010). "Continued Suspense: EC – Hormones and WTO Disciplines on Discrimination and Domestic Regulation Appellate Body Reports: Canada/United States – Continued Suspension of Obligations in the EC – Hormones Dispute, WT/DS320/AB/R, WT/DS321/AB/R, adopted 14 November 2008," *World Trade Review, 9*(1), 151.

Hollis, M., & Smith, S. (1990). *Explaining and Understanding International Relations*: Clarendon Press.

Holtug, N. (2011). "The Cosmopolitan Strikes Back: A Critical Discussion of Miller on Nationality and Global Equality," *Ethics and Global Politics, 4*(3), 147–163.

Horn, H. (2006). "National Treatment in the GATT," *CEPR Discussion Paper, No. 5450.*

Horn, H., Maggi, G., & Staiger, R. W. (2010). "Trade Agreements as Endogenously Incomplete Contracts," *The American Economic Review, 100*(1), 394–419.

Horn, H., & Mavroidis, P. C. (2003). "US – Lamb United States – Safeguard Measures on Imports of Fresh, Chilled or Frozen Lamb Meat from New Zealand and Australia: What Should Be Required of a Safeguard Investigation?" *World Trade Review, 2*(03), 395–430.

(2004). "Still Hazy after All These Years: The Interpretation of National Treatment in the GATT/WTO Case-Law on Tax Discrimination," *European Journal of International Law, 15*(1), 39–69.

(2005). "United States – Preliminary Determination with Respect to Certain Softwood Lumber from Canada – What Is a Subsidy?" in H. Horn & P. C. Mavroidis (Eds.), *The WTO Case Law of 2002: The American Law Institute Reporters' Studies*: Cambridge University Press.

Horn, H., & Weiler, J. H. H. (2005). "European Communities – Trade Description of Sardines: Textualism and Its Discontent," in H. Horn & P. C. Mavroidis (Eds.), *The WTO Case Law of 2002: The American Law Institute Reporters' Studies*: Cambridge University Press.

Howse, R. (1999). "The World Trade Organization and the Protection of Workers' Rights," *Journal of Small and Emerging Business Law*, 3, 131.

(2000). "Democracy, Science, and Free Trade: Risk Regulation on Trial at the World Trade Organization," *Michigan Law Review*, 98(7), 2329–2357.

(2001). "Adjudicative Legitimacy and Treaty Interpretation in International Trade Law: The Early Years of WTO Jurisprudence," in J. H. H. Weiler (Ed.), *The EU, the WTO, and the NAFTA: Towards a Common Law of International Trade*: Oxford University Press.

(2002a). "Back to Court after Shrimp/Turtle – Almost but Not Quite Yet: India's Short Lived Challenge to Labor and Environmental Exceptions in the European Union's Generalized System of Preferences," *American University International Law Review*, 18, 1333.

(2002b). "From Politics to Technocracy – and Back Again: The Fate of the Multilateral Trading Regime," *The American Journal of International Law*, 96, 94–117.

(2002c). "How to Begin to Think about the 'Democratic Deficit' at the WTO," in S. Griller (Ed.), *International Economic Governance and Non Economic Concerns*: Springer.

(2002d). "Human Rights in the WTO: Whose Rights, What Humanity? Comment on Petersmann," *European Journal of International Law*, 13(3), 651–659.

(2002e). "The Sardines Panel and AB Rulings – Some Preliminary Reactions," *Legal Issues of Economic Integration*, 29(3), 247–254.

(2003). "India's WTO Challenge to Drug Enforcement Conditions in the European Community Generalized System of Preferences: A Little Known Case with Major Repercussions for Political Conditionality in US Trade Policy," *Chicago Journal of International Law*, 4, 385.

(2006). "A New Device for Creating International Legal Normativity: The WTO Technical Barriers to Trade Agreement and 'International Standards'," in E.-U. Petersmann & C. Joerges (Eds.), *Constitutionalism, Multilevel Trade Governance and Social Regulation*: Hart.

(2008). "Human Rights, International Economic Law and Constitutional Justice: A Reply," *European Journal of International Law*, 19(5), 945–953.

(2010). "Do World Trade Organization Disciplines on Domestic Subsidies Make Sense? The Case for Legalizing Some Subsidies," in K. Bagwell, G. A.

Bermann, & P. C. Mavroidis (Eds.), *Law and Economics of Contingent Protection in International Trade*: Cambridge University Press.

Howse, R., & Horn, H. (2009). "European Communities – Measures Affecting the Approval and Marketing of Biotech Products," *World Trade Review*, 8(1), 49–83.

Howse, R., & Langille, J. (2012). "The Seal Products Dispute and Why the WTO Should Accept Trade Restrictions Justified by Noninstrumental Moral Values," *Yale Journal of International Law*, 37, 367.

Howse, R., Langille, J., & Sykes, K. (2015). "Pluralism in Practice: Moral Legislation and the Law of the WTO after Seal Products," *George Washington International Law Review*, 48, 81–150.

Howse, R., & Levy, P. I. (2013). "The TBT Panels: US–Cloves, US–Tuna, US–Cool," *World Trade Review*, 12(02), 327–375.

Howse, R., & Neven, D. (2003). "Argentina – Ceramic Tiles Argentina – Definitive Anti-Dumping Measures on Imports of Ceramic Floor Tiles from Italy," in H. Horn & P. C. Mavroidis (Eds.), *The WTO Case Law of 2001: The American Law Institute Reporters' Studies*: Cambridge University Press.

Howse, R., & Nicolaidis, K. (2001). "Legitimacy and Global Governance: Why Constitutionalizing the WTO Is a Step Too Far," in R. B. Porter, P. Sauve, A. Subramanian, & A. B. Zampetti (Eds.), *Efficiency, Equity and Legitimacy: The Multilateral Trading System at the Millennium*: Brookings Institution Press.

(2003). "Enhancing WTO Legitimacy: Constitutionalization or Global Subsidiarity?" *Governance*, 16(1), 73–94.

Howse, R., & Regan, D. H. (2000). "The Product/Process Distinction – An Illusory Basis for Disciplining 'Unilateralism' in Trade Policy," *European Journal of International Law*, 11(2), 249–289.

Howse, R., & Teitel, R. (2009). "Beyond the Divide: The International Covenant on Economic, Social and Cultural Rights and the World Trade Organization," in S. Joseph, D. Kinley, & J. Waincymer (Eds.), *The World Trade Organization and Human Rights: Interdisciplinary Perspectives*: Edward Elgar.

Howse, R., & Teitel, R. (2011). "Global Justice, Poverty and the International Economic Order," in S. Besson & J. Tasioulas (Eds.), *The Philosophy of International Law*: Oxford University Press.

Hudec, R. E. (1992). "Circumventing Democracy: The Political Morality of Trade Negotiations," *New York University Journal of International Law and Politics*, 25, 311.

(1996). "Introduction to the Legal Studies," in J. Bhagwati & R. E. Hudec (Eds.), *Fair Trade and Harmonization: Prerequisites for Free Trade? Volume 2 Legal Analysis*: MIT Press.

(1998). "GATT/WTO Constraints on National Regulation: Requiem for an Aim and Effects Test," *The International Lawyer*, 32(3), 619–649.

(1999). *Essays on the Nature of International Trade Law*: Cameron May.

(2003). "Science and Post-Discriminatory WTO Law," *Boston College International and Comparative Law Review*, 26, 185.

(2011). *Developing Countries in the GATT Legal System* (New ed.): Cambridge University Press.

Hudec, R. E., & Bhagwati, J. (1996). *Fair Trade and Harmonization: Prerequisites for Free Trade?*: MIT Press.

Hufbauer, G. C., & Erb, J. S. (1984). *Subsidies in International Trade*: Institute for International Economics.

Hume, D. (2000). *Treatise on Human Nature* (1738) (David F. Norton & Mary J. Norton eds.): Oxford University Press.

Hurka, T. (1997). "The Justification of National Partiality," in R. McKim & J. McMahan (Eds.), *The Morality of Nationalism*: Oxford University Press.

Hurrell, A. (2007). *On Global Order: Power, Values, and the Constitution of International Society*: Oxford University Press.

Inayatullah, N., & Blaney, D. L. (1995). "Realizing Sovereignty," *Review of International Studies*, 21(1), 3–20.

Irish, M. (2007). "GSP Tariffs and Conditionality: A Comment on EC – Preferences," *Journal of World Trade*, 41(4), 683–698.

Irwin, D. A., Mavroidis, P. C., & Sykes, A. O. (2008). *The Genesis of the GATT*: Cambridge University Press.

Isaac, G. E., & Kerr, W. A. (2003). "Genetically Modified Organisms at the World Trade Organization: A Harvest of Trouble," *Journal of World Trade*, 37(6), 1083–1095.

Jackson, J. H. (1989a). "Perspectives on Countervailing Duties," *Law and Policy in International Business*, 21, 739.

(1989b). *The World Trading System: Law and Policy of International Economic Relations* MIT Press.

(1997). *The World Trading System: Law and Policy of International Economic Relations* (2nd ed.): MIT press.

(2002). "Afterword: The Linkage Problem – Comments on Five Texts," *The American Journal of International Law*, 96(1), 118–125.

(2003). "Sovereignty-Modern: A New Approach to an Outdated Concept," *The American Journal of International Law*, 97(4), 782–802.

(2006). *Sovereignty, the WTO and Changing Fundamentals of International Law*: Cambridge University Press.

Jaiswal, A. K. (2003). "WTO Agreement on SPS: Strategic Implications," *Economic and Political Weekly*, 38(45), 4737–4742.

James, A. (2005). "Constructing Justice for Existing Practice: Rawls and the Status Quo," *Philosophy & Public Affairs*, 33(3), 281–316.

(2012a). *Fairness in Practice: A Social Contract for a Global Economy*: Oxford University Press.

(2012b). "Global Economic Fairness: Internal Principles," in C. Carmody, F. Garcia, & J. Linarelli (Eds.), *Global Justice and International Economic Law: Opportunities and Challenges.*

Joerges, C., & Petersmann, E.-U. (Eds.). (2006). *Constitutionalism, Multilevel Trade Governance and Social Regulation*: Hart.

Johnson, H. G. (1953). "Optimum Tariffs and Retaliation," *The Review of Economic Studies, 21*(2), 142–153.

Johnstone, I. (2003). "Security Council Deliberations: The Power of the Better Argument," *European Journal of International Law, 14*(3), 437–480.

Jonas, D. S., & Saunders, T. N. (2010). "The Object and Purpose of a Treaty: Three Interpretive Methods," *Vanderbilt Journal of Transnational Law, 43,* 565.

Jones, K. (2004). "The Safeguards Mess Revisited: The Fundamental Problem," *World Trade Review, 3*(01), 83–91.

Jörke, D. (2013). "The Power of Reason in International Negotiations: Notes on Risse, Müller, and Deitelhoff," *Critical Policy Studies, 7*(3), 350–363.

Joseph, S. (2009). "Democratic Deficit, Participation and the WTO," in S. Joseph, D. Kinley, & J. Waincymer (Eds.), *The World Trade Organization and Human Rights*: Edward Elgar.

Ju, J., & Wei, S.-J. (2011). "When Is Quality of Financial System a Source of Comparative Advantage?" *Journal of International Economics, 84*(2), 178–187.

Julius, A. J. (2003). "Basic Structure and the Value of Equality," *Philosophy & Public Affairs, 31*(4), 321–355.

(2006). "Nagel's Atlas," *Philosophy & Public Affairs, 34*(2), 176–192.

Kagan, S. (1989). *The Limits of Morality*: Clarendon Press.

Kahan, D. M., Slovic, P., Braman, D., & Castil, J. (2006). "Fear of Democracy: A Cultural Evaluation of Sunstein of Risk," *Harvard Law Review, 119,* 1071–1109.

Kamm, F. M. (1989). "Harming Some to Save Others," *Philosophical Studies, 57*(3), 227–260.

(1992). "Non-Consequentialism, the Person as an End-in-Itself, and the Significance of Status," *Philosophy & Public Affairs, 21*(4), 354–389.

Kant, I. (1991). *Kant: Political Writings* (2nd ed.) (H. S. Reiss ed., H. B. Nisbet trans.): Cambridge University Press.

(1996). *Practical Philosophy.* (M. J. Gregor ed. and trans.): Cambridge University Press.

Kapstein, E. B. (2006). *Economic Justice in an Unfair World: Toward a Level Playing Field*: Cambridge University Press.

Kapterian, G. (2010). "A Critique of the WTO Jurisprudence on 'Necessity'," *International and Comparative Law Quarterly, 59*(01), 89–127.

Karapinar, B. (2011). "China's Export Restriction Policies: Complying with 'WTO plus' or Undermining Multilateralism," *World Trade Review, 10*(03), 389–408.

Kawaharu, A. (2006). "Principles of Non-Discrimination in Tarrif Preferences Schemes: The WTO Appellate Body's Decision in EC-Preferences and the Policy Impact on the European Union," *New Zealand Year Book of International Law, 3*, 43–67.

Keene, E. (2002). *Beyond the Anarchical Society: Grotius, Colonialism and Order in World Politics*: Cambridge University Press.

Kelly, C. (2006). "Power, Linkage and Accommodation: The WTO as an International Actor and Its Influence on Other Actors and Regimes," *Berkeley Journal of International Law, 24*, 79–128.

Kelly, J. M. (1992). *A Short History of Western Legal Theory*: Clarendon Press.

Kennedy, P. M. (1987). *The Rise and Fall of the Great Powers: Economic Change and Military Conflict from 1500 to 2000*: Random House.

Keohane, R. O., & Nye, J. S. (2001). "The Club Model of Multilateral Cooperation and Problems of Democratic Legitimacy," in B. Porter, P. Sauve, A. Subramanian, & A. B. Zampetti (Eds.), *Efficiency, Equity and Legitimacy: The Multilateral Trading System at the Millennium*: Brookings Institution Press.

Keynes, J. M. (1919). *The Economic Consequences of the Peace*: Macmillan.

Khan, M. H. (2005). "Markets, States and Democracy: Patron–Client Networks and the Case for Democracy in Developing Countries," *Democratization, 12*(5), 704–724.

Kim, J. B. (2002). "Fair Price Comparison in the WTO Anti-Dumping Agreement Recent WTO Panel Decisions against the 'Zeroing' Method," *Journal of World Trade, 36*(1), 39–56.

Kirgis, F. L. (1994). "The Degrees of Self-Determination in the United Nations Era," *The American Journal of International Law, 88*(2), 304–310.

Kirshner, J. (2012). "The Tragedy of Offensive Realism: Classical Realism and the Rise of China," *European Journal of International Relations, 18*(1), 53–75.

Kishore, P. (2011). "Conditionalities in the Generalized System of Preference as Instruments of Global Economic Governance," *The International Lawyer, 45*(3), 895–902.

Klabbers, J. (2006). "The Right to Be Taken Seriously: Self-Determination in International Law," *Human Rights Quarterly, 28*(1), 186–206.

Kolers, A. (2009). *Land, Conflict, and Justice: A Political Theory of Territory*: Cambridge University Press.

(2012). "Justice, Territory and Natural Resources," *Political Studies, 60*(2), 269–286.

Koskenniemi, M. (2005). *From Apology to Utopia: The Structure of International Legal Argument (Reissue with a New Epilogue)*: Cambridge University Press.

Kovavic, W. E. (2010). "Price Differentiation in Antitrust and Trade Instruments," in K. Bagwell, G. A. Bermann, & P. C. Mavroidis (Eds.), *Law and Economics of Contingent Protection in International Trade*: Cambridge University Press.

Krajewski, M. (2011). "Legitimising Global Economic Governance through Transnational Parliamentarisation: How Far Have We Come? How Much Further Must We Go?" in T. Cottier & M. Elsig (Eds.), *Governing the World Trade Organization: Past, Present and Beyond Doha*: Cambridge University Press.

Krasner, S. D. (1985). *Structural Conflict: The Third World against Global Liberalism*: University of California Press.

(1999). *Sovereignty: Organized Hypocrisy*: Princeton University Press.

Kratochwil, F. (1986). "Of Systems, Boundaries, and Territoriality: An Inquiry into the Formation of the State System," *World Politics*, 39(1), 27–52.

Krugman, P. R. (1992). "Does the New Trade Theory Require a New Trade Policy?" *World Economy*, 15(4), 423–442.

(1997). "What Should Trade Negotiators Negotiate About?" *Journal of Economic Literature*, 35(1), 113–120.

Krugman, P. R., Obstfeld, M., & Melitz, M. J. (2012). *International Economics: Theory and Policy* (9th ed.): Pearson Education.

Kumm, M. (2013). "The Cosmopolitan Turn in Constitutionalism: An Integrated Conception of Public Law," *Indiana Journal of Global Legal Studies*, 20(2), 605–628.

Kuper, A. (2000). "Rawlsian Global Justice: Beyond the Law of Peoples to a Cosmopolitan Law of Persons," *Political Theory*, 28(5), 640–674.

Kurjanska, M., & Risse, M. (2008). "Fairness in Trade II: Export Subsidies and the Fair Trade Movement," *Politics, Philosophy & Economics*, 7(1), 29–56.

Kymlicka, W. (1996). *Multicultural Citizenship: A Liberal Theory of Minority Rights*: Clarendon Press.

(2002). *Contemporary Political Philosophy: An Introduction* (2nd ed.): Oxford University Press.

Lake, D. A. (2008). "The State and International Relations," in C. Reus-Smit & D. Snidal (Eds.), *The Oxford Handbook of International Relations*: Oxford University Press.

Lamond, G. (2000). "The Coerciveness of Law," *Oxford Journal of Legal Studies*, 20(1), 39–62.

Lamy, P. (2013). "China Should Be More Active in Global Economic Governance, Lamy Tells Beijing Forum," *Speech to the China Development Forum, Beijing*, 24 March 2013: World Trade Organization.

Lamy, P., & Goldin, I. (2014). "Addressing the Global Governance Deficit," *Huffington Post*, 22 March 2014 (Retrieved 16 December 2016)

Lang, A. (2006). "Reconstructing Embedded Liberalism: John Gerard Ruggie and Constructivist Approaches to the Study of the International Trade Regime," *Journal of International Economic Law*, 9(1), 81–116.

(2007). "Reflecting on 'Linkage': Cognitive and Institutional Change in the International Trading System," *The Modern Law Review*, 70(4), 523–549.

(2011). *World Trade Law after Neoliberalism: Reimagining the Global Economic Order*: Oxford University Press.

(2014). "Governing 'As If': Global Subsidies Regulation and the Benchmark Problem," *Current Legal Problems, 67*(1), 135–168.

Lang, A., & Scott, J. (2009a). "The Hidden World of WTO Governance," *European Journal of International Law, 20*(3), 575–614.

(2009b). "The Hidden World of WTO Governance: A Rejoinder to Richard H. Steinberg," *European Journal of International Law, 20*(4), 1073–1076.

Langland, E. (2008). "United States-Final Anti-Dumping Measures on Stainless Steel from Mexico: Row over Zoning Reveals Judicial Quagmire," *Tulane Journal of International and Comparative Law, 17*, 555.

Lee, Y.-S. (2001). "Destabilization of the Discipline on Safeguards? Inherent Problems with the Continuing Application of Article XIX after the Settlement of the Agreement on Safeguards," *Journal of World Trade, 35*(6), 1235–1246.

(2006a). "Comments on the Recent Debate on Safeguards – Difference in Perspectives, Not a Failure of Appreciation," *Journal of World Trade, 40*(6), 1145–1147.

(2006b). "Not Without a Clue: Commentary on 'the Persistent Puzzles of Safeguards'," *Journal of World Trade, 40*(2), 385–404.

Leitner, K., & Lester, S. (2016). "WTO Dispute Settlement 1995–2015 – A Statistical Analysis," *Journal of International Economic Law, 19*(1), 289–300.

Lerner, A. P. (1936). "The Symmetry between Import and Export Taxes," *Economica, 3*(11), 306–313.

Lester, S. (2008). "United States: Final Anti-Dumping Measures on Stainless Steel from Mexico," *The American Journal of International Law, 102*(4), 834–841.

(2011). "The Problem of Subsidies as a Means of Protectionism: Lessons from the WTO EC – Aircraft Case," *Melbourne Journal of International Law, 12*, 345.

Lester, S., Mercurio, B., & Davies, A. (2012). *World Trade Law: Texts, Materials and Commentary* (2nd ed.): Hart.

Lim, C. L. (2012). "The Conventional Morality of Trade," in C. Carmody, F. Garcia, & J. Linarelli (Eds.), *Global Justice and International Economic Law*: Cambridge University Press.

Linarelli, J. (2006). "What Do We Owe Each Other in the Global Economic Order?: Constructivist and Contractualist Accounts," *Journal of Transnational Law and Policy, 15*, 181–218.

Lindauer, D. L., Pritchett, L., Rodrik, D., & Eckhaus, R. S. (2002). "What's the Big Idea? The Third Generation of Policies for Economic Growth," *Economia, 3*(1), 1–36.

Lindsey, B. (1999). *The U.S. Antidumping Law: Rhetoric versus Reality: Trade Policy Analysis No. 7*: Cato Institute Center for Trade Policy Studies.

Lippert-Rasmussen, K. (2008). "Inequality, Incentives and the Interpersonal Test," *Ratio, 21*(4), 421–439.

Lipson, C. (1984). "International Cooperation in Economic and Security Affairs," *World Politics, 37*(1), 1–23.

Livermore, M. A. (2006). "Authority and Legitimacy in Global Governance: Deliberation, Institutional Differentiation, and the Codex Alimentarius," *New York University Law Review, 81,* 766.

Loriaux, S. (2012). "Fairness in International Economic Cooperation: Moving beyond Rawls's Duty of Assistance," *Critical Review of International Social and Political Philosophy, 15*(1), 19–39.

Lovett, F. (2014). "Republicanism," in E. N. Zalta (Ed.), *Stanford Encyclopedia of Philosophy* (Winter 2014 ed.): Stanford University.

Lowenfeld, A. F. (1980). "Fair or Unfair Trade: Does it Matter," *Cornell International Law Journal, 13,* 205.

Lukes, S. (2004). *Power: A Radical View* (2nd ed.): Palgrave Macmillan Ltd.

MacIntyre, A. (1984). *Is Patriotism a Virtue?* (The Lindley Lecture, 26 March 1984): University of Kansas.

Macleod, A. M. (2008). "Rawls's Narrow Doctrine of Human Rights" in R. Martin and D. A. Reidy (Eds.), *Rawls's Law of Peoples: A Realistic Utopia?*: Blackwell Publishing.

Maduro, M. P. (2001). "Is There Any such Thing as Free or Fair Trade? A Constitutional Analysis of the Impact of International Trade on the European Social Model," in Gráinne De Búrca & Joanne Scott (Eds.), *The EU and the WTO: Legal and Constitutional Issues*: Hart, 257–282.

Maffettone, P. (2009). "The WTO and the Limits of Distributive Justice," *Philosophy & Social Criticism, 35*(3), 243–267.

Maggi, G., & Rodriguez-Clare, A. (1998). "The Value of Trade Agreements in the Presence of Political Pressures," *Journal of Political Economy, 106*(3), 574–601.

Mandelson, P. (2010). *The Third Man: Life at the Heart of New Labour.* Harper Press.

Marceau, G. (2002). "WTO Dispute Settlement and Human Rights," *European Journal of International Law, 13*(4), 753–814.

(2013). "The New TBT Jurisprudence in US-Clove Cigarettes, WTO US-Tuna II, and US-Cool," *Asian Journal of WTO & International Health Law and Policy, 8*(1), 1.

Marceau, G., & Trachtman, J. P. (2002). "The Technical Barriers to Trade Agreement, the Sanitary and Phytosanitary Measures Agreement, and the General Agreement on Tariffs and Trade: A Map of the World Trade Organization Law of Domestic Regulation of Goods," *Journal of World Trade, 36*(5), 811–882.

Margalit, A., & Raz, J. (1990). "National Self-Determination," *Journal of Philosophy, 87*(9), 439–461.

Markus, K. (2001). "Democratic Legitimacy and Constitutional Perspectives of WTO Law," *Journal of World Trade, 35*(1), 167–186.

Martin, R. (2006). "Rawls on International Distributive Economic Justice: Taking a Closer Look," in R. Martin & D. A. Reidy (Eds.), *Rawls's Law of Peoples: A Realistic Utopia?*: Blackwell Publishing.

Martin, W., Mattoo, A., & Winkler, D. (2011). "Introduction," in W. Martin & A. Mattoo (Eds.), *Unfinished Business? The WTO's Doha Agenda*: World Bank / Centre for Economic Policy Research.

Maruyama, W. H. (1998). "A New Pillar of the WTO: Sound Science," *The International Lawyer, 32*(3), 651–677.

Maskus, K. E., Otsuki, T., & Wilson, J. S. (2005). "The Cost of Compliance with Product Standards for Firms in Developing Countries: An Econometric Study," *World Bank Policy Research Working Paper*, 3590.

Mastel, G. (1998). *Antidumping Laws and the U.S. Economy*: M.E. Sharpe.

Mathis, J. (2002). "WTO Panel Report, European Communities – Trade Description of Sardines, WT/DS231/R, 29 May 2002," *Legal Issues of Economic Integration, 29*(3), 335–347.

(2006). "Regional Trade Agreements and Domestic Regulation: What Reach for 'Other Restrictive Regulations of Commerce'," in L. Bartels & F. Ortino (Eds.), *Regional Trade Agreements and the WTO Legal System*: Oxford University Press.

Mattoo, A., & Subramanian, A. (1998). "Regulatory Autonomy and Multilateral Disciplines: The Dilemma and a Possible Resolution," *Journal of International Economic Law, 1*, 303.

Mavroidis, P. C. (2007). *Trade in Goods: The GATT and the Other Agreements Regulating Trade in Goods*: Oxford University Press.

(2012). *Trade in Goods: The GATT and the Other Agreements Regulating Trade in Goods* (2nd ed.): Oxford University Press.

Mavroidis, P. C. (2013). "Driftin' too Far from Shore–Why the Test for Compliance with the TBT Agreement Developed by the WTO Appellate Body Is Wrong, and What Should the AB Have Done Instead," *World Trade Review, 12*(3), 509–531.

Mavroidis, P. C., Messerlin, P. A., & Wauters, J. (2008). *The Law and Economics of Contingent Protection in the WTO*: Edward Elgar Pub.

Mavroidis, P. C., & Saggi, K. (2014). "What Is Not So Cool about US–COOL Regulations? A Critical Analysis of the Appellate Body's Ruling on US–COOL," *World Trade Review, 13*(02), 299–320.

Mayeda, G. (2004). "Developing Disharmony? The SPS and TBT Agreements and the Impact of Harmonization on Developing Countries," *Journal of International Economic Law, 7*(4), 737–764.

McCallum, J. (1995). "National Borders Matter: Canada-U.S. Regional Trade Patterns," *The American Economic Review, 85*(3), 615–623.

McCorquodale, R. (1994). "Self-Determination: A Human Rights Approach," *International and Comparative Law Quarterly, 43*(4), 857–885.

McDonald, J. (2005). "Domestic Regulation, International Standards, and Technical Barriers to Trade," *World Trade Review*, 4(2), 249–274.

McGrady, B. (2009). "Necessity Exceptions in WTO Law: Retreaded Tyres, Regulatory Purpose and Cumulative Regulatory Measures," *Journal of International Economic Law*, 12(1), 153–173.

McGrew, T. (2011). "After Globalisation? WTO Reform and the New Global Political Economy," in T. Cottier & M. Elsig (Eds.), *Governing the World Trade Organization: Past, Present and Beyond Doha*: Cambridge University Press.

McIntyre, A. (2001). "Doing Away with Double Effect," *Ethics*, 111(2), 219–255.

(2011). "Doctrine of Double Effect," in E. N. Zalta (Ed.), *The Stanford Encyclopedia of Philosophy* (Fall 2011 ed.): Stanford University.

McMahan, J. (1997). "The Limits of National Partiality," in R. McKim and J. McMahan (Eds.), *The Morality of Nationalism*: Oxford University Press.

Mearsheimer, J. J. (2014). *The Tragedy of Great Power Politics* (Updated edition.): Norton.

Meckled-Garcia, S. (2008). "On the Very Idea of Cosmopolitan Justice: Constructivism and International Agency," *Journal of Political Philosophy*, 16(3), 245–271.

Meckled-Garcia, S. (2014). "Does the WTO Violate Human Rights (and Do I Help It)? Beyond the Metaphor of Culpability for Systemic Global Poverty," *Political Studies*, 62(2), 435–451.

Messenger, G. (2013). *Economic Analysis in WTO Law*. Paper presented at the BIICL 13th Annual WTO Conference, London, 15 May 2013.

(2016). *The Development of World Trade Organization Law: Examining Change in International Law*: Oxford University Press.

Mill, J. S. (1989). *On Liberty and Other Writings* (S. Collini ed.): Cambridge University Press.

Miller, D. (1995). *On Nationality*: Clarendon Press.

(1999a). "Justice and Global Inequality," in A. Hurrell & N. Woods (Eds.), *Inequality, Globalization and World Politics*: Oxford University Press.

(1999b). *Principles of Social Justice*: Harvard University Press.

(2000). *Citizenship and National Identity*: Polity Press.

(2007). *National Responsibility and Global Justice*: Oxford University Press.

(2009). "Justice and Boundaries," *Politics, Philosophy & Economics*, 8(3), 291–309.

(2010). "Why Immigration Controls Are Not Coercive: A Reply to Arash Abizadeh," *Political Theory*, 38(1), 111–120.

(2011). "On Nationality and Global Equality: A Reply to Holtug," *Ethics and Global Politics*, 4(3), 165–171.

(2012). "Territorial Rights: Concept and Justification," *Political Studies*, 60(2), 252–268.

Miller, R. W. (2010). *Globalizing Justice: The Ethics of Poverty and Power*: Oxford University Press.

Miscevic, N. (2010). "Nationalism," in E. N. Zalta (Ed.), *Stanford Encyclopedia of Philosophy* (Summer 2010 ed.): Stanford University.

Moellendorf, D. (2002). *Cosmopolitan Justice*: Westview Press.

(2005). "The World Trade Organization and Egalitarian Justice," *Metaphilosophy, 36*(1-2), 145-162.

(2009). *Global Inequality Matters*: Palgrave Macmillan.

(2013). "Fairness in Practice: A Social Contract for a Global Economy, by Aaron James," *Mind, 122*(486), 548-553.

Moon, G. (2011). "Fair in Form, But Discriminatory in Operation – WTO Law's Discriminatory Effects on Human Rights in Developing Countries," *Journal of International Economic Law, 14*(3), 553-592.

Moore, M. (1998). *National Self-Determination and Secession*: Cambridge University Press.

(2012). "Natural Resources, Territorial Right, and Global Distributive Justice," *Political Theory, 40*(1), 84-107.

Morgenthau, H. J., & Thompson, K. W. (1985). *Politics among Nations: The Struggle for Power and Peace* (6th ed.): McGraw-Hill.

Mosoti, V. (2006). "Africa in the First Decade of WTO Dispute Settlement," *Journal of International Economic Law, 9*(2), 427-453.

Moss, K. (2005). "The Consequences of the WTO Appellate Body Decision in EC-Tariff Preferences for the African Growth Opportunity Act and Sub-Saharan Africa," *New York University Journal of International Law & Politics, 38*, 665.

Motaal, D. A. (2004). "The 'Multilateral Scientific Consensus' and the World Trade Organization," *Journal of World Trade, 38*(5), 855-876.

Mueller, F. (2003). "Is the GATT Article XIX 'Unforeseen Developments Clause' Still Effective under the Agreement on Safeguards," *Journal of World Trade, 37*(6), 1119-1151.

Mulhall, S., & Swift, A. (1996). *Liberals and Communitarians* (2nd ed.): Blackwell.

Muller, H. (2004). "Arguing, Bargaining and All That: Communicative Action, Rationalist Theory and the Logic of Appropriateness in International Relations," *European Journal of International Relations, 10*(3), 395-435.

Murphy, L. B. (1998). "Institutions and the Demands of Justice," *Philosophy & Public Affairs, 27*(4), 251-291.

Musgrave, T. D. (1997). *Self-Determination and National Minorities*: Oxford University Press.

Nagel, T. (1986). *The View from Nowhere*: Oxford University Press.

(1991). *Equality and Partiality*: Oxford University Press.

(2005). "The Problem of Global Justice," *Philosophy & Public Affairs, 33*(2), 113-147.

Naiki, Y. (2009). "Accountability and Legitimacy in Global Health and Safety Governance: The World Trade Organization, the SPS Committee, and International Standard-Setting Organizations," *Journal of World Trade*, 43(6), 1255–1279.

Nanz, P. (2006). "Democratic Legitimacy and Constitutionalisation of Transnational Trade Governance: A View from Political Theory," in C. Joerges & E.-U. Petersmann (Eds.), *Constitutionalism, Multilevel Trade Governance and Social Regulation*: Hart.

Narlikar, A. (2003). *International Trade and Developing Countries: Bargaining Coalitions in GATT and WTO*. Routledge.

Neumann, J., & Turk, E. (2003). "Necessity Revisited: Proportionality in World Trade Organization Law after Korea-Beef, EC-Asbestos and EC-Sardines," *Journal of World Trade*, 37(1), 199.

Neven, D. J. (2001). "How Should 'Protection' Be Evaluated in Article III GATT Disputes?" *European Journal of Political Economy*, 17(2), 421–444.

Nickel, J. W. (2008). "Are Human Rights Mainly Implemented by Intervention?" in R. Martin & D. A. Reidy (Eds.), *Rawls's Law of Peoples: A Realistic Utopia?*: Blackwell Publishing.

Niels, G. (2000). "What Is Antidumping Policy Really About?" *Journal of Economic Surveys*, 14(4), 467–492.

Nielsen, K. (1997). "Liberal Nationalism and Secession," in M. Moore (Ed.), *National Self-Determination and Secession*: Oxford University Press.

Nielsen, L. (2007). *The WTO, Animals and PPMs*. Brill.

Nozick, R. (1974). *Anarchy, State and Utopia*: Basic Books.

Nussbaum, M. C. (2004). "Beyond the Social Contract: Capabilities and Global Justice," *Oxford Development Studies*, 32(1), 3–18.

(2011). "Perfectionist Liberalism and Political Liberalism," *Philosophy & Public Affairs*, 39(1), 3–45.

O'Neill, O. (1997). "Environmental Values, Anthropocentrism and Speciesism," *Environmental Values*, 6(2), 127.

(2000). *Bounds of Justice*: Cambridge University Press.

Odell, J. S. (2006). *Negotiating Trade: Developing Countries in the WTO and NAFTA*: Cambridge University Press.

(2010). "Negotiating from Weakness in International Trade Relations," *Journal of World Trade*, 44(3), 545.

Odell, J. S., & Kell, S. K. (2006). "Reframing the Issue: The WTO Coalition on Intellectual Property and Public Health, 2001," in J. S. Odell (Ed.), *Negotiating Trade*: Cambridge University Press.

Oloka-Onyango, J. (1999). "Heretical Reflections on the Right to Self-Determination: Prospects and Problems for a Democratic Global Future in the New Millennium," *American University International Law Review*, 15, 151.

Onyejekwe, K. (1994). "International Law of Trade Preferences: Emanations from the European Union and the United States," *St. Mary's Law Journal*, 26, 425.

Orford, A. (2013). "Moral Internationalism and the Responsibility to Protect," *European Journal of International Law*, 24(1), 83–108.

Ormonde Driscoll, C. (2005). "Unforeseen Developments – An Unforeseeable Future? The Relationship between GATT Article XIX and the Agreement on Safeguards," *Legal Issues of Economic Integration*, 32(3), 249–258.

Osiro, D. A. (2002). "GATT/WTO Necessity Analysis: Evolutionary Interpretation and Its Impact on the Authority of Domestic Regulation," *Legal Issues of Economic Integration*, 29(2), 123–141.

Özden, Ç., & Reinhardt, E. (2005). "The Perversity of Preferences: GSP and Developing Country Trade Policies, 1976–2000," *Journal of Development Economics*, 78(1), 1–21.

Page, S., & Hewitt, A. (2002). "The New European Trade Preferences: Does 'Everything But Arms'(EBA) Help the Poor?" *Development Policy Review*, 20(1), 91–102.

Pal, R. (2014). "Has the Appellate Body's Decision in Canada – Renewable Energy / Canada – Feed-in Tariff Program Opened the Door for Production Subsidies?" *Journal of International Economic Law*, 17(1), 125–137.

Paliwal, S. (2011). "Strengthening the Link in Linkage: Defining Development Needs in WTO Law," *American University International Law Review*, 27, 37.

Panagariya, A. (2000). "Evaluating the Case for Export Subsidies," *World Bank Policy Research Working Paper*, 2276.

(2002). "EU Preferential Trade Arrangements and Developing Countries," *World Economy*, 25(10), 1415–1432.

Peel, J. (2010). *Science and Risk Regulation in International Law*: Cambridge University Press.

(2012). "Of Apples and Oranges (and Hormones in Beef): Science and the Standard of Review in WTO Disputes under the SPS Agreement," *International and Comparative Law Quarterly*, 61(02), 427–458.

Perdikis, N., Shelburne, W. A. K., & Hobbs, J. E. (2001). "Reforming the WTO to Defuse Potential Trade Conflicts in Genetically Modified Goods," *The World Economy*, 24(3), 379–398.

Perez, O. (2007). "Anomalies at the Precautionary Kingdom: Reflections on the GMO Panel's Decision," *World Trade Review*, 6(2), 265–280.

Petersmann, E.-U. (1992). "National Constitutions, Foreign Trade Policy and European Community Law," *European Journal of International Law*, 3(1), 1–35.

(2002). "Time for a United Nations 'Global Compact' for Integrating Human Rights into the Law of Worldwide Organizations: Lessons from European Integration," *European Journal of International Law*, 13(3), 621–650.

(2008a). "Constitutionalism and WTO Law: From a State-Centred Approach towards a Human Rights Approach in International Economic Law," in D. L. M. Kennedy & J. D. Southwick (Eds.), *The Political Economy of International Trade Law: Essays in Honor of Robert E. Hudec*: Cambridge University Press.

(2008b). "Human Rights, International Economic Law and 'Constitutional Justice'," *European Journal of International Law*, 19(4), 769–798.

(2012). *International Economic Law in the 21st Century: Constitutional Pluralism and Multilevel Governance of Interdependent Public Goods*: Hart Publishing.

Philpott, D. (1995). "In Defense of Self-Determination," *Ethics, 105*(2), 352–385.

(1998). "Self-Determination in Practice," in M. Moore (Ed.), *National Self-Determination and Secession*: Oxford University Press.

Pogge, T. W. (1989). *Realizing Rawls*. Cornell University Press.

(1992). "Cosmopolitanism and Sovereignty," *Ethics, 103*(1), 48–75.

(1994). "An Egalitarian Law of Peoples," *Philosophy & Public Affairs, 23*(3), 195–224.

(1997). "The Bounds of Nationalism," *Canadian Journal of Philosophy, 26*(Sup. 1), 463–504.

(2000). "On the Site of Distributive Justice: Reflections on Cohen and Murphy," *Philosophy & Public Affairs, 29*(2), 137–169.

(2002). *World Poverty and Human Rights: Cosmopolitan Responsibilities and Reforms*: Polity.

(2011a). "Are We Violating the Human Rights of the World's Poor," *Yale Human Rights and Development Law Journal, 14*, 1.

(2011b). "The Role of International Law in Reproducing Massive Poverty," in S. Besson & J. Tasioulas (Eds.), *The Philosophy of International Law*: Oxford University Press.

Polanyi, K. (2001). *The Great Transformation: The Political and Economic Origins of Our Time* (1944) (2nd Beacon Paperback ed.): Beacon Press.

Porges, A., & Trachtman, J. P. (2003). "Robert Hudec and Domestic Regulation: The Resurrection of Aim and Effects," *Journal of World Trade, 37*(4), 783–799.

Porter, D. L., & Bidlingmaier, R. (2013). "Targeted Dumping: The Next Frontier in Trade Remedy Litigation," *Tulane Journal of International and Comparative Law, 21*(2), 485.

Porter, T. (2009). "The Division of Moral Labour and the Basic Structure Restriction," *Politics, Philosophy & Economics, 8*(2), 173–199.

Posner, E. A., & Sykes, A. O. (2011). "Efficient Breach of International Law: Optimal Remedies, Legalized Noncompliance, and Related Issues," *Michigan Law Review, 110*, 243.

(2013). *Economic Foundations of International Law*: Belknap.

Posner, R. A. (1979). "Utilitarianism, Economics, and Legal Theory," *The Journal of Legal Studies*, 8(1), 103–140.

Prebisch, R. (1964). *Towards a New Trade Policy for Development*: United Nations Conference on Trade and Development.

Prevost, D. (2005). "'Operationalising' Special and Differential Treatment of Developing Countries under the SPS Agreement," *South African Yearbook of International Law*, 30, 82–111.

Price, R. M. (Ed.). (2008). *Moral Limit and Possibility in World Politics*: Cambridge University Press.

Primoratz, I. (2008). "Patriotism and Morality: Mapping the Terrain," *Journal of Moral Philosophy*, 5(2), 204–226.

Prusa, T. J. (2005). "Anti-Dumping: A Growing Problem in International Trade," *World Economy*, 28(5), 683–700.

Qin, J. Y. (2003). "'WTO-Plus' Obligations and Their Implications for the World Trade Organization Legal System," *Journal of World Trade*, 37(3), 483–522.

(2010). "The Challenge of Interpreting 'WTO-PLUS' Provisions," *Journal of World Trade*, 44(1), 127–172.

(2012). "Reforming WTO Discipline on Export Duties: Sovereignty over Natural Resources, Economic Development and Environmental Protection," *Journal of World Trade*, 46(5), 1147–1190.

Quane, H. (1998). "The United Nations and the Evolving Right to Self-Determination," *The International and Comparative Law Quarterly*, 47(3), 537–572.

Quick, R., & Blüthner, A. (1999). "Has the Appellate Body Erred? An Appraisal and Criticism of the Ruling in the WTO Hormones Case," *Journal of International Economic Law*, 2(4), 603–639.

Quinn, W. S. (1989). "Actions, Intentions, and Consequences: The Doctrine of Double Effect," *Philosophy & Public Affairs*, 18(4), 334–351.

Quintillhn, S. P. (1999). "Free Trade, Public Health Protection and Consumer Information in the European and WTO Context – Hormone-Treated Beef and Genetically Modified, Organisms," *Journal of World Trade*, 33(6), 147–197.

Quong, J. (2007). "Contractualism, Reciprocity, and Egalitarian Justice," *Politics, Philosophy & Economics*, 6(1), 75–105.

Rauscher, F. (2012). "Kant's Social and Political Philosophy," In E. N. Zalta (Ed.), *Stanford Encyclopedia of Philosophy* (Summer 2012 ed.): Stanford University.

Raustiala, K. (2003). "Rethinking the Sovereignty Debate in International Economic Law," *Journal of International Economic Law*, 6(4), 841–878.

Rawls, J. (1971). *A Theory of Justice*: Harvard University Press.

(1980). "Kantian Constructivism in Moral Theory," *The Journal of Philosophy*, 77(9), 515–572.

(1988). "The Priority of Right and Ideas of the Good," *Philosophy & Public Affairs*, *17*(4), 251–276.

(1996). *Political Liberalism* (Pbk. ed.): Columbia University Press.

(1999). *The Law of Peoples: With, The Idea of Public Reason Revisited*: Harvard University Press.

(2001). *Justice as Fairness: A Restatement* (E. Kelly ed.): Harvard University Press.

Ray, D. (1998). *Development Economics*: Oxford University Press.

Raz, J. (1986). *The Morality of Freedom*: Clarendon Press.

(2006). "The Problem of Authority: Revisiting the Service Conception," *Minnesota Law Review*, *90*, 1003–1044.

Razavi, S. (2013). "Theory of Justice and Asymmetric Trade Liberalization: Limited Reciprocity as a Rule," *Manchester Journal of International Economic Law*, *10*, 108.

Regan, D. H. (2002). "Regulatory Purpose and 'Like Products' in Article III: 4 of the GATT (With Additional Remarks on Article II: 2)," *Journal of World Trade*, *36*(3), 443–478.

(2003). "Further Thoughts on the Role of Regulatory Purpose under Article III of the GATT," *Journal of World Trade*, *37*(4), 737–760.

(2006). "What Are Trade Agreements For? Two Conflicting Stories Told by Economists, with a Lesson for Lawyers," *Journal of International Economic Law*, *9*(4), 951–988.

(2007). "The Meaning of 'Necessary' in GATT Article XX and GATS Article XIV: The Myth of Cost–Benefit Balancing," *World Trade Review*, *6*(3), 347–369.

(2009). "How to Think about PPMs (and Climate Change)" in T. Cottier, O. Nartova, & S. Z. Bigdeli (Eds.), *International Trade Regulation and the Mitigation of Climate Change*: Cambridge University Press.

(2014). "Explaining Trade Agreements: The Practitioners' Story and the Standard Model," *World Trade Review*, *14*(3), 391–417.

(2015). "Explaining Trade Agreements: The Practitioner's Story and the Standard Model" *World Trade Review*, *14*(3), 391–417.

Reid, E. (2010). "Regulatory Autonomy in the EU and WTO: Defining and Defending Its Limits," *Journal of World Trade*, *44*(4), 877–901.

(2012). "Risk Assessment, Science and Deliberation: Managing Regulatory Diversity under the SPS Agreement?" *European Journal of Risk Regulation*, *3*(4), 535.

Reidy, D. A. (2007). "A Just Global Economy: In Defense of Rawls," *The Journal of Ethics*, *11*(2), 193–236.

Reus-Smit, C. (1999). *The Moral Purpose of the State: Culture, Social Identity, and Institutional Rationality in International Relations*: Princeton University Press.

Rigod, B. (2013). "The Purpose of the WTO Agreement on the Application of Sanitary and Phytosanitary Measures (SPS)," *European Journal of International Law, 24*(2), 503–532.

Risse, M. (2006). "What to Say about the State," *Social Theory and Practice, 32*(4), 671–698.

(2007). "Fairness in Trade I: Obligations from Trading and the Pauper-Labor Argument," *Politics, Philosophy & Economics, 6*(3), 355–377.

(2012). *On Global Justice*: Princeton University Press.

Risse, M. and Wollner, G. (2014). "Three Images of Trade: On the Place of Trade in a Theory of Global Justice," *Moral Philosophy and Politics, 1*(2), 201–225.

Risse, T. (2000). "'Let's Argue!': Communicative Action in World Politics," *International Organization, 54*(01), 1–39.

Roberts, D. (1998). "Preliminary Assessment of the Effects of the WTO Agreement on Sanitary and Phytosanitary Trade Regulations," *Journal of International Economic Law, 1*(3), 377–405.

Rodriguez, F., & Rodrik, D. (1999). "Trade Policy and Economic Growth: A Skeptic's Guide to Cross-National Evidence," in B. Bernanke & K. S. Rogoff (Eds.), *NBER Macroeconomics Annual 2000* (Vol. 15): MIT Press.

Rodrik, D. (1995). "Political Economy of Trade Policy," in M. G. Gene & R. Kenneth (Eds.), *Handbook of International Economics* (Vol. 3): Elsevier.

(1997). *Has Globalization Gone Too Far?*: Institute for International Economics.

(2000). *Trade Policy Reform as Institutional Reform*: Inter-American Development Bank.

(2001). *The Global Governance of Trade as if Development Really Mattered*: United Nations Development Programme Background Paper.

(2006). "Goodbye Washington Consensus, Hello Washington Confusion? A Review of the World Bank's 'Economic Growth in the 1990s: Learning from a Decade of Reform'," *Journal of Economic Literature, 44*(4), 973–987.

(2011). *The Globalization Paradox: Why Global Markets, States, and Democracy Can't Coexist*: Oxford University Press.

Roessler, F. (1997). "Diverging Domestic Policies and Multilateral Trade Integration," in J. Bhagwati & R. E. Hudec (Eds.), *Fair Trade and Harmonization, Vol. 2: Legal Analysis*: MIT Press.

Rogowski, R. (2006). "Trade, Immigration and Cross-Border Investment," in B. R. Weingast & D. A. Wittman (Eds.), *The Oxford Handbook of Political Economy*: Oxford University Press.

Rolland, S. E. (2012). *Development at the World Trade Organization* (1st ed.). Oxford University Press.

Ronzoni, M. (2009). "The Global Order: A Case of Background Injustice? A Practice-Dependent Account," *Philosophy & Public Affairs, 37*(3), 229–256.

(2012). "Two Conceptions of State Sovereignty and Their Implications for Global Institutional Design," *Critical Review of International Social and Political Philosophy, 15*(5), 573–591.

Rousseau, J.-J. (1997). *"The Social Contract" and Other Later Political Writings* (V. Gourevitch ed.): Cambridge University Press.

Rubini, L. (2009). *The Definition of Subsidy and State Aid: WTO and EC Law in Comparative Perspective*: Oxford University Press.

(2012). "Ain't Wastin' Time No More: Subsidies for Renewable Energy, the SCM Agreement, Policy Space, and Law Reform," *Journal of International Economic Law, 15*(2), 525–579.

(2014). "'The Good, the Bad, and the Ugly.' Lessons on Methodology in Legal Analysis from the Recent WTO Litigation on Renewable Energy Subsidies," *Journal of World Trade, 48*(5), 895–938.

Ruggie, J. G. (1982). "International Regimes, Transactions, and Change: Embedded Liberalism in the Postwar Economic Order," *International Organization, 36*(02), 379–415.

Saggi, K. (2010). "The Agreement on Safeguards: Does It Raise More Questions than It Answers?" in K. Bagwell, G. A. Bermann, & P. C. Mavroidis (Eds.), *Law and Economics of Contingent Protection in International Trade*: Cambridge University Press.

Salas, M., & Jackson, J. H. (2000). "Procedural Overview of the WTO EC – Banana Dispute," *Journal of International Economic Law, 3*(1), 145–166.

Sangiovanni, A. (2007). "Global Justice, Reciprocity, and the State," *Philosophy & Public Affairs, 35*(1), 3–39.

(2008). "Justice and the Priority of Politics to Morality," *Journal of Political Philosophy, 16*(2), 137–164.

(2011). "Global Justice and the Moral Arbitrariness of Birth," *Monist, 94*(4), 571–583.

(2012). "The Irrelevance of Coercion, Imposition, and Framing to Distributive Justice," *Philosophy & Public Affairs, 40*(2), 79–110.

Sapir, A. (2001). "Who's Afraid of Globalization? Domestic Adjustment in Europe and America," in R. B. Porter, P. Sauve, A. Subramanian, & A. B. Zampetti (Eds.), *Efficiency, Equity, Legitimacy: The Multilateral Trading System at the Millennium*: Harvard University Press/Brookings Institution Press.

Scanlon, T. (1972–1973). "Rawls' Theory of Justice," *University of Pennsylvania Law Review, 121*, 1020.

(1998). *What We Owe to Each Other*: Belknap Press of Harvard University Press.

Schefer, K. N. (Ed.). (2013). *Poverty and the International Economic Legal System: Duties to the World's Poor*: Cambridge University Press.

Scheffler, S. (1997). "Relationships and Responsibilities," *Philosophy & Public Affairs, 26*(3), 189–209.

(2001). *Boundaries and Allegiances: Problems of Justice and Responsibility in Liberal Thought*: Oxford University Press.

Scheuerman, W. E. (2006). "Critical Theory beyond Habermas," in J. S. Dryzek, B. Honig, & A. Phillips (Eds.), *The Oxford Handbook of Political Theory*: Oxford University Press.

Schwartz, G., & Clements, B. (1999). "Government Subsidies," *Journal of Economic Surveys, 13*(2), 119–148.

Scott, J. (2000). "On Kith and Kine (and Crustaceans): Trade and Environment in the EU and WTO," in J. H. H. Weiler (Ed.), *The EU, The WTO and the NAFTA: Towards a Common Law of International Trade*: Oxford University Press.

(2002). "Intergrating Environmental Concerns in International Economic Law," in S. Griller (Ed.), *International Economic Governance and Non Economic Concerns*: Springer.

(2004a). "European Regulation of GMOs: Thinking about Judicial Review in the WTO," *Current Legal Problems, 57*(1), 117–147.

(2004b). "International Trade and Environmental Governance: Relating Rules (and Standards) in the EU and the WTO," *European Journal of International Law, 15*(2), 307–354.

(2007). *The WTO Agreement on Sanitary and Phytosanitary Measures*: Cambridge University Press.

Sen, A. (1985). "The Moral Standing of the Market," *Social Philosophy and Policy, 2*(2), 1–19.

(1999). *Development as Freedom*: Oxford University Press.

(2009). *The Idea of Justice*: Belknap Press of Harvard University Press.

Shadikhodjaev, S. (2014). "Renewable Energy and Government Support: Time to 'Green' the SCM Agreement?" *World Trade Review, 14*(3), 479–506.

Shaffer, G. (2008). "A Structural Theory of WTO Dispute Settlement: Why Institutional Choice Lies at the Center of the GMO Case," *New York University Journal of International Law & Politics, 41*, 1.

Shaffer, G. (2010). "Risk, Science, and Law in the WTO: The Centrality of Institutional Choice," *American Society of International Law Proceedings of the Annual Meeting, 104*, 19–23.

(2016). "Will the US Undermine the World Trade Organization?" *Huffington Post/WorldPost* (23 May 2016).

Shaffer, G., & Apea, Y. (2005). "Institutional Choice in the Generalized System of Preferences Case: Who Decides the Conditions for Trade Preferences? The Law and Politics of Rights," *Journal of World Trade, 39*(6), 977–1008.

Shaffer, G., & Trachtman, J. P. (2011). "Interpretation and Institutional Choice at the WTO," *Virginia Journal of International Law, 52*, 1.

Shapiro, H. S. (2007). "The Rules That Swallowed the Exceptions: The WTO SPS Agreement and Its Relationship to GATT Articles XX and XXI – The Threat of the EU-GMO Dispute" *Arizona Journal of International and Comparative Law,* *24,* 199.

Sharp, B. (2010). "Responding Internationally to a Resource Crisis: Interpreting the GATT Article XX (j) Short Supply Exception," *Drake Journal of Agricultural Law, 15,* 259.

Shaw, M. N. (2014). *International Law:* Cambridge University Press.

Shue, H. (1996). *Basic Rights: Subsistence, Affluence, and U.S. Foreign Policy* (2nd ed.): Princeton University Press.

Simmonds, N. E. (2008). *Central Issues in Jurisprudence: Justice, Law and Rights* (3rd ed.): Sweet & Maxwell.

Simmons, A. J. (1979). *Moral Principles and Political Obligations:* Princeton University Press.

(2001). "On the Territorial Rights of States," *Noûs, 35*(1), 300–326.

Singer, P. (1972). "Famine, Affluence, and Morality," *Philosophy & Public Affairs, 1*(3), 229–243.

Smart, J. J. C., & Williams, B. (1973). *Utilitarianism: For and Against:* London: Cambridge University Press.

Snidal, D. (1985). "The Limits of Hegemonic Stability Theory," *International Organization, 39*(4), 579–614.

Spaulding, J. W. (2006). "Do International Fences Really Make Good Neighbors? The Zeroing Conflict between Antidumping Law and International Obligations," *New England Law Review, 41,* 379.

Spence, M. (2001). "Which Intellectual Property Rights Are Trade Related?" in F. Francioni (Ed.), *Environment, Human Rights and International Trade:* Hart.

Srinavasan, T. N. (2005). "Nondiscrimination in GATT/WTO: Was There Anything to Begin with and Is There Anything Left?" *World Trade Review, 4*(1), 69–95.

Staiger, R. W., & Sykes, A. O. (2010). "'Currency Manipulation' and World Trade," *World Trade Review, 9*(4), 583–627.

(2011). "International Trade, National Treatment, and Domestic Regulation," *The Journal of Legal Studies, 40*(1), 149–203.

Staiger, R. W., & Tabellini, G. (1987). "Discretionary Trade Policy and Excessive Protection," *The American Economic Review, 77*(5), 823–837.

Stamberger, J. L. (2003). "The Legality of Conditional Preferences to Developing Countries under the GATT Enabling Clause," *Chicago Journal of International Law, 4,* 607.

Stegemann, K. (1991). "The International Regulation of Dumping: Protection Made Too Easy," *World Economy, 14*(4), 375–405.

Steger, D. P. (2002). "Afterword: The 'Trade and . . .' Conundrum – A Commentary," *The American Journal of International Law, 96*(1), 135–145.

Stein, A. A. (2008). "Neoliberal Institutionalism," in C. Reus-Smit & D. Snidal (Eds.), *The Oxford Handbook of International Relations:* Oxford University Press.

Steinberg, R. H. (2009). "The Hidden World of WTO Governance: A Reply to Andrew Lang and Joanne Scott," *European Journal of International Law*, 20(4), 1063–1071.

Stevens, C., Bird, K., Keane, J., Kennan, J., te Velde, D. W., & Higgins, K. (2011). *The Poverty Impact of the Proposed Graduation Threshold in the Generalised System of Preferences (GSP) Trade Scheme*: Overseas Development Institute.

Stewart, T. P., & Johanson, D. S. (1998). "The SPS Agreement of the World Trade Organization and International Organizations: The Roles of the Codex Alimentarius Commission, the International Plant Protection Convention, and the International Office of Epizootics," *Syracuse Journal of International Law and Commerce*, 26, 27.

Stiglitz, J. E., & Charlton, A. (2005). *Fair Trade for All: How Trade Can Promote Development*: Oxford University Press.

Strange, S. (1988). *States and Markets*: Pinter.

Summers, J. (2013). "The Internal and External Aspects of Self-Determination Reconsidered," in D. French (Ed.), *Statehood and Self-Determination: Reconciling Tradition and Modernity in International Law*: Cambridge University Press.

Sunstein, C. R. (2006). "Misfearing: A Reply," *Harvard Law Review*, 119(4), 1110–1125.

Suttle, O. (2014a). "Book Review Essay: Poverty and Justice: Competing Lenses on International Economic Law," *The Journal of World Investment & Trade*, 15(5–6), 1071–1086.

(2014b). "Equality in Global Commerce: Towards a Political Theory of International Economic Law," *European Journal of International Law*, 25(4) 1043–1070.

(2016). "Debt, Default and Two Liberal Theories of Justice," *German Law Journal*, 17(5), 799–834.

(2017). "What Sorts of Things Are Public Morals? A Liberal Cosmopolitan Approach to Article XX GATT," *Modern Law Review* 80(4) 569–599.

Switzer, S. (2008). "Environmental Protection and the Generalized System of Preferences: A Legal and Appropriate Linkage?" *International & Comparative Law Quarterly*, 57(1), 113–147.

Sykes, A. O. (1989). "Countervailing Duty Law: An Economic Perspective," *Columbia Law Review*, 89(2), 199–263.

(1991). "Protectionism as a 'Safeguard': A Positive Analysis of the GATT 'Escape Clause' with Normative Speculations," *The University of Chicago Law Review*, 58(1) 255–305.

(1999a). "The (limited) Role of Regulatory Harmonization in International Goods and Services Markets," *Journal of International Economic Law*, 2(1), 49–70.

(1999b). "Regulatory Protectionism and the Law of International Trade," *University of Chicago Law Review, 66*(1), 1.

(2000). "Regulatory Competition or Regulatory Harmonization? A Silly Question?" *Journal of International Economic Law, 3*(2), 257–264.

(2002). "Domestic Regulation, Sovereignty, and Scientific Evidence Requirements: A Pessimistic View," *Chicago Journal of International Law, 3,* 353.

(2003a). "The Economics of WTO Rules on Subsidies and Countervailing Measures," *U Chicago Law & Economics, Olin Working Paper* (No. 186).

(2003b). "The Safeguards Mess: A Critique of WTO Jurisprudence," *World Trade Review, 2*(3), 261–295.

(2004). "The Persistent Puzzles of Safeguards: Lessons from the Steel Dispute," *Journal of International Economic Law, 7*(3), 523–564.

(2006a). "The Fundamental Deficiencies of the Agreement on Safeguards: A Reply to Professor Lee," *Journal of World Trade, 40*(5), 979–996.

(2006b). "International Trade and Human Rights: An Economic Perspective," in F. M. Abbott, C. Breining-Kaufmann, & T. Cottier (Eds.), *International Trade and Human Rights: Foundations and Conceptual Issues*: University of Michigan Press.

(2010). "The Questionable Case for Subsidies Regulation: A Comparative Perspective," *Journal of Legal Analysis, 2*(2), 473–523.

Tamir, Y. (1993). *Liberal Nationalism*: Princeton University Press.

Tan, K.-C. (2000). *Toleration, Diversity, and Global Justice*: Pennsylvania State University Press.

(2004). *Justice without Borders: Cosmopolitanism, Nationalism, and Patriotism*: Cambridge University Press.

(2012). *Justice, Institutions and Luck: The Site, Ground and Scope of Equality*: Oxford University Press.

Tannenwald, N. (2007). *The Nuclear Taboo: The United States and the Non-Use of Nuclear Weapons since 1945*: Cambridge University Press.

Tarullo, D. K. (2002). "The Hidden Costs of International Dispute Settlement: WTO Review of Domestic Anti-Dumping Decisions," *Law and Policy in International Business, 34,* 109.

Tasioulas, J. (1996). "In Defence of Relative Normativity: Communitarian Values and the Nicaragua Case," *Oxford Journal of Legal Studies, 16*(1), 85–128.

(2005). "Global Justice without End?" *Metaphilosophy, 36*(1–2), 3–29.

Teitel, R. G. (2011). *Humanity's Law*: Oxford University Press.

Tesón, F. R. (1998). *A Philosophy of International Law*: Westview.

Thomas, R. D. (1999). "Where's the Beef–Mad Cows and the Blight of the SPS Agreement," *Vanderbilt Journal of Transnational Law, 32,* 487.

Tomasi, J. (2012). *Free Market Fairness*: Princeton University Press.

Trachtman, J. P. (1998). "Trade and … Problems, Cost-Benefit Analysis and Subsidiarity," *European Journal of International Law, 9*(1), 32–85.

(2002). "Institutional Linkage: Transcending 'Trade and …'," *The American Journal of International Law, 96*(1), 77–93.

(2003). "Legal Aspects of a Poverty Agenda at the WTO: Trade Law and 'Global Apartheid'," *Journal of International Economic Law, 6*(1), 3–21.

(2006). "The Constitutions of the WTO," *European Journal of International Law, 17*(3), 623–646.

(2007). "Regulatory Jurisdiction and the WTO," *Journal of International Economic Law, 10*(3), 631–651.

(2008). *The Economic Structure of International Law*: Harvard University Press.

Trebilcock, M. J., & Howse, R. (1999). *The Regulation of International Trade* (2nd ed.): Routledge.

(2005). *The Regulation of International Trade* (3rd ed.): Routledge.

Trebilcock, M. J., Howse, R., & Eliason, A. (2013). *The Regulation of International Trade* (4th ed.): Routledge.

Trebilcock, M. J., & Soloway, J. (2002). "International Trade Policy and Domestic Food Safety Regulation: The Case for Substantial Deference by the WTO Dispute Settlement Body under the SPS Agreement," in D. L. M. Kennedy & J. D. Southwick (Eds.), *The Political Economy of International Trade: Essays in Honor of Robert Hudec*: Cambridge University Press.

Trombetta, M. J. (2008). "Environmental Security and Climate Change: Analysing the Discourse," *Cambridge Review of International Affairs, 21*(4), 585–602.

Turksen, U. (2009). "The WTO Law and the EC'S GSP+ Arrangement," *Journal of World Trade, 43*(5), 927–968.

Tyagi, M. (2012). "Flesh on a Legal Fiction: Early Practice in the WTO on Accession Protocols," *Journal of International Economic Law, 15*(2), 391–441.

Valentini, L. (2011a). "Coercion and (Global) Justice," *American Political Science Review, 105*(01), 205–220.

(2011b). "Global Justice and Practice-Dependence: Conventionalism, Institutionalism, Functionalism," *Journal of Political Philosophy, 19*(4), 399–418.

(2011c). *Justice in a Globalized World: A Normative Framework*: Oxford University Press.

Van den Bossche, P. & Zdouc, W. (2013). *The Law and Policy of the World Trade Organization: Text, Cases and Materials* (3rd ed.): Cambridge University Press.

Van Parijs, P. (2003). "Difference Principles," in S. R. Freeman (Ed.), *The Cambridge Companion to Rawls*: Cambridge University Press.

Verhoosel, G. (2002). *National Treatment and WTO Dispute Settlement: Adjudicating the Boundaries of Regulatory Autonomy*: Hart.

Victor, D. G. (1999). "The Sanitary and Phytosanitary Agreement of the World Trade Organization: An Assessment after Five Years," *New York University Journal of International Law and Politics*, 32, 865.

Voon, T. (2007). "The End of Zeroing? Reflections Following the WTO Appellate Body's Latest Missive," *Legal Issues of Economic Integration*, 34(3), 211–230.

(2010). "Eliminating Trade Remedies from the WTO: Lessons from Regional Trade Agreements," *International and Comparative Law Quarterly*, 59(03), 625–667.

Waincymer, J. (2009). "The Trade and Human Rights Debate: Introduction to an Interdisciplinary Analysis," in S. Joseph, D. Kinley, & J. Waincymer (Eds.), *The World Trade Organization and Human Rights*: Edward Elgar.

Waldron, J. (2006). "The Rule of International Law," *Harvard Journal of Law and Public Policy*, 30(1), 15–30.

(1987). "Theoretical Foundations of Liberalism," *The Philosophical Quarterly*, 37(147), 127–150.

(2004). "Property and Ownership," in E. N. Zalta (Ed.), *Stanford Encyclopedia of Philosophy* (Spring 2012 ed.): Stanford University.

(2010). "Two Conceptions of Self-Determination," in S. Besson & J. Tasioulas (Eds.), *The Philosophy of International Law*: Oxford University Press.

Walt, S. M. (1987). *The Origins of Alliances*: Cornell University Press.

Waltz, K. N. (1979). *Theory of International Politics*: Addison-Wesley Pub. Co.

Walzer, M. (1983). *Spheres of Justice: A Defence of Pluralism and Equality*: Basic Books.

(1994). *Thick and Thin: Moral Argument at Home and Abroad*: University of Notre Dame Press.

Wauters, J. (2010). "The Safeguards Agreement: An Overview," in K. Bagwell, G. A. Bermann, & P. C. Mavroidis (Eds.), *Law and Economics of Contingent Protection in International Trade*: Cambridge University Press.

Weiler, J. H. H. (2009). "Brazil – Measures Affecting Imports of Retreaded Tyres (DS322)," *World Trade Review*, 8(Special Issue 01), 137–144.

Weiler, J. H. H., & Neven, D. J. (2005). "One Bad Apple? A Comment on Japan – Measures Affecting the Importation of Apples," in H. Horn & P. C. Mavroidis (Eds.), *The WTO Case Law of 2003: The American Law Institute Reporters' Studies*: Cambridge University Press.

Weinrib, E. J. (1995). *The Idea of Private Law*: Harvard University Press.

Wenar, L. (2006). "Why Rawls Is Not a Cosmopolitan Egalitarian," in R. Martin & D. A. Reidy (Eds.), *Rawls's Law of Peoples: A Realistic Utopia?*: Blackwell Publishing.

(2008). "Property Rights and the Resource Curse," *Philosophy & Public Affairs*, 36(1), 2–32.

(2011). "Clean Trade in Natural Resources," *Ethics & International Affairs*, 25(1), 27–39.

Wendt, A. (1992). "Anarchy Is What States Make of It: The Social Construction of Power Politics," *International Organization*, 46(2), 391–425.

(1999). *Social Theory of International Politics*: Cambridge University Press.

Wight, M. (1996). *International Theory: The Three Traditions* (G. Wight and B. Porter eds.): Leicester University Press for the Royal Institute of International Affairs.

Wijkström, E., & McDaniels, D. (2013). "Improving Regulatory Governance: International Standards and the WTO TBT Agreement," *Journal of World Trade*, 47(5), 1013.

Wilkinson, R., & Scott, J. (2008). "Developing Country Participation in the GATT: A Reassessment," *World Trade Review*, 7(3), 473–510.

Williams, B. (2005). *In the Beginning Was the Deed: Realism and Moralism in Political Argument*: Princeton University Press.

Winickoff, D. E., & Bushey, D. M. (2010). "Science and Power in Global Food Regulation: The Rise of the Codex Alimentarius," *Science, Technology & Human Values*, 35(3), 356–381.

Wohlforth, W. C. (2008). "Realism," in C. Reus-Smit & D. Snidal (Eds.), *The Oxford Handbook of International Relations*: Oxford University Press.

World Bank. (2015). *World Bank Development Indicators Database*, http://data.world bank.org/data-catalog/world-development-indicators

(2016). *World Bank International Comparison Program Database*. www.world bank.org/en/programs/icp

World Trade Organization. (2007). *WTO Analytical Index: Guide to WTO Law and Practice* (2nd ed.): Cambridge University Press.

(2012a). *GATT Analytical Index*: World Trade Organization.

(2012b). *WTO Analytical Index: Guide to WTO Law and Practice* (3rd ed.): Cambridge University Press.

World Trade Organization, International Trade Centre, & United Nations Conference on Trade and Development. (2012). *World Tariff Profiles*.

Wouters, J., & Coppens, D. (2009). "An Overview of the Agreement on Subsidies and Countervailing Measures," in K. Bagwell, G. A. Bermann, & P. C. Mavroidis (Eds.), *Law and Economics of Contingent Protection in International Trade*: Columbia University Press.

Wren, A. (2006). "Comparative Perspectives on the Role of the State in the Economy," in B. R. Weingast & D. A. Wittman (Eds.), *The Oxford Handbook of Political Economy*: Oxford University Press.

Wright, J. (1999). "Minority Groups, Autonomy, and Self-Determination," *Oxford Journal of Legal Studies*, 19(4), 605–629.

Wu, M. (2008). "Free Trade and the Protection of Public Morals: An Analysis of the Newly Emerging Public Morals Clause Doctrine," *Yale Journal of International Law*, 33, 215.

Zampetti, A. B. (2001). "A Rough Map of Challenges to the Multilateral Trading System at the Millennium," in R. B. Porter, P. Sauve, A. Subramanian, & A. B. Zampetti (Eds.), *Efficiency, Equity and Legitimacy: The Multilateral Trading System at the Millennium*: Brookings Institution.

(2006). *Fairness in the World Economy: US Perspectives on International Trade Relations*: Edward Elgar.

Zanardi, M. (2004). "Anti-Dumping: What Are the Numbers to Discuss at Doha?" *World Economy, 27*(3), 403–433.

Zheng, W. (2012). "Reforming Trade Remedies," *Michigan Journal of International Law, 34*, 151–207.

Zimmerman, D. (1981). "Coercive Wage Offers," *Philosophy & Public Affairs, 10*(2), 121–145.

INDEX